CHRISTOPHER HIBBERT

THE COURT AT WINDSOR

A Domestic History

LONGMANS

LONGMANS GREEN AND CO LTD
48 Grosvenor Street, London W1

*Associated companies, branches and representatives
throughout the world*

© *Christopher Hibbert 1964*
First published 1964

**Printed in Great Britain by
Western Printing Services Ltd, Bristol**

For Kate

CONTENTS

CONTENTS

6. EDWARDIANS

7. WINDSORS

ILLUSTRATIONS

1. THE EARLIEST KNOWN DRAWING OF THE CASTLE
(c. 1450)   *facing page* 18
from a MS. Polychronicon in Eton College Library

This bird's-eye view from the north is part of a composition depicting a
ceremony in connection with the recently begun Eton College Chapel.
King Henry vi and Queen Margaret can be seen kneeling before the
altar in the temporary chapel in the lower part of the picture. About
thirty years after this drawing was done, Edward iv decided to replace
the small chapel shown in the Lower Ward of the Castle by St George's
Chapel. He envisaged this new chapel as a greater and more glorious
building than Eton College Chapel which had been inspired by his rival
and victim Henry vi and had by then been built in full view of the Castle
on the opposite bank of the river. The Lower Ward as it appeared after
Edward iv's work was completed is shown in plate 3.

2. THE CASTLE FROM THE NORTH-EAST *c.* 1570   18
from a drawing by George Hoefnagle in the Royal Library, Windsor Castle

This drawing by George Hoefnagle shows the Castle at a time when it
was said to have been 'verie ould ruinous and far oute of order redie to
fale downe'. The timber work bounding the North Terrace is described
as being 'in verie great ruyn' and for the 'moste parte rotten'. Below
the Terrace (soon to be replaced by the stone structure shown in plate 3)
a stag hunt is in progress.

3. A BIRD'S-EYE VIEW OF THE CASTLE IN 1607   19
from a copy of a survey by John Norden in the British Museum

This survey, done by John Norden, the topographer, shows the improvements and additions carried out for Queen Elizabeth i between 1571 and
1576. The new stone terrace and gallery (see plate 14) can be seen in the
lower left-hand corner – and compared with the timber construction in
plate 2 – also the new brick-enclosed 'Tennyce Court' on the easterly
slope of William the Conqueror's mound. In the middle of the Upper
Ward is a representation of the fountain set up in 1557–1558. This
drawing may be compared with Hollar's bird's-eye view done sixty years
later (plate 7), Sandby's drawing of the Lower Ward done in about
1770 (plate 13), Wyatville's Upper Ward done in about 1840 (plate 29)
and the modern aerial photograph (plate 46).

The Robes of the Order were, perhaps, at this time richer than they had
ever been before or were ever to be again. The high crowned hat with its
immense spray of feathers has now been replaced by a flat cap modelled
on a much earlier style as shown in plate 47.

Charles II sits alone at the high table in the background, an attendant
serving him on bended knee. The Knights sit along the wall on the left
each served by his own attendant. Garter King of Arms stands facing the
King at the head of the twelve Officers of Arms. On his right is the Controller of the Household and on the Controller's right the Treasurer of
the Household. Behind them at the head of the double row of men bearing
the second course is the Server; and at the back of the double row of
attendants stand the Cofferer and the Master of the Household. The
armed figures in the foreground are Yeomen of the Guard. The larger
St George's Hall which visitors to the State Apartments now see was
made by Wyatville who pulled down the wall dividing it from Charles
II's domestic chapel.

This engraving by Wenceslaus Hollar may be compared with Norden's
bird's-eye view (plate 3), Sandby's drawing of the Lower Ward (plate 13)
and the modern aerial photograph (plate 46). The principal towers – to
give them their present names and beginning at King Henry VIII Gate,
the main entrance to the Castle in the bottom left-hand corner, and
working to the east – are Mary Tudor Tower (rising in the middle of
the Military Knights' Lodgings), King Henry III Tower, King Edward
III Tower (at the foot of the mound steps), the Queen's Tower (on the
south-east corner), Clarence Tower, Chester Tower, Prince of Wales
Tower (on the north-east corner), Winchester Tower (opposite King
Henry III Tower), Curfew Tower (on the north-western corner), Garter
Tower and Salisbury Tower (on the south-western corner). The southern

face of the Upper Ward (altered by Hugh May after this engraving was done – see plate 12 – was altered again by Wyatville who made a new gate there (see plate 30). The Queen's Tower was rebuilt in 1680. Subsequently it contained the private apartments of Queen Charlotte and, after being remodelled by Wyatville, of all subsequent queens including Elizabeth 11. The Horseshoe Cloister built by Edward 1v for the priest-vicars at the western end of St George's Chapel can still be seen by visitors to the Castle. The annexe at the eastern end of the Chapel was started by Henry v11 on the site of an earlier building erected by Henry 111 in 1240. It was restored by Queen Victoria in memory of the Prince Consort and is now known as the Albert Memorial Chapel.

8. **THE CASTLE FROM THE NORTH-EAST BEFORE THE ALTERATIONS BY HUGH MAY**   65
from a drawing by Wenceslaus Hollar in the Royal Library, Windsor Castle

This drawing, done by Wenceslaus Hollar in about 1670, shows how plain were the twelfth-century walls and towers of the east and north fronts when Charles 11 first saw them. The way in which Hugh May altered them for him is shown below and more accurately in plate 12.

9. **THE CASTLE FROM THE NORTH-EAST AFTER THE ALTERATIONS BY HUGH MAY**   65
from an engraving published by John Garrett

This engraving, fanciful rather than accurate, was done some years after the drawing reproduced above and shows the work done in the Upper Ward for Charles 11 between 1674 and 1682. The new Star Building (now part of the State Apartments) where the King then lived can be seen in the middle of the north front. The windows of the first floor were round-topped and not rectangular as shown. The lodgings occupied by the King's niece Anne, who married Prince George of Denmark in 1683, are depicted on the far left. One of her many stillborn babies was born here in 1686. Later she moved to the house on the other side of the Castle shown in plate 12 This house was almost entirely demolished in 1778 to make room for Queen's Lodge (see plate 16).

10. **THE QUEEN'S PRESENCE CHAMBER**   80

Another of the rooms made for Charles 11 by Hugh May. The ceiling, painted by Antonio Verrio, represents Queen Catherine of Braganza seated under a canopy spread by Time and supported by Zephyrs. The fireplace was brought by William 1v from Buckingham Palace. George 111 gave concerts here. A bust of his favourite composer Handel is in the left-hand corner.

11. **THE QUEEN'S DRAWING ROOM**   80

This is one of the rooms made for Charles 11 by Hugh May.

Burford House is the large house on the left of the picture to the south-west of Charles 11's tennis court. Once the home of Nell Gwynn, it now belonged to her son by Charles 11 who was created Earl of Burford in 1676 and the Duke of St Albans in 1684. Queen Anne's house is the one with four dormer windows to the south of William the Conqueror's mound. Charles 11's long walk is on the right of the picture. It was not until the reign of George 1v that the Long Walk was taken up into the Upper Ward (see plate 30) and the medieval Rubbish Gate, which can be seen behind Queen Anne's house, was demolished. The Upper Ward as altered for Charles 11 by Hugh May can be compared with the drawing of it in plate 29 which shows the subsequent work of Wyatville. This Ward as it appeared before either architect set to work on it can be seen in Hollar's bird's-eye view (plate 7).

The tower in the middle foreground is King Henry 111 Tower built between 1223 and 1226. On its northern face are the only remaining roundheaded windows incongruously inserted in the Castle walls by Hugh May for Charles 11. The tower on the far right (now called Winchester Tower) was also originally built by Henry 111 but was largely reconstructed between 1357 and 1358 by William of Wykeham. It was again reconstructed by Wyatville who lived in it from 1824, when be began supervising the alterations he carried out for George 1v, until his death in 1840. The buildings in the centre background between King Henry v111 Gate and St George's Chapel were demolished in the 1860s to make way for the present Guard Room. This drawing by Paul Sandby may be compared with Norden's Survey (plate 3), Hollar's bird's-eye view (plate 7) and the modern aerial photograph (plate 46).

On the far left where the soldiers are marching is the tower which Henry v11 built for his Queen. It was here while sitting in the oriel window that Queen Anne received the news of Blenheim in 1704. It now forms part of the Royal Library. Next to it is the gallery that Queen Elizabeth made for her walks when it was too cold or wet to go outside. The tower beyond the line of trees, which conceal a buttressed curtain wall of about 1180, is Winchester Tower (see plates 13 and 17). The position of these Tudor buildings in the north front and the alterations made to them by Wyatville may be seen in plate 28.

ILLUSTRATIONS

This drawing by Paul Sandby, like the one above, indicates the decayed state into which the Castle (a playground for Windsor children) had been allowed to fall during the reigns of the first two Georges. The view through the arch is of the sharp turning in Thames Street where the road coming up south from the river turns west round the Castle walls. It can be seen at the top of Hollar's bird's-eye view (plate 7).

George III and his family are walking on the South Terrace. In the middle of the picture is Queen's Lodge built for the King's large family in 1778 on the site of Queen Anne's almost entirely demolished house (see plate 12). Behind it is Burford House (also to be seen in plate 12) which Queen Charlotte bought from the Duke of St Albans, Nell Gwynn's grandson, in 1777 for £4,000. The high cuspid Castle wall which can just be distinguished in the background above the King's hat was replaced by the present low wall so as to improve the view from Queen's Lodge. Queen's Lodge was demolished in 1823 by George IV after having been in existence for only forty-five years.

The Tudor buildings beneath the Round Tower can be seen more clearly in another of Sandby's drawings in plate 14. The tower on the right beneath the rocket is Winchester Tower (see plate 13).

This engraving was reversed by its original printer but the mistake has been corrected in this reproduction. The Queen's Tower, where Queen Charlotte lived, after regretfully leaving Queen's Lodge, is at the right and the King's comfortless apartments on the ground floor of the north front where the soldier is standing. A more accurate drawing of this front is shown in plate 26.

Formerly Charles ii's private sitting-room, with doors on the right leading to the King's Dressing Room (where he slept) and on the left to the Queen's Drawing Room. This room was redecorated by George iii between 1800 and 1807 when its walls were hung with scarlet cloth and the ceiling was repainted by Matthew Wyatt. The room was remodelled by William iv whose Queen's arms and monogram are on the ceiling which visitors to the State Apartments now see. The large painting above the fireplace is 'The Misers' attributed to Marinus van Reymerswaele and the writing-desk opposite it was used by William iii.

About ¾ mile south of the Castle in the Home Park, Frogmore (then known as Avelyns) was bought for the Crown by Henry viii. It was subsequently let to a succession of tenants and was sold during the Civil War. It did not return into royal hands until almost the end of the eighteenth century. Queen Charlotte improved the house and laid out the grounds with great care and towards the end of her life spent much of her time here. It was subsequently inhabited by Queen Victoria's mother the Duchess of Kent who lies buried in a mausoleum in the grounds as do her daughter and son-in-law Prince Albert. George v and his family lived there for a time when he was Duke of York.

This drawing and the one above it were done shortly before Queen Charlotte's death in 1818. Frogmore is no longer inhabited, being used as a family storehouse and museum.

Hugh May's windows may be compared with the few angular slits in the twelfth-century walls as shown in plate 8.

This drawing on stone by C. Basebee was done six years after the one reproduced above. It shows Wyatville's Gothicisation completed and the 'sunken' garden already established.

The new octagonal tower on the left (Brunswick Tower) and the two towers in the middle were inserted by Wyatville to break up Hugh May's plain front. As can be seen in the lower picture the Gothicisation of the windows in the Star Building had already been done by Wyatville's uncle, James Wyatt, for George III. The squat Round Tower which had existed in the shape shown in the lower picture behind the Tudor building for more than six centuries, was raised to double its height so as to preserve its dominance over the rest of the Castle.

King Henry VII's building is at the far left (for the north front of it, overlooking the river, see plates 14 and 28). The tower to the right of it is King John's Tower. Further to the right is the main entrance to the State Apartments which was brought forward by Wyatville into the Quadrangle. The statues on either side of the big south window are of King Edward III and the Black Prince by Richard Westmacott. Behind is Horn Court which Wyatville roofed in to make the Waterloo Chamber. The Sovereign's Entrance opposite the State Entrance in the southeastern corner is also Wyatville's work. The windows of the upper floor are those of the Oak Dining Room (see page 227). Wyatville's Grand Corridor runs along on either side of it to the west and north. On the western side – on the right of the picture – is the new George IV Gateway leading out into the Home Park by the Long Walk (see plate 30). The Upper Ward as it appeared before Wyatville's reconstruction is shown in plate 12.

Wyatville made this gate to take Charles II's Long Walk into the Upper Ward. The two towers on either side of it are known as York Tower on the right and Lancaster Tower on the left. The rounded tower is King

Edward III Tower. This gate made the medieval Rubbish Gate to the west of it (see plate 12) unnecessary and it was demolished.

This gate is the main entrance to the Castle. It is first mentioned in 1194 and was rebuilt by King Henry VIII who had Queen Catherine of Aragon's pomegranate badge placed over the arch. The gate as it appeared before Wyatville altered it can be seen in plates 7 and 12.

George IV's *cottage orné* in the Great Park was built for him by John Nash. Most of it was demolished by William IV. Around what remained of it George VI built the present house where Queen Elizabeth the Queen Mother now lives.

Formed in the eighteenth century by William Augustus, Duke of Cumberland and Thomas Sandby, Paul's brother, it was a favourite retreat of the Duke's grand-nephew George IV who built the buildings on its shores and who gave parties in the tents which can be seen on the right.

The window looks out upon the East Terrace and George IV's 'sunken garden'. The Prince is wearing the unconventional clothes and boots which the Queen, unlike most of his fellow sportsmen, found so attractive.

This room, which is also the present Queen's sitting room, occupies the western half of the Queen's Tower (see plates 7 and 46). An oriel to the south commands an extensive view of the Park.

The large oriel on the right overlooks the 'sunken garden' (see plate 27).

The State Entrance was built in 1362. The Queen's Audience Chamber and the Queen's Presence Chamber (see plate 10) above the Hall were built by Hugh May for Charles II.

An idea of how the Castle has altered over the past 350 years may be had by comparing this view with Norden's 1607 survey (plate 3) and Hollar's 1670 drawing (plate 7).

Illustrations Number, 2, 8, 10, 11, 13, 14, 15, 17, 19, 20, 26, 28, 35, 36, 38, 41–45 are reproduced by gracious permission of H.M. the Queen, and Numbers 39, 40 by permission of B. T. Batsford Ltd. The plan on p. 6 is modified from Hope, Windsor Castle, by permission of Country Life Ltd. Other illustrations are acknowledged in the list above.

AUTHOR'S NOTE

This is a book about private lives and the Castle and lodges at Windsor in which they were led. No attempt has been made to examine constitutional or political problems; and very little space has been devoted either to architectural details or to the development of the Court. Every monarch from William I to Elizabeth II is mentioned in the book, but only those who have spent long periods at Windsor are discussed at length; and then it is with their personalities, interests, pleasures and with their daily routine that I have been principally concerned.

Inevitably the earlier and later chapters of such a book tend to take the form of a series of anecdotes and character sketches; it is only when dealing with the eighteenth and nineteenth centuries, for which the sources are numerous, detailed and explicit, that it is possible to suggest the atmosphere of life at Windsor as distinct from the atmosphere of life in the other royal palaces.

The book is, of course, designed to entertain rather than to instruct, and source references are given not as an aid to the student but as a means of acknowledging the help the amateur derives from the scholar and for the benefit of those ordinary readers (such as myself) who like to know what sort of authority the writer has for the stories he tells and the opinions he expresses.

Most of the books from which I have quoted are by authors long since dead. Of more recent writers of memoirs, letters and diaries I am particularly grateful to Mabel, Countess of Airlie; Lady Diana Cooper; the Marchioness Curzon of Kedleston; Consuelo Vanderbilt Balsan; Georgiana, Baroness Bloomfield; the Duke of Windsor; Reginald, Viscount Esher; the third Baron Ormathwaite; Lord Ribblesdale; Mohamed Shah; Aga Khan and Sir Frederick Ponsonby whose books are listed in the bibliography.

The quotations from Fanny Burney's letters are from Charlotte Barrett's edition published in 1904; those from Mrs Papendiek's journal from Mrs Vernon Delves Broughton's edition published in 1887; those from Lady Lyttleton's letters from the Hon. Mrs Hugh Wyndham's edition published in 1912; those from the Hon. Eleanor Stanley from Mrs Steuart Erskine's edition published in 1916; and that from the diaries of Colonel the Hon. Fulke Greville from F. McKno Bladon's edition published in 1930. The edition of Charles Greville's diary which I have used is the one published by Macmillan in 1938 and edited by Roger Fulford and Lytton Strachey; and the edition of Miss Knight's autobiography that published by William Kimber in 1960 also edited by Roger Fulford.

AUTHOR'S NOTE

Princess Lieven's letters to Prince Metternich are from *The Private Letters of Princess Lieven*, edited by Peter Quennell for John Murray (1948); and the letters to the Duchess of Manchester from *My Dear Duchess*, edited by A. L. Kennedy also for John Murray (1956). *The Journal of Mrs Arbuthnot* was edited by Francis Bamford and the Duke of Wellington and published by Macmillan (1950).

The description of George IV by Queen Victoria is from *The Letters of Queen Victoria* (1st Series) edited by A. C. Benson and Lord Esher (1908) and Lord Randolph Churchill's letter to his father about Edward VII and Queen Alexandra from *Lord Randolph Churchill* by Winston Churchill (1907). Eleanor Roosevelt's account of an evening at Windsor after the Second World War is from her autobiography *On My Own* (Hutchinson, 1959). And Mr Dermot Morrah's views about the British attitude towards monarchy from his book, *The Queen at Work* (William Kimber, 1958).

What knowledge I have acquired and imparted about the architectural history of the Castle comes almost entirely from W. H. St John Hope's monumental *Windsor Castle* (published in two volumes by Country Life in 1913) and from Sir Owen Morshead's *Windsor Castle* (Phaidon Press, 1951).

I have to acknowledge the gracious permission of Her Majesty the Queen to reproduce prints, drawings and paintings in her private collections.

For their help in a variety of ways I also thank Mrs Joan St George Saunders of Writers' and Speakers' Research, Mrs Peter Crane, Mrs Stephen O'Malley, Miss Georgina Stonor, Mr Roger Fulford, Professor Arthur Aspinall, Miss Scott-Elliot and my wife. I am particularly grateful to Miss Olwen Hedley, on whose unrivalled knowledge of the Castle's history I have been able to call, for her kindness in having read the manuscript.

C.H.

1

Normans and Plantagenets

FORTRESS AND FEASTING HALL

He came from the Devil, it was said of him, and to the Devil he would return. There was a legend that the blood of Satan himself ran through his veins and his sons did not deny it. 'Do not deprive us of our heritage,' they protested when stopped from fighting each other. 'We cannot help acting like devils.'[1]

When he was angry their father, Henry II, the first of the Angevin kings, would throw himself to the floor, and grind the rushes that covered it between his teeth; and once in his rage he fell screaming out of bed and crammed his mouth with the stuffing of his mattress.

He could never bear to be still; he sat down only in his horse's saddle or when he had to eat, and he always ate impatiently without apparent pleasure. All his business he transacted standing up, walking backwards and forwards on strong, bowed legs, cleaning or mending his hunting gear. Even during Mass, which he attended daily, he fidgeted and talked in a harsh, cracked voice, and scratched himself and scribbled orders, notes and messages. After a whole day spent riding or walking so hard that his legs and feet were covered in sores and blisters, he would stay up half the night talking and arguing. He had more learning than any other European king of his time and he was constantly increasing it. Yet he never seemed tired nor ever satisfied.

He was short and rather fat and a big hard round head, with reddish hair cropped very short, grew out of a neck like the neck of a bull. His grey eyes were prominent and occasionally bloodshot and his hands were large and coarse. He hunted with such ferocious energy, he said, to keep his weight down; but one of the chroniclers at his court thought it was to dispel his erotic dreams. His sexual appetite surprised even his contemporaries.[2]

His Court, though, was almost oriental in its complete seclusion from female influences.[3] And it was, indeed, not a Court that held much appeal for most women, for it was so often and so uncomfortably on the move; while the food provided was apparently almost inedible. The bread, grumbled Peter of Blois, was 'not neaded, nor leavened, made of the dregs of beer; bread like lead, full of bran and unbaked'. The wine was 'thick, greasy and rancid' and tasted of pitch. 'I have sometimes seen wine so full of dregs put before noble-men,' he went on, 'that they were compelled rather to filter than to drink it, with their eyes shut and teeth closed. The beer at court is horrid to taste and filthy to look at. On account of the great demand, meat is sold whether it be fresh or not. The fish one buys is four days old, yet the fact that it stinks does not lessen the price.'[4]

But to the King neither food nor comfort was important. He seemed to despise them both in his anxiety to keep moving and never to waste time. Impatient, energetic, industrious and wary, he was not a man to trust others to do things he could do himself. He had possessions abroad as well as in England and his marriage, two years before he became King in 1154, to Eleanor of Aquitaine, the divorced wife of Louis VII, greatly extended them. A strong taste as well as a real talent for legislation and administration urged on his restless nature to govern these possessions, as his son John was to try to govern them, by direct and personal rule. And so the long straggling lines of the horses and pack animals, the wagons and carriages of the Royal Household became a familiar sight on the roads of England.

There were many animals and carts, for it was not only a household on the move but a government, not only the court of a king but of a man who had to prove himself a king. The Lord High Steward, the Lord High Chancellor, the Lord High Treasurer, the Lord President of the Council, the Lord Great Chamberlain, the Lord High Con-stable, the Keepers of the Seals and the King's Marshal – these were the Crown's most powerful officers; but they were also, when the King needed them to be, members of his peripatetic Household, with household duties to perform and with stipulated allowances of food, wine and perquisites. The poulterers and fruiterers, the bakers, cooks and confectioners who prepared this food and the servitors who served it, the butlers who looked after the wine and the Keepers of the Cups who poured it out, the Usher of the Spithouse and the Keeper of the Dishes, the Master Steward of the Larder and the Workmen of the Buttery, all had to travel when the King travelled. Nor was it only the staffs of the kitchen, the buttery, the larder and the spithouse who had to do so. Chaplains, clerks, limners, ushers, lawyers, hornblowers, watchmen, guards, archers and huntsmen, Cat Hunters and Wolf Catchers, Keepers of Gazehounds and Keepers of Brachs, all had to follow the Court. There had to be a Keeper of the Tents and a Chamberlain of the Candles, a washer-woman to wash the King's clothes and a water-carrier to give him his bath. And rumbling along over the rough roads, in clouds of dust in summer, splashing through the mud in winter, were the wagons and pack animals, the horses and the oxen, with their bundled bags and leather pouches, their barrels of silver pennies, their boxes of jewels, their documents and kitchen utensils, hunting-spears and altar cloths, chalices, quills and parchment, tables and feather beds, chamber pots and scent bottles.[5]

Riding along beside and behind this royal caravan were all sorts of scholars and artists as well as 'actors, singers, dicers, confectioners, huxters, gamblers, buffoons and barbers', and hurrying along ahead of it were express messengers whose duty it was to give warning of its approach and to advise the owners or tenants of estates on the route to collect provisions or to provide accommodation. Under feudal law grants of lands were frequently made conditional upon the performance of some service, and a common service required was *firma unius noctis* – one night's entertainment for the travelling Household of the King. Often, of course, there was a royal castle on the route – there were, apart from hunting lodges, about sixty castles more or less permanently in royal hands towards the end of the twelfth century[6] – and special apartments were always kept ready for the arrival of the King and his entourage (as well as at West-minster and in the Tower) at Winchester, Nottingham, Ludgershall, Marlborough, and Windsor. And it was to Windsor in 1184 that the King and his Court came for the Christmas holidays.

*   *   *

The Castle was by then already a massive structure whose walls, built of immensely thick slabs of heath-stone, were commanded by a dominating tower in which the archers, looking through their high arrow-slits, could see for miles across the river valley to the south and west, and to the north as far as the hills of Buckinghamshire.

The site, covering about thirteen acres in the Manor of Clewer, had been chosen by Henry's great-grandfather, William I, who, attracted by a position at the top of a steep hill high above the river, from which a subject and unfriendly people could be constantly reminded of their intimidating Norman conquerors, had built a fortress there to close a ring of other fortresses that secured the safety of his chosen capital in London.

Round the summit of this hill, except on the northern side where the sheer slope up from the river made it unnecessary, and from north to south across it, Norman soldiers and native labourers had dug a deep ditch; and the earth and chalk removed had been thrown up to make a high mound in the middle of the hill's crest.[7] The quadrangular baileys or wards formed on either side of the mound were protected by the ditch on three sides and the escarpment on the fourth. Beyond the ditch a palisade of felled trees, whose branches had been lopped off and whose ends had been sharpened to points, followed the line of a rampart of earth and stones. The fortification was approached by means of the drawbridge in the south-western

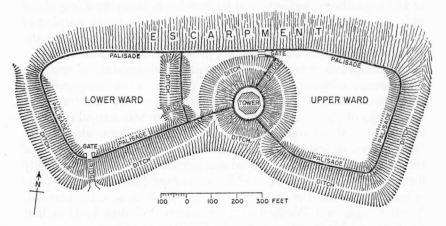

Probable arrangement of the Norman earthwork.

corner (in the position now occupied by King Henry VIII gate – see plate 31) and the Upper Ward was approached from the Lower by means of another drawbridge across the ditch which divided them and through a gate placed between the bottom of the mound and the edge of the escarpment. The Upper Ward was, therefore, the safer and it was accordingly here that the King's houses developed.

The Castle became for William I, though, as for most of his successors, a great deal more than a fortress. For around it, farther than the eye could stretch, lay a vast expanse of uncultivated country of heath and forest where wild oxen and boars, red and fallow deer, foxes, wolves and hares, roamed and ran, bred and multiplied beneath skies alive with the movement of birds. The Saxon kings had hunted there, chasing the wild boar with bows and arrows, and returning at night to a royal manor house in the parish of Wyndleshore (now Old Windsor) down by the river.[8] And William I and his two sons, William II and Henry I, had all followed the example of their Saxon predecessors, hunting by day and returning at night to their new Castle on the hill. They enclosed tracts of woodland and appointed a parker;[9] they instituted a system of fines for tenants on the royal desmesne who failed to drive their deer for them;[10] they built kennels for the royal hounds and mews for the royal falcons; and so Windsor became for the Norman kings a place of pleasure as well as of defence.[11]

The new buildings that developed inside the palisade were for the most part still of wood. There were huts for the soldiers of the garrison and for the huntsmen and falconers; there were gatehouses by the drawbridges; there were stables; there were cages for prisoners; there were secret subterranean passages to provide outlets in time of siege; there was a great hall and a kitchen; there were houses for the king and his court; and there must have been – although nothing remains to indicate its position – a chapel, for the Bishop of Salisbury insisted that it was his right and not the Archbishop of Canterbury's to marry Henry I to his second Queen there in 1121.* But there was very little masonry until Henry II, in the twelfth year of his reign, having rescued England from the chaos into which the civil war of Stephen's time had plunged it, began an ambitious building programme which was to last for six years.

*   *   *

Hard heath-stone blocks of a silicate and crystalline composition, washed so clean by every shower of rain that they were to retain their pristine freshness for eight centuries, were brought up from quarries near Bagshot; lead for the roofs was brought down three hundred miles from Cumberland; workmen – obliged by law, when impressed by a sheriff, to work for the King – were brought from wherever they could be found. Soon large buildings developed in the Upper Ward, stone walls stretched for half a mile, and an immense stone tower was built on the artificial mound which had now settled firmly enough to bear its great weight.[13]

---

* It was decided that the Sovereign must always be a parishioner of the Archbishop of Canterbury. The Archbishop, however, was so old and feeble that his right to marry the King was delegated to the Bishop of Winchester; but Ralph Cantuar, determined to play his part, came to the chapel. He was rather late and when he arrived the crown had already been placed on Henry's head. It had been arranged that this should be done by the Archbishop, who crossly asked the King the name of the man that had presumed to usurp his authority. Henry said he had not been taking much notice so could not say. The Archbishop lifted the crown up, so that he could put it back on the royal head himself.[12]

By 1184 when the King came to Windsor for the Christmas holidays, the new Castle was a home as well as one of the most powerful strongholds in England. Henry did not, of course, have either the time or the temperament to use it as a home. Nor did his son Richard I, a tall, commanding, gifted homosexual of savage and cruel temper, immense courage and churlish arrogance, who was preoccupied with plans to rescue the holy places from the infidel and to secure his Continental possessions from French attack. But Richard's youngest brother John who succeeded him in 1199 was a frequent visitor at Windsor.

A man with his father's restless energy and ruthless determination to govern his kingdom personally, John rarely stayed long and never for more than a week.[14] His visits, though, were memorable events, for his tastes, unlike his father's, were far from frugal, while his love of hunting was quite as intense. When he came to the Castle to enjoy the pleasures of hunting in the Forest and hawking along the banks of the river, he took pains to ensure that his guests were lavishly entertained. At Christmas in 1213 the Sheriffs of the surrounding counties were ordered to send to Windsor 2,000 capons, 15,000 herrings, 1,000 eels, 1,000 pounds of almonds and 6,000 gallons of wine,* as well as quantities of spices, wagonloads of wood and coal, pitchers, cups and dishes, and rolls of cloth for his tailor to make up into towels and table-napkins and into new surcoats for his loyal knights.[19]

The provision of clothes, as well as sport and entertainment, for these knights was, indeed, one of John's most regular expenses.[20] And it was necessary that this should be so. For, having 'the mental abilities of a great King, but the inclinations of a petty tyrant',[21]

---

* Gascony wine was then about 1¼d. a gallon (there was a vineyard on the slopes of the Castle hill but it was not large enough to provide sufficient wine for all the household) and a fat hog cost about 3s. Although it is impossible, of course, to make any satisfactory or even remotely relevant comparisons, money was, perhaps, worth roughly sixty times its present value. Even so, wine and pork were not cheap for the ordinary labourers and poor clerks, and in winter when meat was scarce owing to lack of fodder they could rarely afford it, although the royal Norwegian gerfalcons were regularly fed on pork as well as on chicken and doves.[15] Fish was still fairly cheap, for eel and salmon and roach abounded in the Thames between Gravesend and Henley bridge, but the clumsy methods of fishing employed (including a trained polar bear)[16] were gradually destroying the fry; and by the second half of the fourteenth century an average salmon cost as much as 10s.[17] Watchmen at Windsor received 2d. a day and gardeners 2¼d., building labourers got 1s. a week, skilled carpenters 2s. a week and skilled masons 4s. In 1155 the Castle's chaplain (there was only one until the reign of Henry III but thereafter the numbers of chaplains grew as new chapels were built within the Castle walls and new chantries endowed) received 1d. a day.[18]

John had alienated most of those who might otherwise have supported him and was driving the feudal classes to revolt. In 1215 he was forced to open negotiations with the representatives of these classes at Runnymede, an island in the Thames four miles downstream from Windsor, and to approve a Great Charter renouncing his ambitions for a personal dictatorship. Each evening, after the long and aggravating discussions of the day, it is said that he rolled on the floor in his rage, in the characteristic Angevin manner, clawing at the air, gnawing sticks and straw, his face mottled with blue spots.[22]

He signed the Charter, but only to deny its validity; and civil war broke out. The Castle, however, defended by Engelard de Cicogné, its energetic Constable, a man 'very skilful in the art of war', who owed everything he had to the King, withstood all the onslaughts that were made upon it. The great tower and the high stone walls were pounded for nearly three months by the immense balls thrown at it by the besiegers' *perrière*, the beam of which was twice cut in half by Engelard's raiding parties, who crept out at night through the secret passages which led into the Castle ditch.[23] Several buildings, most of them on the western side of the Upper Ward, were reduced to rubble,[24] but the main defences held firm; and at the end of September 1216 the siege was abandoned.

Not until the Great Rebellion was the Castle that John had 'loved above all others' attacked again.[25] And for a hundred years, throughout the reigns of his son Henry III, of his grandson Edward I (whose Queen, Eleanor, spent most of her time in England at Windsor)[26] and of his great-grandson Edward II, Windsor Castle, growing and changing all the time, provided a background for the pleasures and business of a royal court and a setting for royal charity,* rather than a stronghold for a threatened royal garrison. New towers, no longer square but D-shaped (since the experience of the Crusaders had revolutionised the science of military architecture) were built into the outer wall, for the Castle, like all others, had still to have the strength and appearance of a fortress and had still to contain a strong garrison whose service to the Crown was accepted as an alternative to service in the field.[28] But behind those towers and that faceless, threatening wall, a palace was taking shape – a palace with walls and towers gaily painted on the outside as well as within, with fine

---

* Henry III, whose distributions to the poor were immense, provided in 1239 for feasts for the poor in the great hall of the Castle at Christmas and in the small hall on St Stephen's Day and at Epiphany. Poor clerks and chaplains were also feasted on St Thomas's Day and poor children on Innocents' Day.[27]

rooms overlooking fine gardens, and beyond the gardens a beautiful park where foreign visitors could be entertained with hunting parties and with tournaments. Windsor Castle was, in fact – so a chronicler said towards the end of the thirteenth century – the 'most magnificent palace that existed in all Europe'.[29] And the entertainments that were given there were as renowned all over Europe as the buildings themselves.

At a splendid tournament in 1277 gilded armour, emblazoned tunics and surcoats, with aiguillettes fixed to the shoulder with silk cords, were provided for all the knights who came to take part in the 'peaceable jousts'. The knights were presented also with specially painted shields, richly embroidered saddles and swords whose pommels and hilts were gilded with pure gold. Finely woven fabrics for their ladies' dresses came, together with silk and furs, from Paris at a cost of over £600; and for the occasion the King himself, Edward I, ordered seven new carpets for his bedroom, several carved ivory combs and half a dozen pairs of buckskin gloves.[30]

Magnificent and extravagant as this entertainment was, however, its splendour was soon to be surpassed when the King's grandson, Edward III, returned to Windsor to enjoy the spoils of his foreign wars and to found the 'greatest military Order in Christendom'.

[ii]

KNIGHTS OF THE GARTER

Chivalry, Bishop Stubbs decided, was 'the gloss put by fine manners on vice and selfishness and contempt for the rights of man'.[1] But for Edward III chivalry was far more than a gloss; it was an instrument of power. Handsome, brave, ambitious and self-indulgent, by turns revengeful and forgiving, flamboyantly pious without true religious feeling, of limitless energy and great physical strength, he was himself the epitome of the medieval knight. And it was by his successful appeal to the selfish instincts of the aristocratic classes that his triumphs were achieved. These classes did not want peace or retrenchment; they wanted the excitement and danger, the prestige and rewards of war. Edward, a fierce nationalism urging him to make France and Scotland dependent on England's will, was able to indulge them.

He gave them war and he shared with them the pleasures that followed war. They supported him because he was one of them; and no one knew better than he how strong are the bonds of friendship forged by pleasures shared. There is more than an element of propaganda in 'the most brilliant inspiration of the Age of Chivalry'.[2]

This inspiration was not a sudden one. Towards the end of 1343, after defeating the Scots at Halidon Hill and destroying the French navy off Sluys, Edward went to his favourite castle at Windsor where he had been born thirty-one years before. Here he decided to hold a magnificent tournament, lasting four days, to which 'a great array of earls, barons, ladies and damoiselles' would be invited. The feast was to be 'most grand and noble with good cheer and good joustings'.[3]

On 1 January 1344 letters of safe conduct were drawn up and sent out; and about three weeks later, from all over England as well as from 'parts beyond the seas', there came to Windsor 'an indescribable host of people to delight in so great a solemnity'. On the first evening the ladies were shown to their places in the great hall of the Castle by the King himself, who arranged them according to their rank. His good and gentle wife Queen Philippa was there and his mother Queen Isabella and so many other 'countesses, baronesses, as well as ladies and gentlewomen' that they 'could not easily be counted'. There was, in fact, not enough room for the men to sit down with them and a tent had to be put up in the courtyard.

The meal was lavish, 'abounding in the most alluring of drinks', and as the guests ate and drank, minstrels wearing new tunics provided by the King specially for the occasion played music in the gallery.[4] And afterwards, as a satisfied guest remembered, 'dances were not lacking, embraces and kissings alternately commingling'.[5]

This was, at that time, the manner in which the evenings after feasts and tournaments were commonly spent, since according to the ethos of chivalry, an act of infidelity was no disgrace. Indeed, a knight who got married without first having made love to the wife of another knight, preferably one of a higher rank than himself, was not considered worthy of his spurs.[6] In an age when most marriages were *mariages de convenance* contracted at a very early age – for the average life of a nobleman was less than forty years[7] – adultery had become an accepted social diversion of the upper classes, with a recognised code of behaviour compatible with chivalrous ideals. The knight must be prepared to observe the manners of polite society as well as to fight and die for the object of his passion, but otherwise he might behave as he liked. 'Woman-hunting was, it may be said, a normal sport.'[8] Chastity girdles were not worn by ladies in fourteenth-century courts, as the virtue of a lady, if it were to be protected at all, must be preserved by the sword and not by the key in the manner of an Italian merchant,[9] just as her heart must be won, not by money, nor by wit, nor by subtle appeals to her sexual appetite, but by feats of strength and daring. The tournament, then, as well as an exercise in arms, was a form of love-play. The men, gorgeously dressed in coloured silk surcoats over their armour, with bells jingling on horse bridles which were bound round with gold thread, charged at each other with long gilded spears whose blunted tips shone brightly in the sun, and swung at each other with swords of whalebone covered with silvered parchment, while sitting above them in their silk-draped stands the women watched and judged.

In former times these displays had taken the form of mock battles or *mêlées* fought in open fields, with numerous knights on each side lashing out at each other indiscriminately and ferociously in their efforts to unhorse their opponents. But now they were more usually tests of individual skill, performed in boarded enclosures and preceded and followed by the ceremonial of an elaborate pageantry in which the presence of women was an essential part. They were still dangerous, for the antagonists rode full tilt at each other and were sometimes thrown to the ground with such force that they never recovered; but although barriers to prevent the horses colliding were not in common use until the fifteenth century,[10] many rules had grown up to limit the sorts of weapon which might be used in close-quarter combat and the manner of using them, and these rules were rigidly enforced. The indiscriminate violence of the battlefield was giving way to the formal pageantry of the *plaza del toros*.[11]

Each knight had a 'favourite fair one who was not only esteemed by him as the paragon of beauty but supplied the place of a tutelar saint to whom he paid his vows and addressed himself on the day of peril'.[12] He prayed to her for victory, and to Our Lady that, after victory, his prowess in the lists might be rewarded by an opportunity to demonstrate his prowess as a lover.[13] And if he had fought well the ladies who had watched him fight might formally express their hope that his prayers would be fully answered. For at the end of the day, after he had taken off his helm in front of them, bowed and returned to his room to have his armour removed, they decided who

should win their prizes and were required by the regulations governing these occasions to deliver their verdict in these words: 'Sir,
theis ladyes and gentilwomen thonk you for your disporte and grete
labour yt ye have this day in their presences. And the seide ladyes
and gentilwomen seyen that ye, Sir —— have done the best joust
this day. Therefore the seide ladyes and gentilwomen gevyn you this
diamonde and send you much worship and joy of yor lady.'[14] Sometimes, indeed, the ladies did not merely give away the prizes but
constituted the prizes themselves.[15]

*   *   *

After the third day of the jousts at Windsor in 1344, the King,
having himself won three of the six prizes,[16] asked all his guests to
remain in the Castle until the following morning as he had an
announcement to make. And when he came out of his chapel after
Mass on Thursday morning nobody could doubt that the announcement would be an important one. He was wearing a cloak of 'very
precious velvet and the royal crown was placed upon his head' and
the royal sceptre was in his hand. The Earl of Derby, Seneschal of
England, and the Earl of Salisbury, Marshal of England, went before
him, and the Prince of Wales, later to be known as the Black Prince,
and the Queen, stout and rather plain but 'most nobly adorned',
followed him.

'At the place appointed for the assembly' the King solemnly
placed his hand upon the Bible and 'took a corporeal oath that he
would begin a Round Table in the same manner and condition as the
Lord Arthur, formerly King of England, appointed it, namely to the
number of 300 knights, a number always increasing, and he would
cherish it and maintain it according to his power'.[17]

The Round Table was one of chivalry's most treasured legends
and purest ideals. By the time of Edward III it had admittedly come
to mean little more than an association of knights who met from time
to time, as Roger Mortimer's friends had done at Kenilworth, to
joust during the day and to feast at night, sitting with their shields
at their backs, at a table which set aside all distinctions of rank and
quality, every place being equally honourable. But as originally
conceived by King Arthur – that 'stout and successful Martialist, of
incredible courage and gallantry, the most famous and renowned of
all the British Kings', whose miraculous exploits in the sixth century
were already the legends of a forgotten age – the Round Table was
an expression of the eternal principles of knighthood. The knights

of the first Round Table were bound, in the words of Sir Thomas Malory, 'never to do outrageousity, nor murder, and always to flee treason. Also by no means to be cruel, but to give mercy unto him that asketh mercy . . .; and always to do ladies, damsels, and gentlewomen succour upon pain of death.'[18] This conception of the true knight's obligations to behave as a noble and gentle man was a real step forward into the light out of the shadows of the Dark Ages; and, although the knight did not in fact often live up to his high ideals, and although chivalry itself was dying in Edward III's time, in the face of the rising power of those outside the aristocratic class and in the choking smoke of gunpowder, the King's announcement at Windsor that January morning was an attempt to restore to the Round Table its early ideals and *mystique*.

It was also, of course, an excuse to bind his supporters more closely to his cause, and it was – this was no doubt of more immediate interest to those staying in the Castle at the time – an excuse for further festivities.

Indeed, as soon as the oaths were taken, binding the knights to each other and to the service of the weak and the wronged, the trumpets and kettle drums sounded 'all together, and the guests hastened to a feast; which feast was complete with richness of fare, variety of dishes, and overflowing abundance of drinks: the delight was unutterable, the comfort inestimable, the enjoyment unalloyed, the hilarity without care'.[19]

*   *   *

Within a few days, work began on a circular building in the great courtyard of the Upper Ward in which the feasts of the Round Table could, in future, regularly be held. The bridges over the Castle ditch were covered with sand and heather to protect them from the wheels of the heavy wagons which were to come rumbling across with loads of stone and timber; and the King's carpenter and mason and their deputies were sent out as far afield as Kent and Norfolk with letters authorising them to collect materials, to impress workmen and to 'arrest and take as often as there may be need' all punts on the Thames between Gravesend and Henley.[20]

By the beginning of March there were over 700 men at work, including 131 men cutting and shaping stone in the quarries at Bustlesham (Bisham) south of Marlow, and 40 men in sand and lime pits. Working at the Castle itself were 170 cutting and laying masons, 15 carpenters, 3 smiths and 361 labourers. Their wages varied from 9d. a week paid to the junior smith, to 4s. paid to a skilled cutting mason. Skilled carpenters received 2s. a week, junior carpenters 1s. 3d. The master mason and master carpenter were paid 7s. a week and the labourers 1s.

Materials came from many different parts of the country and from abroad. Stone shipped from Caen in Normandy came up-river from London, the softer English stone of Bustlesham came downstream from Marlow, and by wagon from Reigate and from the quarries of Kent. Immense loads of timber came from Kingston and Reading, Easthampstead and Hartley Park.

A well was sunk for water for the masons' mortar; a forge was built for the smiths; a limekiln was tended throughout the night. For five weeks the men were kept hard at work; and then, as suddenly as it had begun, the activity ceased. A fortnight before Easter nearly all the men were sent away and by the autumn the building of the great feasting hall was abandoned altogether.[21]

For the King was at war again. He had decided that 'much treasure must be got together for other affairs',[22] and he could no longer afford the weekly wages bill and the cost of the materials still required at Windsor. On a hot August day in 1346, however, he defeated the French army of Philip VI at Crécy, and two months later various northern lords who were not serving with him in France routed the Scots at Neville's Cross and captured the young King David, afterwards sending him to Windsor Castle where so many other distinguished prisoners had been and were to be held.* The following year, after a long siege, Calais was captured and Edward could return home once more in triumph to revel in his plunder.

---

* These prisoners had included Robert de Mowbray, Earl of Northumbria, and were afterwards to include many French and Scottish noblemen captured in the wars. James, the eldest surviving son of Robert III of Scotland, was a prisoner for eleven years in the Castle where he fell in love with Joanna Beaufort, daughter of the Earl of Somerset, whom he had seen one day walking in the Moat Garden below the Devil's Tower where he was imprisoned. His poem *The Kingis Quair* has for its main theme his love for this girl whom he was eventually allowed to marry in 1424 after he had succeeded his father as James I of Scotland. These well-born captives were treated chivalrously. King David and his fellow Scottish prisoners were permitted to take part in a tournament in 1348 and were provided with decorative harnesses by Edward III.[23] John, King of France, taken prisoner at Poitiers in 1356, was permitted to 'hunt hawk and take what other diversions he pleased in that neighbourhood, as well as the Lord Philip his son'.[24] King James of Scotland was provided with an allowance of £700 a year by Henry V. The numerous lesser prisoners – workmen who had run away from the Castle to earn better wages than the King paid, witches, and men convicted of offences against the Forest Laws – who were incarcerated in the 'Colehous' in the Lower Ward were, of course, treated far less mercifully.

He had never appeared more happy, more confident, or more successful. 'A new sun seemed to have risen in England' when he and his friends came back to Windsor, with clothes and furs and feather beds and the spoils of foreign cities, to abandon themselves to pleasure and to 'many deeds of love and nobleness, of pleasantry and of prowess'.[25] The wild extravagance of their celebrations seemed, however, to some chroniclers wickedly wanton. Women paraded themselves in expensive dresses 'without thought of the French ladies' from whom they had been looted; and others 'of the most beautiful, but not of the best of the kingdom' appeared in 'divers and wonderful male apparel', with chequered tunics and tight belts and with their hair bound up in turbans, to 'vex their bodies with scurrilous wantonness'.[26]

For the King himself, though, continuous pleasure was never enough. The unfinished feasting hall for the knights of the Round Table, its walls covered by tiles to protect them from the frost, still stood in the Upper Ward to remind him of his obligations as a knight and as a leader and sovereign of knights. And soon his restless ambition drove him to consider a far greater enterprise 'more particular and more select'.[27]

* * *

The early statutes of the Order of the Garter have been lost, and for centuries men have speculated as to its origins. The most pleasant and romantic story is well known. It is that the King was dancing at a ball with Joane, Countess of Salisbury, when her garter fell off. Edward stooped down quickly and picked it up. Some of the other dancers saw him do so and began to tease him. He replied sharply, '*Honi soit qui mal y pense*'* and added, when they continued laughing and snatching the garter out of each other's hands, that in a short time they should 'see the garter advanced to so high honour and estimation, as to account themselves happy to wear it'.

The earliest authority for this traditional story is Polydore Vergil, who did not arrive in England until the next century. The chronicles of Jean Froissart, the Flemish courtier who came to Edward III's court with a letter of introduction from the Count of Hainaut, Queen Philippa's uncle, do not mention it, although Froissart did say that Edward fell in love with the Countess of Salisbury when he rescued

---

* Edward III is believed to have been the first King after the conquest (with the possible exception of Henry I) to have a little English; but it was not a language he used in ordinary conversation.

her from a castle in the north of England which was being besieged by the Scots during her husband's absence in France.

The story, in fact, came to be dismissed as a 'vain and idle romance derogatory both to the founder and to the Order'.[28] And Elias Ashmole, the seventeenth-century antiquary, whose history of the Order remains the most authoritative, thought it a 'vulgar' invention. Ashmole recorded another legend – although he thought it equally unfounded – which suggested that it was the Queen's garter which slipped from her leg as she was going to her room and that the King, after telling an attendant to pick it up, said to him, 'You make but small account of this garter, but within a few months I will cause the best of you all to reverence the like.' The motto, according to this legend, was the Queen's answer to the King's question as to what men would think of her for losing a garter so indecorously.[29]

There was a legend, too, that Richard I had once inspired some of his fellow Crusaders, worn out by days of fighting in the burning sun, to further efforts by tying round their legs, with his own hands, a leather thong to remind them that he relied upon them for the 'successful conclusion of his noble enterprise'. Ashmole concluded, however, that it was not Richard I in the Holy Land but Edward III himself at Crecy who had used the symbol of the Garter, as being one of 'unity and society', to encourage his knights on the battlefield and afterwards to reward them for their victory. The motto, Ashmole believed, was intended as a reflection of shame upon those who did not think well of his determination to gain the French crown by force of arms,[30] and a later historian of the Order has supported this view.[31]

In more recent years, however, Dr Margaret Murray put forward a quite different and startlingly original theory. It was her belief that in Edward III's time Christianity had not yet overthrown the old religion of witches and devil-worshippers and that the garter was a symbol of deep significance in that old religion. 'The confusion of the Countess,' she wrote, 'was not from the shock to her modesty – it took more than a dropped garter to shock a lady of the fourteenth century – but the possession of that garter proved that she was not only a member of the Old Religion but that she held the highest place in it.'[32] Edward III's words on picking it up, Dr Murray thought, were to indicate to his guests that he understood the garter's significance and that he, too, was a devotee of the old religion.

While this view of the Order's origin has not found wide acceptance, it does not seem necessary to turn back to a specifically military origin. A garter certainly represented, as Ashmole said, a 'badge of unity and concord'; but it was also the sort of favour which was not only worn by knights at a tournament as a compliment to their ladies – and was constantly used by Edward III himself for this romantic purpose – but which frequently became the device of medieval orders of chivalry. In fact, two of the greatest Knightly orders of Europe have badges with similar associations. The Order of the Annunziata, Italy's highest order of knighthood, dedicated to the honour of the Fifteen Mysteries of the Virgin, was once known as the Order of the Snares of Love, since the letters F.E.R.T., supposed to represent, *Frappez, Entrez, Rompez, Tout,* were inscribed on the collar of the Order, a collar which was designed in the shape of a bracelet, with love knots made from tresses of hair that the founder had received from his mistress.[33] Similarly, the Order of the Knights of the Golden Fleece was instituted by Philip II, Duke of Burgundy, who, so it was said, finding in the bedroom of his golden-haired mistress ('a most beautiful lady of Bruges') an undergarment of coarse country wool, made it the emblem of an Order, membership of which was to be denied to those who had derided his loved one's simple taste.[34]

Sir Harris Nicolas has said that nothing is more likely 'than that in a crowded assembly a lady should accidentally have dropped her garter; that the circumstance should have caused a smile in the bystanders; and that, on its being taken up by Edward, he should have reproved the levity of his courtiers by so happy and chivalrous exclamation, placing the garter at the same time on his knee, as "Dishonoured be he who thinks ill of it". Such a circumstance occurring at a time of general festivity, when devices, mottoes and conceits of all kinds were adopted as ornaments or badges on the habits worn at jousts and tournaments, would naturally have been commemorated, as other royal expressions seem to have been, by its conversion into a device and motto.'[35]

The most recent research supports this contention and it now seems certain that Edward III's dancing partner did drop her garter. She has been satisfactorily identified as Joane, Countess of Salisbury, in Froissart's opinion, '*la plus belle dame de tout la roiaulme d'Engleterre, et la plus amoureuse*'. She was probably Chaucer's model for the heroine of *Troilus and Criseyde*, and she married Edward III's son, the Black Prince, in 1361.[36]

Recent research also supports Sir Harris Nicolas's argument that the garter was originally no more than a badge worn by two teams

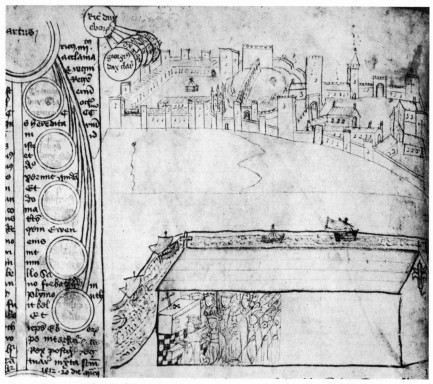

1. The earliest known drawing of Windsor Castle
from a MS Polychronicon in Eton College Library

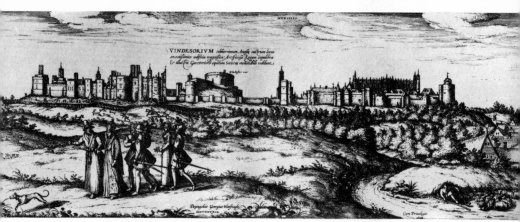

2. The Castle from the north-east *c.* 1570
from a drawing by George Hoefnagle in the Royal Library,
Windsor Castle

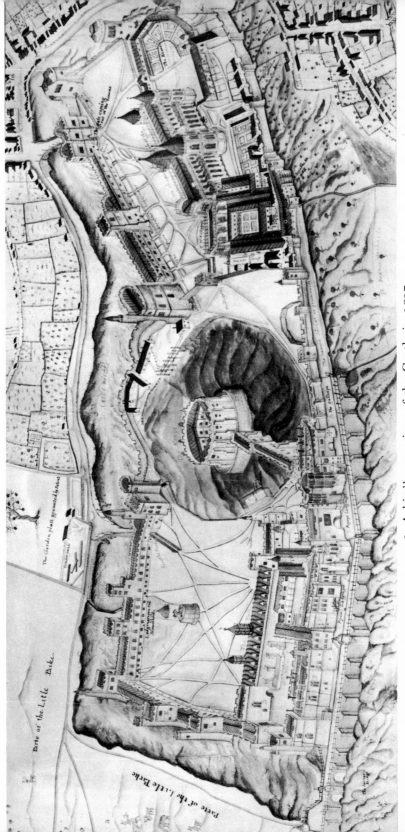

3. A bird's eye view of the Castle in 1607
from a copy of a survey by John Norden in the British Museum

Parte of the Litle Parke.

Parte of the Little Parke.

The Garden platt grauntedby fatent

of twelve knights, one team led by the King, the other by the Black Prince, during the tournament held at Windsor in the spring of 1348. And certainly the men chosen to be the first members of the Order lend weight to this theory, for some of them were very young and almost unknown as soldiers, while more distinguished knights, who had fought well in the recent war, were not at first elected.[37]

There were never to be more than twenty-five knights in all, with the King as Sovereign of the Order, for its exclusiveness, Edward decided, would be its guarantee of worth and nobility – a nobility to be enhanced by the splendour of its robes. The colour of these robes was to be blue, the colour of the arms of France – until the time of George iii, English kings followed Edward iii's example and always gave themselves the additional style of King of France – and they were all to be alike, for the equality of the Round Table was to be faithfully observed. The Sovereign's mantle, made of fine woollen cloth, 'to give a reputation to that homebred and native Commodity', was, however, unlike the others, to have a long train; and his surcoat, as well as being lined with miniver, as were those of the other knights, was to be bordered with ermine.

In time the style of the robes changed and became more elaborate than ever, and the materials from which they were made became richer and more rare. Mantles in the fifteenth century were made of velvet and lined with white damask. Surcoats were powdered all over with little garters, of silk and gold plate, carrying the Order's motto delicately embroidered in each. It became customary to embroider a larger garter on the left shoulder and to attach long silk cords to the collar. The hood was replaced by a cap of black velvet which later became a high crowned hat with a brim tacked up with immense jewels and a plume of white feathers, 'a stately Heron's feather rising in the middle' (see plate 4), and then it returned once more to its present shape of a sixteenth-century cap. Eventually a collar of gold, of thirty ounces troy weight, with a bejewelled image of St George, the martyred hero of the early Christian Church who was one of the Order's patrons,* was added to the robes; and another image, known as the Lesser George, was worn on a silk ribbon before the breast and, after this position was altered by Charles ii, under the right arm.[38] The garter itself, worn on the left leg a little below the knee, also became more elaborate as the years passed; and the garter presented to Gustavus Adolphus, King of Sweden, in 1629

* The other three patrons were the Holy Trinity, the Blessed Virgin Mary, and Edward the Confessor.

19

had, in addition to the usual gold buckle, the motto of the Order picked out upon the strap in 411 diamonds.[39]

Although it was originally the Sovereign himself who bore much of the heavy costs incurred by English as well as foreign knights, paying for their surcoats as well as for the robes of those of their ladies who were received into the Order as *Dames de la Fraternité de St. George*, the more elaborate the robes and insignia grew and the less the Sovereign contributed towards them, the more expensive it became to be elected to the Order. Nor did the expense end with these cloaks of silk and fur and velvet, these lavishly jewelled images and garters, these plumed hats with their cascades of rubies and pearls and diamonds; for each knight had to provide a helm, crest and sword to be hung up over his stall in the chapel of the Order. The helm, larger than the real one upon which it was modelled, was to be of steel 'parcel gilt with fine Gold in Oyle, wrought with Rabeskys and other works, and burnished with fine Gold'.[40] The mantlings were to be cloth of gold lined with sarcenet, and beneath them gilt knobs had to be placed on which could hang tassels of gold and silver intertwined with silk of the main colour of the knight's arms. The pommel, cross and chape of his sword had to be gilded and the scabbard had to be of cloth of gold. Embroidered banners became obligatory later.[41]

The installation fees rose with the passing of the years until, by the middle of the seventeenth century, election to the Order cost as much for a duke as a year's wages for thirty of his servants. Apart from fees due to the canons and choir of the chapel and to various minor officials of the Order, £38 had to be paid to the Register (the Dean of Windsor) towards the cost of his crimson satin robes, £90 to Garter King of Arms and £20 to the Gentleman Usher of the Black Rod.[42]

These last two dignitaries were, and have remained, more than picturesque figures created to enhance the Order's elaborate ceremonial. Garter King of Arms, an officer created by Henry v, is chief of the Heralds and the principal officer within the College of Arms. By the constitution of the Order framed by Henry viii, he was to be 'a person of gentile Blood, of an honest Name, bearing Ensigns, and superior to all the other Officers of Arms'. The Gentleman Usher of the Black Rod, who must be 'a gentleman, famous in Arms and Blood, and born within the Dominions of the Sovereign,' is 'for the honour of the Order' appointed the Chief Usher of the Kingdom. He carries his Black Rod before the Sovereign 'at the feast of St George within the castle of Windsor, and at other solemnities and chapters of the Order', and has the duty of touching with it any knight who has to be degraded.[43]

This rare punishment of degradation is to be inflicted not on knights found guilty of felony or immorality, but on those who are heretics or traitors, who flee from the field of battle, who waste their estate so prodigally that they can no longer afford to maintain their honour, or, lastly, who are discovered in the offence of 'not being a gentleman of blood'. The ceremony is a solemn one. Garter King of Arms is required to take from the offending knight his collar with its image of St George, and his garter; then to go to the chapel of the Order with 'such knights as are ordered to accompany him' and to read the formula for degradation. When he reaches the words, 'expelled and put from among the Arms', a Herald climbs a ladder, snatches up his crest and banner and sword and hurls them down into the choir. And the other knights kick them out of the Chapel through the Castle gate.[44]

*   *   *

For the first century and a half of the Order's history, the chapel where this awesome ceremony was performed was the one built in 1240 by Henry III, who had personally supervised the painting of it.[45] At the time of the Order's foundation, however, the building had fallen into disrepair, and it appeared to Edward III, who had been baptised in it, of 'convenient' but not of sufficient beauty. And so 'because it is a good way of merchandise, whereby, with a happy bartering, transitory things are exchanged for eternal', as the King's letters patent frankly and characteristically expressed it, the chapel was to be repaired and renovated and its establishment of eight chaplains was to be increased, with the Pope's consent, to that of a college comprising twelve canons, twelve priest-vicars (or, as they were later known, minor canons) and a *custos* (or Dean). And further, because it became the 'majesty of a king to delight always in acts of piety' so that when he stood before the tribunal of the Most High King he should not be 'condemned with the reprobates, as a slothful and unprofitable servant', the King announced that he would provide for the maintenance of twenty-four Poor Knights, 'impotent of themselves or inclining to poverty', who would daily attend Mass and pray for the souls of the Knights of the Garter.[46]

Although excused by these poor proxies from daily attendance to pray for their own souls, the Knights of the Garter were, however, required to celebrate a set number of Masses whenever one of their number died. The number laid down for the King, as Sovereign of the Order, was one thousand,[47] and the rule was, it seems, constantly observed until the reign of Henry VIII, when the Masses were compounded for a money compensation, ranging from £8 6s. 8d. for the Sovereign to 16s. 8d. for a Bachelor Knight. It was intended that the money handed over by the Knights should be devoted to charity and public works, but there was apparently always difficulty in collecting it. In the reign of Charles I, however, a considerable sum was collected. It was spent, though, not in the way originally intended but on the provision of new plate for the chapel altar.[48]

By then the College of St George was not nearly so rich as it once had been and could not perhaps otherwise have afforded the large sum involved. From its foundation the College had been endowed with lands and advowsons and freed from the payment of many taxes; and as the years passed many private grants had been made to it. But some of these grants were no more profitable than that made by the Corporation of Yarmouth which, on consideration that the Corporation were 'taken into their prayers', allowed the Canons every year 'a last of red herrings, well dried and cleansed'.[49] Also, since the Reformation, the College's most profitable source of income had ceased; for pilgrims no longer came to give offerings to its relics.

At one time these treasures had been numerous. In the fourteenth century, when faith in the power of relics of the earthly lives of Christ and his saints was still almost universal, they had included a thorn of Christ's crown, parts of his supper table, some of his mother's milk, and a piece of the Holy Cross which Edward I had been given by a former Crusader while campaigning in Wales. The marvellous collection was from time to time increased by the acquisition of parts of the skulls of St Bartholomew and St Thomas the Apostle, the shirt and some of the blood of St Thomas of Canterbury, arm bones of St William of York, St George, St Osytho and St Richard, various other parts of the skeletons of St Thomas of Hereford, St Margaret, St David, St William of England, St Maurice, St Elizabeth, St Vitale, Archbishop Edmund and St Gerard, part of the jaw bone of St Mark containing fourteen teeth, a rib of one of the eleven thousand virgins, part of the brain of St Eustace, a stone which had touched St Stephen, a white girdle given by St John the Evangelist to St Mary, a candle end which had belonged to the Blessed Virgin Mary and a piece of her tomb.*[50]

* There were so many bones in the collection that when the roof of the Chapel was repaired in Queen Victoria's reign and quantities of broken skeletons were found secreted

In 1414 the collection was further augmented by the Emperor Sigismund, brother-in-law to Richard I, who generously presented the very heart of St George together with his fingers.[52] By the end of the century the body of the holy king, Henry VI, was also in the chapel having been sent there with some of his armour, clothes and other possessions by Richard III in 1484.[53]

These relics of Henry VI were amongst the chapel's most treasured possessions, and pilgrims came from as far away as Cornwall to worship at the tomb on which they were placed. 'Seely betwitched People' – so a contemptuous writer said, looking back with horrified disdain upon the 'late Tyme of general Darkness when no place was free from one Sorte of superstitious Mawmetrie or other' – flocked to 'this Churche of Wyndsore' being 'persuaded that a small Chippe of his Bedsteade (which was kept heare) was a precious Relique, and that to put upon a Man's Heade an olde red Velvet Hatte of his (that lay heare also) was a Sovereign Medicine against the Head-ache.'*[54]

Nor were the remains of Henry VI, although the most distinguished that the chapel possessed, the only ones that were revered by ailing pilgrims. For on the south side of the altar, opposite the tomb of Edward IV, who was buried in the chapel at his own request, lay the bones of John Schorne, a parish priest who, in addition to a remarkable ability to cure the ague, had also possessed the even more remarkable power of forcing the devil into a boot.[56]

Strong iron money-boxes received the offerings of the pilgrims who came to worship at John Schorne's tomb. These boxes, still to be seen in St George's Chapel, were provided not only with numerous coin slots, but also with four different locks,[57] a precaution which seemed justified. For, according to the Poor Knights, the behaviour of the Canons was outrageous. They misappropriated the donations

in it, the canons believed they must be saintly relics. They had been found in deep holes in the pinnacles where once heraldic beasts had stood. These stone beasts, placed there in the reign of Henry VII, were decayed two centuries later and Christopher Wren, on a visit to Windsor, suggested that they should be replaced by representations of pineapples, a fashionable motif since Charles II's gardener had succeeded in growing one. The beasts had come down (those there now were put up during the restoration of the Chapel in 1921–30) but the pineapples had never gone up in their place, and it seemed that at the time no one had noticed the holy bones hidden in the hollow pinnacles. One canon, more sceptical than the others, did not believe they could be holy bones at all and he sent some of them to London to be analysed. The report came back: they were the bones of stags picked up in the Park by jackdaws, who had dropped them into the crevices.[51]

* The kissing of Henry VI's spurs, after having made an offering to them, was also a common practice; and in the nineteenth century, possibly as a result of this, as well as because they sometimes made a ringing noise on the stone floors, people wearing spurs in St George's Chapel were required to pay a fine to the choir-boys.[55]

and, having collected fines from the Poor Knights whenever they missed a Mass, they misappropriated the fines as well. Adorned in their gorgeous vestments and surrounded by the most lavish assortment of silver images, candlesticks, illuminated books, bells, jewelled chalices, staves, crosses, morses and paxes, they gabbled through their offices, and as soon as they had collected enough money, they went home. One of them spent the time of Mass gossiping with his neighbour, another was out most of the day hunting and fishing, a third was often to be found in bed with another man's wife.[58]

The Poor Knights' charges were investigated by the Chancellor, who found there was much justice in them. He also found, though, that some of the Knights themselves were far from blameless and one at least, when he did attend Mass, was nearly always late, went to sleep immediately he got into the chapel, and could only with difficulty be aroused to receive the sacrament. Whether or not either side in the dispute was as lax or unscrupulous as the other suggested, it is at least certain that this fourteenth-century quarrel was the first of many and that until recent years the Poor Knights were frequently regarded as a troublesome and somewhat sordid appendage to an otherwise glorious Order.

Henry VIII did what he could to raise their standing and self-respect and in his will provided for thirteen additional Poor Knights who were to be given a shilling a day for ever and, once a year, 'a long gown of white cloth, with the Garter upon the breast, imbrothered with a shield and cross of St George within the Garter, and a mantle of red cloth'.[59] By 1720, however, their total number had fallen to eighteen, and these forlorn old men as they walked to chapel twice a day, each from 'a little cell round the square', under the shadow of crumbling, ivy-covered and rook-infested walls, seemed to a visitor a sad reminder of those more splendid days when Edward III first chose the Garter as the symbol of his Most Noble Order.[60]

[iii]

KNIGHTS FOR THE BODY

As Edward III, senile at sixty-four, lay helpless in the room in which he was soon to die, talking of hunting and hawking, deserted by opportunist courtiers and in the end by his mistress, Alice Perrers, who waited only long enough to take the rings from his fingers before leaving him with a priest,[1] the structure of society which he had so much admired and tried so hard to preserve was already crumbling.

The Black Death had carried off almost half his country's five million people, most of them poor labourers and their families;[2] and the survivors soon learned the value of their labour. They demanded higher wages and were met by a statute which made it illegal for them to receive the increases. The braver amongst them marched on London and, having executed the King's Chancellor and his Treasurer and carried their heads through the streets on pikes, were met by promises which were immediately broken.[3]

Quarrels between employer and employed, master and servant, landlord and tenant, had for long been exacerbated by statutes which, whatever the official reason for their enactment and however impossible it proved to enforce them, proclaimed the difference between the rich courtier and the ordinary man. Men were told what they might not eat and what they might not wear; but the regulations were openly ignored by the rich and in many cases were not even intended to apply to them, being directed against men who wore clothes unsuitable to their estate and against 'common lewd women' who presumed to dress like 'good noble dames and damsels'.[4]

And yet the courtier in Edward III's time, and even more extravagantly in the time of his successor Richard II, dressed in a fashion as outrageously provocative as that of the early twelfth-century Norman courtier, who, according to William of Malmesbury, 'put on false tresses' and attempted 'to rival women in delicacy of person and to mince their gait'.[5] The coat sleeves of the courtier at Windsor in Richard II's reign were tipped with fur and worn so long that they trailed on the ground; the points of his shoes were usually far longer than the feet themselves and had to be held up by gold chains stretched from the end of the toes to the knees; golden ribbons with wide bows were tied round his legs which were clothed in stockings of vividly contrasting colours; velvet bands were tied round hair that grew thick and long upon his shoulders; precious stones sparkled all over him and upon the rings which he wore round the fingers of his scented gloves. Even the clergy curled and powdered their hair, wore caps with tippets of a wonderful length, furred cloaks, chequered shoes, and knives in scabbards so long that they looked like the scabbards of swords.[6]

The Queen, Anne of Bohemia, and her ladies wore horned and

pearl-studded head-dresses of an astonishing size. And on Anne's death, the governess of Richard's second Queen, the nine-year-old Isabella of Valois, kept several goldsmiths and furriers constantly at work making her own dresses as lavish as her pupil's.

The meals at court – ten thousand of which were served every day[7] – were quite as sumptuous as the clothes. And so were the entertainments provided by the King's musicians, jugglers and comedians. There was a royal band with trumpeters, pipers and singers, a fiddler, a citoler, a tambouretter, a clarion-player and a kettle-drummer. The strolling *joculatores,* who recited epic stories and romances of inordinate length, were no longer such popular performers in an impatient and sybaritic age which found greater pleasure in less exacting and more titillating entertainers. Although disapproved of by the Church (whose servants nevertheless regularly indulged in the *Festum Fatuorum* and the *Festum Puerorum,* celebrations of 'foul voluptuosity'[8]) the travelling players with their bawdy songs and comic or lascivious acts, were gradually replacing in the favour of the rich those reciting minstrels whose principal stocks in trade were a loud voice and a good memory.[9] The versatile minstrels who could juggle and walk on a tight-rope, who were prepared to 'distort their bodies by lewd dance and gesture or strip themselves and put on horrible masks'[10] were the ones most welcome in fourteenth-century households. Dwarfs and simpletons were always welcome, too; although most noble households had resident freaks and fools of their own.

These poor creatures, dressed in absurd particoloured clothes, sat at table with their owners, whose digestion was helped by the laughter evoked by their appearance and antics, by their inhuman sounds and uncoordinated, spastic movements. Freaks and simpletons also provided a butt for the coarse humour of the jester whose repertoire seems usually to have been limited to preposterous insults and practical jokes. Indeed, the recorded buffooneries of the court jester Scoggin[11] – in comparison with whom Shakespeare's fools must be considered humorists of rare genius – are a valuable commentary on the fickleness of comedy. Scoggin who, so he said, had been a student at Oxford but had not taken a degree, having decided that a 'Master of Art was not worth a Fart', was once found greasing a fat sow with unnecessary generosity. He explained his behaviour by saying, 'I do as Kings and lords do and everyman else do; for he that hath enough shall have more and he that hath nothing shall go without, and this sow needeth no basting nor greasing for she is fat enough, yet shall she have more than enough.' While the humour of the comment, much prized at the time for its smart irreverence, does not, of course, wear well, its aptness as a social criticism was certainly undeniable.

For the wasteful extravagance of the Royal Household was prodigious. It continued long after the abdication of Richard II, until, in the next century, Edward IV, although well aware that splendour not only bolstered the royal authority but was 'an essential attribute of kingship itself', felt constrained to regulate the numbers of attendants at Court, which had grown to many hundreds, to limit their allowances, which had become a matter of dispute, and to establish rules for the observance of their duties, which had frequently been unperformed. He decided, in fact, as he put it himself, that he would have his goods 'dispended but not wasted'.[12]

Ordinances, of course, had been issued before to regulate the conduct and ceremonial of the Royal Household; but they had never been strictly observed. The courts of Henry IV and Henry V were less lavish than those of their immediate predecessors, while that of Henry VI, a kind and studious man, who had been born at Windsor in 1421, was comparatively modest. Henry VI, founder of King's College, Cambridge, and of Eton, was a man preoccupied with religious observances and education. He loved to send for the scholars of Eton when he was at Windsor and, when still sane enough to do so, to give them his advice, to tell them to be 'good boys, gentle and teachable', and to forbid them to come to his Court lest 'the young lambs should come to relish the corrupt deeds and habits of his courtiers'.[13] He himself certainly never came to relish the habits of his courtiers, and the story is told that 'at Christmas time a certain great lord brought before him a Dance or show of young ladies with bared bosoms who were to dance in that guise before the King . . . who very angrily averted his eyes, turned his back upon them, and went out to his chamber, saying "Fy, fy, for shame".'[14]

Edward IV, a man of voracious sexual appetite, would never have objected to such performances. He did, however, object to the waste that Henry's weakness had allowed to continue in the Royal Household, a waste that was at least partly responsible for an increase in expenditure from £13,000 in 1433 to £24,000 in 1449.[15] And, so, *The Black Book of the Household* was issued. In this book the rights and duties of all those who attended upon the King at Windsor and at his other royal palaces, from the Knights of the Body to the Servants of the Kitchen, were carefully stipulated. It was, though,

27

far more than a measure to enforce an economy which the Crown's increasing financial problems had rendered necessary. In an age when the worth and power of men was judged by the grace and splendour of their hospitality, a king could not allow a subject to outdo him. A nobleman who entered London as the Earl of Warwick did, accompanied by six hundred attendants all wearing his livery and badge, was a real threat to the King's prestige. And foreign visitors – such as those who came over with the Queen of Bohemia's brother in 1466 and were entertained by the King at a dinner with fifty courses, and on subsequent days by two Earls who each provided them with sixty courses – were likely to remember and discuss this sort of evidence of the superior standards of seigniorial munificence. Nor was it only magnificence which was recognised as an important political instrument and social ideal. Courtly manners and etiquette, raised by symbolism and allegory to an esoteric art, were also regarded as essential to the preservation of order and respect in a competitive and ever-changing society. 'It is no accident that the fifteenth century, when the number of *"bourgeois gentilhommes"* was quickly increasing, saw the appearance of more books on etiquette than ever before, telling one how to behave in courtly circles and devoting special attention to subtle differences and equivalencies of rank. Feudal tenures had lost their *raison d'être*; but the trappings of chivalry grew more splendid.'[16]

These books on etiquette prescribed rules of behaviour which turned a meeting between two noblemen into a sort of ritualistic dance. The number of steps which hosts of varying ranks should take to greet their guests, for instance, and the number of times places of precedence should be offered to inferiors before their refusal of them was finally accepted, were laid down with as much elaboration as the rules for polite eating prescribed for princes and noble pages. These young men were advised – and clearly they needed some advice – that wine must not be drunk while the mouth was full of food; that the upper part of the body must not lean forward over the table with the head hanging over the dish; that neither the nose nor the teeth nor the nails must be picked at table; that salt should be put on the plate and not taken out of the cellar whenever required with a knife; that dirty soup spoons should not be put down on the tablecloth; that the knife must never be used to carry food to the mouth; and that when the meal was finished the guest must 'ryse uppe with-oute lauhtere, japynge, or boystrous worde'.[17]

The rules laid down by the Black Book, and the Ordinances which

28

preceded and followed it, dealt with all this and more. They had to be extensive for the Household was still an extensive one, the King's Chamber at Windsor alone, for example, being served by the attendance of more than four hundred men of varying rank presided over by the Lord Chamberlain. The Chamber, both constitutionally and architecturally, was divided into three – an Outer or Audience Chamber, where the King held receptions and talked to foreign ambassadors, an Inner or Privy Chamber, where he could have more private discussions, and a Bedchamber, where he could relax. At the top of the hierarchy of attendants upon the King in his Chamber were the Knights for the Body who had tours of duty lasting eight weeks. These were followed by the King's Knights and the Squires for the Body. Then there were Squires for the Household, twenty of whom were required to serve each day at table, and Gentlemen Ushers who enforced the protocol and supervised the activities of the Yeomen of the Crown and the Yeomen of the Chamber, the message carriers and torch-bearers. Lastly came the Grooms of the Chamber and the Pages, young sons of noble families who combined lessons in horsemanship and languages with more menial tasks, which included making sure that the dogs did not dirty the floors.

In the morning the King was dressed by the Squires for the Body, who had slept on truckle-beds in his room, and he was attended when eating breakfast, as at all meals, by twenty squires for the Household and at least one Gentleman Usher. A Server, who was required to be 'ful cunyng' in the ceremonial of presenting the dishes, went to fetch the meat from the kitchen, accompanied by the Squires, and on his return asked the Ewer for a towel and a basin of water so that the King could wash when he had eaten. A 'Doctoure of Physyque' stood nearby to advise the King as to 'wich dyet is best according, and to the nature and operacion of all the metes'. And throughout the meal thirteen minstrels played in the gallery.

The regulations governing the making of the King's bed were even more elaborate than those laid down for feeding him. Two Squires for the Body stood at the head and two Grooms of the Chamber at the foot while a Yeoman of the Chamber carried in the bedclothes and a Gentleman Usher held back the curtains. The manner of putting on, shaking out and striking down the lower sheet was as minutely described as the way in which the fustian upper sheets and ermine counterpane were to be laid above it and then rolled down 'the space of an ell'. When the Yeomen had beaten the pillows well and thrown them to the Squires to place in position, the bed was to be sprinkled with holy water.[18]

There was inevitably, of course, a wide difference between practice and precept, for Edward, intelligent and wonderfully energetic, was not a man to allow restricting codes of behaviour to interfere with his pleasures. Handsome, extremely tall, autocratic, and exuberantly sensual, he had married Elizabeth Woodville, universally considered of too humble an origin for a queen-consort, when he had failed to overcome her strong will and force her to accept him as her lover – by threatening her, so it was said, as he held a dagger at her throat–and he filled his Court with her relations.[19] After his marriage he had countless mistresses, many of them from far humbler homes than his wife's, including Jane Shore, the wife of a London mercer, who was to lend her name to some of London's most squalid eighteenth-century brothels and flash-houses. When he and his Court went hunting at Windsor, no tiresome rules of precedence were allowed to spoil the atmosphere of gay abandon. 'Tables heavy with roasted meats and sugared dainties were stretched in the shade of the trees, and silken tents grew like gargantuan flowers on the lawns. The King and his courtiers glided on the Thames in gilded barges', jousted and feasted, 'made love by moonlight and torchlight, rose at dawn to hear Mass, broke their fast with a mess of meat and ale, and quickly took horse to be beforehand of the sun in their pursuit of royal disports.'[20] Edward's infectious enthusiasm and affable manner made him a delightful companion; and he made good use of these attributes not only in flattering courtiers and citizens whose wives he intended to seduce, but also in the entertainment of foreign visitors whose good opinion of him might help his cause. Louis de la Gruthuyse, Governor of Holland, for instance, who came to England in September 1472 and was entertained at Windsor Castle in the lavish manner which the opulent standards of the Court of Burgundy had made *de rigueur* in Europe, found Edward an entrancing host. One of the King's heralds, Bluemantle Pursuivant, wrote an account of the visit.

Louis was met inside the Castle gate by Lord Hastings, the Chamberlain, who showed him to a set of chambers, hung with arras, where he and his servants had supper. When he had finished his meal, Lord Hastings took him to the King, who greeted him warmly and led him to Queen Elizabeth's rooms where he found her and her ladies-in-waiting playing *marteaux* – a game like bowls – and throwing balls at ivory ninepins. There were minstrels there and some of

4. Charles II in his robes as Sovereign of the Order of the Garter
from the engraving by W. Sherwin in Elias Ashmole, *Institutions, Laws
and Ceremonies of the Most Noble Order of the Garter*, 1672

5. The procession of the Knights of the Garter in the reign of Charles II

from engravings by Wenceslaus Hollar in Elias Ashmole, *Institutions, Laws and Ceremonies of the Most Noble Order of the Garter*, 1672

6. The Knights of the Garter feasting in St. George's Hall in 1663

the ladies were dancing and the King took his eldest daughter in his arms and swung her round the room. She was seven then, and thirteen years later, after her two little brothers had been murdered in the Tower, she was to marry Henry, the first of the Tudor kings.

The following morning after Mass, which was 'melodyousely songe', the King gave Louis a present. It was a gold cup encrusted with pearls and with a big sapphire on the lid. Inside was a 'great Pece of an Vnicorne's horne', an antidote to poison. When breakfast was over Edward brought his baby son out into the courtyard to introduce him to the distinguished visitor and then the two men went out to hunt together in the Little Park. In the Park the King gave Louis another present, a crossbow, with a velvet-covered case bearing the royal arms, together with a set of gilt-headed arrows. They had little luck hunting, and before their midday meal, which was served in the lodge, they succeeded in killing only a single doe. But in the afternoon several deer were killed and half a dozen bucks which Edward gave to his guest. 'By that tyme yt was nere night, yett the Kinge shewed him his garden, and Vineyard of Pleasour, and so turned to the Castell ageyne, where they herde evensonge in their chambres.'

That night the Queen gave a banquet in her dining room. At her table, with the King and Louis and her daughter Elizabeth, sat her sister the Duchess of Buckingham and her husband, her sister-in-law, Lady Rivers, and the King's sister, the Duchess of Exeter. Lower down the table were 'divers ladyes and certeyn nobles of the Kinges owen courte' including Lord Hastings and Lord Berners, Constable of the Castle. At a separate table, all sitting down the same side of it, was a 'great Vue' of other ladies; and in an outer room sat a long row of the Queen's gentlemen facing the servants of the foreign visitor. After dinner there was dancing and at 'aboute six of the clocke, the Kinge and the quene, w^t her ladies and gentlewomen, brought the sayde Lord Grautehuse to iii chaumbres of Pleasance, all hanged w^t Whyte Sylke and lynnen clothe, and alle the Floures covered w^t Carpettes'. Here, in the first silk-lined chamber, was a gorgeous bed with a soft down mattress, a cloth of gold canopy and curtains of white sarcenet; in the second chamber was a feather-stuffed sofa inside a tent; and in the third chamber were two baths each enclosed in tents of white cloth. When the King and Queen had shown him these chambers and provided him with dishes of green ginger and sugared sweets, with bottles of liqueurs and spice-flavoured wine, they left him to enjoy the pleasures of the bath, and of the bed.[21]

The Castle, in which these gracious and exciting entertainments were provided, had altered much since Edward iii had died a hundred years before. In Edward's lifetime William of Wykeham, the founder of Winchester College and of New College, Oxford, who was appointed Surveyor of the King's Works in 1356, had organised the construction and completion of many 'fair and sumptuous' buildings, work on some of which had been abandoned during the time of the Black Death.[22] And after William left Windsor, where he had so pleased the King that, although not yet ordained, he had accumulated several ecclesiastical benefices including two good livings in Norfolk, a deanery of St Martin-le-Grand, and canonries at Lichfield and Lincoln, his work was continued by William of Mulsho, and by Adam of Hartington, who by the time of Edward iii's death had supervised the entire rebuilding of the royal apartments in the Upper Ward.[23] In the following reign, Geoffrey Chaucer, clerk of the King's works in the Palace of Westminster, and already the author of his century's most celebrated poems, was instructed to repair the Chapel of St George, which was 'threatened with ruin and on the point of falling to the ground'.[24] Considerable works of repair were carried out, under the supervision of Chaucer (who was paid two shillings a day), but not enough to prevent its being again in decay in 1478 when Edward iv decided to pull it down and 'replace it by another and altogether more glorious building'. If this should outshine the chapel lately built just across the river at Eton by his rival and victim, King Henry vi, so much the better.[25] The new chapel which was finished in about 1525 was, indeed, altogether more glorious, and now remains as one of the most beautiful examples of the Gothic perpendicular taste in the world.

Here, after the smoke and fury of the Wars of the Roses had brought the Middle Ages to a close, the body of Elizabeth, the widow of Edward iv, was buried in her husband's vault in accordance with her last request. Accompanied only by her chaplain and one of her long dead husband's numerous bastard daughters, she was buried at 'ix o'clocke at night wtoute any solempne dirge or the ringing of any bell'.[26]

Not for more than a hundred and fifty years was there to be another funeral in the chapel so quiet and restrained. For when Elizabeth Woodville died, her son-in-law, Henry vii, had already secured the success of a dynasty for which so modest a ceremony was to hold little appeal.

2

Tudors

THE NEW APOLLO AND HIS CHILDREN

In the winter of 1547 when Elizabeth Woodville's grandson died, the funeral ceremony was far less restrained. The King's body was taken to Windsor from Westminster along roads specially cleared and swept and in some places widened, on a carriage drawn by eight black-trapped horses, on each of which a page sat carrying the Royal banner. The effigy which it was customary to place on top of the coffin was clothed in crimson velvet, trimmed with miniver and powdered with ermine. There was a crown on its head placed over a 'night-cap of black satin, set full of precious stones'. There were precious stones, too, in the gold bracelets which encircled the wrists, and in the numerous rings on the fingers of the velvet-gloved hands. As the cortège, four miles long, approached the Castle hill and entered between the barriers, draped with black cloth and studded with escutcheons, the choir began to sing. Three bishops in pontificals approached the coffin, which was carried into the chapel by sixteen yeomen bearing long black staves. The senior officers of the Royal Household carried white staves which they broke into three pieces and threw down upon the coffin when it had been lowered into the vault.[1]

It was a final act of homage to a magnificent and cataclysmic career. Forty years before, this dead king, Henry VIII, whose immense corpse and coarsened face now lay in St George's Chapel next to his 'true and loving wife Queen Jane', was a boy of great intelligence, excessive self-confidence, and numerous accomplishments. Despite a large and ugly high-bridged nose he was also considered extremely good-looking. He had the fair skin, faint eyebrows, and auburn hair which his contemporaries so much admired and his 'round face' was so 'very beautiful', a Venetian thought, that it would have become a 'pretty woman'.[2] He was lazy and inclined to be frivolous, but he brought to physical pursuits a seemingly tireless energy. Every day he was up early, hunting, shooting, hawking, riding, jousting, or wrestling. He was a most agile dancer, leaping about like a stag in the energetic style which southern Europeans found so astonishing an oddity;[3] he loved singing; he could play recorder, flute and virginals with equal grace and facility; he composed music; he wrote anthems. He was at once dashing, strong and charming, and his shrewd and clever Welsh father, who within five months of his defeat of Richard III at Bosworth Field in 1485 had united the houses of Lancaster and York by marrying Elizabeth, eldest daughter of Edward IV, was determined to make good use of this tall, virile son, this 'new Apollo', that the Queen had given him.

One day at the beginning of 1505 a ship on its way from the Netherlands to Spain was forced by bad weather to take shelter in a Cornish harbour, and Henry, Prince of Wales, was given an early lesson in the art of hospitality.

On board the damaged ship were Juana, the new Queen of Castile – La Loca, the mad one – and her husband Philip the Handsome, Archduke of Austria and heir to the Holy Roman Empire. Juana was the daughter of Isabella of Castile and Ferdinand of Aragon, and her youngest sister Catherine had been married to Prince Arthur, Henry VII's elder son, who had died at the age of sixteen three years before. King Henry had originally wanted the young widow Catherine to marry his other son, the new Prince of Wales, but now that Isabella, her mother, was dead the match was not so favourable a one. The King decided instead that a marriage between Prince Henry and the Archduke Philip's daughter Eleanor and perhaps, a second marriage between his daughter Mary and Philip's son Charles would be far more useful. The fortuitous arrival of Philip in England gave him an opportunity to further these ambitions.

As soon as he heard of Philip's landing, he sent the Earl of Arundel to ask him and Juana to come to Windsor, which was, as it had been and would remain for centuries, 'an ideal settynge' for the arrangement of the treaties and alliances that the English King had in mind. Philip said that he would come at once and that his wife would come later. He was met, five miles from the Castle, by 'five hundred persons all gorgeously apparelled' led by the Prince of Wales, who, although not yet fourteen, 'received him after the most honourable fashion'.[4]

Prince Henry watched his father greet the Archduke inside the Castle gate. The minstrels were playing beneath the grey walls in the cold winter air; and to the sound of trombones the two men went through the extravagant rites which court etiquette demanded.

Philip made as if to dismount first but Henry refused to accept the gesture; and so they stepped to the ground together. Henry, noticing that Philip had taken his hat off, quickly took off his own and declined to put it on again until Philip was ready to do the same. Once more they acted in unison.

When Philip said that the King need not accompany him to his lodgings, Henry insisted on doing so. The Archduke said that he would agree only if he were allowed to accompany his host back to the royal apartments afterwards. This was at last agreed, but, having completed the two journeys, Henry made as if to go back with Philip to the rooms which he had just showed him. Philip, however, 'wolde not suffere it, and so they saluted the one the other and departed; the Kynge remained in his Chamber, and the Kynge of Casteele wente to his and so they both wente to dynner every eiche in his own Chambre for it was ffastynday and our Lady's evene'.

On Sunday morning the King went to Mass at his chapel and then went to Philip's room where a private Mass had been said by the chaplain. 'And at the meetynge the Kynge of Casteele Tooke off his Bonnete and made a Lowe Curtesye and bade the Kinge god morrowe, and the Kynge said to him that he could not have welle dined that day unlese that he had seene him and bad him good morowe. The Kinge of Casteele thanked the Kinge of his greate Curtesye and payne, and so with diveres other goode words they both proceeded together to the Kynge of Casteel's dininge Chambere, and both stood by the fyere together.'

After dinner that day Henry asked Philip if, as it was Sunday and they could not go hunting, he would like to see the ladies dancing and he took him to a room next to his dining-room where Catherine danced with another Spanish girl, both in their national costumes; and Princess Mary danced with an English girl. Catherine asked her brother-in-law, Philip, to dance with her but he said he was too clumsy and preferred to watch. His eyes were fixed on Mary, performing with such liveliness and grace. She was only nine but she could play the lute and clarabel as skilfully as she could dance, and although he had previously declined to consider the proposed marriage between her and his son Charles, he was induced during this visit to Windsor to change his mind.

Philip stayed twelve days in the Castle and everything possible was done to impress him. The chapel, where he and Henry attended Mass daily, was hung with cloth of gold and lit by hundreds of beautifully moulded tapers. In the tennis court he and his host sat on cloth of gold cushions while they watched the players below, and Philip was persuaded to believe that he was better than any of them and he challenged the Marquess of Dorset to a match, giving himself a handicap of fifteen points. Henry created him a Knight of the Garter and presented him with robes of exceptional splendour. He was entertained with the spectacle of a fine horse being baited to death beneath the windows of the delicately painted towers in which his lodgings were; and whenever the weather was fine he was taken out into the Park to hunt deer with a cross-bow.[5]

* * *

A day's hunting in the Park, always one of the most exciting pleasures that Windsor had to offer, was also usually an occasion for the King to demonstrate the lavish excellence of English food. At the banquets held in the Castle the meals were sumptuous, of course, but the atmosphere of formality, the effort to make polite conversation, the necessary observances of etiquette, took some of the pleasure out of eating, whereas at the hunting lodge in the Little Park hungry men and women could eat without restraint. There is no record of what Henry vii and Philip ate there in 1505; but a few years later, when Prince Henry was King, the fare supplied to thirty of his guests would have surprised Gargantua himself. In addition to fine English beef, veal, lamb and bacon, capons, hens, plovers, woodcock, partridges, herons and snipe, in addition to leverets, rabbits and larks' tongues, there was enough fruit for each guest to eat ten oranges, seven pears and six apples as well as quantities of pippins, quinces, prunes, raisins, almonds and dates; and there was enough English ale and beer as well as French, German and Greek wine for each of them to drink twenty pints. There were eight hundred eggs, ninety dishes of butter, eighty loaves of chestnut bread and three hundred wafers for marzipan, in addition to an immense variety of spices and fifty pieces of gold leaf for gilding the gingerbread.[6]

Henry viii brought to eating, as he brought to everything he did, a wonderful zest and lustiness. His father, by discipline and a calculating policy, by forcing men to fear a scarcely human King whom he dared not let them like or even understand, had restored the ravaged fortunes of the Crown. He had spent no more than the traditional necessity for occasional displays of lavish entertainment and ostentation demanded; he had kept profitable appointments in royal hands and employed cheap professional deputies; he had hoarded treasure and money, cut court expenses to a minimum while keeping a necessarily 'sumptuous table', and had left his son a fortune of £1,250,000.[7]

Such parsimony was not for Henry VIII, nor was it necessary. The Court at Windsor became, and could afford to become, as splendid a place as it had been at the beginning of the previous century. The number of servants and attendants grew each year. There were constant entertainments, dances, tournaments, games and banquets. But if it was a rowdy place, extrovert and uninhibited, it was also a place of learning. Erasmus found it more like a home of the Muses than a court.

Catherine of Aragon shared her husband's interests and pleasures. She too enjoyed riding and hunting, jousting, dancing, conversation and music. And he himself, so far as respect for the Queen allowed, delighted not only in the company of scholars and sportsmen but also in that of her lively ladies-in-waiting. He had a son by one of them, Elizabeth Blount, and he fell in love with another, Anne Boleyn, and having divorced Catherine, to whom he was, according to Francis Bacon, 'no indulgent husband', he married Anne on a winter's morning when she was pregnant with his child.

Anne Boleyn, swarthy and flat-chested but exciting and excitable, witty, provocative and calculating, had come to Windsor from the Court of Francis I where she had been a lady-in-waiting to Queen Claude, and the King was captivated by her dark, flashing eyes, her long, loose black hair, and her vivacity. She refused to become his mistress until she was certain that he would marry her; but not long after she was crowned, the King was excited by someone else. Charged with having committed adultery with five different men, one of whom was her brother, Anne Boleyn, who had failed to provide her husband with a male heir, was convicted of high treason and beheaded on Tower Green on 19 May 1536. The King, who was out hunting, reined in his horse to listen to the sound of the guns and married one of her ladies-in-waiting, Jane Seymour, the next morning. The following year the new Queen, having given birth to a son, died of puerperal fever and for the first time in his life the King knew the grief of losing someone he loved. He left Hampton Court immediately for Windsor, 'too broken to be able to consider the arrangements for the lying-in-state or the funeral'. [8]

He had aged much since his coronation. He danced and hunted and jousted as energetically as ever, but men believed he did so no longer because he enjoyed these activities but because he wanted to show that he was still as strong and jovial as he had been in his youth. In fact he had become grimly masterful and inordinately selfish. He suffered increasingly from feverish headaches and depression; he had an ulcer on his thigh which broke out spasmodically, giving him such pain that at times he was speechless and his face grew black; he had, also, perhaps through some glandular maladjustment, become immensely fat. 'He had a body and a half, very abdominous and unwieldy with fat. It was death to him to be dieted, so great his appetite and death to him not to be dieted, so great his corpulency.'[9] In five years, if his armour provides an accurate guide, he added seventeen inches to his waist measurement.[10] At Windsor and his other royal palaces, machines with ropes and pulleys had to be provided for him as he could no longer get up the stairs.[11]

His Court, though, remained the glittering place that he had made it. And so it had to be, for like the Court of his daughter Elizabeth, it was the world, the power and the glory, 'the fountain of power and influence, the source of fortune, magnet of all eyes . . . a centre of education, in the arts of culture and manners, in worldliness and sophistication, intrigue and treachery'.[12] It was still the seat of government as well as the royal setting. Its splendour and liveliness were necessary both as a means of impressing foreign visitors and of attracting young men of energy and talent into the service of the Crown, and of keeping them out of mischievous employment elsewhere. It had to provide a home not only for many high officials of state but also for boys and girls of good birth finishing their education there. It had to open its doors to important ambassadors as well as to the hundreds of lesser functionaries who came there to eat at the tables of their masters. And consequently it had, of course, to be prepared to supply prodigious quantities of food.

The cost of the food was to some extent met by the royal right of purveyance by which counties had to provide cattle, corn and other provisions at fixed prices to the officers of the Household; but the whole business of preparing, cooking and issuing this food when the Court was at Windsor had to be done in the Castle. Every man in the King's service had a right not only to lodging but to 'Bouche' or 'Bouge of Court', an allowance of food (which ranged from sixteen dishes at dinner and eleven at supper for the Lord Chamberlain, to four at each meal for servants and porters) and of fuel and candles. In addition to this allowance, most officials had a share in the growing number of perquisites, in salmon tails and pigs' heads, for instance, in the skins of cattle and the feathers of birds, in bread chippings and in the traditional candle ends.

Cheating and trickery over these perquisites were common at Windsor, as in all large households, and impossible to prevent. It became customary for the Yeoman of the Pantry to increase his profit from bread chippings by chopping off 'great pieces from the bottoms of loaves' and selling them back to the household as dog food; for the Yeoman of the Ewery to get the Chandler to make his candles with a long, solid, wickless bottom.[13] Sometimes lesser servants ran away with whole dishes prepared for the tables of other servants' masters, or even with pewter and silver. The King's servants were not only dishonest but dirty, and it was necessary to forbid scullions in the royal kitchen to go about 'naked or in garments of such vileness as they now do', and to warn servants waiting at table in the King's chamber against wiping their greasy fingers on the tapestries and against putting dishes down 'upon the King's bed for fear of hurting of the King's rich counterpoints that lie thereon'.[14]

By 1526 the Court, according to Cardinal Wolsey, who drew up the Eltham Statutes in that year in an effort to reform its abuses, had become a resort of 'vile and unmeet persons', whores, 'vagabonds and mighty beggars' who came to eat the food and steal the goods of better men. Wolsey's proposed reforms, although never very conscientiously carried out, were far-reaching. Ushers were enjoined to make sure that nothing whatsoever was stolen in future; the Knight Harbinger was instructed to banish lewd women from the Household; unkennelled mastiffs, greyhounds and ferrets were also to be banished. Strict mealtimes were in future to be observed. Pages, Yeomen and Esquires were told to keep regular hours and to perform their duties with dispatch; barbers were warned against keeping company with 'misguided women' and transmitting their infection to the King by breathing on him; the Comptroller of the Household was reminded of the scales of stabling and beds laid down for visitors – twenty-four horses and nine beds for a duke, three horses and two beds for a chaplain.[15] The scales had to be carefully stipulated, for many visitors had been in the habit of coming to Windsor not only with secretaries, chaplains and servants but with their own minstrels, actors and fools. These, Wolsey felt, might well have been left at home; for there were many entertainers in the Royal Household including Jane, a female fool, and Will Somers, one of the most famous jesters of his time.

Somers could send guests in the hall at dinner time into paroxysms of laughter by grinning through a gap in the arras and then making his way to the tables 'in such a rolling and antic posture, holding his hands and setting his eyes that was past describing unless one saw him'. Usually attended by a monkey which sat on his shoulder and did funny tricks, he told joke after joke, laughing helplessly and infectiously at each one and screwing his cheerful, malicious face into cruel caricatures of the people he was deriding.[16]

The King himself, despite an increasing insistence on the rights and pleasures of privacy, was still also expected to be part of the show at Court. He was rarely alone even in his Withdrawing Chambers. Access to his Privy Chamber was supposedly limited, but it was frequently full of people who had no business there, merely wishing to see what the King looked like. And the Presence Chamber was, in effect, a stage. Here, sometimes, he was expected to eat, watched by curious spectators who were permitted also to witness the ceremonial method of bringing in the board, laying the table and tasting the food and wine and assaying the salt and the water in the hand basins. To assay the salt, the Carver uncovered the cellar, dipped a piece of bread inside, made a 'floryshe over it', and gave it to the Panter to eat. All the dishes had to be treated in the same way as they were brought in, and always with a flourish of the hand.[17] And all the while the spectators watched and marvelled.

To live for ever, as it were, in a goldfish bowl, to be gazed at in public and to be attended by numerous servants and officials in private, continued to be necessary attributes of kingship for generations. Throughout the sixteenth century, as in the time of Edward iv, the choreographic ceremonial laid down by the Household Ordinances denied the monarch the comfort of all but the most artificial seclusion. He dressed in the morning in a room where Gentlemen and Grooms were required to warm his linen before a fire (which must on no account be smoking), to pass the garments (clean and brushed) from hand to hand, to set in their respective places a chair and a cushion for His Majesty's feet, to place a handkerchief over his shoulders before combing His Majesty's hair. He undressed at night – after the bed had been ritually made, a Yeoman of the Chamber had prodded the palliasse with a dagger, another Yeoman had made his requisite 'tumble over it for the search thereof', and a third had set his sword up at the bed-head – in the company of attendants who stood by to receive the discarded clothes, who laid out the bowl of water for washing and the cloth for cleaning his teeth, who combed his hair, who put on his night cap, who saw him to bed, who drew the curtains, who put in its place the light that was to burn throughout the night, who made sure there were no dogs or cats still in the room, who bowed, and at last went out to sleep on pallets outside the door.[18]

Regulations as rigid as these, whether strictly observed or not, were laid down also for the households of royal princes, so that a naturally reserved and introspective boy like Jane Seymour's son and Henry's successor, Edward vi, could live and die in loneliness without ever having known what it was like to be left alone.

Edward succeeded his father at the age of nine and died three months before his sixteenth birthday. Extremely pale and very fair, solemn and precociously learned, potentially, perhaps, the ablest of the Tudors but potentially, too, the least attractive,[19] he grew up in the shadow of a father held up to him as 'the greatest man in the world', and in the company of men whose struggles for power drew out of an essentially generous nature characteristics both equivocal and unappealing. He did not like Windsor. 'Methinks I am in prison', he said of it when he was twelve. 'Here be no galleries, nor no gardens to walk in.'[20] And it was not only at Windsor that he felt this burden of restraint. Energetic, yet so solemn he is reported to have laughed only once, capable of a disarming responsiveness yet remaining warily cold and withdrawn, at once priggish and intro-spective, he had neither the temperament nor the physique to lead the life expected of him. Finally, in June 1553, poisoned by the medicine that had at first so stimulated him, with swollen legs and arms and darkened skin, with fingers and toes touched by gangrene, his hair and nails began to fall out, and on 6 July he died, too weak to cough, murmuring a prayer.[21]

Convinced of the 'divine right of Protestantism', he had agreed to exclude from the accession in his will his Catholic half-sister Mary, the daughter of Catherine of Aragon, in favour of Lady Jane Grey. It was, however, as Queen that Mary came to Windsor in the summer of 1554, after Lady Jane Grey had been beheaded, to prepare herself for her marriage with Philip ii, King of Spain, grandson of Philip the Handsome who had been entertained at Windsor by her grandfather Henry vii half a century before.

Philip ii came to Windsor in August and was installed as a Knight of the Garter and afterwards he and his wife went hunting in the Forest. Mary was obviously in love with him, or at least 'in love with what he represented – the prospect of a Catholic heir, reunion with Rome, her martyred mother's Spanish dynasty, the Spain that stood for centuries of knight-errantry against the infidel'.[22] 'All the affection, all the passion that her starved and thwarted youth had been unable to spend, she now threw at the feet of this restrained, courteous young husband.'[23] She was eleven years older than he was, and Philip's friend, Ruy Gomez, thought she looked older even than that. She was a 'dear thing' and perhaps if she had dressed in the

Spanish fashion she might not have looked 'so old and flabby'; but, as another young Spaniard said, she was 'not at all beautiful, small . . . of white complexion, and fair, and has no eyebrows'.[24] She had tight, thin lips and a somewhat spatulate nose and few remaining teeth; and she spoke in a deep, loud voice 'almost like a man's.' Her eyes were 'greyish and pale and so short-sighted that to read she must hold the page close to her face'; and she was quick-tempered and imperious, obstinate, unworldly and narrow-minded. Her husband – who went home to Spain as soon as he could – apparently found her unattractive and lacking 'all sensibility of the flesh'.[25]

Yet she was, beneath that unprepossessing exterior and despite her many faults, much more the 'dear thing' that the young Spaniard had called her than the 'Bloody Mary' that new generations were to decry. The Venetian ambassador while noting that she was of 'low stature, with a red and white complexion and very thin', thought that the 'great benignity and clemency' that illumined her face made her almost 'bella'. 'She is of very spare diet,' he continued, 'and never eats until one or two o'clock, although she rises at daybreak when, after saying her prayers and hearing Mass in private, she transacts business incessantly until after midnight, when she retires to rest.'[26]

She was not cruel. She knew her way to God and could not conceive that there was any other way. Men suffered for their refusal to accept it, not to be punished but to be saved. It was not that she had no sensibility, but that she had no judgment. Courageous, unshakably loyal to those she loved and to the religion which was the mainstay of her life, capable of passionate affection, yet virtuous, conscientious and devout, she appeared more like a practical housewife or even a nun than a queen. She loved jewels and gay clothes, but her principal preoccupations were people, babies and religion. During her visits to Windsor as a young woman, she had gone out almost every day visiting the old and sick with her ladies, dressed as they were dressed so as not to be recognised; she had enjoyed riding and long walks which she felt were good for the amenorrhoea that troubled her intermittently throughout her life; she had stood as godmother to numerous babies, had attended Mass with unfailing regularity, had played cards and listened to music. She had lived, in fact, the life of quiet innocence for which her character and capacities suited her.[27] It was fortunate for her country that, after her brief sad reign was over, there was waiting to follow her a half-sister whose temperament and talents were so different from hers.

QUEEN ELIZABETH I

'She readeth here now at Windsore,' Roger Ascham, her tutor, said of the young Elizabeth, 'more Greek every day than some Prebendaries of this Church do read in a whole week.'[1] She could read Latin as well, and she could speak it without stopping for a word. She spoke French, Spanish and Italian, too, and even Welsh. Ascham had never known a woman with a quicker apprehension or a more retentive memory. She had, he said, a mind which seemed to be free from female weakness, and her power of application was like a man's. She could talk intelligently on any intellectual topic and liked to spend three hours a day reading history. She spent hours, too, with a pen or a needle between her extraordinarily long, white fingers until her handwriting and her needlework were both of an exquisite beauty.

Her concentrated study, however, undermined her health. Already the nervous shock of her mother's execution and the events that had surrounded it, followed by the execution of Catherine Howard, a stepmother of whom she had been particularly fond, and the excitation of her awakening sexual instincts by the outrageous Lord Seymour, who had married another stepmother, Catherine Parr, after her father's death, had contributed, it seems, to do Elizabeth's 'nervous system and her sexual system an injury from which they never recovered'.[2] Her menstrual periods were very few or none; she suffered from painful eyestrain, agonising headaches and frequent breathlessness. The paleness of her skin, 'though tending to olive' when she was young, became so white through bleaching that it appeared almost to glow; and its whiteness was emphasised by the large pupils of her very bright eyes under faint, highly arched eyebrows and by straight reddish gold hair, which, like her clothes, plain and unadorned, scorned the current fashion.[3]

Despite her hair and clothes, though, and her rigorous devotion to duty, she was far from either staid or unworldly. Indeed, it may well be that her modest demeanour and 'maidenly apparel' were calculated rather than instinctive, for the scandalous rumours that were spread about concerning her relationship with her stepmother's husband, Lord Seymour, were a threat to her future. Also, she was well aware that 'in the reign of her prim and Protestant little brother

demureness was the becoming wear', while in Mary's reign 'the
simplicity of her tastes helped her to make friends with what might
be called the mammon of righteousness, that is, with the incipient
Puritan party'.[4] Certainly when she became Queen herself and Lord
Robert Dudley, tall, dark-skinned, handsome and selfish, came to
renew his friendship with her and to indulge her susceptibilities, he
was immediately admitted to her service as Master of the Horse,
an office – worth £1,500 a year and a table at Court – ideally suited
to his talents, both as an expert in the riding, judging and maintaining of horses and as a showman. Dudley, created Earl of Leicester in
1564, retained the Queen's favour for thirty years, surviving the
scandal of being sent away from Windsor when his wife was found
with her neck broken at the bottom of a staircase in a lonely house in
Oxfordshire, and surviving even his marriage to Lettice Devereux,
which drove the Queen to fury. He was the epitome of those dashing,
virile, gifted young men with whom the Queen delighted to adorn
her brilliant if often vulgar and self-consciously dashing Court –
men like the arrogant, versatile Walter Raleigh, the clever, love-sick
Thomas Heneage, the robust and passionate Christopher Hatton,
the young Earl of Oxford, and the Earl of Essex who, on Leicester's
death, was made Master of the Horse.

She loved these men to tell her – they were expected, in fact, by a
tiresome and elaborately stylised convention to tell her – how
beautiful she was, that they would die of the passion that they had for
her, that her skin (which she kept 'white as Albion rocks' with a
lotion made of white of egg, powdered eggshell, poppy-seeds, borax
and alum) was paler than snow. Indeed, as she grew older, her sus-
ceptibility to flattery, her delight in compliments however outlandishly extravagant, her inordinate vanity, were the talk of Europe.
'With her all is falsehood and vanity,' complained the Spanish
ambassador maliciously, and Raleigh believed that if Essex had not
said angrily that she had 'a crooked carcase' he need not have died.[5]
When the vile Robert Topcliffe said that he had been allowed to
put his hand on Elizabeth's bosom and that he had seen her naked
thighs,[6] he was making an outrageous claim to favours that the
Queen was rumoured to have bestowed elsewhere. Certainly she was
always excessively proud of her body and liked men to see it. The
French ambassador once noted in his journal how, one day during
a private audience towards the end of her life, she kept pulling open
the front of her white damask dress and lawn chemise so that he
could see her belly 'even to the navel'.

She was sixty-four then. The gaps between her black teeth made it hard to understand what she said, her uncovered bosom was 'somewhat wrinkled', and she wore a 'great reddish-coloured wig'.[7]

And yet she was not absurd; nor ever had she been absurd. She was not beautiful. Her nose was too long and her mouth too thin. She could not, apparently, feel a normal sexual passion, or perhaps it was that she was physically incapable of consummating it. But there was something in the liveliness of her conversation, her responsiveness, her ability to make men feel that she needed them, her spirit and energy and quick reactions, that was captivating. Her personality was more than strong; it was magnetic. She was, in fact, an 'amazing Queen, so keenly intelligent, so effervescing, so intimate, so imperious and so regal. She intoxicated Court and country, keyed her realm to the intensity of her own spirit. No one but a woman could have done it, and no woman without her superlative gifts could have attempted it without disaster. In part instructive, it was also conscious and deliberate.'[8]

Her courtiers and advisers often found her irritating and difficult, of course. For she was 'a great *prima donna*' in the realm of politics, and she had many personal foibles. She hated, for instance, to be ill or to be thought ill. In 1587 when a tooth was giving her pain and needed to be pulled out, her physicians dared not tell her so because she herself 'doth not or will not think so'.[9] Eventually the Council decided that the tooth must come out, having listened to the opinion of a tooth-drawer who said that the only other possibility was to dress it with fennygreek, but that might make the neighbouring teeth fall out as well as the painful one; and a body of councillors went to persuade the Queen that she must agree to the extraction. She refused to do so, however, until the Bishop of London allowed the surgeon to pull one of his own teeth out to demonstrate the ease with which the operation could be performed.[10] Some years later 'she had a "desperate ache" in her right thumb, but the gout it *could* not be, it *dare* not be; in fact she had no ache, but she would not sign letters.'[11]

Illness was a personal affront, and she would never be affronted. Even in church she checked preachers who seemed to be disrespectful towards her. 'Do not talk about that,' she once called out to a dean who in a Lenten sermon attacked images and implicitly called attention to the crucifix. '*Leave that*,' she called out in an even louder voice when, not having heard her, he continued his sermon.

'Leave that! It has nothing to do with your subject and the matter is now threadbare.'[12]

But although she was dictatorial, high-handed and could be irritable, ungrateful and cruel, she had the endearing qualities of a gentler, less assertive and self-confident woman. She loved flowers and children and jewels; she changed her mind far more frequently than diplomacy required, although 'her vacillation and her neurotic fear of irrevocable decisions happened by sheer luck to be in the national interest';[13] she had a deep sympathy for those who were old or ill. She would refuse to take men into her service at Windsor if they were ugly and once refused employment to an otherwise handsome man who had a front tooth missing; but 'she was never known to desert them for age or other inferiority after they were once enrolled in her service'.[14] They were paid 'good pensions', although her dislike of spending more money than she could possibly avoid was notorious.

It was, indeed, her parsimony which, intensified by the dictates of a shrewd financial policy, induced her to move her Court so often at the expense of her richer subjects. This was not the only reason, of course. She had, for instance, an extremely sensitive nose and the smell of a house occupied too long by too many people was peculiarly offensive to her. There were baths and jakes in most large houses – there were fine bathrooms at Windsor with ceilings and wainscots of looking-glass[15] – but the water-closet installed at Richmond Palace in 1597 to the design of the Queen's godson, John Harington, was the first in any of the royal palaces.[16]

There was, too, the smell of the horses. Henry III had felt compelled to regulate the number of horses that could be stabled at Windsor as they were considered a danger to Prince Edward's health; and in 1519 the regulation was repeated 'in consideration of a scarcyte and straitness of Lodgings as well as in avoyding and eschewing of the corrupt air'.[17] For reasons of sanitation, therefore, the Royal Household had to be a mobile one, and Henry VIII, who was in the opinion of the French ambassador, Marillac, 'the most timid person in the world' when there was a threat of plague,[18] forced it to move often enough, to trail from house to house with hundreds of carts carrying clothes and linen, table-ware and documents, jewels and even furnishings, for many of the houses were too bare for a court. Not until the reign of Elizabeth, however, did it move so often, for no previous monarch had combined so sensitive a nose with so restless a determination to force the country's rich families to entertain the Household in the interests of royal economy, or had combined so strong a desire for movement and activity with so great a gift for winning the hearts of the people she would meet on her way.[19] Elizabeth's visits to Windsor were consequently never prolonged.

Her affection for the place was, however, undoubted. She was particularly happy there in the summer – in the winter she found it terribly cold[20] – and she built a fine stone terrace beneath the windows of her apartments on the northern side of the Upper Ward, in place of the decaying planks and rails that had formerly covered the earth and stones at the top of the escarpment. Here in the evenings she liked to walk, moving very fast, as though she were hurrying away from a ghost or trying to keep warm in ice-cold air, but never losing her dignity or appearing to bustle as her sister Mary had done. She built, too, a gallery (see plate 14) next to the tower which her grandfather had built for his Queen, where she liked to walk when the weather was too bleak for exercise outside in the garden, 'full of meanders and labyrinths' that she made below the new North Terrace. She also liked to hunt in the Park, wearing clothes and jewels more suitable for the audience chamber than the hunting field, and riding her horse so fast that she tired out her frightened companions. She was capable of killing the 'great and fat stagge with her owen Hand'.[12] And even when she was sixty-six she was not content to watch the greyhounds driving the deer along the coursing paddock, a long strip of narrow ground to the north-east of the Castle, and to shoot at the quarry from the stands as her ladies preferred to do. She insisted on riding with the men. She was still 'excellent disposed to hunting' and rode for long periods 'every second day'.[22]

The contrasts between her fragile figure and her strong will, her graciousness and her robust beer-drinking, spitting, swearing, coarseness, between her courage and her lapses into fear, her kindness and her cruelty, were contrasts to which her courtiers soon grew accustomed. They knew that she could not bear loud noises, that she slept badly and had a poor appetite, that she was sometimes as hysterical as her mother; but they knew, too, that she had her father's genius for authority, and that as an employer she was rigidly exacting – Leicester, Heneage and Hatton as members of the Council, and not only the Cecils and Walsingham as Secretaries, were all hardworking men. They knew that she did not shrink from giving instructions for men to be tortured, and that although she could forgive a man who had created a disturbance in the Sovereign's presence by firing a shot in her direction and could reprieve him at the gallows'

foot in the Castle courtyard, she could not forgive the Puritan John
Stubbs for suggesting that she was too old to marry, insisting,
rather, that his right hand should be cut off, saying she wished he
could be hanged.[23]

She was a woman of her time. In her room at Windsor she read
and talked and laughed and played her virginals as any woman
might have done. She sat on a cushion 'most curiously wrought by
Her Majesty's own hands'. She slept in an immense and gorgeous
bed 'covered with curious hangings of embroidery work'.[24]

She would come to the window in her négligé to look down at
Leicester's fool shouting on the Terrace[25] and she would smile at
Leicester himself when he came to see her in the morning and kissed
him as he handed her her shift.[26] But beneath that beautiful room,
beyond the curve of the grey stone wall, was a place she knew in
Windsor where the gallows were put in the time of the plague to
hang anyone from the infected area who disobeyed the Council's
order and came near the Queen's most precious person.[27]

3

Stuarts

[i]

JAMES I

Three days after the Queen died, a messenger spattered with mud and 'be-blooded with great falls and bruises', stumbled into the ante-chamber of King James VI of Scotland to tell him that the day for which he had been so impatiently waiting had come at last. Queen Elizabeth was dead and he was King of England. Almost immediately he set out to claim his rich inheritance.

The reports about him that had come through to the English Court during the Queen's last years had not been reassuring. He was graceless, conceited, lazy and a coward. He was slovenly in his dress and he rarely washed. His narrow jaws and large tongue made it difficult for him to eat or drink without noisy and distasteful splashing. He spoke 'in the full dialect of his country' and in a very loud voice, expressing his opinions with a tiresome, irritating dogmatism. He hated to be beaten at games or, in fact, surpassed at anything. He was nervous, excitable and restless and walked up and down on his weak legs with a strangely erratic gait. His whole appearance was undistinguished – he was rather plump and looked ungainly even when he was standing still; his eyes were large and protuberant, 'ever rolling after any stranger that came in his presence'; he had a ruddy complexion with a skin left slightly pitted by smallpox, and thin sandy coloured hair; his small, trowel-shaped beard was 'scattering on his chin and very thin'. He was terrified of witches and naked steel, and he hated the sea and pigs. He had an almost obsessive interest in freaks and monstrosities of nature and in sexual perversions, and he loved to listen to obscene stories and to recount them. He was married to Anne, the youngest daughter of King Frederick II of Denmark, an enterprising, ambitious, rather masculine, cheerful and affectionate blonde woman, given to childish tantrums and expensive and frivolous conceits; but he preferred the company of handsome young men whose cheeks he would pinch and kiss and whose clothing he would fondle as if it were the coat of a lap dog.

There were those who could find excuses for his unattractive failings in the effects of a narrow and unhappy childhood. His mother was Mary Stuart, the vivacious, passionately emotional Queen of Scots, and his father was Lord Darnley, drunken, faithless, unintelligent and insolent, although 'the lustiest and best proportioned long man' that Mary had ever seen. And when Mary was pregnant with James, this Darnley had helped to murder David Rizzio, Mary's Italian secretary, in her presence. This pre-natal shock alone, it was felt, accounted for much of her son's fears and physical peculiarities. In addition he had been handed over as a child to the care of George Buchanan, the Scottish scholar, once one of the most celebrated European humanists but now a dour and crabbed old man who poured into him the prejudices of a severely Calvinistic mind. At the age of four, James's syllabus included Greek, dialectic, and astronomy. By the time he was eight he could speak Latin and French, translate the Bible into either language with equal facility, and discuss high theological questions. But there was no affection in his life, no development of that understanding which makes learning both useful and admirable. Buchanan, about whom James continued to have nightmares at the age of fifty-three, did not like women and thought them all stupid and vain, and his pupil 'through all his life entertained most lofty views of the superiority of the male'.[1]

He entertained also the most lofty views of his own superiority in particular, both as a person and as a king. 'The supreme consolation for everything he lacked lay in his kingship. The intense self-centredness which was to become his most dominating characteristic had its root in the importance which everybody else attached to his person and the kingship which it embodied.'[2] He held that his subjects should 'fear and obey him as God's lieutenant on earth',[3] and his English courtiers soon discovered that this belief in a divine mission made flattery, however grotesque, not merely acceptable but obligatory. Eventually, it was said, he 'ignored words spoken to him unless they were prefaced by such titles as most sacred, pleaseful, wise or learned'.[4] The Venetian ambassador reported that they were 'almost adoring His Majesty'. Even women had to kneel down when presented to him.[5] And the whole charade was rendered even more absurd by the King's embarrassing lack of natural dignity. Sir Henry Wotton had noticed in Scotland how 'extremely familiar' he was with his domestic servants – he was very mean with them too – and how he would linger on at table after the meal was over 'listening to banter and to merry jests' in which he took great delight.[6] In England his Court retained all the superficial vices of Elizabeth's, while losing most of those virtues that had made hers so virile and aggressively undegenerate. James's Court had vulgarity without panache.

The behaviour of Elizabeth's courtiers was governed not only by her own wishes, tastes and prejudices but also by standards which were beginning to be accepted throughout Europe as essential to the conduct of a gentleman. Authorities such as Castiglione's *Book of the Courtier*, first published in England during her reign, were having a widespread influence on the manners of courts by insisting that politeness and manliness were not contradictory. Castiglione condemned the courtier who powdered his face, curled his hair, plucked and dyed his eyebrows and kept a looking-glass inside his hat, but he also attacked the courtier who indulged in horseplay and hearty laughter and accepted stupid and degrading bets. The true gentleman was a healthy, chivalrous, quick-witted sportsman with an instinct for self-advancement. Queen Elizabeth's ideal courtier was just that. King James's young friends, on the contrary, were encouraged to be all that Castiglione disliked. The most successful of them, according to one observer, 'exceeded any part of womankind' with their mincing walk and wanton gestures.[7] Horseplay and practical jokes were *de rigueur*. The Earl of Pembroke disliked frogs, so the King put one down his neck; the King disliked pigs, so Pembroke put one in his bedroom. The royal jesters Archie Armstrong and David Droman, cantered about Windsor Castle on the backs of other fools pretending to be chargers. Sir George Goring, 'master of the game for fooleries', once led into a party 'four brawny pigs, piping hot, bitted and harnessed with ropes of sausages, all tied to a monstrous pudding'.

Both the King and Queen delighted in masques and at one staged in 1606 for King Christian IV of Denmark, during whose visit the ladies of court were seen to abandon all 'sobriety and roll about in intoxication',[8] there was more lack of 'good order, discretion and sobriety' than Sir John Harington had ever seen.[9] The Queen herself often took part in such displays, for she loved dressing up and appeared in several of Ben Jonson's brilliant and ingenious masques, together with some of her heavily scented and lavishly bejewelled ladies, in extremely provocative dresses. The King encouraged them to do so for he liked watching women 'being immodest'.[10]

His taste was for satire, low comedy and burlesque; and it seems that he liked best these aspects of the comedies of William Shakespeare, whose company continued to receive the royal patronage, as it had done in the time of Elizabeth when the Queen's wish that

Falstaff might fall in love, had been, so it was said, the inspiration of *The Merry Wives of Windsor*.

The extravagance of these court entertainments was inordinate. One masque alone cost over three thousand pounds and Ben Jonson's *Metamorphosed Gipsies*, which James saw for the third time at Windsor in 1621, cost little less.[11] During a Christmas holiday, in which another of Jonson's masques was performed, the Queen wore jewels worth £100,000.[12] The King himself, despite his lack of interest in his own clothes and his insistence that his wife ought to make do with those outmoded ones that he had discovered in his predecessor's wardrobes,[13] also spent immense sums on jewels with which he loved to decorate his clothes and his outlandish hats. He bought £92,000 worth in the first four years of his reign.[14]

Meals would be served on the occasions of masques and holidays with 'dishes as high as a tall man could well reach, filled with the choicest and dearest viands sea or land could afford, and all this, once seen and having feasted the eyes of the invited, was thrown away and fresh set on to the same height, having only this advantage of the other that it was hot'.[15]

Such extravagant waste at Court would have appalled Elizabeth. Her clothes (she had over two thousand dresses) and her jewels were magnificent; the splendour of her receptions and entertainments was dazzling; the ceremonial processions she held on Sundays when she was at Windsor were overwhelmingly impressive as she walked 'grandidly' by, gorgeously clothed and smelling of rose water and marjoram, stopping to say a few words to some kneeling spectator who had caught her eye. Such grandeur she believed essential to the maintenance of her position. But the Castle, as all her palaces, was run with the most severe economy. She had an annual budget of no more than £40,000 allocated to the Household and was very angry with the clerk comptroller when it was found not to be enough.[16] The salaries of officials were kept as low as they had been during her father's time, and her maids of honour slept in an unheated room without a ceiling, open to a leaky roof and with a partition low enough for servants to look over.[17]

These maids of honour were expected to do more than put up with disagreeable accommodation in the hope of making a good marriage. They had to entertain the Queen whenever she required them to do so, and they were expected to behave with the strictest propriety. The Queen was not above slapping them when they annoyed her, and she would have them put in the Tower if they became pregnant as Sir

Nicholas Throckmorton's daughter did by Sir Walter Raleigh. She interfered with all their love affairs and became furious if they contemplated marriage without her consent, not so much because she was jealous – as sometimes, though, she may have been – as because 'like their manners and morals, their marriage was a royal responsibility, and it was a breach of duty as well as a gross personal affront to their Sovereign to marry without her leave'.[18] They were required to obey the Queen in everything, to compose their inevitable and frequent quarrels for her sake, and to contribute as much to her fortunes as she did to theirs.

For James, such relationships were impossible. He could rarely command anything but the pretence of admiration, and so, abandoning himself to the pleasures of generosity and with little conception of the value of money, he lavished gifts on those whose affection he craved. He once presented one of those numerous Scottish friends – whose presence in England 'creeping into English lordships and English ladies' beds'[19] enraged the English – with an order for £20,000; and on another occasion when walking along a corridor with one of his forty-eight Gentlemen of the Bedchamber and passing some servants carrying three thousand pounds in gold, he stopped them and made them take it to the lodgings of his companion who said he wished he had as much to spend.[20]

Such munificence could not, of course, gain respect; nor could it be allowed to continue. James Hay, a favoured Scottish crony whose debts were settled by the King, was obliged to retire from the Wardrobe in favour of Sir Lionel Cranfield, who immediately made a saving of £14,000 a year. James, however, was not impressed. And when another of his officers had wanted to confess on his death bed that he had been cheating him, the King forgave him immediately. 'I wonder much', he said, 'that all my officers do not go mad with the like thoughts, for certainly they have as great cause as this man hath.'[21]

That James was fundamentally good-natured few men denied. Nor could it be said of him that he had an essentially vulgar mind. He swore with a lurid zest for obscenity and blasphemy; he never tired of lewd stories; but he had an acute intelligence and although his humour and puns were often too heavily facetious for even his contemporaries' taste, he was often genuinely funny. 'He was very witty,' Weldon, who did not care for many of his other characteristics, said of him, 'and had as many jests as any man living, at which he would not smile himself, but deliver them in a grave and serious manner.' He did not like music – he was far too clumsy to dance –

and his poetry was mechanical; but he had a sincere love of literature and wrote a vigorous prose himself. His *Counterblaste to Tobacco*, for instance, in which he suggests that smoking originated with the Indians, who indulged in the habit as an antidote to syphilis, is a fine piece of sustained tendentious polemics. He was undoubtedly lazy and governed England personally and self-indulgently in his spare time and mostly by correspondence; but his excuse that when he did work he could do a whole day's business in an hour or two was not entirely groundless. He had a real talent for business and made up his shrewd mind quickly. He also displayed an unexpected courage in moments of crisis. The fact remained, however, that the King's virtues seemed swallowed up by the vulgarity of his behaviour and the gracelessness of his manner.

What did the people want? he asked crossly when they crowded round him in the street soon after his accession to catch a glimpse of their new King, frightening him with their numbers and staring, curious faces. They came of love to see his face, he was assured. But he had already grown tired of this adulation which he had at first found exciting, believing it to spring from love of himself rather than from pleasure in the occasion of welcoming a new King, and he cried out in Scottish, 'God's wounds! I will pull down my breeches and they shall also see my arse.'[22]

It was, as his courtiers had quickly learned, a characteristic remark. Deal with 'this pantaloon', he once commanded Salisbury when an ambassador interrupted him with a business matter when he was out hunting, an activity which revealed far more unpleasant aspects of his character than the intimidation of crowds did.

He had an overwhelming passion for hunting. The discovery of so great a store of deer and game at Windsor was one of the most exciting pleasures of his first tour of his royal palaces.[23] And within a few weeks of his arrival in England he was out after them. He hunted down the quarry with a fury which appeared insanely vindictive, riding after the hounds at a wild gallop, often with the ribbon of the Garter dangling above his left boot, disdainful of his customary timid caution, dismounting eagerly as soon as the stag was brought down to run at it and cut its throat. Then he would rip its belly open, put his hands and sometimes his feet inside and daub his companions with blood.

He seemed to take a strange delight in the death of all animals. Not only did he hunt stags with frenzied enthusiasm, not only did he enjoy killing hares and catching larks, pursuing game with hawks and cormorants, but he loved to see cocks fighting and bears and bulls being baited to death. To see lions baited he had a special pit made and once matched a lion with a bear who was to be punished for killing a child, but the lion refused to fight and the bear had to be baited to death by dogs instead. [24]

He liked to be accompanied, while indulging these tastes by a few handsome young men. 'Handsomeness,' Sir Richard Bulstrode said, 'went a long way in our court.' For the King 'loved young men, his favourites, better than women, loving them beyond the love of men for women'. Sir John Oglander had never seen 'any fond husband make so much or so great dalliance over his beautiful spouse' as he had seen 'King James over his favourites, especially Buckingham'. [25] Abroad he was sometimes referred to as Queen James, King Elizabeth's successor. [26]

That anything more physically satisfying than kissing and petting took place between the King and these young men, most of his contemporaries doubted, although when he was old and feeble the French ambassador said of him, that by comparing his friendships to those of antique heroes, he endeavoured to 'conceal scandalous doings' and because his strength had deserted him for these activities he 'fed his eye where he could no longer content his other senses'. [27] This was, however, a minority view as well as a malicious one. Just as the King rarely got drunk, preferring to sip the strong, sweet Greek wine and Scottish ale he loved throughout the day, so, perhaps, he had always preferred to sip at the men he loved.

When they married he continued to pet and fondle them in public as he had done before. The first morning after the Earl of Montgomery's marriage to Lady Susan Vere the King was in their room at an early hour and even, it was believed, in their bed. [28] When Robert Carr, who had come from Scotland as the King's page and was created Earl of Somerset, went to face his trial for the murder of Sir Thomas Overbury which his wife had committed in order to marry him, King James 'hung about his neck, slabbering his cheeks, saying, "For God's sake, when shall I see thee again. On my soul I shall neither eat nor sleep until you come again . . . For God's sake, let me, shall I, shall I?" – then lolled about his neck. "Then for God's sake give thy lady this kiss for me"; in the same manner at the stair's head, at the middle of the stairs, and the stairs' foot.' [29]

After the King realised that, in Bishop Goodman's phrase, 'a choice of dishes best pleaseth the palate', and discarded the peevish Somerset in favour of George Villiers who was the 'handsomest bodied man in England' and had a 'very lovely complexion', he became more infatuated than he had ever been. Villiers, an energetic, talented and ambitious, as well as an extremely good-looking man, with 'that rather overripe masculine attraction that trembles on the verge of femininity', an 'exquisitely curved mouth, and the dark blue eyes of the highly sexed',[30] was made a Gentleman of the Bedchamber in 1615, a Knight of the Garter and a viscount in 1616, an earl in 1617, and a marquess in 1618. By the time he was raised to the dukedom of Buckingham in 1623, he was one of the richest men in England and the country's virtual master. To the King he was 'Steenie' – he was said to look like St Stephen – his 'sweete boye', his 'dear child and gossope'. 'I wear Steenie's picture,' he confessed, 'in a blew ribbon under my wastcoate, next my hairte.'[31] After Buckingham married, the Duchess, a pretty, kind, adoring woman, became 'Dere Dad's' pet, his 'Baby Kate', and even her children – although he had never shown any particular fondness for his own – became his pets, too, 'so that little ones would dance up and down the privy lodgings like fairies'.[32]

Neither the King's own children nor the Queen came to Windsor often. There was little in the Queen to make the King uxorious, Bishop Goodman thought, and although she tolerated his peculiarities, 'they did not much keep company together'.[33] She lived mainly at Greenwich and at Somerset House, then called Denmark House as a compliment to her native country, and she gave birth to seven children, four of whom died young. The eldest son, Henry, influenced by his mother, had little respect for his father who, in turn, was so jealous of his gifted, athletic and popular son that, when he died at the age of seventeen, cruel rumours circulated that his father had had him poisoned.[34] The King's only surviving daughter, Elizabeth, was married to Frederick, Count Palatine of the Rhine when she was sixteen. And his son Charles, when he was old enough to make the choice, kept as far away as he could from a court whose behaviour disgusted him. He disliked Buckingham, until the Duke, recognising, no doubt, the danger of 'quarrelling permanently with the heir to the throne of an ageing King',[35] began to exercise his compelling charm over the son as well as over the father; and King James's appearance and manners cannot fail to have distressed so fastidious a boy as Charles.

As the King grew older and more infirm this appearance and these manners grew increasingly distasteful. 'His skin was as soft as taffeta sarsnet,' Weldon said, 'because he never washed his hands, but only rubbed his fingers' ends slightly with the wet end of a napkin.'[36] He was always scratching himself, and as he was subject to over-heating and sweated profusely he had his clothes cut very loose. He also had them made stiletto-proof with 'breeches in great plaits and full stuffed; he was naturally of a timorous disposition which was the reason of his quilted doublets'.[37] When he got too hot he would throw his outer clothes off, and so he caught cold and was for ever sneezing and blowing his nose. He lost all his teeth and, being unable to chew, bolted his food and so suffered from indigestion and heart-burn. He was excessively fond of fruit and when he was brought the first strawberries, grapes or cherries of the season out of the Windsor gardens he would never wait till the man from the spicery had finished his speech of 'complimental words' and risen from his knees, but plunged his hands impatiently into the basket,[38] so he suffered from intermittent diarrhoea as well. He also had arthritis and gout which he attempted to cure by standing up in the belly of bucks and stags slaughtered in the hunting field.[39]

Hunting was one of the few pleasures that remained to him and he continued up till the last year of his life to insist on the observance of many forest laws and restrictions that had long since fallen into disuse. He had discovered at the beginning of his reign that the inhabitants of Windsor had, during the late Queen's time, been in the habit of walking through the Park with their dogs, shooting the little game, particularly hares, and collecting sticks and firewood. This he took as an affront and an importunity and he did all he could to prevent it. The old laws were revived and the brothers Richard and Jeffrey Richbell, who were imprisoned in 1621 for riding in Windsor Forest at night with 'staves and greyhounds', were neither the first nor the last to suffer for breaking them.

One day while he was hunting, the King was approached by the Vicar of Windsor, the Mayor and four aldermen who presented him with a petition on behalf of the Vicar whose living did not constitute, so they maintained, 'a competent menes of livelyhood'. The King took the opportunity to lecture the petitioners about the 'complaintes that had been made unto him by some of his keepers concerning the Poore of our Towne fetching wood in the Parkes and Forests'. He said to the Mayor, '"Am I any ill naighbor to you? Doe I doe you any hurte? Doth my coming be any hinderance to you? Why then do you vex me by permitting and suffering your poore to cutt downe and carey awaye my woodes out of my parkes and grounds?" and he commanded the aforesaid Mr Maior to punish the offenders by whipping of them.'[40]

The King's denial of what the people of Windsor had come to regard as their traditional right was only one of many selfish actions which made them dislike him. He allowed his officers to abuse his right of purveyance; he and his huntsmen and courtiers trampled down crops without regard to the farmers' profits; he even attempted to revive the ancient elaborate ceremony of the Forest Courts by expecting each forester and each woodward to kneel before him and present him with their horses and hatchets which they did not receive back until they had paid a fine of 6s. 8d.[41]

The King, however, had never much cared about the esteem of the public and as he grew older he cared less. He grew, indeed, indifferent to most things. He became ever more repellent physically, hiccupping and sneezing and belching, with sores on his lips from the 'bitter humours boiling from his mouth', with stones in his bladder and disease in his liver; and his devotion to Buckingham, now his 'sweete childe and wife',[42] became ever deeper, more frenzied and more emotional, alternating between moods of angry reproach and tearful reassurance.

In March 1625 the King was attacked by a tertian ague and although it was agreed to be 'without any manner of danger if he wold suffer himself to be ordered and governed', the only people who had any control over him at all were Buckingham and Buckingham's fussy, managing mother. These two, apparently against his physicians' advice, decided to give him patent powders obtained from a doctor in Essex and to apply plasters to his wrists and stomach; and within a short time he was dead.[43] The Buckinghams were naturally accused of having killed him, but when the doctors opened his body they found no poison. All his vitals were 'sound, as also his head, which was very full of brains; but his blood' – and this provided a sad and fitting epitaph – 'was wonderfully tainted with melancholy.'[44]

[ii]

CHARLES I

Charles, Prince of Wales, was twenty-four when his father died and everyone who had talked with him and looked into those sad, dark, reproachful, rather protuberant eyes knew that his Court would be a very different place from that of his father. And so, indeed, it was. Charles had no intimate companions apart from his 'sweet Steenie' for whom he conceived an affection which filled his whole horizon, as it had filled his father's.[1] The sister whom he had loved was married and in Germany; the brother whom he had idolised was dead; the fifteen-year-old French wife he married within two months of his accession found at first his Protestant people tedious and himself at once solemn, priggish and unfriendly. Reserved, melancholy, restless, with little sympathy and less humour, meticulous, 'intellectual without being intelligent',[2] disingenuous, so shy that he blushed at the sound of a coarse word, so hesitant and stammering when he spoke in his falsetto voice with its pronounced Scots accent that he infected most of those he met with his own ill-disguised embarrassment, he was not a man likely to inspire close friendship.[3]

Compelled by the Duke of Buckingham's overpowering personality to assume a romantic bravura quite out of keeping with his character, as Dr J. P. Kenyon has pertinently said, 'all his adult life he was acting a part; he was the nervous man afraid of seeming nervous, the shy man afraid of seeming shy. He always over-acted slightly; he was always advancing to occupy untenable positions, then defending them with pathetic heroism against impossible odds. The end-product is the martyr-King of Van Dyck's portraits, with the heavy-lidded eyes, the compressed mouth, the long, handsome wistful face and effeminate hair, a composition in suffering and Christ-like resignation.'[4]

Immediately on his accession he let it be known that whoever had occasion to come to Court 'must never approach him by backstairs or private doors'.[5] The Court became as ostensibly sober and moral as the King himself was, both in appearance and in fact. It also became rigorously formal. Every official was reminded of his duty, 'at which table to take meat, when to attend prayers, when the King would rise, when sleep, when ride, when give audience, and who, with staff or office in hand or napkin on arm, should walk before him or stand behind his chair'.[6] No other King in Europe was served on bended knee, and when the French ambassador asked for a chair to be brought for his wife, as would have been done for the English ambassador at the Court of Louis XIII, he was told that on official occasions no lady at the English Court, except the Queen herself, was allowed to sit in the royal presence.[7]

But although severely formal and exactingly decorous, it was not a parsimonious Court nor was it always a dull one. And after 1628 –

when the murder of the Duke of Buckingham removed what had formerly been an insurmountable obstacle to a happy marriage between the King and the jealous, stubborn but eventually self-confident and charming little Queen Henrietta Maria – it became in the words of the Venetian envoy '*la piu sontuosa e la piu allegra del mondo*'.[8]

It was an abode of beauty as well as of 'ceremony, elegance and learning. The noble ladies in silks of pale saffron, and coral pink, sky-blue, willow-green and oyster, their ringletted hair framing plump, oval faces' were rowed in barges on the Thames to have their portraits painted by Van Dyck,[9] while the smaller luxuries which surrounded them were 'etched in loving detail' by Wenceslaus Hollar, the royal children's Bohemian drawing master, one of whose carefully detailed pictures of Windsor Castle is shown in plate 7.

The King was not merely a patron of painters; he also had a real understanding and appreciation of their work. He was fond of music, too, and of the theatre. He liked hunting and riding as well as masques; he enjoyed swimming and tennis as well as dancing. He did not dismiss Archie Armstrong until the brash jester called Archbishop Laud a monk and a traitor, and when Armstrong was dismissed he was replaced by Muckle John.[10] Both he and the Queen liked to have dwarfs about them. The Queen had several, including Jeffrey Hudson, the son of a bull-baiter, who was often at Windsor, and Anne Shepherd, who married King Charles's dwarf, Richard Gibson, and bore him nine children – five of whom were of normal stature – before dying at the age of eighty-nine. Both Anne Shepherd and her husband were less than four feet in height – the King himself was only about 5ft. 5in. – but they were tall compared with Jeffrey Hudson, who was said to have stood no higher than eighteen inches when he jumped out of a pie on to the dining-table one day, in his miniature suit of armour, to bow politely to the Queen. He grew a little in the years which followed this youthful performance, but he remained small enough to fit into the pocket of the King's gigantic porter whose pretence of eating him as a tasty morsel between the two halves of a loaf of bread was greatly enjoyed at court masques.[11]

In general, though, 'the fools and bawds, mimics and catamites of the former Court grew out of fashion; and the nobility and courtiers who did not quite abandon their debaucheries, yet so reverenced the King as to retire into corners to practise them.'[12]

The reverence increased as the King grew older. For it seemed to those who knew him well that his chastity and sobriety, his deep

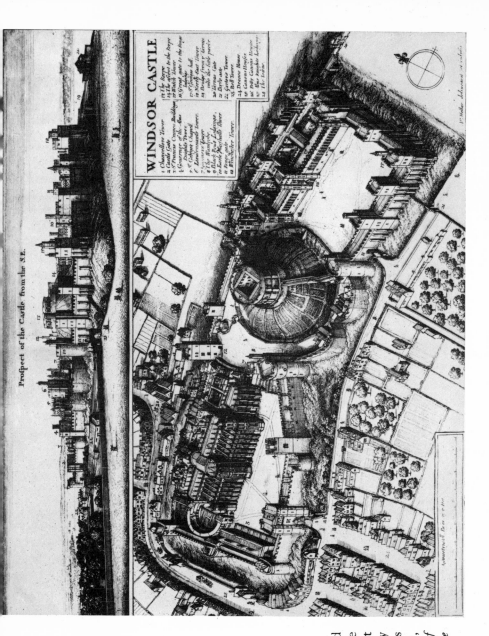

7. A bird's eye view and a prospect of the Castle from the south-east from the engraving by Wenceslaus Hollar in Elias Ashmole, *Institutions, Laws and Ceremonies of the Most Noble Order of the Garter*, 1672

8. The Castle from the north-east before the alterations by Hugh May from a drawing by Wenceslaus Hollar in the Royal Library, Windsor Castle

9. The Castle from the north-east after the alterations by Hugh May from an engraving published by John Garrett

religious sense, his perfect manners and gentleness, his insensibility to flattery, were not, after all, the affectations of a prig but the manifestations of a noble spirit. Even those whom his disastrous policies had made his enemies were as conscious of this nobility as they were exasperated by his 'ultimate power of complete refusal' to believe that his motives might be less pure, his friends less worthy of his loyalty, and his means less justified than he supposed them to be. But although he was reverenced as a good man, he was not greatly loved. Remote, sad, and mystical, he completely lacked the common touch. He expected his people to do their duty as his subjects, but what little he knew about their lives as human beings came by report and from books; he expected his servants at Windsor to be as stately and punctilious as he was and, so long as they were, he treated them justly and considerately; but the devotion those who remained in his service displayed towards him in his later years came not so much from affection as from pity. When the Civil War began and Windsor opened its gates to the forces of Parliament, many other servants came down from the Castle to fight against him.[13]

* * *

For eighteen years after the first battle of the Civil War was fought at Edgehill, Windsor Castle was a garrison and a prison. Colonel John Venn, a 'broken silk-man in Cheapside' as a Royalist historian[14] described him, took possession of the Castle in the name of the Parliament in October 1642.[15] There was no opposition to his occupation and a week later, when Prince Rupert's artillery, firing from the grounds of Eton College, had failed to do any appreciable damage to the walls after a bombardment lasting seven hours, the Royalists withdrew from the siege amidst scenes of 'great jubilation'.[16]

Venn was instructed to 'take care that there be no disorders and disturbances made in the chapel at Windsor; and that the evidences, registers, monuments there, and all things that belonged to the Order of the Garter may be preserved without defacings'.[17] And despite the charges made by many Royalist writers, he did his best to ensure that this injunction was obeyed. It seems unlikely that he 'caused St George's Hall to be filled with straw and hay or that the Chapel, where services were held throughout the Commonwealth, was used as a stable.[18] The altar plate was taken to help pay the cost of maintaining the Parliamentary troops, as were many rich vestments, hangings, velvet chairs and brass ornaments. The metalwork of the unfinished tomb intended for Henry VIII, and Edward IV's

F   65

coat of mail were both removed and melted down. The valuable Garter which had been sent to Gustavus Adolphus, King of Sweden, and returned to Windsor at his death, was taken from its hiding place and sold.[19] But both the Chapel and the Castle were plundered and damaged far less than has been maintained and far more circumspectly than many other churches and houses were damaged and plundered by the Parliamentarians in their hatred of ornamentation, of stained glass and 'superstitious pictures', and in their need for money.[20]

The lack of money was felt no more strongly anywhere than at Windsor where the garrison's pay was ninety weeks in arrears by March 1646. The soldiers, constantly verging on mutiny, took to shooting the deer in the Park for food and tearing up the fences for fuel,* and it was not until the summer of 1648, after General Fairfax had insisted on the 'great necessity of some present assignment of moneys for the better fortifying and victualling' of the Castle, that they could at last be paid.[22] By then the fate of the defeated King had been decided.

At Windsor Castle on 11 November 1647 a meeting of the General Officers of the Army 'resolved that the King should be prosecuted for his life as a criminal person'. The decision was reached after 'earnest prayers, made at the very council by Cromwell or Ireton, or some other *inspired* person',[23] and was followed some weeks later by a 'solemn fast' held at the Castle where the officers 'prayed very fervently and pathetically; this continued from nine in the morning till seven at night'.[24]

A few days before Christmas 1648 the King was brought from Hurst Castle to Windsor while preparations for his trial were being made in London. He rode into the Castle on 25 December, a plot

---

* The severity with which the Forest Laws were interpreted during the reigns of James I and Charles I had already led to onslaughts upon the protected game and the railings in the Parks and Forest. The royal deer had caused havoc to crops in many parishes where the inhabitants had taken to protecting their property with guns and crossbows as well as with greyhounds and nets and all sorts of traps. There had been riots in the Forest in 1641, and at the beginning of 1642 the Constable of Windsor Castle, the Earl of Holland, had told the House of Lords of 'the great destruction and killing of His Majesty's deer in the Forest of Windsor, where the people of the Country, in a riotous and tumultuous manner have lately killed a hundred of His Majesty's Fallow Deer, and besides Red Deer, and do threaten to pull down the pales of the Great Park'. The Sheriff of Berkshire was ordered to attend at the House and explain why he had not prevented the riots. Several men were eventually sent to prison; but a few months later the Civil War began and the Constable and Sheriff had other matters to occupy them. By the end of the War so many animals had been destroyed that Charles II had to restock the Parks with deer from Germany.[21]

prepared for his escape on a fast horse in Windsor Forest having miscarried when the animal was lamed by a kick from another horse and the King found himself surrounded by a hundred cavalry soldiers each carrying a pistol 'ready spanned' in his hand.[25]

Twenty pounds a day were allowed 'for the daily expenses of the King and his attendants'. And Colonel Christopher Whitchcott, who had succeeded Venn as Governor of the Castle, was instructed by the House of Commons to 'discharge and turn out such of the attendants who wait upon the King, as are malignants'.[26]

He was well treated, though, being allowed a choice of rooms in the royal apartments in the Upper Ward and as many visitors as he wished to receive. 'His Majesty hath three new suits,' *The Perfect Weekly Account* reported, 'two of them are of cloth with rich gold and silver lace on them, the other is of black satin, the cloak lined with plush. Since the King came to Windsor he shows little alteration of courage or gesture, and, as he was formerly seldom seen to be very merry, or much transported with any news, either with joy or sorrow; so now, although he expects a severe charge and tryal, yet doth he not shew any great discontent.'[27]

On the fourth day of his captivity 'came the order that he was no longer to be treated with the ceremonial of kingship. The cup was not to be offered to him with a genuflection, nor his dishes brought covered to the table, nor the trumpets sounded at his meals. Therefore, for what he could save of his dignity, he determined to dine alone. . . . His exercise was pacing up and down the long terrace, and for his solace he would pass hours in what Milton so curiously condemned in him, the reading of Shakespeare's plays.'[28]

Dignified and adamant to the end, his head was cut off on the morning of 30 January 1649. 'The blow I saw given,' wrote a spectator, 'and can truly say with a sad heart, at the instant whereof, I remember well, there was such a grone by the Thousands then present as I never heard before and desire I may never hear again.'[29]

The body was embalmed, wrapped in cere-cloth 'into the folds of which a quantity of unctuous or greasy matter mixed with resin' was melted so as to 'exclude as effectually as possible the external air,'[30] and an order was issued by Parliament that it 'should be buried at Windsor in a decent manner, provided that the whole expense should not exceed five hundred pounds'. The Duke of Richmond, the Marquess of Hertford and the Earls of Southampton and Lindsay were granted permission to attend the funeral, and the Bishop of London was permitted to officiate.[31]

The Bishop was in tears when the coffin, covered by a black velvet cloth and carried by the four noblemen, was brought down towards the chapel from the darkened room where it had been kept while the vault, in which the bodies of Henry VIII and Jane Seymour lay, was being prepared to receive it. It was bitterly cold and the Thames below was frozen over from bank to bank. The sky, at first serene and clear, darkened; and then snow began to fall into the courtyards of the Castle. 'By the time the corpse had reached the west end of the chapel, the black pall was white.'[32]

[iii]

CHARLES II

On the afternoon of 15 March 1660, just before the Exchange closed, a workman 'with a ladder upon his shoulder and a pot of paint in his hand, set the ladder in the place where the last King's statue had stood'. The statue had been taken down by order of the Government and in its place an inscription had been written: '*Exit Tyrannus, Regum Ultimus*' – The tyrant is gone, the last of the Kings. The workman painted out the inscription, and 'as soon as he had done it threw up his cap and cried, *God bless King Charles the Second*, in which the whole Exchange joined with the greatest shout'.[1]

A few weeks later King Charles II returned home after his long exile and the people greeted him with such enthusiasm that his head was 'so dreadfully stunned' by their acclamations, so he told his beloved sister Minette who was still with their mother in Paris, that he did not know whether he was writing sense or nonsense.[2] He did not disappoint his excited subjects however, either by his behaviour or by his appearance.

He had an ugly mouth and his expression was seen sometimes to relax into one of mocking cynicism, but he bowed, he smiled, he took off his hat, he turned from left to right; he was tall and dark and slim and graceful; he was thirty and a bachelor. 'His face is rather grave than severe which is very much softened whenever he speaks', one of his servants said of him in this year. 'His complexion is somewhat dark, but much enlightened by his eyes, which are quick and sparkling. Until he was near twenty years of age, the figure of his face was very lovely; but he is since grown leaner, and now the majesty of his countenance supplies the lines of beauty. His Haire, which he hath in great plenty, is of a shining black, not frizled, but so naturally curling into great rings, that it is a very comely ornament.'[3]

Pleased as most of his people were to have their King back, however, there were soon to be few of them not shocked by the behaviour of his Court. At Whitehall, that magnificent and sprawling palace which was almost entirely destroyed by fire soon after his death, the King could be seen walking very fast up and down the galleries, doing his best to avoid the dreary, the impecunious and the ambitious, or, having been stopped, carelessly granting some expensive favour to an improbable-looking suitor. He could be seen in the Chapel Royal, kneeling on velvet cushions and going to sleep during the sermon; and in his Physic Garden, picking herbs for his laboratory where his chemists manufactured the famous King's Drops that made 'cunning tongues babble secrets'; and he could be seen in the Banqueting Hall, showing himself to his people as he dined in state. And everywhere he seemed to be surrounded by dogs and epicene courtiers and pretty pages and by expensive women, lush and wanton. Even at Windsor, where life was lived rather less publicly, people soon learned of the King's recklessly carefree behaviour – his dining 'almost every night' with the gorgeous Barbara Palmer,[4] whose husband had been created Earl of Castlemaine (the honour to be tied up with the heirs of Lady Castlemaine's body), his getting so drunk after hunting in the Forest that he and his courtiers 'all fell a-crying for joy' in Sir George Carteret's house at Cranbourne, 'being all maudlin and kissing one another . . . and in such a maudlin pickle as never people were'.[5]

He took no trouble to hide from the world the pleasure he took in women and the presents and honours he bestowed upon them. Samuel Pepys was told how the King did 'doat upon his women, even beyond all shame'; and, in later years, John Evelyn, who said that he would never forget 'the inexpressible luxury and profaneness, gaming and dissoluteness of the Court', saw him 'sitting and toying with his concubines . . . a French boy singing love songs, in that glorious gallery, whilst about twenty of the great courtiers and other dissolute persons were at Basset round a large table, a bank of at least 2,000 in gold before them'.[6]

When he married, the King promised one of these concubines, Lady Castlemaine, that she should be a Lady of the new Queen's Bedchamber. The Queen angrily struck her name off the list of her Ladies, and the Lord Chancellor, the Earl of Clarendon, warned the King that his subjects would think him heartless, as indeed they did; but although he did not, perhaps, mean to be unkind, he was determined not to be 'argued out of justice to an old friend',[7] and behaved,whether consciously or not, with that 'rather feminine cruelty, usually hidden from the world'.[8]

The trouble was, of course, that the Queen had fallen deeply in love with her husband within a few days of first seeing him, 'a solecism none of his mistresses was so careless as to commit' for they had learned that the King was a man 'easily irked by demanding affection'.[9] The King's own passions were never aroused by this small, dark, nervous daughter of John of Portugal. He had chosen her not so much because her face in a miniature seemed 'not unhandsome' as because he needed a rich wife; and while he assured Lord Clarendon, having seen her in person, that there was 'not anything in her face that in the least degree could shame one' and that her conversation conducted in 'a most agreeable voice' was 'very good', he spoke of her in a less complimentary way to his courtiers. To Colonel Legge he complained that 'they had brought him a bat instead of a woman'.[10] But although she was indeed 'a very little woman', as Sir John Reresby said, and with her sallow skin and prominent teeth and her 'very nervous distemper' could not hope to 'stand in competition with the charms of the Countess of Castlemaine', she had what Pepys called a good, honest and innocent look and was far more handsome than her formidable maids of honour – 'six frights' according to Count De Grammont[11] – with their 'monstrous fardingales', their stern refusal to offend their virginity by sleeping in sheets once touched by a man and their entourage of 'very pious, very dirty Portuguese monks'.[12] She might indeed have given 'little additional brilliancy to the Court, either in her person, or in her retinue', yet she was far from being the haughty, bigoted, parsimonious, unimaginative frump some writers have described.

Realising that the King would not give up Lady Castlemaine for her sake, that he not only continued to make love to this mistress but was trying to seduce Frances Stewart at the same time, that he had other women besides, and that – or so she was advised – she would never change him, but might by changing herself win his love, she gave in. She stopped sitting alone and aloof, declining to join in the pleasures of the Court and going early to bed when she could bear no longer the insulting whispers and disdainful glances of her husband's friends. By 1668 she was apparently taking part in all the 'fashionable freaks' of the Court, going about the town masked or disguised as an orange girl, entering into houses to dance there 'with a great deal of wild frolic'. And 'once the Queen's chairmen, not knowing who she was, went from her; so she was alone and much disturbed' and had to get home in a hackney-coach. 'Some say it was in a cart.'[13]

This complete and astonishing change in the Queen's behaviour was noticeable, too, in her clothes. She abandoned her sombre and gigantic skirts held out by hoops of a vast circumference; she wore no more the high, stiff ruffs that concealed her throat; and she yielded to her husband's entreaties that she should conform to the current fashion of his Court. That fashion was continually changing. At the beginning of the reign, the King, in introducing his courtiers to the elaborate techniques of French manners, had also induced them to adopt a French style of dressing; but within a few years he had 'put himself solemnly into the Eastern fashion of dress resolving never to alter it, and to leave the French mode, which had hitherto obtained to our great expense and reproach'. Despite the King's enthusiasm, this fashion was, however, 'shortly after abandoned' also.[14]

But, whatever the fashion, the Queen's clothes not only reflected but exaggerated it. At a time when it was fashionable for a dress to be cut so low that the swell of the breasts was seen even to the nipple's aureola, the Queen 'exposed her breast and shoulders without even . . . the slightest gauze; and the tucker instead of standing up on her bosom, is with licentious boldness turned down and lies upon her stays'.[15]

Now it was not only the King who could shock his subjects by receiving Holy Communion with three bishops on one side of him and three illegitimate sons by three different mistresses on the other, but the Queen who could also shock them by appearing at a party with the King, Lady Castlemaine, and a pretty boy, James Crofts (afterwards created Duke of Monmouth), the King's son by Lucy Walter, and by going home afterwards with them all in the same coach, happily affectionate.[16]

To those who knew him well there was nothing surprising about the Queen's surrender to the King's wishes and her rare objections to the insulting activities of his mistresses, for his bland charm was ultimately irresistible. He was self-indulgent, sometimes sarcastic, and often impatient; he had a tendency, without being permanently indolent, to dismiss serious matters with a flippant jest; and he also had a tendency, as Bishop Burnett said, to make 'fair promises, in which he was liberal to excess, because he intended nothing by them but to get rid of importory, and to silence all further pressing upon him';[17]

he was affected and he could be deceitful and unreliable, insensitive and even vindictive; he was capable of alarming outbursts of anger and moods of surly ill-temper, particularly as he grew old. But his innate kindness and generosity, his friendliness and tact, his love of children and animals, his tolerance, his ironical humour and conversation, his evident and disarming delight in all the pleasures of living, cast his failings into shadow. He may have been a 'lazy Prince' but he was a delightful man. He 'never lost his affability and courtesy. He touched people for the evil without evincing either nausea or a temptation to mirth. But on solemn occasions he could never play the King. He read his speeches to Parliament like a schoolboy. . . . If he saw an acquaintance at play, in the park, or even in a State procession, he would nod to him with the easy familiarity of an equal; and if the gentleman happened to have a handsome wife with him, he would cast on the husband a glance of significant meaning.'[18] And yet for all his carefree ways, he never forgot that he was King. Pepys was told by Sir Herbert Cholmly that King Charles never allowed the companions of his debauches to take advantage of him the following day,[19] and while he would receive visitors willingly at any hour and would always – as his brother declined to do when he succeeded him – stand up to greet them with his hat in his hand,[20] he was no less dignified because of his easy courtesy. Nor did he allow his courtiers to behave disrespectfully towards his wife; and one day when the Queen asked him, 'What do you English mean, when you squeeze a lady by the hand?', he said he would tell her, if she would tell him whose conduct had made her ask the question. She said it was Edward Montague, her Master of the Horse, who squeezed her hand whenever he helped her into her coach. Montague was sent from Windsor and never returned.[21]

The Household at Windsor was governed by rules which were occasionally relaxed but never abandoned. Many of his courtiers would have liked these rules to be more closely modelled on those of the French Court of Louis xiv which they had so much admired during their exile. When Louis 'rose from his bed, two officers helped him on with his dressing gown. The first Valet-de-Chambre helped him put on the right sleeve of his shirt, the first Valet of the Wardrobe helped him put on his left sleeve. A *Cravatier* arranged the neck cloth, but the Master of the Wardrobe put it on'.[22] Charles, who did so much to change the tastes and attitudes of Englishmen admired the French. He brought back from the Continent with him a love of French music, of French food and French architecture. He saw in the polite manners of French society far more than a superficial elegance.

But he had little patience with the fantastic extravagance of formal etiquette that enforced upon French courtiers when performing their duties correctly – which it must be said they did not often do – the stylised movements of a parodied ballet. And when a visitor denied him the respect traditionally due to a King he would make a joke of the breach of etiquette rather than take offence, as he did with William Penn who 'thinking proper to bring his sectarian prejudices into the presence of royalty' kept his hat on when introduced and, seeing the King remove his own, asked, him 'Friend Charles, why dost thou not keep on thy hat' ? ' 'Tis the custom of this place,' the King replied, 'for only one person to remain covered at a time.'[23]

Charles's daily life was consequently far less rigidly formal than many of his Francophil friends would have liked it to be, and his Bedchamber, where the most secret affairs of State were transacted, frequently contained men and women whom a strict observance of court protocol would have denied entrance. To his closet only he and his trusted servant William Chiffinch had a key, but this was not so much because court etiquette required it as because Chiffinch was entrusted with the task of conducting women of the town into it; and here, when his male friends were admitted, the conversation, as in the Bedchamber and the Withdrawing Room, was gay and uninhibited. When he went to the lavatory, which he did every night before he went to bed, he liked to be accompanied by two attendants, one to hold the candle, the other to hold the paper, not because the rules governing his conduct required their presence, and certainly not because he shared the views of the King of Spain who would 'not piss but another must hold the chamber pot', but because he enjoyed their company.[24]

He did not comb his hair or shave himself, but when these duties were being performed he was talking, flipping over the pages of a book, or sitting with his knees against the window looking out at his gardens and parks and planning alterations. There was always something to do or something to be said or seen, and the room in which he was, was never silent for long. Even at night when the Gentlemen and Grooms of the Bedchamber had seen him into bed and themselves lain down to sleep, there were few quiet hours. 'Several circumstances made the lodging uneasy,' said Lord Bruce, a Gentleman of the Bedchamber, 'the great grate being filled with Scotch coal that burnt all night, a dozen dogs that came to our beds, and several pendulums that struck at the half, quarter, and the hour and all not going alike, it was a continual chiming.'[25]

The King slept soundly through it all and nearly every morning, whether he had been making love in the night or not, he got up early; and nearly every day he went outside to take some sort of exercise and so preserve his excellent health. He took pleasure in all kinds of sports, and at Windsor, where he could scull and swim as well as ride and hunt and play tennis in the new court he had built there, he was particularly happy.

*   *   *

The better he knew Windsor, the more he liked it. During the first few years of his reign, the duties and diversions of London life occupied most of his time and he came to the Castle but rarely, and never stayed long. For although the squatters who had moved into the Castle after the Civil War had been turned out, much of the fabric was still 'ragged and ruinous',[26] and many of the items of repair, listed by a Commission of Inquiry into allegations of negligence and misappropriation of funds made against King Charles I's surveyor in 1629, remained neglected.[27] After the King's execution the House of Commons had even resolved that 'the Castle of Windsore, with all the Houses, Parks and Lands there, belonging to the State, be sold for ready money'.[28] But although a Bill was brought in, it was thrown out after a debate in which the price of £2,700 (for a fine house and 472 acres) obtained a few years before for Sunninghill Park nearby, apparently influenced many Members against taking so drastic a step for so small a price.[29] It had been decided to sell the 'Little Parke and meadowes there' only. Within a short time, however, these were re-purchased for the Protector, and so passed back with the rest of the Windsor estates into royal ownership at the Restoration.[30]

The Constable of the Castle at the time of the Restoration was Bulstrode Whitelocke, who set out for the benefit of his successor the customary duties and perquisites of this office. The Constable 'is Keeper and Governour of the Castle,' Bulstrode wrote, 'and commands any Garison or under officers there. Hee may make use of any Lodgings or Roomes in the Castle whereof the King hath not present use; Hee is Judge of the Castle Court for tryell of Suites of any value arising within the honor. . . . He is Keeper of the Forest which is 120 miles compas, and hath care of the Vert and Venison there when it is stored, and power to hunt and dispose of them as he shall thinke fitt, not prejudicing the King's Pleasure.' He had power to punish and imprison in the Castle's Colehouse all those who killed game without a licence or cut down any trees. He might dispose of the 'several

74

Lodges and walkes in the Forest to whom he pleaseth' and was responsible for the collection of rents. His salary was only £20 a year and 'Tenn Load of wood for fuell and 40s. yearly to defray the charge of cutting it', so that, as Whitelocke complained, the office, although of 'very great antiquity, honour, power and pleasure', was of 'very little profit'.[31]

The widespread belief that it was also an office with privileges which its holders still abused as they had done in the past was given fresh evidence by Whitelocke's successor, Lord Mordaunt, who was impeached for his savagely vindictive treatment of William Tayleur, his clerk and the Castle's surveyor. Mordaunt had, it seems, conceived a passion for Tayleur's daughter and when a proposition he made to her was virtuously refused he 'swore by a most dreadful Oath and Imprecation, He would persecute her, and her Family to all Eternity'. He arrested Tayleur and had him imprisoned; he ejected Mrs Tayleur, who was pregnant, from their lodgings and 'frightened a young child of the said Mr Tayleur out of his wits; whereof it soon after died'. And all this, according to the Earl of Anglesey, was 'because Mr Tayleur's daughter would not prostitute herself to His Lordship's Lust'.[32]

The King rendered the repetition of such conduct impossible by revoking Lord Mordaunt's patent and appointing Prince Rupert as Constable in his place. Prince Rupert was prematurely old then and a sick man with a 'dry hard-favoured visage, and a stern look, even when he wished to please,'[33] but his life was as crowded and active as it had ever been. He hunted with vigour; he reorganised the garrison and tightened up its discipline; he experimented with mezzotint engraving; he wrote long letters to friends in Germany; he received visits from his mistresses;[34] and, as John Evelyn noticed on a visit in August 1670, he began 'to trim up the keep, or high round tower, and handsomely adorned his hall with furniture of arms, which was very singular, by so disposing the pikes, muskets, pistols, bandoliers, holsters, drums, back, brest and head-pieces, as was very extraordinary. Thus those huge steep stairs ascending to it had the walls invested with this martial furniture, all new and bright, so disposing the bandoliers and drums, as to represent festoons and that without any confusion, trophy-like. From the hall we went into his bedchamber, and ample rooms hung with tapestry, curious and effeminate pictures, so extremely different from the other.'[35] The Castle, Evelyn was glad to learn during this visit, was at last 'going to be repaired'.

A few years before, Elias Ashmole, the antiquarian, had walked round it while gathering materials for his projected history of the Order of the Garter and had taken with him the engraver, Wenceslaus Hollar, whose most important engraving was the large bird's eye view of the Castle (see plate 7). This engraving, illustrating the Castle's severe lines and its absence of windows in the outside walls, shows clearly how little its architecture can have appealed to Charles ii, whose taste had been formed during his exile in Holland and France. The palace at Versailles and the Louvre, where the new Baroque style, born further south, was being revealed to admiring architects and patrons from all over the world, seemed to him incomparably finer than the severe lines of Windsor Castle which had remained largely unchanged in their main contours for five centuries. Christopher Wren, who visited Paris in the summer of 1665 and found a thousand hands at work on the Louvre, where twice a month 'an academy of painters, sculptors, architects, and the chief artificers' met to give magnificent reality to Bernini's design, thought that here indeed was the best school of architecture in Europe.[36]

Wren had lived at Windsor for over twenty years, for his father had been Dean between 1635 and 1659; but he was not appointed Comptroller of the Works until 1684 when Charles ii had only another year to live. All the work that was carried out in the Castle during the King's lifetime was supervised by another architect of far less fame but of considerable talent, Hugh May.

May was the friend of both Pepys and Evelyn. He was, Pepys thought, a most ingenious man;[37] and although Horace Walpole did not include him in his list of architects, his designs for Berkeley House, Piccadilly, and for Cassiobury, 'a very noble place' in Evelyn's opinion,[38] together with his work at Windsor, which was responsible for 'introducing the grand Baroque conception into the domestic architecture of the country',[39] entitle him to high regard.

At Windsor, he entirely rebuilt the royal suite in the Upper Ward, known today as the State Apartments; and while from the outside this new Star Building – as it was called from the huge Garter Star on its northern face – presented an appearance which was plain to the point of dullness (see plate 9) its interior was of an astonishing beauty. On the ground floor, facing inwards towards the quadrangle, the fourteenth-century Gothic entrance hall was retained (see plate 41), but above this the domestic chapel, St George's Hall and the new saloons, (see plates 10 and 11) reflected all the rich exuberance of the Baroque taste. Delicately painted ceilings by the Neopolitan Antonio

Verrio, in which the allegorical figures – one of which was of Charles himself in the unlikely company of Prudence, Temperance and Fortitude – seem to move and float, and richly carved cornices and frames by Grinling Gibbons, in which the leaves and fruit, the fish and game have a graceful asymmetry at once intricate and sensual, give to those rooms, which have survived both the erosion of time and the Gothic revival, a splendour which is unexcelled.

John Evelyn on a visit to Windsor in the summer of 1683 was delighted with the newly finished works. Verrio's invention was 'admirable,' he thought, 'his ordnance full and flowing, antique and original'. With 'the stupendous and beyond all description the incomparable' work of Grinling Gibbons he was particularly delighted, for he had himself discovered the artist, while walking near his home one day, in a 'poor solitary thatched house' which he had stumbled upon by 'mere accident'. He had happened to look through the window and seen Gibbons at work and some time later he had introduced him to the King. Seeing his work at Windsor he felt sure that he was 'without controversy, the greatest master both for invention and rareness of work, that the world ever had in any age'.[40]

Evelyn was delighted also with the surroundings of the Castle. The terrace on the north side had been taken round the south and east flanks and had been made 'clean, even, and curiously turfed'. The Long Walk, an avenue three miles long was not laid out and planted until 1685, but already other 'avenues to the new park had been planted with elms and limes'. There was 'a pretty canal and receptacle for fowl: nor less observable and famous' was 'the throwing so huge a quantity of excellent water to the enormous height of the Castle, for the use of the whole house, by an extraordinary invention of Sir Samuel Morland'.[41]

Morland, a most versatile man credited with all sorts of inventions from the drum capstan for weighing heavy anchors to the speaking trumpet as well as with this machine for raising water, placed his remarkable engine beneath the base which Grinling Gibbons had carved for Josias Ibach's statue of Charles II in the Upper Ward. Morland amazed his contemporaries by forcing water 'in a continual stream at the rate of above sixty barrels an hour up to the top of the Castle'.[42] There had been a fountain in the Upper Ward for generations and in Norden's drawing of the Castle done in 1607 (see plate 3) the Tudor fountain under its curious canopy occupies an imposing position; but Morland's seemed 'the boldest and most extraordinary experiment ever performed by water in any part of the world'.[43]

The King enjoyed watching the machine at work and would stand by it with his watch in his hand, measuring the rate of flow. He had always been interested in mechanics and science and spent longer hours than ever in his laboratory as he grew older.

It was a quiet life at Windsor. 'Ther was little resort to him,' Sir John Reresby said after being shown round the Castle when the improvements were in their final stages, 'and he passed his day in fishing or walking in the parks which indeed he naturally loved more than to be in a crowd or in business.'[44]

And in these summer weeks, although he got up early as was his usual practice in London, he did little business. Occasionally there were days when he was obliged to discuss affairs of state; sometimes there was a visit from a foreign prince; and once the curious Ambassador from the King of Bantam came with 'several of his Retinue carrying Launces, and two of them umbrellas, besides two of his master's servants, who also carried two umbrellas over his letter of credence'.[45] But most days were spent in quiet pleasure: fishing at Datchet, swimming in the river, hawking in the Forest, long walks in the Park, planting trees, playing tennis and bowls, watching cock-fights, looking at his pictures or the illustrations in his books, watching his exotic birds in their beautiful cages and, in particular, admiring 'Cockatoo', whose cage was kept in his eating-room, amusing his friends by his conversation, well informed and witty, and his store of anecdotes, embellished each time they were repeated. In the evening he would watch a play in St George's Hall or go to the Queen's apartments to play a game of basset or downstairs to the apartments assigned to the Duchess of Portsmouth to play crimp.[46]

The Duchess of Portsmouth, formerly Louise de Kéroualle, an exceptionally pretty baby-faced Breton girl who had been his sister's maid-of-honour, was now his most favoured mistress, and perhaps, even, his closest friend. Lady Castlemaine, created Duchess of Cleveland in 1670 and the acknowledged mother of six of his numerous illegitimate children, rarely came to Windsor after the alterations were completed; while the other mistresses of his later years, the Duchess Mazarin, healthy, strong and masculine, 'a natural and glorious lover',[47] who was 'toujours entourée d'un cercle d'adoratrices', Catherine Peg and Moll Davis, the actress, were also more often to be seen with the King in London. One of the Duchess of Portsmouth's rivals was, however, frequently at Windsor, where she lived in a fine house called Burford House after her son, who was created Earl of Burford in 1676 (see plate 12).

The story of the elevation of this little boy to the peerage, whether true or not, is characteristic both of his father, the King, and of his mother, Nell Gwynn. Pepys first saw the lively little Cockney comedienne standing outside her door in Drury Lane. He admired her 'smock-sleeves and bodice' – something of a fetishist, he once confessed that it had done him good to look upon Lady Castlemaine's 'smocks and linnen petticoats' hanging up to dry – and he decided that Nell was a 'mighty pretty creature'. The King thought so too, and found her not only exciting and lovable as a mistress but enchanting as a companion. The daughter of a woman who had drowned herself when drunk, she had been brought up in a brothel and had been an orange girl in a theatre before becoming an actress. She was a clever and impudent mimic and a mistress of tart and vulgar repartee. Once when her carriage was stoned by the mob who mistook it for the unpopular Duchess of Portsmouth's, she put out her head and shouted 'Don't hurt me, good people! I'm the Protestant whore';*[49] and once when this rival went into mourning for a French prince to whom she was in no way related, Nell Gwynn dressed herself in even deeper mourning for, so she said, the dear departed Cham of Tartary.[51] In Charles's presence she is said to have called to his son, 'Come here, you little bastard', and when Charles reproached her for using such a rude word, she replied that she had no other name to give him. Immediately he was made Earl of Burford and afterwards Duke of St Albans.[52]

Such stories delighted a people who detested the King's less honest and far less faithful mistresses. For, claiming no special privileges, Nell Gwynn excited no popular jealousy. She was appointed one of the Queen's Ladies in 1675,[53] some years after the King's munificence had enabled her to leave the stage; but few except the Duchess of Portsmouth, who could tell she had once 'been an orange-girl by her swearing', begrudged her either this honour or her new-found wealth. 'Her joyous laugh, her wild extravagance of speech, her warm-hearted disposition, and imperturbable good-nature' established her not only in the affections of her Charles the Third (as she fondly called him, referring to her two previous lovers, Charles, Lord Buckhurst and Charles Hart, the actor) but also in the affections of her fellow people. She was, in fact, in her own time, 'the picaresque heroine she has ever since remained'.[54]

* The Duchesses of Cleveland, Portsmouth and Mazarin were all Roman Catholics, the two last by birth, the first by conversion, an event which induced her relations to ask her lover to intervene. 'Oh, no!' replied the King, he could not, for as to the *souls* of ladies, he never interfered with them *there*.[50]

Despite the presence of the Duchess of Portsmouth in the Castle and of Nell Gwynn at Burford House, the Queen appeared to like Windsor as much as her husband did. She had long become resigned to his selfishness and constant unfaithfulness. Once going to his bedroom and noticing a tiny slipper beside his bed, she laughed and withdrew quickly, lest 'the pretty little fool', whoever it was, hiding behind the curtain, should catch cold.[55]

She loved to go out into the Park on hot afternoons and share a picnic with her ladies and servants in the shade of the trees. 'All the Queen's servants treated her by everyone bringing their dish,' Lady Chaworth wrote, giving an account in a letter of one such alfresco meal, 'and she eat under a tree. Lady Bath's dish was a chine of beef, Mrs Windham's a venison pasty, but Mr Hall bought two dozen of ruffs and reeves and delicate baskets of fruit, Mr Chiffinch, for his daughter's behalf, twelve dozen of choice wine. The Queen wonderfully pleased and merry, and none but herself and servants.'[56]

Informal as both the King and Queen liked to be, however, when taking their meals on ordinary occasions, the banquets given for the Knights of the Garter in the tapestry-hung St George's Hall at the time of the Feast of St George were as magnificent as they had ever been.

The celebrations lasted three days and at each meal the fare provided was a splendid display of English food and cooking at their superb and lavish best. For one Feast in 1670 the gravy alone accounted for 249 lbs of beef, 74 lbs of bacon, four cases of veal, two of mutton and one of pork, ten dozen pullets, nine dozen sheeps' tongues, eighteen dozen sweetbreads, seven dozen marrow bones as well as veal cauls, haggis bags, calves' caldrons, sheeps' feet, blood and the 'small guts of an Ox'. Apart from the different sorts of meat garnished by the various gravies made from these ingredients, twelve thousand prawns, fifteen hundred crawfish, 136 large lobsters, 118 large crabs, 400 scollops, twelve quarts of oysters and sixteen barrels of pickled oysters, eight pounds of caviare, eight quarts of cockles, sixty mullets and twelve mess of sturgeon, were provided during the course of this same Feast, together with 123 dozen capons, pullets and chickens, thirty-five dozen ducklings, twenty-four dozen pigeons, fifteen dozen green geese, nine dozen turkey chickens, thirty dozen quails, two dozen godwits, four dozen pheasants, twenty-four ruffs, thirty-five dozen rabbits, one hundred dried tongues, seventy Westphalia gammons, two hundred artichokes, two thousand eggs and six thousand sticks of asparagus, as well as immense

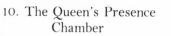
10. The Queen's Presence
Chamber

11. The Queen's Drawing
Room

12. A prospect of Burford House, Windsor, in the reign of Queen Anne from the engraving by Kip after Knyff in *Britannia Illustrata*, 1709

quantities of China oranges, Duke cherries, red and white strawberries, dried fruits and confectionery, ice cream and liquid sweetmeats, at a total cost of £2,394 17s. 8½d.

At each meal during the Feast an astonishing variety of succulent and more or less esoteric dishes was provided by the cooks: from Pies of Paris and Custard Plancyd to Bawdrets, Wildboar Pye, Bisk of Shellfish and Jagot Multon, from frosted Chicken Pye, Stump Pye and Umble Pye to Turkies aladob, Olives Luke, and CocksCombs.[57]

This is the bill of fare of one relatively modest supper:[58]

First Course

1. *Ducklings* boyled xii
2. *Veal* Arago
3. *Salmon* boyled i case
4. *Pidgeon* Pye
5. Green *Geese* xii
6. Gammon *Bacon* with iiii *Pullets*
7. *Pike* with *Prawns, cockles* and oysters
8. Bisk *Pigeons*
9. *Venison* Pye
10. Chines *Mutton* and *Veal* iii
11. *Chickens* boyled xii
12. *Hens* with Eggs Hasht vi
13. *Carps* Great iii
14. *Oyster* Pye
15. *Tongues* and *Udders* iiii
16. *Capons* boyled ii
17. *Kid* i case
18. *Pullet* a Granow iiii
19. *Beatilia* Pye
20. *Capons* fat v
21. Petty *Paties*
22. *Rabbits* fryed xii
23. *Sallet*
24. *Capon* good *per Sallets* iiii
25. *Rabbits* marrionated
26. Hashed *Sallet*
27. Cold *Sparagrass*
28. Pickled *Sallets*
29. *Sweet breads* Arago

Second Course

1. *Veal* Soust ii
2. *Salmon* col
3. *Pullets* Great vi
4. *Tongue* Pye
5. *Ducklings* xii
6. *Leverets* vi
7. *Lobsters* vi
8. *Chickens* fat xii
9. *Pheasants* with Eggs vi
10. *Skerret* Pye
11. *Partridges* xii
12. Turkey *Chicks* xii
13. *Crabs* buttered vi
14. *Tarts* sorts
15. Gammons *Bacon* ii
16. *Pigeons* tame xii
17. *Chickens* marrionated xii
18. *Lamprey* Pye
19. *Pullets* soust vi
20. *Sallet*

21. *Tongues* iiii
22. *Leich*
23. *Anchovis, caveare,* and pickled Oysters
24. *Eggs* of Portugal
25. *Blamange*
26. *Creame* Pistache
27. *Sparragrass*
28. *Jelly*
29. *Prawnes*

The meals 'most costly and delicate, completely royal and set forth with all befitting state and grandeur', were eaten in a suitably ceremonious manner. While an orchestra played in the gallery the King entered the Hall to be handed a basin of water and a towel by his attendant noblemen; and, the Sovereign having washed, the Prelate of the Order said grace. Then the King sat down alone at his table, which was raised on a dais and divided from the other tables by a rail and banisters (see plate 6). After he was seated the Knights, all dressed in their full robes, washed as ceremoniously as the King had done. Between the first and second courses all the spectators were removed from the Hall and the following ritual was observed: the Sovereign stood up and drank to the Knights; they then stood up and took their plumed hats off; Garter King of Arms, accompanied by Clarenceaux and Norroy, the Heralds and Pursuivants, bowing twice on their way, went up to the dais and cried *'Largesse!'* three times, whereupon the King stood up again. Garter then announced, in Latin, French and English, the Sovereign's styles and titles of honour – the Queen and her Ladies having come in to observe this part of the ceremony. When he had finished Garter cried *'Largesse!'* a fourth time and gave another bow which was the signal for the Treasurer of the Household to put £10 in gold into his hat as a gift for the Officers of Arms. After this presentation it had been customary in past reigns for the Sovereign to make a speech, or for a poem to be read, but Charles ii usually allowed Garter and his attendants to retire, in silence and at once, walking backwards and bowing after every three yards.[59]

All the other ceremonies of the Feast of St George – the installation of new Knights, the meetings of the Chapter, the processions (see plate 5) between ranks of attendants and chanting choristers to St George's Chapel, which was specially decorated for the occasion 'with peculiar and most rich furniture' – were performed with the same solemn yet elaborate ritual. For King Charles was determined to restore to the Order those ancient trappings of splendour which had never fully recovered their former ostentation since new statutes passed in the reign of Edward vi had deplored the activities of that 'olde serpente Sathan, a contynuel adversarye to mankynde' who, conceiving a 'grate envye' of the Order, 'busyly labored to deface and utterly to destroy so grate an encouragement and occasion of vertue by filling and stuffing the Order with many despicable ceremonies of a Papist origin' and with 'many obscure, supersticious and repugnante opinions'.[60]

The new Statutes, which removed all these repugnant practices from the ceremonial of the Order, were repealed by Mary, but Elizabeth had again interfered with the ancient regulations by permitting the Feast of St George to be held not necessarily at Windsor but wherever the Sovereign happened to be on 23 April. James i had brought the Feast back to Windsor but he, unwilling, or so it was believed, to see the English Knights outdoing his Scottish ones, had drawn new limits to magnificence and decreed that no Knight could be accompanied to Windsor by more than fifty attendants.[61] Charles i, in his turn, had repealed these new provisions of his father's, and the Earl of Northampton had arrived for the Feast in 1629 preceded by trumpeters, liveried grooms, yeomen and pages, by his secretaries, steward, comptroller and chaplain, by his Gentlemen of the Horse, his Pursuivants at Arms, Ushers and Heralds, and followed by a suite of noblemen and Knights and their servants and their servants' servants to the number of eighty men.

As the Civil War approached, however, the Feasts gradually became less and less grand and imposing, and by the time of the Restoration the number of Knights had dwindled to half the statutory strength and there seemed even a danger that the Order itself might lapse into decay. Through the efforts of Charles ii it did not do so. Within a year of his return to England he had restored the Order to its 'proper condition'; he had filled up all its vacancies and he had even 'thought it not unworthy' his care to 'descend unto the particulars of its clothing' by decreeing that undergarments which 'followed too much the modern fashion' should not be worn beneath the upper robes of the Order and thus detract from their 'decency, gravity and stateliness'. In future all undergarments, whether 'Trunk-hose or Round Breeches' should be made of 'Cloth of Silver'.*[62] The effect

---

* Another change made by Charles was in the manner of wearing the Lesser George. Previously this had been worn hanging on its blue ribbon on the centre of the breast. After the Duchess of Portsmouth had presented her twelve-year-old son, the Duke of Richmond

of all this was, unfortunately, far from decent, grave and stately, for the Knights became so proud of their new clothes that, so Evelyn told Pepys, they 'did wear them all day till night, and then rode into the Park with them on. Nay,' Pepys went on indignantly, Evelyn 'tells me he did see my Lord Oxford and Duke of Monmouth in a hackney-coach with two footmen in the Park, with their robes on; which is a most scandalous thing, so as all gravity may be said to be lost among us.'[64] Evelyn was also shocked by the way the 'banqueting stuff was flung about the room profusely' to the spectators, after the Knights had eaten as much as they could. He stayed 'no longer than this sport began for fear of disorder. The cheer was extraordinary, each Knight having forty dishes to his mess, piled up five or six high.'[65]

While Pepys and Evelyn were both distressed by the conduct of the Knights who disregarded the King's wishes for their dignified appearance and behaviour, they were both gratified that the restoration of the Order had led to the restoration also of St George's Chapel, 'a noble place indeed' in Pepys's opinion, with 'a good Quire of voices'. 'Great bowing by all the people, the poor Knights in particular, to the Altar,' he noticed when taken to a service there one day by the organist. There were those who were shocked by these repeated obeisances; but Pepys made no complaint. It was a memorable day and he was happy that the Stuarts had come back. And Windsor, after all, was truly the 'most romantique Castle in the world'.[66]

[iv]

JAMES II

Although most Englishmen shared Pepys's view of the Restoration, few of them could look forward happily to the accession of Charles ii's brother, James, Duke of York, who, since it seemed unlikely that Queen Catherine would ever have a son, would regrettably be his successor.

and Lennox, K.G., to his father with the ribbon over his left shoulder, 'Charles was so pleased with the conceit, that he decreed the fashion – which in fact has ever since been adhered to – should be generally adopted.'[63]

Once when taking one of his long walks with two of his friends, Charles came across the Duke of York returning from hunting in his coach. The Duke expressed surprise at seeing his brother endanger his life by walking about with 'so small an attendance'. 'No kind of danger, James,' said the King, 'for I am sure no man in England will take away my life to make you King.'[1]

It might well have been true, for the Duke of York, as Burnet said of him, had the 'strange notion' that no regard was 'to be had to the pleasing of the people'.[2]

When Charles died in 1685 the Duke was fifty-one and he had the reputation of being as great a threat to female virtue as his brother had been, without any of his brother's charm or taste. James's extraordinarily unattractive mistresses, Charles had once said, referring in particular, no doubt, to Catherine Sedley, must surely be inflicted upon him by his priests as a penance. 'I do not believe there are two men who love women more than you and I do,' Charles told the French Ambassador, 'but my brother, devout as he is, loves them still more.' Indeed, according to De Grammont, the Duke of York's principal if not his only occupation was adultery.[3]

He had few other vices, apart from an impenetrable obstinacy which made him believe that all those opposed to him were guilty of treason or worse and deserved the most ferocious punishment; but his virtues were not attractive ones. He was provident, but it was a providence close to parsimony; he was rarely drunk but was censorious of those who were; he was a firm friend but 'a heavy enemy'; he was brave but entirely lacking in understanding of what makes some good men cowards; he was sincere but self-righteous; he was industrious but unimaginative; he was desperately concerned about the strength of his sexual needs, but it was the concern of one whom Maurice Ashley has described as a 'remorseless masochist'.[4] He was believed at the time of his accession to be suffering from a venereal disease which had impaired his mental faculties, and certainly the loss of what little sense of proportion he had previously enjoyed, his erratic impulses and excessive *hauteur* can be thus explained.[5] Apart from a passion for hunting which rivalled that of his grandfather – he was one of the earliest of aristocratic fox-hunters, foxes previously being considered fair quarry for yeomen farmers and the lesser gentry but not for noblemen who had confined their attention to stags and hares – he had few other interests. Music appealed to him a little, but literature and painting scarcely at all. Like most egotists he had no humour. The principal objects of his life – the conversion of England to Roman Catholicism and the establishment of a monarchy on the model of Louis xiv's – were never realised, and the means he took to achieve them resulted in his final exile and the Glorious Revolution of 1688.

In his younger days he had served with distinction in the French and Spanish armies, both of which he had for some time commanded, and had proved himself, as Lord High Admiral in England, a good naval commander as well as an excellent administrator. He had demonstrated his skill in military tactics at Windsor, when, with the Duke of Monmouth, 'at the foot of the long Terrace below the castle' he attacked with a little army a representation of the City of Maestricht, 'newly taken by the French. Bastions, bulwarks, ramparts, palisadoes, graffs, horn-works, counterscarps, etc., were constructed', John Evelyn, one of the spectators, wrote in his diary. 'On Saturday night they made their approaches, opened trenches, raised batteries, took the counterscarp and ravelin, after a stout defence; great guns fired on both sides, grenadoes shot, mines sprung, parties sent out, attempts of raising the siege, prisoners taken, parleys; and, in short, all the circumstances of a formal siege, to appearance, and, what is most strange, all without disorder, or ill accident, to the great satisfaction of a thousand spectators. Being night, it made a formidable show.'[6]

But admirable as James may have been as a tactician, his interest in the Army after his accession was taken as being a threat to the constitution, and his determination to have a large standing army as a means of establishing an arbitrary power and himself as supreme ruler of a Roman Catholic state.[7]

How far he was prepared to go in realising his ambition was demonstrated in July 1687 when the Papal Envoy was received in State at Windsor. 'The Duke of Somerset [one of the lords of the bedchamber] being in waiting refused to attend in that ceremony, for which he was forbid comming to Court and lost all his places. Five of the six gentlemen of the Privy Chamber were put out of their imployments for the same caus.'[8] Already the King, who had publicly celebrated Mass at Windsor and bought vestments and candlesticks and a new organ[9] out of Secret Service money, had discharged the 'Dean of the Chappell and the Chaplaines from attendinge any more at that office'. Now he and his second wife, Mary of Modena, were to the horror of most of their subjects prepared to 'parade the Papal Envoy' if not before the 'vast population of the capital' at least before the 'great multitudes that flocked' to Windsor to see the long procession of thirty-six coaches each drawn by six horses led by the Knight Marshal's men and 'a long train of running footmen'.[10]

It was one of James's last acts of provocation towards a people far from ready to accept the kind of religious toleration he advocated; and when in the following year seven bishops were tried for refusing to read in their pulpits a Declaration of Indulgence, which exempted Catholics and Dissenters from penal statutes, and a son was born to the Queen, an invitation was sent to William of Orange, James's nephew and the husband of his daughter Mary by Anne Hyde, the King's first wife.

William landed at Torbay on 5 November 1688 and made his way to Windsor, which became the 'Dutch headquarters'.[11] Here as the year and James's reign ended, William of Orange demonstrated a gift for statesmanship which his father-in-law had never possessed.

[v]

WILLIAM III AND MARY II

Apart from a strong taste for hunting and an autocratic manner, there was little in common between James II and his nephew. The new King was thirty-eight and his character had long ago 'been shaped in the iron mould of disillusionment'.[1] He had grown up among enemies and was distrustful, cold, artful, always severe and on occasions ruthless. 'He hid his slow brain, his growing distrust of men, behind an impassive exterior. He heard his Ministers out in chilling silence, chewed over their advice until they had almost forgotten it themselves, then acted, relying only on his powerful memory and his exact judgment of men in politics.'[2]

His father had died eight days before he was born, and his mother, the eldest daughter of Charles I, had quarrelled both with his grandmother and the government about his custody. At the age of nine he was taken to the University of Leyden, where he showed himself to be a conscientious pupil, a good linguist, a strict Calvinist and precociously conscious of his stern destiny. Married to King James's daughter Mary at St James's at eleven o'clock on the night of his twenty-seventh birthday, he had consistently treated her with a harshness which she appeared never to resent or even to regret.[3] She was pious and charitable, modest, gracious, sweet-natured and retiring. She loved to work and, as Horace Walpole was sardonically to observe, she 'contented herself with praying to God that her husband might be a great hero, since he did not choose to be a fond husband'. Her court at The Hague had been 'remarkable only for dullness and decorum' and when she returned to England to be proclaimed joint-sovereign with her husband she ran about, talking a great deal and 'looking into every closet and conveniency, and turned up the quilts of the beds, just as people do at an inn, with no sort of concern in her appearance'.[4]

Much as her new courtiers despised her, however, they considered her husband's behaviour far more unseemly than that of their tall, gentle Queen with her interests in housework, gardening, music and collecting porcelain. William kept his mistress, the Countess of Orkney, out of public sight. But his two close and extravagantly rewarded Dutch friends, Hans Willem Bentinck (created Earl of Portland and given, among many other sources of revenue, the Rangership of Windsor Great Park) and Arnoud van Keppel (created Earl of Albemarle, a Lord of the Bedchamber, Keeper of the Robes, and a Knight of the Garter), were believed to be something more than friends. According to the Duchess of Orléans, the King was 'in love with Albemarle as with a woman . . . and used to kiss his hands before all the Court';[5] while Portland's jealousy was obvious to everyone and was believed to be impossible to explain outside the context of a homosexual affection. The King, however, provided his many enemies with no satisfactory proof of an illicit relationship. And more sympathetic observers might have seen in his emotional attachments to these two men the sad hunger for friendship of a man without friends, the desire for a father of a man who had never known his own father, the desire for a son of a man who did not have one.

Aloof and unsociable, with a 'coldness in his way' that damped 'a modest man extremely', so reserved that often at dinner he would eat the entire meal in silence, by turns phlegmatic and irritable, seldom laughing 'but when he had outwitted others and then it was in the most ungraceful manner',[6] he struck most of the English nobility with his awkward movements, his pitted face, his slow speech and constant cough as a thoroughly distasteful interloper. Unprepared to recognise his qualities as a brave soldier, a statesman and a diplomatist, or to sympathise with his high aims and ideals, they disliked him for the apparent callousness of his means – pointing to the massacre of Glencoe as a characteristic example – they despised him for his atrocious manners and lack of any social graces, and, as Sir Charles Petrie has observed, the world, in any case, 'detests a morose adulterer'.[7] One of Princess Anne's ladies has given an instance of his vulgar behaviour at his own table: 'There happened to be a plate of peas, the first that had been seen that year. The King, without offering the princess the least share of them, ate them every one himself. Whether he offered any to the queen I cannot say; but he might do so safely enough, for he knew she durst not touch them. The princess confessed, when she came home, she had so much mind to the peas that she was afraid to look at them, and yet could hardly keep her eyes off them.'[8]

The Court, reformed by James II, who had curbed its drunkenness, its waste and its occasional outbursts of violence, became as unutterably dull as only five years before it had been gaily licentious. The King avoided it as much as he could. He suffered badly from asthma and found the air of London oppressive; nor did he feel either well or at ease at Windsor and was 'never so happy as when he could quit the magnificence of the Castle for his far humbler seat at Loo.'[9] Occasionally he came to Windsor for the hunting, but after his wife died in 1693 he visited it less and less.

Queen Mary's death, in fact, had a profound effect upon him. During her sickness he had been 'in an agony that amazed us all,' Bishop Burnet wrote, 'fainting often, and breaking out into most violent lamentations. When she died his spirits sunk so low that there was great reason to apprehend that he was following her . . . He turned himself much to the meditations of religion and secret prayer. He entered upon solemn and serious resolution of becoming in all things an exact and exemplary Christian.'[10] He married off his mistress to an army officer and he kept his wife's wedding ring and a lock of her hair next to his heart.[11] He began to drink heavily, usually alone, and his voice, already weakened by his asthma, became fainter than ever. His body shrank to a pitiful thinness, while his legs swelled to an immense size. When he pointed this out to his lugubrious physician, Dr Radcliffe heartlessly replied, 'I would not have your Majesty's two legs for your three kingdoms.'[12] His manners became gentler and he who had been known to lash out at servants with his cane now treated them with marked consideration. One day when driving from Windsor in his coach a woman ran up close to the windows to see him. 'Is *that* the King?' she said to a friend in a voice which surprise had made louder than she had intended, 'Why my husband is a handsomer man than he.' William 'stooped towards her and said, very seriously, "Good woman, don't speak so loud; consider I'm a widower."'[13] To his sister-in-law, Anne, with whom both he and his wife had been on the worst possible terms, he gave the dead Queen's jewels.

As his character seemed to change towards the end of his life, so did his people's attitude towards him. Their indifference and even their dislike developed into a wary respect. 'Superficially it appeared that he was a failure. But he had restored a nation; he had confirmed its essential Protestantism, and he had put it on the course leading directly to the maritime supremacy of the world. He had come to an England at the mercy of her King; he left an England well able to look after herself.'[14]

[vi]

ANNE

His sister-in-law's dislike of William long outlived him. She could not forgive him for being so rude both to her dearest confidante and to her husband. When she became Queen she continued on occasions to refer to him as 'Mr Caliban' and the 'Dutch Monster'. Anne was, of course, no Miranda herself. As a child her mother, who, according to De Grammont was 'one of the greatest eaters in England', encouraged her daughter's good appetite and she had grown extremely podgy. When she succeeded William III in 1702 at the age of thirty-seven, although not as stupendously fat as she later became, she was nevertheless a very stout woman whose early good looks had long since been lost.

Her husband, Prince George of Denmark, was also fat, and on asking Anne's uncle how he might stop himself from becoming more so, Charles II had replied, 'Walk with me, hunt with my brother and do justice to my niece.'[1] And no one could deny that he had followed the last part of this advice. During her life Anne became pregnant nearly twenty times. She miscarried frequently, however, and most of the babies that survived their birth died of hydrocephalus in their infancy, and the one that lived longest, the Duke of Gloucester, died at Windsor, also of hydrocephalus, shortly after his eleventh birthday had been hopefully celebrated with an exciting party and a magnificent display of fireworks.[2]

These painful experiences seriously affected the health of a woman who had never been strong. She suffered recurrently from gout, and her round and serious face, always ruddy, eventually became so discoloured and blotchy that she was obliged to paint her skin to disguise it, and she often felt too ill to get up in the morning. Because of this it was often suggested that she was a heavy and secret gin drinker, but the rumours, in the opinion of the Duchess of Marlborough, a far from sympathetic observer at the time of its expression, were 'utterly groundless'. She had, in fact, most of the virtues of her father with few of his peculiar vices. She was deeply attached to her husband, the good-humoured rather stupid, quiet, asthmatic George with his kindly ways, his love of the bottle and his atrocious accent, and she was deeply affected by his death. Her passionate attachments, first to Sarah Jennings (whom as a mark of intimacy she called Mrs Freeman and was in turn called Mrs Morley) and in later years to Abigail Hill, were whispered to be homosexual, as, indeed they no doubt were, although she was probably not even conscious of the sexual root of her love for them.

Sarah Jennings, who married the future Duke of Marlborough in 1678, had clearly fascinated her when they were both young girls. She was pretty, lively, strong-willed and amusing. The friendship of so vivacious and unusual a girl was flattering and exciting. Anne and Sarah 'were necessary to each other', Dr A. L. Rowse has written. 'Sarah, in all her pride and flourish of her spring; Anne still a girl, unsure of herself, but ready to give her heart unstintingly. All the more so to someone so self-confident and positive, when Anne was as yet so negative . . . She had need of Sarah; Sarah no such need of her. Anne was in love, Sarah not.'[3]

As soon as Anne became Queen she heaped honours on both Sarah and her husband. He was made Captain General of the Forces and a Knight of the Garter; she became Groom of the Stole, Mistress of the Robes, Keeper of the Privy Purse and, in place of the Dutch Earl of Portland, Ranger of Windsor Park, with emoluments totalling £5,600 a year. The Rangership of the Park carried with it the use of an attractive house, Byfield House (later to be known as Cumberland Lodge), so that the Queen was to have her dear friend close to her whenever she made one of her frequent visits to Windsor, which she loved.

Preferring a quiet country life to any other, she had spent as much time at Windsor as she could before her accession. She had lived for some years in Burford House after Nell Gwynn's death; and when Nell Gwynn's son, the Duke of St. Albans, had come of age and taken over the house that had been given to his mother, Anne bought another house nearer to the South Terrace on Castle Hill (see plate 12). This 'little retreate out of the Palace', as the energetic traveller Celia Fiennes called it, was a charming house, all the rooms in which were panelled in plain unvarnished oak, which looked 'very neate'. The chairs were covered in white, crimson and yellow damask and there were beautiful marble chimney-pieces and pier glasses between the windows.[4]

At both Burford House and this house on Castle Hill, Sarah Jennings had been a frequent visitor; and both Sarah and Anne, for their different reasons, continued to find their close companionship enjoyable for the first few years of the reign. By 1707, however, it had become evident that the Duchess was finding the Queen increasingly tiresome and that the Queen was finding the Duchess insupportable. It was clear that their uneasy relationship would soon be damaged beyond repair. And then suddenly it was. The Duchess discovered that she had a rival, who 'came often to the Queen when the Prince was asleep'. One day Sarah had been in the Queen's room in the Castle when a woman 'unlocked the door in a loud familiar manner', and tripped 'across the room with a gay air' until, catching sight of the Duchess, 'she immediately stopped short and acting a part like a player, dropped a low curtsey . . . and in a faint low voice cried "Did your Majesty ring?"'[5] The woman was Abigail Hill, a poor relation of the Duchess who had been introduced to Anne by Sarah herself. Sarah discovered that this plain and red-nosed girl, who nevertheless possessed her 'own share of the Jennings' charm,'[6] had secretly married Samuel Masham, one of Prince George's attendants, and that Anne had been present at the ceremony without telling her anything about it. The quarrel became an open one, and often it seemed to those who knew of it that the Queen's obsessive passion for hunting was a means of escape from the bickering of her erstwhile friend.

Being now too fat to ride, she drove after the hounds in Windsor Forest at a furious pace, 'like Jehu' Jonathan Swift told Esther Johnson, the 'Stella' of his *Journal*. The Queen drove herself in a narrow one-seated, one-horsed calash with extraordinarily high wheels which carried her rattling through cornfields and across the most formidable obstacles. The taking of the quarry was celebrated by a loud blowing on a great number of horns and a knife was presented to the highest ranking man present who cut off the animal's head. Young spectators were smeared all over with blood, and in 1696 the six-year-old Duke of Gloucester was given a lavish 'baptism of blood' from hands dipped into the carcase of a deer that had been brought into the yard and killed for this specific purpose.[7]

After the Duke's death Anne became more addicted to hunting than ever and drove as many as fifty miles on the hottest summer days. She built new kennels for the hounds at Windsor and restocked the Forest with deer. Apart from hunting and racing – she was responsible for transferring the main local race meeting from Datchet Mead, where Charles II had 'appointed races to be made' to Ascot in August 1711[8] – she had, however, no compelling interests. She had strong, indeed often obstinate views, but she never seemed to understand what was happening in the world or even in her own country. She paid little attention to the art, the drama or the literature which were making her reign a time of fresh renaissance. She is said to have been fond of music and she played the guitar as a girl, but in her later life she did not even listen to her own band.[9] Her conversation was the conversation of a good-natured, unambitious, and unimaginative woman who liked her food, enjoyed playing cards and gambling, and was excessively concerned with the niceties of etiquette. She spoke, in a very pleasant voice (and with a disarming habit of 'blushing frequently'), chiefly 'upon fashions,' the Duchess of Marlborough said, 'and rules of precedence, or observations upon the weather, or some such poor topics, without any variety of entertainment'. She had an extraordinarily retentive memory, 'but chose to retain in it very little besides ceremonies and customs of courts, and such like insignificant trifles'.[10]

Her knowledge of court procedure and protocol was, in fact, immense; and her Court was consequently at once peculiarly dull and extremely ceremonious.

Her behaviour at one of the tedious receptions at Windsor has been described by Swift: 'There was a drawing-room today at Court but so few company that the Queen sent for us into her bedchamber, where we made our bows, and stood about twenty of us round the room while she looked at us round with a fan in her mouth and once a minute said about three words to some that were nearest to her; and then she was told dinner was ready, and went out'.[11] She noticed at once if anyone present was improperly dressed and would express her disapproval of any man who appeared before her in the wrong sort of wig. Once Lord Bolingbroke came to her in a tie-wig instead of a full-bottomed one, and although she had sent for him in the greatest haste she was thoroughly disconcerted. 'I suppose,' she said crossly, 'that the next time his lordship appears at Court he will come in his nightcap.'[12]

With regard to her own dress she was particularly careful and, despite the dullness of the result and her negligence when she was feeling ill, she spent a great deal of time each day at her toilet, an operation performed with all due ceremony, the clothes being handed by the bedchamber woman to a Lady of the Bedchamber who helped the Queen put them on.

'When the Queen washed her hands, the page of the back stairs brought and set down upon a side-table the basin and ewer,' according to Mrs Masham. 'Then the bedchamber woman set it before the Queen and knelt on the other side of the table over against the Queen, the bedchamber lady only looking on. The bedchamber woman poured the water out of the ewer upon the Queen's hands.

The bedchamber woman pulled on the Queen's gloves . . .

The page of the back stairs was called in to put on the Queen's shoes.'[13]

Rigorous as she was in the observance of etiquette, however, and susceptible as she was to even the most outlandish flattery, Queen Anne was, as the Duke of Marlborough said of her, 'a very good sort of woman'. She was extremely conscientious, deeply religious, self-restrained and more ready to spend money on presents or pensions for others than on herself or on her palaces.

Most of the money she spent at Windsor was in improving the lay-out of the grounds and gardens, in which she took much interest, rather than in improving the Castle itself.[14] William III who had spent a great deal at Hampton Court 'contemplated improvements to the Castle in a similar style, and on an equal scale of grandeur' and the 'talents of Sir C. Wren were called upon for a design to convert the Castle, as far as might be practicable, into a regular edifice and to connect with it an extensive and magnificent suite of gardens'.[15] Nothing came of the scheme, however, and many parts of the Castle towards the end of the Queen's reign began gradually to fall into disrepair, while many encroachments were made not only in the Castle ditch where several 'Tenants and others pretended to have Interest',[16] but also within the walls of the Castle itself where there was even a small shop, the building of which inside the Gate in the Lower Ward had been permitted by Wren, then Comptroller of the Works, as it did not render any 'inconvenience to passage'.[17]

* * *

The Queen, growing fatter and more gouty in her advanced middle age, lived on at the Castle a sadly pathetic figure. She could not manage to walk up the stairs during her last years and had to be carried up and down in her chair and eventually to be lowered through a trap-door into the room below and hauled up again by means of ropes and pulleys as Henry VIII had been. For a time she hoped that the waters which she had brought up to the Castle every day from a well near Chalvey on the far side of Eton would cure her dropsical complaint, but they proved useless.[18] She spent long hours looking out across the fields and woods, sitting in the window where in 1704 the messenger with the news of Marlborough's victory at Blenheim had found her in her large and heavy chair. Her once beautiful hands were red and swollen and swathed in bandages and it was 'only with the greatest difficulty that she could sign her name'.[19] Her face was more blotchy than ever. On a cold rainy day in February 1714 she left Windsor for the last time, a dying woman. Throughout the spring she insisted on touching for the King's Evil, a scrofulous disease which it was believed could be cured by contact with the royal hands.*

Throughout the early summer the Queen's death was intermittently reported and on 1 August she died. As her servants wept for this 'entirely English' queen, messengers were already on their way to Hanover to inform her German distant relative that he was, by

* The miraculous properties of the monarch's hands had supposedly been inherited from Edward the Confessor, the saintly Saxon King, and were shared with the Kings of France who inherited their powers from Clovis. After Edward the Confessor had shown how palliative and sometimes actually curative was the force of faith, English Kings followed his good and rewarding example. Edward III gave public displays of his attribute; Henry VII had the 'Ceremonies for the Healing' inserted in the Service Book. Elizabeth laid her long white fingers on the diseased flesh of thousands of her subjects; and James I, although he clearly found the whole process distasteful, did the same. Charles II is believed to have touched over 100,000 strumous people and special certificates had to be obtained by the applicants who flocked to Windsor every summer that he was there. William III had discontinued the practice, informing all sufferers that they must apply to his exiled predecessor.[20] But Anne had revived the custom with a dedicated enthusiasm, and during this last spring of her life the exertion was too much for her, fasting as she did, for long periods before and after each ceremony.[21] The belief in the healing power of the Monarch has survived into our own times. Before the Second World War, afflicted people in Norfolk pressed round George VI in the hope of curing themselves by touching him.[22]

virtue of his Protestantism and his descent from a daughter of James
I, their new King. George I came to England to claim his inheritance,
accompanied by a large retinue of German attendants, two Turkish
valets and an uncertain number of German mistresses. And for sixty
years Windsor was virtually abandoned as a royal home.

4

Hanoverians

[i]

GEORGE III – THE ROYAL FARMER

Shortly after seven o'clock on the morning of 25 October 1760 George ii, having drunk his customary cup of chocolate, went into his water-closet. A few moments later 'the German *valet de chambre* heard a noise, listened, heard something like a groan, ran in, and found the hero of Oudenarde and Dettingen on the floor, with a gash on his right temple, caused by falling against the corner of a bureau. He tried to speak, could not, and expired'.[1]

His son Frederick, Prince of Wales, 'a nauseous little beast' to his mother and 'the greatest ass and the greatest liar, the greatest *canaille* and the greatest beast in the whole world' to his father, had died, unlamented, in the arms of a dancing-master nine years before; and so it was to George ii's twenty-two-year-old grandson that the Crown now passed.

The new King, it was generally admitted, was an honest, healthy and good-natured young man. Despite his bulging eyes, the rather flabby lips and undershot chin characteristic of his family, he was not bad looking. He spoke well in public; he was dignified; he was religious; and his morals, compared with those of his father and grandfather, were beyond reproach. He was, however, as his tutors had already noticed, indolent, prejudiced, moody and stubborn. He was also – and the fault was his tutors' as much as his own – appallingly ill educated, being unable to read English at the age of eleven and never mastering the rules of its grammar or learning how to spell it. One of his governors, Lord Harcourt, a 'civil, sheepish' fellow, as Horace Walpole described him, was 'said to have been perfectly satisfied that he had done his duty so long as he was unremitting in his exhortations to his royal pupil to turn out his toes'.[2] Another governor, Lord Waldegrave, was, in George's own opinion a 'depraved, worthless man' who taught him little and did not disguise in his private conversations the antipathetic relationship that existed between himself and a pupil who, as Waldegrave said, was 'uncommonly full of princely prejudices, contracted in the nursery, and improved by bed-chamber women and pages of the back-stairs'.[3] It was a justified and well considered judgment, for although Lord Waldegrave was unsuccessful in an appointment which he did not want and for which he was wholly unsuited, he was a thoughtful and perspicacious man who understood his charge's character and recognised in it the germs of a disastrous career. The tragedy of that career, as Dr J. H. Plumb has said, lay in the King's temperament. His obstinacy and the narrowness of his intellect might have been forgiven, 'if only they had been exercised on the trivialities of politics – the promotions of ensigns, the appointment of deans, or the ritual of the royal lives. But they were not. They were exercised on fundamental questions of policy and personalities.'[4]

However misguidedly he was to behave as a King, though, however ruthless or underhand he was to be in the prosecution of what he took to be his duty, however faithlessly he was to deal with his supporters and however vengefully with his enemies, George III was, nevertheless, in his private life, a good and amiable man. And it is at Windsor, where he loved to be, that he is to be seen at his best. Here, surrounded by a respectful family and a restful country-side, he had no longer to strive to be a king, an occupation which called for greater talents than he possessed, but he could instead behave as a country squire, a way of life more suited both to his temperament and to those undoubted capabilities which could find expression nowhere else. Like most men who suffer from a recurrent sense of inferiority and a consequent need for self-assertion, he often appeared to be less intelligent than he was and more brusque than he intended to be. At Windsor, however, retired from a life which he did not fully understand and removed from people he did not trust, he could feel at ease. His brusque rudeness was softened into the acceptable abruptness of an acknowledged and beloved eccentric; his celebrated conversational method became no longer an object of ridicule but an endearing and highly personal idiosyncrasy. Away from those who thought him stupid, he did not seem stupid. He was at home.

He did not discover the pleasures of this home until he had been King for several years. As his grandfather and George I had both preferred Hampton Court and Kensington Palace to Windsor, most of the Castle had remained neglected since the death of Queen Anne, and several parts of it were occupied by families with real or pretended claims upon royal favour.[5]

The courtyards, the gateway, the ditch and the terraces had become playgrounds. 'The deserted courts of the Upper Quadrangle often re-echoed on the moonlit winter evenings' with the shouts of running children. 'The rooks and a few antique dowagers,' the son of a local bookseller remembered, 'were the only personages who were disturbed by our revelry. In the magnificent playground of the Terrace, away we went along the narrow wall, and even the awful height of the north side could not abate the rash courage of *follow my leader.'* [6]

While children played, visitors, beggars, idle soldiers, higglers selling fish and vegetables, women crying out oysters and oranges, all passed unhindered through the gates into the courts, and 'disorderly persons and women in red clogs or pattens' wandered up and down along the terraces shouting to each other and making assignations. [7]

Some buildings in the Lower Ward, and in the Canons' Cloister where Horace Walpole had rented a house for a short time in 1746, were in ruins; parts of the Round Tower were 'almost entirely useless'; [8] and in the Upper Ward a visitor reported in 1766, there was 'little worthy of one's observation'. It was all 'so very unneat' that it hurt her to see 'almost the only place in England worthy to be styled our King's Palace so totally neglected'. [9] Another visitor found St George's Chapel 'neglected, dirty and disregarded to such a degree as to become a nuisance to the eye, and a reproach to the sextons'. The floors would have been 'disgraceful to a barn' and the monuments were not only cracked and dusty, but some of them were tied up with rope. [10] Of the Chapel's seven junior canons, two were described by Lord Hertford, in a report to the King, as being 'pretty fully emploied' elsewhere; one was a 'bad reader', another 'a very heavy and indifferent reader', one was superannuated, one was unfit for duty and the seventh, 'a bad reader with a kind of thickness in his speech' was 'at times so near mad as to be capable of making a worse use of the Book than that of reading the service ill out of it'. [11]

For almost twenty years the King left the Castle, and those who lived within its walls, undisturbed, using his mother's house at Kew as a retreat from St James's Palace where he did most of his work, and from Buckingham House which he bought for the Queen from Sir Charles Sheffield for £21,000. *[12] The Queen also had the use of Ormond Lodge in Richmond Old Park which had been set aside for her by Parliament, together with the generous promise of £100,000 a year, in the event of her husband's death. These four houses satisfied his never extravagant tastes so long as his family remained small, but as year followed year and the Queen gave birth to children with

---

* The appearance of this fine red brick house, afterwards known as Buckingham Palace, was completely altered in 1824 when the work began on its reconstruction and extension.

seasonal regularity, a larger country house became essential. He had never cared for Hampton Court which, like Kensington Palace, was associated with the family quarrels that had disturbed his childhood, and so his mind turned to Windsor Castle. Instead of turning out its occupants, however, and making it suitable for a King and Queen who by then had eleven children, he decided in 1776 to build a new house on the site of the one on Castle Hill which Queen Anne had occupied. He had taken over this house on its being relinquished by the Lord Steward, Lord Talbot, as the Queen had 'expressed a strong wish' to have it;[13] but it was too small to extend and Sir William Chambers, Governor General to the Board of Works, was asked to design a much larger one, making use of what few features in the original one he could. The new building, constructed at a cost of £44,000[14] and more like a barracks than a country house, was referred to by its architect and by some local people as the Upper Lodge to differentiate it from the Lower Lodge, the new name given to Nell Gwynn's house (Burford House) immediately to the south of it which was bought by the Queen from the Duke of St Albans for the younger princesses at a price of £4,000, a figure, which was, so the Duke was told, 'far above the Value' as the Queen well knew, but she did 'not chuse to Negociate'[15] (see plate 16).

By the summer of 1778 King George was able to move into Upper Lodge, or Queen's Lodge as it was more generally called, with the rest of his still growing family; and for the first time in his life he seemed to be happy. He loved his good-looking children passionately (particularly the girls) when they were young, frequently weeping when they were ill or when he was parted from them,[16] and his elder sons, who were soon found suitable apartments in the Castle itself, were not yet causing him the distress they were to do later. He was not a good father to them as they grew older, for his strict enforcement of a well-intentioned, although stultifying and provocative régime allowed no imaginative modifications; but for the moment he ruled benevolently over an apparently contented family. And he seemed, at this time, to be fond of Charlotte, his wife.

He had married her in 1761 on an evening in September, a few hours after he had seen her for the first time. She had been chosen for him because she was a Protestant princess likely to bear children, and Prince George, who had recently fallen passionately in love with the beautiful Lady Sarah Lennox, took her as his wife without marked enthusiasm. She was small and thin and plain. Her skin was pale, her nose rather flat, her mouth excessively large. Her beautiful, fine brown hair, her 'pretty' eyes and her regular teeth were all that those who have described her appearance have found to praise in it. But George soon overcame his initial reluctance. She was young – only eighteen – and her expression was lively and her movements graceful. She seemed sensible and friendly; and although as the daughter of the Duke of Mecklenburg-Strelitz she had, as she herself confessed, led a life of 'extreme retirement' in Germany and was consequently not very entertaining, her husband did not appear to resent the fact. She could not talk English when she was married and, in fact, never did learn to speak it idiomatically, but her French was tolerable and the King could talk to her in German, which remained throughout their lives the language they always used together when they were alone.[17]

Sharing a taste for a life of quiet regularity, the King and Queen introduced at Windsor a form of court life more uncompromisingly domestic and virtuous than ever before had been known there. Those chosen for court appointments were accordingly compelled to spend weeks on end in stupefying boredom. Life at St James's, as Lord Hervey had complained, was bad enough. There were 'constant avocations without any employment, and a great deal of idleness without any leisure; many words pronounced, and nothing said; many people smiling, and nobody pleased; many disappointments and little success; little grandeur and less happiness'.[18] But at Windsor where no Drawing Rooms were held as they were at St James's; where few dances ever took place, as they quite often did at Buckingham House; where, in fact, scarcely any entertaining of any sort was done, there was nothing to relieve the appalling monotony of the days.

*   *   *

For the attendants it was a life of misery. Fanny Burney, who was one of them, had never conceived how miserable she would be.

The choice of this remarkable woman for such unsuitable employment seemed to her contemporaries extraordinary. She was the second daughter of Dr Charles Burney, the musical historian, at whose house in London she had met many of the leading actors, musicians, painters and writers of the day, including Garrick, Burke, Sir Joshua Reynolds and Dr Johnson. She herself had written two novels, *Evelina* which had had an immense success – to the great surprise of her father who did not even know that she was the author of it until six months after it had been published – and the less successful *Cecilia*.

In 1783 she met Mrs Delany, an old widow who was indirectly to alter her whole life.

Mrs Delany was then eighty-three. A niece of Lord Landsdowne, she had been married twice, first at the age of seventeen to a drunken old Cornish squire, and then to Dr Patrick Delany, an Irish clergyman. In spite of her undistinguished husbands, she had become a familiar figure in the drawing rooms of the eighteenth century's most celebrated hostesses. And it was at Bulstrode, while staying with her friend the Duchess of Portland, that she met the King and his family, who immediately took to this 'charming old lady with her pretty ways and her pretty accomplishments',[19] and her delightful habit of blushing like a young girl.[20] The King, who was never at his ease in the drawing-rooms of fashionable hostesses, who preferred the company of such rough squires of 'unrefined and rustic' manners as Pen Portlock Powney, his neighbour at Windsor,[21] who was conscious of the ridicule with which his clumsy mind and clumsy manners were treated by the society he shunned and by the satirists whose drawings and poems made such savage fun of him, was particularly grateful for the affection and respect of aristocratic old ladies, virtuous and decorous, like Mrs Delany.

When one of the Queen's German attendants retired and Leonard Smelt, the Prince of Wales's sub-governor, suggested that Miss Burney should replace her, both Her Majesty and the King looked with favour upon the suggestion, for Miss Burney was a young friend of Mrs Delany's. The choice of Miss Burney seemed advisable for another reason as well: her father had been disappointed when he had not been made Master of the Queen's Band. Here was an opportunity of 'benefiting Dr Burney through his daughter',[22] by giving her a Court appointment which commanded a salary of £200 a year, the services of her own footman, her own maid, and the use of a coach.[23]

And so Fanny Burney at the age of thirty-five became Assistant Keeper of the Wardrobe to Queen Charlotte. She took over this unenviable position from Mrs Hagerdorn who had accompanied the Queen from Strelitz, and she was placed in the charge of another German, Mrs Schwellenberg (or Madame Schwellenberg as she preferred to be called), Keeper of the Wardrobe, a pretentious and intolerably self-satisfied woman of very uncertain temper who, to Lord Macaulay's horror, kept pet toads in a glass-house. Like Mrs Hagerdorn she was a spinster, but custom required that she should style herself as a married woman and custom ruled Mrs Schwellenberg's life. It was clear from the beginning that she resented Miss

Burney's invasion of what she considered a German province, and that she was jealous of anyone who seemed likely to undermine the strong influence she possessed over the Queen, whom she had known since childhood.[24] She was careful to ensure that the nervous, delicate and short-sighted Miss Burney strictly observed all the habits that had previously regulated the daily life of the Household, many of which she had instituted herself. Of course, Fanny Burney was not an ideal assistant; and the long, introspective entries in the journal she kept at Windsor reveal a great deal more than she can have intended to expose. Her extreme shyness and frequent blushing, her nervous uncertainty and occasional absentmindedness were, for instance, disabilities of which she seems to have been unconsciously proud; and Mrs Schwellenberg may well have been justifiably irritated by what appeared to be wilful efforts to exaggerate them. Whether or not she was as 'utterly unfit for any place requiring punctuality, neatness and manual dexterity' as one antagonistic commentator[25] has maintained, she was certainly often to be seen racing half-dressed down the windy corridors of Queen's Lodge to Her Majesty's apartments and she never did manage to tie the bow of her necklace without getting the Queen's hair caught up in the knot.[26] She was also, if this same commentator is to be believed, capable of expressing herself in the most absurd way 'when she desired to be especially eloquent, and particularly courtly. On one occasion when she had been laid up by violent head-ache, to which she was often subject, one of the attendants told her that His Majesty had asked if she was better, or how she was. "Give my duty to His Majesty," said Miss Burney, "and tell him the little machine has not yet quite ceased to vibrate".'[27]

Sometimes, though, she thought it *would* cease to vibrate. For her days were not merely emotionally exhausting but physically exhausting too – and the exhaustion was increased by her not being allowed to wear spectacles, for this would have been a breach of court etiquette.

She got up each morning at six o'clock and waited for the bell to ring, giving her the first of her daily summonses to attend the Queen. The summons usually came at half-past seven and Fanny immediately rushed to the Queen's apartments. When she arrived there, Her Majesty's hair had already been dressed by her wardrobe-woman, who handed Fanny the clothes that were to be worn that day. No maid was allowed in the Queen's room while it was occupied, so Fanny always had to do all the dressing herself.

By eight o'clock the Queen was dressed and ready to go to prayers in the now cleaned and restored St George's Chapel with the King and Princesses; and Fanny, unless she was asked to look after the Queen's favourite dog, Badine, was free to return to her room. The next hour, while she read a book alone at her breakfast table, was the only pleasant one in the day.

After breakfast a long time had to be spent preparing her own clothes. On an 'ordinary' day at Windsor her dress 'required no finery' but merely had to be 'neat, not inelegant, and moderately fashionable'; but there were so many days that were not ordinary. There were Court-Days; there were the numerous birthdays of the Royal Family, all of which necessitated a new dress; and there were days when a journey had to be made to London or to Kew. Sometimes Fanny had not finished getting her clothes ready until a quarter to twelve when she was called again to attend the Queen. On Wednesdays and Saturdays she was called earlier, for on those days Her Majesty's hair had to be curled and craped, an operation which took the hairdresser, who always needed about two hours for the normal daily treatment, an additional hour to perform. While the hairdresser was at work, the Queen read the newspapers, occasionally reciting a paragraph aloud to lessen the boredom of her attendants. Fanny liked listening to her voice, which she described as very prettily foreign with a 'varying emphasis' which gave an interest to everything she said; and she thought that the Queen's insistence that she should go away during the process of powdering so as not to spoil her clothes was yet another example of a 'consideration' which one would not have expected 'belonged to her high station'.

The labours of the toilette were over at about three o'clock and Fanny was set free to get ready for dinner, which was served at five o'clock. It was a dispiriting meal, sometimes eaten alone with the forbidding Mrs Schwellenberg, more often with the attendants of any guests whom the King and Queen might have staying with them, or with the guests themselves; but it was always eaten in tedium. After dinner, coffee (which Fanny did not like) was served upstairs in Mrs Schwellenberg's room; and when the Royal Family had finished their habitual evening stroll on the Terrace – usually at eight o'clock – the poor woman, almost stupefied by boredom, came down again to the dining-room to have tea with the equerry and any gentleman that the King or Queen might have invited for the evening, as it was 'only a very select few' that could eat with Their Majesties, and those few were always ladies, 'no men, of what rank soever, being permitted to sit in the Queen's presence'. An hour later the equerry led the guests away to the concert room and left Fanny with Mrs Schwellenberg for two more long hours during which, every evening, she was obliged to play picquet.

At eleven o'clock she had supper and then waited, as after breakfast, for the bell to ring. As soon as she heard it she ran along the corridor again to the Queen's room to take Her Majesty's clothes off.

Only occasionally was the dreary routine altered or enlivened by a visitor; very rarely did she see any of those entertaining people who had made her earlier life so much more stimulating. Even when one of them did come to Windsor she was hesitant about allowing him to come to see her for fear of what her mistress or Mrs Schwellenberg would think. Once James Boswell came to stay with the Bishop of Carlisle in the Canons' Lodgings and it was suggested that he should be brought down to Queen's Lodge to see Miss Burney. But although she 'really wished to see him again', not only for the amusement which his own oddity and good humour gave her but also out of respect for the 'object of his constant admiration', her revered Dr Johnson, she dared not permit a visit and felt constrained to suggest what might appear to be a chance meeting outside St George's Chapel after evening service.

This, however, was quite as embarrassing. 'I am extremely glad to see you, indeed', Boswell told her in his loud and cheerful voice. 'But very sorry to see you here. My dear ma'am, why do you stay? It won't do, ma'am! You must resign! We can put up with it no longer! I told my good host the Bishop so last night. We are all grown quite outrageous.'

Laughing nervously, Fanny hurried away from him terrified that these 'treasonable declarations' would be heard. Boswell, not in the least put out, however, followed her, continuing his advice with that deep and urgent seriousness that heightened the effect of his humour.

'If you do not quit, ma'am, very soon, some violent measures, I assure you, will be taken. We shall address Dr Burney in a body; I am ready to make the harangue myself. We shall fall upon him all at once.' Fanny stopped him by asking after Sir Joshua Reynolds and then about Edmund Burke's forthcoming book, *Reflections on the French Revolution*. Oh! Boswell assured her, Sir Joshua was very well and Burke's book was the best in the world after his own which would also come out soon. Brought to his favourite topic, Boswell pulled a sheet of proofs out of his pocket and asked for Miss Burney's advice. 'You must give me some of your choice little notes of the Doctor's,' he said. 'We have seen him long enough upon stilts. I want to show

107

him in a new light.' Excitedly he began to read one of the great man's letters. He read it very well, Fanny thought, in strong imitation of Johnson's manner but without caricature. By now, though, Fanny was thoroughly alarmed. Mrs Schwellenberg was looking out of her window, the Royal Family were coming towards them from the Terrace, and a crowd was gathering round the railings. She made a quick apology and hurried inside, immediately to be asked who the unknown and uninvited gentleman was and to be warned that she must never allow him to come beyond the limit of the railings.[28]

*   *   *

In the hours that remained to her between dressing and undressing, having her hair done, and eating and sleeping, the Queen, herself, had a no less uninteresting time than Fanny Burney. She did a little embroidery; she occasionally read a book; she took a great deal of snuff; she shared her husband's liking for music and sometimes sang to her own accompaniment on the spinet; she usually went for a walk or a ride in the afternoon and in the evening played a game of cards, although her husband did not altogether approve of women enjoying themselves in this way; she professed a taste for conversation but had few opportunities to indulge it, as she found difficulty in expressing herself in English. With her husband she could speak German, but conversation with George was never easy. She does not, though, appear to have been an unhappy woman in these early years,[29] and according to her Chamberlain, Colonel Desbrowe, the 'bloom of her ugliness' began to wear off.[30] She never appeared to resent the fact that the King, who never discussed politics with her, forbade her to make many acquaintances in England where, so he said, 'there never could be kept up a Society without party, which was always dangerous for a woman to take part in'.[31]

Fanny Burney, who could not – it remains a national idiosyncrasy – judge her Queen as a woman without regard to her queenship and was always acutely conscious of her 'condescension', thought her 'a most charming woman'. She remembered vividly her kindness, forgetting – or, at least, rarely recording – her contradictory meanness and selfishness; she remembered her good nature, dismissing her frequent peevishness; she remembered that she had told her how the 'fatigue and trouble of putting' her jewels on and the fear of losing them had made her 'long for her earlier dress', but she did not say, as others knew, that her passion for them was almost pathological. Yet the picture of a fundamentally contented woman which Fanny Burney has drawn has not been satisfactorily contradicted. The Queen was lonely, of course, and her pleasure on seeing the King whenever he came upon her unexpectedly was moving and unfeigned. Her life was bound up with his and with those of their children; and to be told that amongst the many effigies of her eldest son which she possessed was a wax model of his naked form which she kept upon a crimson cushion under a dome of glass where she could see it every day,[32] is to understand something of her loneliness.

* * *

The King was not so lonely, and far more self-contained. He had, in fact, an extraordinary variety of interests apart from all the normal duties and recreations of a country squire. He was interested in botany as well as music, in architecture as well as genealogy. He was devoted to fireworks and to the history and traditions of Eton College. He had a little-known but deep concern for social reform and both Robert Raikes, the Sunday School enthusiast, and John Howard, the prison reformer, had long conversations with him at Windsor. He had a passion for pottering about with bits of machinery. He could use a lathe with skill and even managed, so it was said, to turn out several respectable buttons.[33] He loved to take clocks and optical instruments to pieces.[34] and it was his deep interest in telescopes that led to his appointing Sir William Herschel as Royal Astronomer and to providing him with a house and observatory at Slough. It was, of course, the detail and predictability of machinery that appealed to him, for he was a man who detested uncertainty, unpunctuality, untidiness and change. Any suggested alteration in the details of a military uniform or the prescribed customs and trivialities of etiquette disturbed him profoundly. When the shape of the hats worn by the Guards at Windsor was changed, he was deeply shocked. 'What!' he protested to the Duke of Richmond, 'What, Richmond! Who ever saw Guards in round caps?' 'Oh, yes, Sire,' said the Duke. 'My own hat is round.' 'Aye! And so is my night-cap.'[35]

He loved uniforms. He spent hours studying military prints until he could recite the details – as he could recite the names of all the ships in his Navy – by heart.[36] He often wore the uniform of the Royal Horse Guards because he liked the colours so much and he created a special Windsor troop and made himself a captain. In 1778, borrowing perhaps an idea of Frederick the Great's, he designed a purely personal uniform to be worn at Windsor, blue like that of the Horse Guards – and like the livery worn at Wilton by the servants of Esther, Lady Pembroke, a woman he deeply admired – with scarlet and gold accessories.*[37] (See plate 19.) Even when he went out riding or walking through the royal estate he often wore a uniform, a less striking variation of the Windsor uniform made in country colours of country cloth.[39] When he went hunting with the Princesses they all wore 'blue habits faced and turned up with red, white beaver hats and black feathers'.[40] Sometimes he found a black jockey's cap more suitable, for eighteenth-century rides were often fast and long – eighty miles being a not uncommon distance – and by modern standards, ferociously cruel to the horses. At the end of one ride which lasted six hours, the 'stag dropped down dead before the hounds; not twenty of the horses out of 150 were in at the death; several horses died in the field, and tired ones were seen crawling away to every village'.[41]

The King loved the country. He had a sound knowledge of agriculture, writing letters under a pseudonym to the *Annals of Agriculture*,[42] and the farms in the Great Park were well and profitably run. He was never so much at his ease as he was with country people. He would stroll into their cottages unannounced and talk to them about simple things in a friendly, wholly natural way. If they were poor he did his best to help them.

In many respects he was niggardly, and the tips he gave to servants frequently amounted to a single penny produced after a long search between the folds of a leather purse, while the hospitality usually offered at the Castle was severely economical if not actually parsimonious.[43] But his heart was moved by poverty. A mill in the Park ground corn at a special rate for the needy; and it was his habit to leave money behind him when he left a cottage whose tenants seemed in want of some comfort they could not afford. A committee appointed to examine the state of his private finances during his first long illness discovered that nearly a quarter of his personal income was given away in charity.[44] The smaller, spontaneous gifts were made with the greatest good humour and without a hint of patronage. Once at harvest time when passing a field where only one woman was at work he stopped

---

* Charles II had tried to introduce a court uniform, too, but it was abandoned when Louis XIV ridiculed it by dressing all his footmen in an identical way. The Windsor uniform was again abandoned by William IV but revived by Victoria; and the Duke of Windsor can remember wearing it at Windsor station 'with dark, or even pepper and salt, trousers and top hat' when meeting distinguished guests. George V confined its use to evening wear with knee-breeches. It is still worn at Windsor in the evenings occasionally, particularly during Ascot week, by Prince Philip and other members of the Royal Family and Household.[38]

to ask her where the other labourers were. The woman said they had gone to see the King and added, 'I wouldn't give a pin to see him. Besides the fools will lose a day's work by it, and that is more than I can afford to do. I have five children to work for.' 'Well, then,' said the King, putting some money in her hands, 'you may tell your companions who are gone to see the King, that the King came to see you.'[45]

He took great pleasure in talking to country people in this easy, familiar way. 'He had an extraordinary faculty for recognising everybody, young or old,' wrote Charles Knight, who, as a little boy gathering mushrooms in the short grass of the Home Park, often used to bow to the King when he walked quickly by on his way to his dairy at Frogmore. 'He knew something of the character and affairs of most persons who lived under the shadow of the castle.'[46]

He knew all his servants, too, and often spoke to them about their lives and families. He did not allow his guests to give them vails (to tip them) as was the custom in most other big houses – and this led to a demonstration by his London servants at a theatre where the King 'bore all their taunts and uproar with the greatest composure'[47] – but he insisted that they received all the other perquisites which were due to them. And it was for this reason, more than for reasons of economy, that as soon as the last evening card game was over in Queen's Lodge and as soon as the benediction was pronounced in St George's Chapel, he saw to it that the candles were immediately blown out, for partly used candles were still an important part of the perquisites of royal servants.[48] He was considerate in other ways, too; and the story was told that one evening when the fire was getting low he rang for the page-in-waiting and asked him to go for some more coal as the scuttle was empty. The page considered this task too menial and rang for an old footman whose job it properly was. Immediately the King picked up the scuttle himself, told the page to show him where the coal was kept, filled the scuttle, went back to the fire, tipped the coal on to it and, handing the empty scuttle to the page, he said, 'Never ask an old man to do what you are so much better able to do yourself.'[49]

Of course, the holders of quite profitable appointments like the pages – who were paid £200 a year, when £1 was worth about ten times its present value – were prepared to accept these remonstrances. And lower servants were also prepared to put up with the King's eccentricities, even to wait for long periods before they received their wages, for their perquisites, in addition to candles (on which by 1812 the Household at Windsor was spending £10,000 a year[50]) were considerable and included all unconsumed food and wine once it had been laid upon a table.

The servants had to wait for their wages because George III spent so much of his £800,000 income on maintaining a political party prepared to support his policies. The monarchy had, of course, an immense patronage which the King manipulated for political purposes granting appointments to his supporters and dismissing from their posts those who failed to vote in his favour, but this patronage was not as profitable as it appeared.

There were numerous appointments in the King's gift, ranging, for instance, from Master of the Buckhounds (£2,341 a year), Master of the Ceremonies, Master of the Great Wardrobe, Master of the Harness, Master of the Revels, Master of the Barges, Master of the Tennis Court and Master of the Music, to Keeper of the Lions, Lionesses and Leopards in the Tower, Surveyor of His Majesty's Revenues Arising by Fines, Forgetfulness and Sums of Money called Greenway Money, Keeper of the Fire Buckets, Groom of the Confectionery, Tuner of the Ryals, Pumper at the Mews and the Embellisher of Letters to the Eastern Princes.[51] But not all these appointments were sinecures and the King, having secured support by disposing of an appointment which entailed specific duties, then had to pay someone for doing the work which the office holder would not or could not do.

Edmund Burke, in determined prosecution of a Plan of Economic Reform first proposed by him in 1779, eventually brought about a long overdue change in a system under which there was 'scarcely a family so hidden and lost in the obscurest recesses of the community which does not feel that it has something to keep or to get, to hope or to fear, from the favour or displeasure of the Crown'.[52]

The habits of centuries are not, however, changed quickly; and the Royal Household continued much as before. The immediate result of the abolition of many ancient posts was merely that the King increased the amount of income he spent on buying political support, so that the royal servants had to wait longer than ever for their wages. But they, making up their wages in other ways as they had always done, were never unduly discontented. Certainly the King himself did his best to make them feel at home. All new servants were likely sooner or later, usually in the first week of their employment, to be startled by His Majesty appearing suddenly in front of them to make some cheerful and friendly if confusingly inconsequential remark.

13. A view of the Lower Ward from William the Conqueror's Mound *c.* 1770 from the coloured drawing by Paul Sandby in the Royal Library, Windsor Castle

14. A view of the North Terrace looking west *c.* 1770
from the coloured drawings by Paul Sandby in the Royal Library, Windsor Castle

15. A view of the town through Queen Elizabeth's Gate *c.* 1770

'Well, boy, what?' he called happily one morning while on his way o make his usual early visit to his stables. 'What do you do? What do they pay you, what?'

'I help in the stable, but I have nothing but victuals and clothes.'

'Be content. I have no more.'[53]

Inside the stables another morning he found the grooms arguing so urgently that they did not notice his arrival. 'I don't care what you say, Robert,' one of them said, 'but everyone else agrees, that the man at the Three Tuns makes the best purl in Windsor.'

'Purl? Purl? Purl?' whispered the King in his quick excited way to Robert who was standing next to him. 'Purl? What's purl, Robert?'

Robert said it was a tankard of warm beer with a glass of gin in it.

'I dare say a very good drink, grooms,' said the King so loudly that they all turned round and recognised him, 'but, grooms, too strong for the morning. Never drink in the morning, grooms.'

He never expected that they would take his advice, and many years later, arriving at the stables much earlier than usual, he found them deserted except for a small lad who did not know him.

'Boy! Boy!' the King asked, 'Boy! Where are the grooms?'

'I don't know, sir, but they'll soon be back because they expect the King.'

'Aha! Then run, boy, run, and say the King expects them. Run to the Three Tuns, boy. They are sure to be there, boy, for the landlord makes the best purl in Windsor.'[54]

He often went down to the town himself. He liked strolling along the streets, tapping the stones with his long stick, looking in the shop windows, occasionally walking in to give the tradespeople instructions on how to vote in a local election.[55] Sometimes he was to be seen sitting on a high stool at the counter of Charles Knight's bookshop, looking over the latest publications. One afternoon his eye caught Paine's *Rights of Man* and he picked it up and began to study it intently. Absorbed, he 'continued reading for half an hour', the bookseller's son remembered, 'and he left the shop without saying anything; but he never afterwards expressed his displeasure.'[56] In fact, when he returned to the shop later, he was as good humoured as ever. On another occasion, though, the title of Bishop Watson's *Apology for the Bible* upset him. 'What! What! What! Apologise for the Bible! What! What! What!'[57]

He was profoundly and sincerely religious, with the Low Churchman's belief in the virtues of a straightforward simplicity of worship.

He refused to wear his crown when attending Holy Communion after his coronation, and he later decided that new Knights of the Garter should not be required to attend that part of the service after their installation because the Sacrament was not to be 'profaned by our Gothic institutions'.[58] Every morning at Windsor, before his visit to the stables at seven o'clock, he devoted an hour to reading the Bible and to solitary prayer; and every day he went to St George's Chapel, where he accompanied the time of the music with the printed form of the service rolled up into a baton. Anyone near him who showed the slightest symptom of having lost his place in the prayer book he was sure to put right, and a visitor once received a few smart taps on the back of the head for having sat in the wrong place.[59]

Despite the rigidity of his political views he was not the religious bigot he appeared to those who did not know him. He refused to countenance any measures designed to remove the disabilities imposed upon Roman Catholics, but this was more due, it seems, to a confirmed belief that to do so would be to deny his coronation oath rather than to any violent prejudice against their religion.[60] To Nonconformists he was openly sympathetic. The Methodists, he believed, were 'a quiet, good kind of people and would disturb nobody'. And one day finding a maid-servant at Windsor in tears he asked her what the matter was. She had been refused permission to attend a dissenters' meeting, she told him. Immediately he sent for the housekeeper and talked to her severely. He would 'suffer no persecution' during his reign, he warned her, and later added that if he heard that anyone in his employment supported the persecution of Methodists they would be straightaway dismissed.[61] Towards the end of his life he told one of his doctors that the Lutheran religion was superior to that of the Church of England.[62]

It was, of course, the simple virtue of the Noncomformists that made its appeal to him. One of his first acts as King had been to issue a proclamation 'for the Encouragement of Piety and Virtue, and for preventing and punishing of Vice, Profaneness and Immorality'. Addressed to 'all persons of whatsoever degree or quality', it was particularly intended for 'those who were employed near [the] royal person'. And it was the Court that suffered most. Playing at dice, cards and other games was theoretically prohibited everywhere on Sundays; but it was only at Court that the prohibition was strictly observed. Here, gambling died away on week days as well as on Sundays, and the Sunday Drawing Rooms became entertainments of the past.[63]

The abolition of Sunday receptions could be justified, so it seemed to the King, on other grounds, too. They were expensive. And an economic Court he was determined to have. He himself set the example. People could point as they liked at the great number of his costly children, but no one could say that his own life was an indulgent one. He refused to have a carpet in his bedroom, and there was no heating in the passages of any of his apartments. St George's Chapel was always fearfully cold. 'Princesses, governesses, equerries, grumbled and caught cold; but cold or hot, it was their duty to go; and wet or dry, light or dark, the stout old George was always in his place to say amen to the chaplain.'[64]

One of the equerries, Colonel Goldsworthy, warned Miss Burney at the outset of her career that she would certainly die of cold. He himself, like every other equerry when in waiting, had always to be ready to accompany the King whenever he felt like going out for a ride. It was the King's 'delight to mount his horse before the equerry-in-waiting could possibly be aware of it; often in severe or unpleasant weather which rarely deterred him'. Sometimes the King was half-way down Windsor Hill before the equerry had had time 'to pull up his stockings under his boots'.[65]

'Oh, Ma'am,' Colonel Goldsworthy lamented, 'what lives we do lead!' Of course, he comforted her, 'You won't have the hunting, to be sure, nor amusing yourself with wading a foot and a half through the dirt, by way of a little pleasant walk, as we poor equerries do! It's a wonder to me we outlive the first month.' And the final hardship was that 'after all the labours of the chase, all the riding, the trotting, the galloping, the leaping, the – with your favour, I beg pardon, I was going to say a strange word – the, the' – he was not allowed to say sweat – 'wet perspiration, and – and all that – after being wet through over head and soused through under foot, and popped into ditches, and jerked over gates', they were expected to get warm again by drinking – barley water.

'Running along in these cold passages,' he went on despairingly, 'bless us! I believe in my heart there's wind enough in these passages to carry a man o'war! And there, you'll have your share, ma'am, I promise you that! You'll get knocked up in three days, take my word for that.'

Fanny protested disbelief.

'Oh, ma'am, there's no help for it. . . . Stay till Christmas. Only stay till then, and let's see what you'll say. You'll be laid up as sure as fate! You may take my word for that. One thing, however, pray let me caution you about – don't go to early prayers in November. If you do, that will completely kill you.'

Oh yes, everyone got regularly knocked up by that chapel business. First the Queen, then the Princesses, then all the poor attendants. 'One after another,' the Colonel said with a kind of gloomy satisfaction, 'like so many snuffs of candles; till, at last, dwindle, dwindle, dwindle – not a soul goes to the chapel but the King, the parson and myself; and there we three freeze it out together.'[66]

But at least Colonel Goldsworthy could not complain of the food in the Castle. There was always enough to eat, for the equerries did not have to share the King's table, which was exceedingly plain and very sparse,[67] since the King, as he had once told a friend, dreaded becoming as fat as so many members of his family had been. His uncle the Duke of Cumberland was so grotesque in his later years that when once he fell over while dancing at Lord Sandwich's 'he lay like a tortoise on its shell; his face could not reach the ground.'[68] King George took great pains never to allow himself to suffer the indignities of such obesity. He not only rode and hunted with furious energy; he not only often walked twelve of the twenty-three miles between Windsor and London; he not only drank little but water, lemonade, barley water or very weak wine, but he ate nothing which he thought might lead to corpulence. Frequently his dinner was limited to cold mutton, green salad and stewed pears. Only occasionally were there plovers' eggs or cherry tart. On Sundays, like any English farmer, he had a plate of roast beef with plenty of vegetables. This, though, was a rare treat. His one regular indulgence was fresh fruit which, as it grew plentifully in the Windsor orchards, he did not consider an extravagance.

Banquets were, of course, events of extreme rarity except on royal birthdays, although, when they were given, the guests admitted that they had been well treated. And the King himself would go round the kitchens, ensuring 'that all was going on right, and that proper cheer was provided, not merely for the higher orders, but even for the soldiers in attendance'.[69]

Friendly and hospitable as he appeared to his guests, however, he never forsook the custom of dining alone with his family at a table raised to a slightly higher level than the other tables in the room,[70] for life at Court, simply as the Royal Family usually lived and much as the King insisted on the virtues of plainness and economy, was bound by the strict regulations of an invariable etiquette.

*   *   *

Every guest or attendant at Windsor was obliged to retire to the nearest wall and stand quite still as soon as any member of the Royal Family appeared in sight. And even amongst themselves the Family maintained this severe formality. When the King entered one of their rooms, preceded by a page who made that 'particular kind of scratch' which had to be used on royal doors instead of knocking, the Princesses were expected to stand up and they were not allowed to say anything unless asked a question. Nor were they allowed to leave a room — walking backwards as everyone else did — until they were dismissed with the formal command, 'Now I will let you go.' They could sit down with permission, but the Ladies-in-Waiting, whose rules went so far as to forbid them to walk past the open doorway of a room which contained a royal personage, had always to remain on their feet, sometimes for hours on end. Even Her Majesty's Reader had to stand up at a lectern while she read to the Queen who, in her efforts to demonstrate that the standing circle around her was less formally constrained than it appeared, always had a small table at her elbow on which she could place her needlework or tea cup.[71]

Those who formed this circle had to maintain a deep and decorous silence.

'If you find a cough tickling your throat,' the Assistant Keeper of the Wardrobe told her sister-in-law in an ironic letter in December 1785, 'you must arrest it from making any sound; if you find yourself choking with forbearance, you must choke — but not cough.

'In the second place, you must not sneeze. If you have a vehement cold, you must take no notice of it; if your nose-membranes feel a great irritation, you must hold your breath; if a sneeze still insists upon making its way, you must oppose it, by keeping your teeth grinding together; if the violence of the repulse break some blood-vessel, you must break the blood-vessel — but not sneeze.

'In the third place, you must not, upon any account, stir either hand or foot. If, by chance, a black pin runs into your head, you must not take it out. If the pain is very great, you must be sure to bear it without wincing; if it brings the tears into your eyes, you must not wipe them off; if they give you a tingling by running down your cheeks, you must look as if nothing was the matter. If the blood should gush from your head by means of the black pin, you must let it gush; if you are uneasy to think of making such a blurred appearance, you must be uneasy, but you must say nothing about it. If, however, the agony is very great, you may, privately, bite the inside of your cheek, or of your lips, for a little relief; taking care, meanwhile, to do it so cautiously as to make no apparent dent outwardly. And, with that precaution, if you even gnaw a piece out, it will not be minded, only be sure either to swallow it, or commit it to a corner of the inside of your mouth till they are gone – for you must not spit.'[72]

The etiquette observed during the Royal Family's evening stroll on the Terrace was always strictly observed, although on one occasion there was an unpleasant scene when many persons had to be 'turned off, being in a state of intoxication'. One man refused to take his hat off when the King passed by, and when the Marquess of Thomond did it for him the man flew at him with his fist and kicked him.[73] Such a spectacle, however, was a rarity. Usually the Royals walked sedately up and down, the spectators backing away from their path, while two bands played alternately. The King wore his Windsor uniform with a star on his chest and a hat with a gold button and loop, mounted by a black cockade, which marked him out 'conspicuously from the rest of the company'. A police officer was in attendance with a little switch to keep 'individuals from pressing too much on the King' when he stopped to talk to anyone. But this was done 'with the greatest urbanity'.[74] Even on less formal occasions if a visitor happened to come across any member of the Royal Family while walking in the grounds, he was expected to back away respectfully[75] (see plate 18).

Inside the Castle or Queen's Lodge a visiting Minister was rarely asked to sit down. And Pitt was once kept standing for two hours when suffering painfully from an attack of gout.[76] Later the King asked Pitt if he had had any ill effects from his having to stand so long; but he seems not to have considered the possibility of asking him to sit down. He had, in any case, little sympathy for the sick, and Fanny Burney recorded how one day he refused to allow that one of his equerries was ill. He had a 'very good colour' and looked strong, so the man *must* be well!

Only Mrs Delany, being very old and a devoted friend, was excused from observing the more tiring rules of etiquette, which applied equally stringently whether the King and Queen were hosts or visitors. If they called at a house in Windsor, as soon as they entered the drawing room everyone had to stand up, move away towards the walls and remain standing in a circle. When the mistress of the house went out to fetch tea – a duty she was expected to perform herself – she had to walk backwards out of her own doorway and return with tea, bread and butter and cake, carrying a napkin over her arm for the royal fingers. When the Royals left, all the people they had spoken to were expected to see them out to their carriage to receive 'their last gracious nods'.[77]

Conversation on these occasions was appallingly difficult. Although the King was nearly always pleasant and good-humoured, he had no idea of how to make educated people feel at ease with him and often asked them to repeat several times things he found amusing, laughing just as much the last time as the first.[78] His tastes were as limited as his opinions were erratic, and he expressed himself forcibly, talking very fast in a series of questions which expected no answer and interrupting most of them with a series of rapidly repeated ejaculations.

'Was there ever,' he once asked Fanny Burney, expressing a celebrated and understandable opinion, 'such stuff as great part of Shakespeare? Only one must not say so! But what think you? What? Is there not sad stuff? What? – What? . . . Oh, I know it is not to be said! But it's true. Only it's Shakespeare and nobody dare abuse him.'

Then he enumerated many of the characters and parts of plays that he objected to; and when he had run them over, finished with again laughing, and exclaiming: 'But one should be stoned for saying so.'[79]

Despite this, however, and although he thought Voltaire a 'monster', he was not the philistine that most of his ancestors were. He did not hate all 'boets and bainters' as George I confessed he did. In fact he wanted to institute a new order for writers and scientists – the Order of Minerva. 'The Knights were to take rank after the Knights of the Bath, and to sport a straw-coloured ribbon and a star of sixteen points. But there was such a row among the *literati* as to the persons who should be appointed, that the plan was given up.'[80]

His interest was, of course, more that of a patron than a devotee. He accumulated a good library at Buckingham House and a smaller one at Windsor, but he did not use either of them much. His interest in a book soon waned after he had looked up the names in the index and he confessed, 'laughing heartily', to Fanny Burney that he was surprised and disappointed, having seen her name in the index to Boswell's *Life of Johnson*, that the book contained so little about her.[81] Mostly he read newspapers and even they sent him to sleep in less than half an hour.[82]

His taste in other respects was not well formed. He admired Sir Joshua Reynolds who became the first President of the Royal Academy founded in 1769; but he preferred the less subtle Benjamin West, whom he put to work on an immense representation of the Resurrection for the east window of St George's Chapel. He had a passion for Handel, but was content to listen to the same facile work of lesser composers time after time. He played the flute himself, but not very well. He went regularly to the theatre, but he enjoyed a simple farce

better than anything else. He delighted in the broad comedies performed at the little theatre in Windsor and roared his appreciation of
the actors of whose familiar faces and antics he never grew tired.[83]
He preferred Mrs Siddons to Garrick, and asked her frequently to
come to Windsor to read a play for his family – and characteristically
he did not pay her anything for doing so.[84]

These limited interests, his lack of general knowledge and slow
understanding all added to the difficulties of talking to him – difficulties which have been well described by Fanny Burney, whose own
extreme shyness emphasised them.

Fanny had met him for the first time at the house near Queen's
Lodge in which the King had installed Mrs Delany as a life tenant.
The old lady had already given Fanny a short lecture on how to talk
to the Queen, whose service she had not yet entered. The Queen,
Mrs Delany said, often complained that she could not get any conversation and when she did she not only had to 'start the subjects,
but, commonly, entirely to support them' for people could often think
of nothing to reply to her except 'yes' or 'no'.[85] Fanny experienced
a similar difficulty with the King.

She was in the drawing room with Mrs Delany's great-niece
Georgiana, a little girl who was Georgiana's cousin, and the little
girl's father, when the noisy Christmas game they were all playing
was interrupted by the entrance of Mrs Delany followed by a large
man in deep mourning with a glittering star on his chest.

'The King! – Aunt, the King!' Georgiana called out nervously
while Fanny retreated to the wall, intending to slip out of the door as
soon as she had sidled near enough to it. But before she could fulfil
this design she heard the King's loud whisper: 'Is that Miss Burney?'
Mrs Delany said that it was and the King, with 'a countenance of the
most perfect good humour', approached her.

'How long have you been come back, Miss Burney?' the King
asked her.

'Two days, sir,' Miss Burney answered in a very soft voice.

'Unluckily he did not hear me,' she wrote later in her diary, 'and
he repeated his question; and whether the second time he heard me or
not, I don't know, but he made a little civil inclination of his head and
went back to Mrs Delany.'

Fanny was eventually to become accustomed to the King's unnerving manner of conducting a conversation, his habit of walking
about a room to ask a question of one person in a tone of voice at once
good-natured and hectoring, and then to turn away and repeat the

answer to someone else; but for the time being it confused her pitiably.

After telling Mrs Delany that Princess Elizabeth, his tragically fat fifteen-year-old daughter, was recovering from a recent illness, having been blooded twelve times in a fortnight, and after reminding her that the fault of his own constitution was a tendency to excessive fat which he kept under control by the most vigorous exercise and the strictest attention to a simple diet, he went up to a table to look at a book of prints which had caught his eye. He turned over a leaf or two, and then said, 'Pray, does Miss Burney draw, too?'

'The "too" was pronounced very civilly.

'"I believe not, sir," answered Mrs Delany; "at least she does not tell."

'"Oh!" cried he, laughing, "that's nothing! She is not apt to tell, she never does tell, you know! – Her father told me that himself. He told me the whole history of her *Evelina*. And I shall never forget his face when he spoke of his feelings at first taking up the book! – he looked quite frightened, just as if he was doing it that moment! I can never forget his face while I live!"'

Then going up close to Fanny, he said in his abrupt and alarming way, 'But what? What? How was it?'

'"Sir," Fanny said nervously, not knowing what he meant.

'"How came you? How happened it? What? – What?"

'"I – I only wrote, sir, for my own amusement – only in some odd idle hours."

'"But your publishing – your printing – how was that?"

'"That was only, sir, – only because –"'

She hesitated, as she confessed, 'most abominably, not knowing how to tell him a long story, and growing terribly confused at these questions'. She was also trying not to laugh at the urgently repeated '*What? What?*' that followed so many of his questions.

Another '*What?*', more earnest than ever, suddenly burst from his lips and Fanny stammered out, '"I thought – sir – it would look very well in print." It was, she thought, the silliest speech she had ever made, but she felt compelled to say something for fear of laughing. It was, however, the King who laughed. And he laughed, she remembered, very heartily and walked away from her, crying out, 'very fair, indeed! That's being very fair and honest.' Then, as was his custom, he turned abruptly round and went back to her to continue the investigation of her motives, occasionally going over to Mrs Delany to tell her what the girl had said.

Why had she written nothing since *Evelina*, he asked her.

'"I – I believe I have exhausted myself, sir."'

He laughed again at this 'and went and told it to Mrs Delany, civilly treating a plain fact as a mere *bon mot.*'

Then returning to Fanny again, he said, more seriously, '"But you have not determined against writing any more."

'"N-o, sir –"

'"You have made no vow – no real resolution of that sort?"

'"No, sir."

'"You only wait for inclination?"

'"No, sir."'

He appeared well pleased with this last reply and went back to the middle of the room where he addressed its occupants in general upon the different motives for writing, finally summing up:

'"I believe there is no constraint to be put upon real genius; nothing but inclination can set it to work. Miss Burney, however, knows best."' And then, hastily returning to her, he added violently, '*What? What?*'

The conversation, to Fanny's relief, was then turned by the King to painting to please Mrs Delany who afterwards turned it to hunting to please the King.

Suddenly a 'violent thunder' was made at the door. Fanny felt certain it was the Queen and longed again to escape. Georgiana backed out of the drawing room into the hall to light Her Majesty in.

'Oh!' said the Queen as she came into the room, making her husband a low curtsey as etiquette demanded, 'Your Majesty is here!'

'"Yes, I ran here without speaking to anybody."'

The Queen crossed the room towards Mrs Delany holding out both her hands; then she turned – or Fanny's weak eyes registered the impression that she turned – and made another curtsey. Not being sure that the Queen had made it to her, if, indeed, she had made it at all, and whether or not, therefore, she ought to return it, Fanny became more nervous than ever. She knew that etiquette forbade a formal introduction except at a court Drawing Room. The King saw her distress and said something to his wife about her so that Fanny would know she must curtsey. She did so, the Queen curtseyed again and 'with a very smiling countenance' went up to her. 'But she could not speak, for the King went on talking, eagerly, and very gaily,' repeating to his wife every word Fanny had said during his conversation with her.

When tea was brought in and the Queen went to sit down, the

122

King began all over again, with marvellous energy, on a different tack:

'"Are you musical?"'

'"Not a performer, sir."'

He rushed to the Queen with this intelligence: 'She does not play.'

He stayed with his wife a few minutes to tell her some encouraging news he had had about Princess Elizabeth from the doctor, and then returned to Fanny.

'"Are you sure you never play? Never touch the keys at all?"'

'"Never to acknowledge it, sir."'

'"Oh! That's it,"' cried he; and flying to the Queen, cried, '"She does play – but not to acknowledge it."'

He returned once more to Fanny with increased eagerness and began to examine her more closely. Fanny terrified that she might be asked to perform in public, denied vehemently that she had ever done so.

'He repeated all this to the Queen, whose answers I never heard,' Fanny said, 'but when he once more came back, with a face that looked unwilling to give it up, in my fright I had recourse to dumb show and raised my hands in a supplicating fold, with a most begging countenance to be excused. This, luckily, succeeded; he understood me very well, and laughed a little, but made a sort of desisting, or rather complying, little bow, and said no more about it. I felt very much obliged to him, for I saw his curiosity was all alive. I wished I could have kissed his hand.'[86]

Soon, indeed, she gew extremely fond of him, for, in spite of all his foibles and the disastrous effects of his misguided sense of duty, he was undeniably a lovable man. Her heart could not fail to warm to him when she saw how much he adored his children. It was ridiculous, of course, to allow the three-year-old Prince of Wales to make a short speech of thanks to a charitable organisation and to allow him to hold a Drawing Room after he had been created a Knight of the Garter at the age of seven. It was absurd to permit Princess Amelia to march along the Terrace at Windsor in front of the rest of the family, 'in a robe coat covered with fine muslin, a dressed close clip, white gloves and a fan', turning from side to side to watch the spectators retreat before her, as a celebration of her third birthday.[87] But the King's so obvious delight in his 'little darling', the way he held her hand and picked her up to kiss her, his concern for her and all her sisters when they were ill, his excitement and pride when his second son the Duke of York and his next one the Duke of Clarence came back as young

officers to Windsor, the one from Germany where he had been studying military science, the other from his service in the Navy,[88] all the
pleasure that he took in being a father, and most of the mistakes he
made as a father, were too moving for ridicule.

Fond of him as she became, Fanny Burney could not, therefore, fail
to be deeply shocked and upset when in the spring of 1788 it became
clear that the King was in danger of losing his reason.

[ii]

GEORGE III – THE ROYAL PATIENT

The King's behaviour in the past had often given cause enough for
alarm. Outbursts of disconcerting hilarity had been followed by moods
of silent depression. He had always been liable to violent headaches
and attacks of overwhelming nervous excitement, accompanied by
palpitations and sweating, when worried about something, however
trivial it might be. The problem of what to do about Lady Beaulieu's
application for the Earldom of Montague, reduced him, for instance,
as he confessed himself, into 'the greatest state of uneasiness' he ever
felt, an uneasiness no less intense than that he endured when General
Burgoyne surrendered at Saratoga bringing nearer the dreaded day
when the independence of the American rebels would have to be recognised, and, with that precedent set, the Empire would begin to
crumble. His feverish illnesses in 1765 and 1766 had been accompanied by excessive nervous agitation and a delirious incoherence.
But all this had been little known outside his family and Court. In
1788, however, his behaviour and appearance became too outlandish
for secrecy.

Middle-age had emphasised the peculiarities of his face. His eyes
no longer merely protruded, they goggled; his complexion was not
so much healthy as florid. Thickened lips and a flabbier chin made
his rapid speech even more difficult to follow than it usually was.
When he walked, waving his arms, nodding his head and rolling his
shoulders, he looked like a drunken penguin. In the spring of 1788 his
Principal Equerry, General Benjamin Carpenter, committed suicide
and after this shock the King became more erratic than ever. Sir

George Baker, his doctor, alarmed by his 'up and down condition' which today might be diagnosed as a psychotic disorder of a manic-depressive type, consulted other physicians who 'prescribed a regimen without riding, to which His Majesty refused to submit, and the mildly purgative waters of Cheltenham, to which he consented.'[1] The holiday seemed to do him good, but one day in the summer after his return an alarming scene was said to have taken place in the Great Park. The King, it appeared, was taking the Queen for a drive, when suddenly he cried out, 'Ah! There he is!' He stopped the carriage, gave the reins to his wife and walked towards an old oak tree.

'At the distance of a few yards,' reported a servant who claimed to have been accompanying him, 'he uncovered and advanced, bowing with the utmost respect, and then, seizing one of the lower branches, he shook it with the most apparent cordiality and regard, just as a man shakes his friend by the hand.

'The Queen turned pale with astonishment, the reins dropped from her hands. Never was I in such a consternation lest the horses in the carriage, finding themselves under no control, should run headlong to destruction. Nor did I dare call for assistance, lest the attendants should witness a scene that I desired to keep from their view. At last Her Majesty became attentive to her situation, and, as the reins were happily within reach, they were recovered, and the Queen commanded me to dismount, and to go and intimate, in a soothing voice and suppliant terms, that Her Majesty wished for his company. On my approach, I perceived the King was in earnest conversation, for His Majesty anticipated the answer from his royal friend, and then made a reply. It was the King of Prussia with whom His Majesty enjoyed this rural interview: continental politics were the subject. What I heard it would be unpardonable to divulge. I cannot, however, withhold a remark that must fill every loyal bosom with pleasure; His Majesty, though under a momentary dereliction of reason, evinced the most cordial attachment to freedom and the Protestant faith.

'I approached with reverence.

'"May it please your Majesty . . ."

'"Don't you see I am engaged?" answered the King.

'I bowed and withdrew.

'"Go again," said the Queen.

'I went.

'"May I presume to inform your Majesty that . . ."

'"What is the Matter?" said the King, in great surprise.

'"Her Majesty is in the carriage, and I am commanded to intimate her desire of your Majesty's company."

'"Good lack-a-day," said the King, "that is true. Run on and inform Her Majesty I am hastening to her." '[2]

He was pathetically conscious of his predicament. Repeatedly he insisted that he was really quite all right, but unaccountably nervous and excited. Some weeks after his hallucination in the Park he stopped Miss Burney, who was on her way from the Queen's room to her own, and talked about his health for nearly half an hour 'still with that extreme quickness of speech and manner that belongs to fever'. He was 'all agitation, all emotion,' Miss Burney said, 'yet all benevolence and goodness, even to a degree that makes it touching to hear him speak. He assures everybody of his health.'[3]

He admitted, though, that he could not sleep any more; and once, in the Queen's dressing-room, Miss Burney heard him tell his wife 'at least a hundred times' not to speak to him when he got to his own room next door for he was greatly in need of rest.[4] He lost weight through lack of sleep, and began to look very frail. Soon he was unable to get about without a stick. 'My dear Effy', he said sadly to Lady Effingham, one of the Queen's Ladies of the Bedchamber, 'you see me, all at once, an old man.'[5] A looking-glass in one of the corridors was covered with green cloth so that he could no longer upset himself by looking in it as he passed, to see how much he had changed.[6] Even music now failed to comfort him, for it hurt his head to listen to it and one day he suddenly burst into tears after riding in the Park and cried out, 'I wish to God I may die, for I am going to be mad.'[7]

On 16 October he got up early and went outside for a walk. He returned with his shoes and stockings wet but refused to change them before riding up to London where he ate four large pears before going to bed. About one o'clock in the morning he was seized with a violent cramp which rendered him speechless for several minutes, and his illness began to reach its climax. The following week his condition was still critical, according to Sir George Baker, but he insisted on holding a levee to prove there was no cause for alarm. His appearance in London with his disordered dress, his legs wrapped up in flannel, his vacant gestures, his lips moving so quickly as he talked away in a hoarse, scarcely coherent voice, had, of course, quite the opposite effect. In chapel the next Sunday, in the middle of the sermon, he stood up suddenly, so it was reported, threw his arms round the Queen and the Princesses and said loudly, 'You know what it is to be nervous. But was you ever as bad as this?' The following day Sir George Baker wrote in his diary of the King's 'great hurry of spirits and incessant loquacity' which caused 'great uneasiness to the Queen'. During the concert that evening the King 'talked continually, making sudden and frequent transitions from one subject to another'.[8]

At the beginning of November he seemed a little better. On the 5th he went for a ride in his chaise with the Princess Royal and, although he gave numerous orders to the postillions and got in and out of the carriage several times with an agitation which was painful to watch, he was smiling cheerfully when he set off.[9]

That afternoon, however, the Prince of Wales arrived at Windsor from Brighton and at dinner the King in a delirium of rage seized his infuriating son by the collar and threw him out of his chair against the wall. The Queen, who for weeks had been close to a nervous breakdown herself, fell into violent hysterics. The Prince burst into tears and was only prevented from fainting by his distracted sisters who rubbed his forehead with Hungary water.[10]

That night a most uncommon stillness 'reigned over the whole house. Nobody stirred; not a voice was heard; not a step, not a motion. . . . There seemed a strangeness in the house most extraordinary.'[11] Fanny Burney, alone in her room, waiting for the ring of the bell, could bear the stillness no longer and opened her door to listen in the passage. But she could hear nothing. Her apartment 'seemed wholly separated from life and motion. Whoever was in the house kept at the other end, and not even a servant crossed the stairs or passage.'

Shortly after one o'clock a page came to her room to tell her that the Queen wanted her.

'My poor Royal Mistress!' Fanny Burney wrote in her diary next day. 'Never can I forget her countenance – pale, ghastly pale she looked; she was seated to be undressed, and attended by Lady Elizabeth Waldegrave and Miss Goldsworthy [the equerry's sister and the royal children's sub-governess]. Her whole frame was disordered, yet she was still and quiet.

These two ladies assisted me to undress her, or rather I assisted them, for they were firmer, from being longer present; my shaking hands and blinded eyes could scarce be of any use.

I gave her some camphor julep, which had been ordered by Sir George Baker. "How cold I am!" she cried, and put her hand on mine; marble it felt! and went to my heart's core!'

Fanny offered to spend the night in the little room next door but the Queen would not let her. The King himself was in the second dressing-room and would be sure to wander about in the dark. The previous night he had got up in sudden fear that his wife had left the house, and had spent half an hour looking at her through the curtains of her bed, a candle in his hand, muttering to himself. He was still talking the next morning (one day some weeks later he was to talk without stopping for sixteen hours[12]) and the Queen asked Miss Burney to listen and tell her what His Majesty was saying.

'I am nervous,' Fanny heard him say. 'I am not ill, but I am nervous. If you would know what is the matter with me I am nervous. But I love you both very well; if you would tell me the truth: I love Dr Heberden best, for he has not told me a lie: Sir George has told me a lie – a white lie, he says, but I hate a white lie! If you tell me a lie, let it be a black lie!'

The King's voice rambled on, and Fanny read the morning service to the Queen, who felt too ill to get up and go to the Chapel. Fanny had burst into tears when entering her room that morning and the Queen, infected by the sound of her uncontrollable sobs, had herself broken down in a 'perfect agony of weeping'. She began to cry again after breakfast when the King refused to be examined by Dr Richard Warren, the Prince of Wales's physician, whom the other doctors, worn out by their night-long vigil, had summoned to assist them. And she broke down for a third time when the Prince of Wales came to see her in the new apartments, further down the corridor from the King's, to which the doctors had insisted she move because His Majesty was always trying to get out of bed to go and see her. 'The Queen is my physician,' he had told Fanny Burney, 'and no man can have a better. She is my *friend*, and no man can have a better.'

He was an appallingly difficult patient, and no one had courage enough to be firm with him. In the middle of the second night after his attack on the Prince of Wales he insisted on walking into the next room, where he found the Prince and another of his sons, several of his attendants and all of the doctors sitting on chairs and sofas round the walls. He began talking in praise of his favourite son, Frederick, Duke of York, in terms which reflected no credit on anyone else. Sir George Baker was urged to lead him back to bed, but the old doctor dared not approach him and contented himself with making a few timid suggestions. The King thereupon penned him in a corner and told him he was a mere old woman and knew nothing of his complaint. The Prince of Wales dared not approach him either and left it to an equerry to take his father by the arm and forcibly lead him back to bed.[13]

The Prince of Wales, in fact, according to Mrs Papendiek, whose German father, Frederick Albert, and whose husband, Christopher Papendiek, were both in the royal service, behaved throughout his father's illness very heartlessly. He took over the running of the Household in the most high-handed manner, coming constantly to

16. The Queen's Lodge in 1783
from the engraving by James Fittler after George Robertson

17. The Round Tower from the river on a Rejoicing Night *c.* 1770
from the coloured drawing by Paul Sandby in the Royal Library,
Windsor Castle

18. George III and the Royal Family walking on the East Terrace
from an engraving after O'Neal

Queen's Lodge to give his orders 'without any consideration or regard for his mother's feelings'.[14]

The possibility of the King's cure was, of course, a political issue in which the Prince was interested as heir to the throne; and any doctor who believed that the King would not recover was naturally encouraged and supported by those who wished to see the Prince made Regent. One of these men, Richard Brinsley Sheridan, was given hope by Captain Jack Payne, Comptroller of the Prince of Wales's Household, who wrote to assure him, without much regard to truth, that the King's illness was now characterised by 'all the gestures and ravings of the most confirmed maniac, and a new noise in imitation of the howling of a dog.'[15] The King had also, apparently, tried to jump out of a window.[16]

William Massey — who derived most of the private information about the Court given in his *History of England during the reign of George III*, from Elizabeth, Countess Harcourt, one of the Queen's Ladies of the Bedchamber — says that the Prince of Wales, who had a talent for mimicry,

was in the habit of amusing his companions by taking off, as the phrase was, the gestures and actions of his insane father. That which he did himself, he suffered his friends to do; and the standing topic in the prince's circle was ridicule of the king and queen. The Duke of York vied with his brother in defamation of his parents; but he was wholly destitute of the lively talent which sometimes carried off the grosser parts of the most ribald discourse; and the brutality of the stupid sot disgusted even the more profligate of his associates.[17]

Massey says that the King in his delirium was frequently starved and beaten — a common contemporary treatment of maniacs — chained to a stable and enclosed in a strait-jacket, that his care was entrusted to a German page named Ernst who treated him with contempt and struck him frequently.

Although stories of the King's ill-treatment became much exaggerated in the telling, there can be no doubt that in the early stages of his illness the methods used to combat his insanity were both painful and humiliating. He was continually given overpowering purges and emetics until the Queen in looking at his eyes could compare them to 'nothing but black-currant jelly. The veins in his face were swelled, the sound of his voice was dreadful. He often spoke till he was exhausted and, the moment he could recover his breath, began again while the foam ran out of his mouth.'

After Sir George Baker, worn out by his duties, handed over the case to Dr Warren and Sir Lucas Pepys, the King's shaven head was blistered 'to draw the noxious substances from the brain to the skin surface'. And this treatment was so painful that it led to paroxysms 'so violent that his attendants had to sit on him to hold him down'. Often a strait-jacket had to be applied to prevent him tearing off the bandages.[18]

While the King struggled with his pages and they retaliated by 'behaving with a degree of familiarity and insolence that often irritated and hurt him',[19] the doctors argued about the best way of dealing with their patient. On only one matter could they agree; and that was that perfect quiet must be maintained throughout the house.

The silence and gloom within the walls of the Lodge was something terrible [Christopher Papendiek told his wife]. Every precaution was taken to preserve this state of quiet. No bells were rung, and all arrangements were made among the attendants that the necessary changes should take place at stated hours without any bustle or confusion. The park gates were locked and no stranger was permitted to enter. Three gentlemen porters were added at the Royal entrance-gate, and four sergeant porters at the gate in the Home Park, and an additional number of kitchen boys was ordered down from London to fetch everything from these gates.[20]

While the Queen spent her days sitting at a table with her suddenly greying head resting on her outstretched arms, refusing to eat anything and drinking nothing but barley water,[21] the King in his calmer moments energetically performed a succession of imagined duties with determined industry. He wrote despatches, he bestowed orders, he kept a journal, filling it with details of everything that took place around him and every conversation that he overheard.[22] Occasionally, for brief intervals, he would talk rationally. Once he asked if Lord North had been to enquire about him, and when told that he had been, he said, 'He might have recollected me sooner. However, he, poor fellow, has lost his sight, and I my mind. Yet we meant well to the Americans, just to punish them with a few bloody noses, and then make bows for the mutual happiness of the two countries. But want of principle got into the army, want of energy and skill in the First Lord of the Admiralty, and want of unanimity at home. We lost America. Tell him not to call again. I shall never see him.'[23]

And then his mind wandered and he began talking about something else.

By the end of the month there was so little improvement in his condition that it was decided, at last, to call in an acknowledged expert in mental diseases. There was only one man in the whole country who was considered to deserve this title — Francis Willis, an old clergyman who had taken a medical degree at Oxford and acted both as priest and doctor to his parishioners. Dr Willis had shown himself so skilful in his long career in treating symptoms of madness and so many patients had come to him for help, that he had founded an asylum in Lincolnshire where his treatment, based on kindness and sympathy rather than upon forcible subjection, had had remarkable results.

'Doctor Willis keeps a madhouse,' Lord Sheffield wrote disdainfully. 'He is considered by some as not much better than a mountebank, and not far different from some of those that are confined in his house.'[24] It was not an uncommon opinion.

He came with his two sons to attend the King and they were greeted with predictable suspicion.

Wasn't he ashamed of himself, the King asked the father in a lucid moment, to exercise the profession of medicine when he was an ordained clergyman?

'Sir,' said Dr Willis, 'Our Saviour Himself went about healing the sick.'

'Yes,' agreed the King, adding with a rude wit which promise his ultimate recovery, 'but *He* had not £700 for it.'[25]

Eventually, however, the King was persuaded to accept the help of the Willises on condition that they allowed him to shave himself, to cut his own nails and to have the use of a knife at meal times. Previously the King had been shaved by one of his pages and the operation of clearing the cheeks alone had taken nearly two hours, owing to the patient's compulsive need to talk all the time.[26]

The King himself was not much quicker, and although he managed to do it without cutting his skin too badly, he was glad, having asserted his authority, not to have to handle the razor again.

Before the Willises took charge of his case a suggestion had been made that the King should be taken to Kew. Here there were 'grounds and gardens in which His Majesty could take air and exercise privately, and without any annoyance, while at Windsor the whole of the private garden could be seen from the Terrace; and to exclude the public suddenly from what they had hitherto had the privilege of using would give rise to comments and surmises that were best avoided'.[27]

The King, unfortunately, in recent years had taken a dislike to Kew and when the move was first suggested to him he had been 'very vehement in his objections'. The Willises felt sure, though, that the change must be made whether he liked it or not; and it was settled that the Queen and the Princesses should leave Windsor quietly without his knowledge so that when he discovered he had been left behind he might more easily be persuaded to follow them.

On Saturday morning 29 November at about ten o'clock they left. The Queen, 'drowned in tears', climbed softly into the leading carriage with Lady Courtown and two of the Princesses, who were also in tears, while Lady Charlotte Finch, the royal governess, and another Princess got into the next one. Fanny Burney thought that a more melancholy scene could not be imagined. 'There was not a dry eye in the house. The footmen, the house-maids, the porters, the sentinels – all cried bitterly as they looked on.'[28]

These servants were instructed to follow later, as Dr Willis insisted that the King should have as few new faces around him as possible; but one of the footmen, Fortnum, 'begged to resign from ill health'. He was given leave to do so and soon afterwards went to help in his family's grocery shop in Piccadilly.

When the King was told that the Queen had left Windsor he was extremely angry. At first he refused to get out of bed and insisted that the Queen must return and beg his pardon. His physicians and equerries and even the Prime Minister pleaded with him to be reasonable, but it was not for several hours that he was at last persuaded to pull back the bed curtains and get dressed.

He came out to his coach in his Windsor uniform and while 'sentries, footmen and porters wept as though they would never see him again, he drove off with an escort of cavalry'.

An equerry, Colonel Robert Fulke Greville, accompanied him in the coach and described the journey in his diary:

On Entering the Home Park through which we went, in the way to Datchet Bridge, about 20 Loyal Inhabitants at Windsor and These I saw cheifly Tradesmen, appeared; As the Kings Carriage drove by Them they bowed respectfully and took a melancholy leave. The King on seeing Them bowed most Kindly and He felt the greatest Emotion which I have yet observed. When He bowed the 'Big Tear' started in his Eye, and putting his hand before his Face, He said with much feeling 'These good People are too fond of Me,' and He then added with affecting sensibility 'Why am I taken from a Place I like best in all the World'. . . . As he proceeded on his

journey his flow of spirits became high, and He had frequent fits of laughing –
He talked without ceasing but the topics and his manner marked too plainly
his derangement.[29]

*   *   *

Gradually that winter at Kew, under the skilful and sympathetic care
of the Willises, the King's health began to improve. At first the
weather was fearfully cold and he was kept inside, breathing the
powerful fumes of musk in whose therapeutic qualities Dr Willis
believed so strongly that the whole place was pervaded with them.[30]
But as the warmer weather came at the beginning of 1789, he was
allowed out more often to walk in the garden, where he occasionally
caught sight of the Princesses watching him anxiously from the
windows. He peered back at them and complained to Dr Willis that
his eyesight was not good enough to see his dear Amelia as clearly
as he would have liked.[31]

The exercise did him good. He began to look better and to walk
with more control over his limbs. He talked as quickly as ever but
more sensibly than before. He had, however, one intermittent
delusion which, becoming persistent later, caused profound grief
to the Queen, and that was that he was no longer married to her.

His real Queen, he sometimes now insisted, was Esther, Lady
Pembroke, that beautiful and admired woman who had adorned the
Court of his youth and whose blue livery he had copied for the
Windsor uniform. He refused to see Charlotte, complaining that,
while he had always respected her and paid her every attention, she
had deserted him in his moment of need and 'left him to the care of
those who had used him ill'.[32]

One day Dr Willis persuaded him to see the Queen, and when he
saw her he kissed her and burst into tears. He wanted to tell her 'of
all his sufferings, but she said she was aware of them, and had
known of all that had passed both by day and by night'.[33] The
interview was short; and although they saw each other every day
from then on, their behaviour towards each other, even after the
King's recovery, never again suggested that 'most cordial confidence
and happiness' that Fanny Burney had noticed three years before.[34]
At the crisis of his illness he had repeatedly insisted not only that he
was going to retire to Hanover – he had threatened this before,
preparing the most elaborate details of the new liveries to be worn
there[35] – but that all marriages were to be dissolved both there and
in Britain by Act of Parliament.[36] It was an obsession that Charlotte,

133

now so stout that she looked, so it was said, as if she were bearing all her fifteen children at once, found it impossible to forget.

As spring approached, however, the King stopped talking about Queen Esther and showed so much improvement that the Regency Bill, although passed by the Commons, seemed unlikely to pass into law. One day Fanny Burney came across the King in the gardens at Kew and noticed this appreciable improvement.

She was strolling on the lawn when she saw a group of figures, whom she took to be gardeners, approaching her. Because she was so short-sighted, the men were almost level with her before she realised her mistake and recognised one of them to be the King. As Dr Willis had given instructions that the King's walks were on no account to be disturbed, Fanny turned and fled. Terrified, she heard the men run after her. Then she heard shouts and the King's voice, loud and hoarse, calling her name, and then a shriller voice: 'Stop! Dr Willis begs you to stop.'

'I cannot! I cannot,' she called back.

'You must, ma'am. It hurts the King to run.'

And so at last she did stop, and turned round to see the King between two panting doctors hurry on towards her.

'Why did you run away?' he called out.

Not knowing how to answer him, she overcame her fear and walked up to him. He put out his arms and she felt a sudden horror that he was going to crush her like a bear. But he put his hands on her shoulders and to her relief and astonishment he kissed her fondly on the cheek.

He was overcome by the pleasure of seeing her alarmed but friendly and familiar face and he talked to her with an excitement that was almost feverish. He spoke of anything that came into his mind, and although he still had little control over his speech he was, Fanny thought, nearly in his perfect state of mind as to his opinions. 'I am your friend,' he kept telling her. 'Never mind her' – referring to Mrs Schwellenberg – 'Don't be oppressed! Don't let her cast you down!'

Thinking him too elated, the doctors came up to suggest that Miss Burney should walk on. 'No, no, no, no,' the King protested, repeating the word countless times in a single breath; and they gave in to him. He spoke of his pages, and in particular of the rough and disrespectful Ernst, of the Prince of Wales, of Fanny's father, and the thought of Dr Burney brought him to his favourite theme – Handel. He recounted numerous anecdotes of the great composer and 'ran over most of his oratorios, attempting to sing the subjects of several airs and choruses but so dreadfully hoarse that the sound was terrible'.

Again Dr Willis came up, but the King waved him away and began to talk of Mrs Delany who had recently died. 'I loved her as a friend,' he said. 'I made a memorandum when I lost her – I will show it to you.' He pulled out a pocket-book and rummaged in it, but he could not find what he was looking for. There were tears in his eyes. And seeing him wipe them away, Dr Willis protested once more.

'No, no! I want to ask her a few more questions. I have lived so long out of the world. I know nothing.'

He walked away from the doctor with Fanny by his side, asking about other people whom she knew. This reminded him of his Ministers and he told her how dissatisfied with them he was and how he would alter things as soon as he was able to 'get loose again'. He took a paper from his pocket and showed her his list of names for a new Government. 'When once I get away,' he said passionately, 'I shall rule with a rod of iron.'

Hearing the vehemence in his voice, the doctors became alarmed again and insisted, this time successfully, that the conversation must stop. Fanny hurried back to the house, 'inexpressibly thankful to see the King so nearly himself'.[37]

In March he returned to Windsor, where he was welcomed with unfeigned enthusiasm by cheering crowds. The following month he drove in state from Buckingham House to St Paul's for a service of thanksgiving for 'God's Mercy in giving the King his health and reason once more'. And as the bells pealed and the guns boomed, the crowds cheered him more wildly than ever. He had never been so popular. Disliked and distrusted before his illness, all was forgiven him now by a people with a traditionally sincere and spontaneous sympathy for the afflicted and the ill-used. His two elder sons, chatting unconcernedly during the service in St Paul's, were greeted coldly when they came out of it; but the applause for the King was deafening.

Nothing could have done more to hasten his full recovery. He drove back to Windsor in the highest spirits and allowed the Princess Royal to organise a gala, at which all the ladies wore bandeaux with 'God Save the King' embroidered in front; and the dinner – there were no fewer than twenty different sorts of soup alone – was adjudged the best that had been given there for a hundred years.[38]

In July the Royal Family went for a summer holiday to Weymouth where the King, cheerful and relaxed, could enjoy once again the company and obvious loyalty of simple people. When he played cards in a private apartment in the Rooms, he left the door open so that everyone could see him; when he went to the theatre he leant forward in his box to acknowledge the cheers; when he went bathing in his blue serge costume followed by a machine filled with fiddlers playing 'God Save the King', he waved happily to his female companions, upon whose bonnets as well as upon the cumbersome sashes they wore round their waists, were embroidered letters expressing the same universally popular sentiment.[39]

On his return to Windsor the King seemed as happy as he had ever been. He resumed the habits of his former quiet life with contentment. He walked; he rode; he hunted; he farmed; he listened to concerts in the new music room overlooking the Terrace; he pottered about, fiddling with Herschel's telescope and the Castle's recently erected organ; he played chess and backgammon with his equerries; he read his newspaper; he dozed. Usually in the summer after the races at Ascot and Egham he went to Weymouth. He never seems to have considered going anywhere else. The idea of foreign travel appalled him – indeed, few Kings can have travelled less in their own country than he did. Regularly, out of a sense of duty, he attended his levees in London, where his manners were as startlingly unconventional as ever. Once when a Scots colonel was presented and bowed so low that his ill-fitting kilt came up at the back to an embarrassing height, he called out in a loud and cheerful voice, 'Keep the ladies in front! Keep the ladies in front!'[40] This, no doubt, was innocent enough. On other occasions, though, he could be distressingly ungracious. To refuse at Windsor with sardonic abruptness a horse dealer's impressively drawn up pedigree because it would serve very well for the next horse he sold, was merely to emphasise how like he was to a bluff yet amiable squire;[41] but to go up to a gentleman from Yorkshire at a Drawing Room in London and say suddenly, 'I suppose you're going back to Yorkshire, Mr Stanhope? A very ugly county, Yorkshire!' was not to lessen an unfortunate reputation for blindly insensitive tactlessness.[42]

It was nevertheless a tactlessness which those who knew him best in these years found it easy to forgive, for his fundamental good-nature was as always unquestionable.

Dr Johnson, a man also without much tact, decided that George III was the 'finest gentleman' he had ever seen.[43] As the holder of a royal pension, Johnson was predisposed to this opinion, of course, but others shared it who had no cause for gratitude. John Adams, for instance, the first envoy to the English Court from the United States of America, to whom the King confessed that he was the 'last to consent to the separation' of America from Britain but now was the 'first to meet the friendship of the United States as an independent power', thought that George III had all the 'affability of Charles II' with all the 'domestic virtues and regularity of Charles I'. And although the subsequent interviews were less pleasant because the Queen was so cold and aloof, Adams continued to hold the King in high regard. Benjamin Franklin thought him 'the best King any nation was ever blessed with'.[44]

*　　*　　*

When Fanny Burney became ill, as Colonel Goldsworthy, indulging his taste for the pleasures of *schadenfreude*, had cheerfully prophesied she would, and she was obliged to give up her appointment, she parted from the King and Queen with a deep and sincere regret. The Queen, with characteristic and, perhaps, unconscious selfishness, had insisted she stay at Windsor for another fortnight, which the poor girl was clearly unfit to do. Her Majesty's 'cordiality and condescension' towards her far from satisfactory attendant, previously so satisfying to Fanny's susceptible emotions, had given way to an unspoken displeasure which arose, Fanny thought, from an opinion that she 'ought rather to have struggled on, live or die than to quit her'. The displeasure may also have arisen because the Queen felt – this, at least was the opinion of others in the Household, although Fanny herself does not record the fact – that Miss Burney appeared to be increasingly less interested in her duties and more in her writing, and because Her Majesty, whose feelings were not consistent with the encouragement or even sanctioning of novel writing 'particularly under her own roof', was 'certain that whenever she rang her bell, the pen was laid down with regret'.[45] When the time came to say good-bye, though, the Queen, who, despite Fanny's protests, insisted that she would continue to pay her half her present salary as a pension, had to keep dabbing her eyes with a handkerchief and Fanny, too, was almost in tears.

'The King then came into the room,' Fanny recorded. 'He immediately advanced to the window, where I stood, to speak to me. I was not then able to comport myself steadily. I was forced to turn my head away from him. He stood still and silent for some minutes, waiting to see if I should turn about; but I could not

137

recover myself sufficiently to face him, strange as it was to do otherwise; and perceiving me quite overcome he walked away, and I saw him no more.

'His kindness, his goodness, his benignity, never shall I forget.'[46]

*　　*　　*

Even those who had cause to detest him as a King found it difficult to maintain their hatred of 'Farmer George' as he pottered about at Windsor in his political retirement. They warmed to him when they heard that he had said to Colonel Landmann, 'I should like to fight Bony single-handed. I'm sure I should. I should give him a good thrashing. I'm sure I should. I'm sure of it.'[47] For they knew he meant it; and the thought of that emphatic voice and those emphatic gestures as the excited figure in his Horse Guards uniform regularly inspected the Volunteers drawn up under the Round Tower at Windsor during the autumn of 1803, when a French invasion seemed imminent, was curiously inspiring.[48]

But he was growing old now and each new crisis in his public or family life seemed to threaten a return of insanity. Pitt, on whose calm good sense he had grown accustomed to rely, shocked him profoundly when he sought to bring about the long overdue emancipation of the Roman Catholics, and he was soon 'in the height of a phrenzy fever – as bad as the worst period' of his former attack.[49] According to the Prince of Wales he spoke of abdication and again of retirement to Hanover and now even of going to live in America.[50] He got better but it was only a temporary recovery, and as his fear of permanent insanity grew he became increasingly suspicious of all those around him who seemed to be watching him to discern symptoms of its onset. He began to hate his doctors; he refused to see the Prince of Wales, whom, although he loved as his son, he 'hated as his heir';[51] he took pains to avoid the company of his wife, whose nervousness increased the cold hostility of a dying marriage. He took to dismissing servants for imagined slights or insults.

Once more he lay in bed at night unable to sleep, talking breathlessly to himself. In the daytime, too, he was now as compulsively voluble as ever he had been and would stop people in the Castle grounds and hold them in conversation, or in effect talk at them, for an hour on end. Sometimes he would stop in the middle of a sentence and burst into tears.[52] By 1804 it seemed certain that he would soon lose his reason completely.

He rallied a little, however, the next year when there were whole weeks during which he seemed happy and, despite his always hurried speech, unruffled.

Colonel Herbert Taylor, who was appointed his secretary in 1805 because of the King's failing sight, said that his 'unutterable good humour' was daily increasing.[53] By the end of the year he was 'handing round the muffins to the ladies in his old jocose and good-humoured manner'.[54]

He had moved now from Queen's Lodge and was living in the Castle itself, on the north side overlooking the Terrace, where all his predecessors had lived, while his wife and daughters occupied apartments in the southern wing, changing, so the Queen lamented to Lady Harcourt, 'from a very comfortable and warm habitation to the coldest house, rooms and passages that ever existed'.[55] Their life there soon became set into a rigid pattern.

The King got up at half-past seven and walked over towards the Queen's apartments where one of the Princesses, who took it in turns to attend him, met him and accompanied him to chapel. At breakfast he sat at the head of the table with the Queen, the five Princesses sitting, in order of seniority, down the side.

After breakfast he went riding if it was fine or played chess if it was wet. He dined at two o'clock and at five visited the Queen and the Princesses (who dined at four) for a glass of wine thinned with water. Then he went back to his study to transact business with his secretary, and afterwards he played cards in the Queen's drawing-room. Occasionally guests were invited but they never stayed long, for at the stroke of ten they were expected to retire. When they had gone supper was laid out; but that was 'merely a matter of form', because no one ate anything.[56]

The King always went back to his apartments in the north front at an early hour and was soon in bed. His ground-floor bedroom was still uncarpeted but it was otherwise 'neatly furnished partly in a modern style' and was newly decorated.[57] Indeed, the whole Castle was now gradually changing its appearance.

James Wyatt, a young architect who had made his reputation with several fine buildings at Oxford and some beautiful country houses all in the classical style, had succeeded Sir William Chambers as Surveyor-General to the Board of Works in 1796.[58] By then he had turned his attention to Gothic architecture which had become so fashionable since Horace Walpole's extravagant fancies at Strawberry Hill and Gray's elaborate house at Stoke Poges had caught the imagination of a class to whom the severe lines of Palladio were becoming arid and lifeless. Wyatt, although he was never fully in sympathy with the Gothic taste, was one of its most influential popularisers, and he found in George iii and Windsor Castle both a client and a building sympathetic to his ideas.

Work began in 1800 to give the buildings round the Upper Ward – which were then as plainly unornamented as Hugh May had left them in the time of Charles ii – the more elaborate appearance suggested by the romantic details of Gothicism. Rectangular windows were taken out to be replaced by arched openings with surrounds and transoms cut from Portland stone; and in the entrance tower to the State apartments a new staircase, wide, tall and gloomy, approached from a vault under the Queen's Guard Chamber, took the place of the two staircases whose ceilings had been painted by Verrio in 1678. [59]

The new Grand Staircase was far from being an improvement, but it seemed to the King a more suitable setting for the Garter ceremonial in which he was now taking a renewed interest. And in April 1805, when the new Knights were installed, they were able to walk up a staircase which resembled those built during the days of their Order's founder.

This installation was, in other respects, a memorable occasion, for the King had been determined to revive as many as possible of the ancient customs associated with the Feast of St George. The dinner which began at six o'clock was even more splendid than that held in the Castle to celebrate his recovery in 1789. The royal princes sat at the Sovereign's table, on which there was £12,000 worth of gold plate and a 'variety of splendid ornaments consisting principally of several figures of knights on horseback, composed wholly of silver, surmounted by the Star and Order of the Garter in solid gold'. After the meal, eighteen tables were set out in the Castle yard covered with provisions and nine hogsheads of ale. Police officers from Bow Street helped to keep the crowds outside in order, but when the gates were opened the scene of confusion which ensued exceeded 'all description. Everyone being more anxious to plunder than to eat, they carried off that which came soonest to hand.' [60]

The King, watching the tumult from one of the windows of the Queen's apartments, was seen to be extremely agitated. All the excitement, particularly the anxious supervision in the kitchen of the roasting and spicing of a baron of beef, weighing 162 pounds, had clearly been too much for him. In St George's Chapel, surrounded by an array of Knights whose dispiriting appearance, 'fat, limping and leaden', [61] took much from the splendour of the scene, the King's face was 'unusually red and anxious' and the vast, outmoded, powdered and curled periwig he wore gave the impression of a man in the most absurd fancy dress.[62]

He was no longer able to withstand the effects of these exciting alterations in the rhythm of an unvaried routine. So long as he observed this routine and so long as nothing surprised, worried or shocked him he was able to control the agitation which otherwise overwhelmed his mind. But as he refused to shut himself away in the care of a crowd of detested doctors, he suffered the consequences. In 1809 his favourite son, the Duke of York, Commander-in-Chief of the Army and a man who in that position had shown himself possessed of a far greater talent than his detractors would allow, was accused, without possibility of contradiction, of having commissioned and promoted officers on the recommendation of his consequently rich mistress. This shocking scandal, preceded by the retreat of the British Army under Sir John Moore to Corunna and followed in the same year by the disastrous expedition to Walcheren, had its predictable effect on the King's health. And then, in the following year, his fifth son, the Duke of Cumberland, was involved in a criminal case which received widespread publicity.

The Duke, a strange and ugly man of the most reactionary opinions, had, so he claimed, been woken up in bed one night at St James's Palace by a light blow on the head which he thought at first had been caused by a bat attracted into his bedroom by the light of the lamp that was kept burning there all night. He sat up and his eyes caught the flash of a sabre blade. He reached up, gripped the blade and almost severed his right thumb. He felt for the bell rope, could not find it, jumped out of bed and ran next door to his page's room, pursued by his assailant, who managed to cut him superficially on his buttocks and thigh and more seriously on his head. Hearing the Duke shout 'I am murdered! I am murdered!' other servants and some soldiers ran into the room and he immediately asked them where Sellis, his Corsican valet, was. Sellis was found in his room, half undressed and with his throat cut.[63] The official verdict was suicide but there were many who thought that Sellis had not cut his own throat, and that the Duke, who was reported not only to have been once found in bed with Mrs Sellis, but also to have been blackmailed by her husband after the Duke had made homosexual advances to him, was the murderer.*

* In the Royal Archives at Windsor there is a document, deposited there in the 1930s, which contains a 'confession' by the Duke to his secretary, Captain Charles Jones, that he

This was in the summer of 1810 and the King had scarcely recovered from the shock of it all when in November his beloved Amelia died at Windsor. Towards the end of her illness the King had become progressively more distracted and unbalanced, talking so loudly while out riding on a horse led by a hobby groom – for he was almost blind now – that his voice could be heard a long way off, and then relapsing into paroxysms of weeping. As often as he could he would go into Princess Amelia's room and 'hold her hand and bend over her to scan the face in which he was too blind to discern the onset of death'.[66]

One evening a few days before she died, he shocked Miss Cornelia Knight, the precise, humourless, literary companion of the Queen, by the 'dreadful excitement in his countenance' when he came into the drawing-room.

As he could not distinguish persons [Miss Knight wrote in her memoirs], it was the custom to speak to him as he approached, that he might recognise by the voice whom he was about to address. I forget what it was I said to him but shall ever remember what he said to me: 'You are not uneasy, I am sure about Amelia. You are not to be deceived, but you know that she is in no danger.' At the same time he squeezed my hand with such force that I could scarcely help crying out. The Queen, however, dragged him away. When tea was served I perceived how much alarmed I had been, for my hand shook so that I could hardly take the cup.'[67]

When Princess Amelia knew she was going to die she gave instructions to Rundell and Bridges, jewellers to the Royal Family, to put a valuable stone she possessed into a ring for her father to wear in remembrance of her. She put the ring on his finger herself one night when he came to see her. As well as the jewel there was a lock of her own hair pressed under a little crystal window and an inscription cut into the gold: *Remember Me.* He had not been prepared for the emotional scene and he broke down.[68] He wrote her a letter but his writing, usually clear and easy to read, was appalling now, and only a word here and there is decipherable.[69] He accepted the news of her death with a low mumble of incoherent talk and although he recovered sufficiently to arrange 'everything relating to the cere-

did murder Sellis. The confession, however, is believed to be an invention.[64] A surgeon at the inquiry did say, though, that Sellis, who was left-handed, could not have cut his throat in the way it was cut. On the other hand the foreman of the jury was Francis Place, a man in no way sympathetic to the Royal Family in general or to the Duke of Cumberland in particular. The Corsican – some reports describe him as a Piedmontese – seems to have been goaded to fury by the Duke's taunts at him for being a Roman Catholic.[65]

mony of the funeral'[70] except for short intervals he was never sane again.

He lived on for nine more years, a shrunken old man with a white beard, dwelling in a world of his own imagining. It was difficult to tell how much he knew of the real world outside, for when he was not violent he rarely showed emotion now and even cried silently. The doctors were at first concerned to prevent him learning anything which might upset him, though they soon understood that their concern was unjustified. They had dreaded, for instance, his discovering that Princess Amelia had left all her possessions to General Fitzroy, one of his equerries, of whom she had been so fond that there were rumours of a secret marriage, and to whom she, at any rate, so she told her brother, the Duke of York, 'considered herself married'.[71] But when the King learned the contents of the will he seemed unperturbed, contented even.[72] Later he believed Amelia to be still alive, happily married and living in Hanover;[73] and he tried to comfort one of his doctors whose wife had died by assuring him that she was perfectly all right and had gone to stay with his daughter there.[74]

He believed that he himself – it was a persistently recurrent delusion – was married to Lady Pembroke, 'Queen Esther', whose continued absence from Windsor grieved him deeply. 'Is it not a strange thing, Adolphus,' he said one day to his youngest son, the Duke of Cambridge, 'that they still refuse to let me go to Lady Pembroke, although everyone knows I am married to her?' And what was worse, 'that infamous scoundrel', Sir Henry Halford, his new doctor, was at the wedding and now had the effrontery to deny it to his face![75]

Queen Charlotte was all but forgotten. For years it had been known that they no longer slept together, and that she went so far as to lock her door against him.[76] She never dined with him now and refused to see him alone. When she did go to see him, she was usually accompanied by one of her daughters. 'I went down with the Queen,' wrote Princess Mary after one of these distressing visits, 'and it was shocking to hear the poor, dear King run on so, and her unfortunate manner makes things worse.' Princess Mary thought that this 'unfortunate manner' of her mother's was attributable partly to 'extream timidity' and partly to an inborn deficiency in 'warmth, tenderness, affec.'[77] The Queen seemed to find her husband frightening as well as distasteful and in her unhappiness she made others unhappy too. She quarrelled with the Princess Royal, who decided that she was a 'silly woman'.[78] She quarrelled with the Princess of Wales, whose daughter Charlotte was brought up at Windsor in the care of her grandparents. She behaved badly to her attendants.[79] She became increasingly ill-tempered, withdrawn and aloof.

She spent much of her time at Frogmore, a small estate in the Park which, known orginally as Avelyn's after the family that had long owned it, was bought for the Crown by Henry viii and had subsequently been let to a succession of tenants. Queen Charlotte acquired the adjoining estate, Little Frogmore, in 1790 and Avelyn's, by then called Great Frogmore, in 1792. She demolished Little Frogmore and added its grounds to Great Frogmore. Here, in her 'little paradise' (see plate 23) she retreated from the formal and aggravating life of the Castle and found pleasure in creating the lovely gardens which still exist. In earlier years she had entertained here and given fêtes; but now she came only for peace.[80] Sometimes her daughters came with her, but whenever they could they excused themselves and stayed behind at the Castle, sometimes spending their afternoons in a hexagonal cave in the slopes beneath the North Terrace. This cave, ventilated by a chimney which opened on to the turf above their heads and made less gloomy by walls of looking-glass, no traces of which remain, was their favourite hiding-place from a difficult mother, who died in 1818, a sad, unloved old woman, after a long and painful illness.

The King still lingered on, although he sometimes believed himself to be dead as well. The thought did not seem to distress him; often indeed, he seemed strangely happy. He walked about his rooms in his flannel dressing-gown and ermine night-cap, holding conversations with Ministers long since dead. He still liked to play his flute and his harpsichord and when he had given an uncertain rendering of one of his favourite tunes he would say that he had been very fond of that particular tune when he was in the world.[81] His meals often appeared before he was expecting them and he would say, 'Can it be so late? How time flies!' He had a good appetite, particularly for cold meat, which he usually ate standing up; and Miss Lucy Kennedy, an old lady who had lived in the Castle for over thirty years the previous century and still heard all the news of it at her house in the town, recorded in her diary with evident pleasure that one 'Teusday he eat 3 jellys'.

He did not lose his appetite and until the last few weeks of his life he never lost the pleasure of dressing up. Every afternoon he

19. George III in Windsor
uniform
from the painting by Peter
Edward Stroehling in the Royal
Collection

20. Queen Charlotte
from the painting by Peter
Edward Stroehling in the Royal
Collection

21. The Great Kitchen *c.* 1810
from the engraving by W. J. Bennett after C. Wild in W. H. Pyne,
History of the Royal Residences, 1819

22. The King's Closet *c.* 1810
from the engraving by W. J. Bennett after I. P. Stephanoff in
W. H. Pyne, *History of the Royal Residences,* 1819

changed for dinner, wearing his Orders, up to the day of his death. Occasionally he decided to wear mourning 'in memory of George III, for he was a good man'.[82] He found comfort in praying to God and on at least one occasion, apparently, he administered Holy Communion to himself.[83] He liked to believe that he possessed supernatural powers and he would sometimes stamp his foot when one of the doctors annoyed him and say that he would send him down to hell.[84]

But he was rarely upset now. It irritated him when he was denied his favourite meal or when it was proposed to shave his beard. If they insisted on shaving him, he warned them once with magnificent authority, he would have the battle axes-called in.[85] It was a rare outburst, though. Most of his days were passed quietly and without complaint in the dark room overlooking the Terrace, where he refused now to go because he could no longer see the countryside beyond it which he loved. On the evening of 29 January 1820, quietly and without complaint, he died.

[iii]

GEORGE IV – THE *COTTAGE ORNÉ*

For several weeks the Prince Regent had been seriously ill himself at Brighton and he had begun to fear that he too might be dying. He was already fifty-seven. The handsome, chubby young man who had fallen so helplessly in love with 'Perdita' Robinson at the age of seventeen and who had secretly contravened the Royal Marriage Act by marrying the handsome, devout and intelligent Roman Catholic Mrs Fitzherbert when he was twenty-three, had become gouty and immensely fat. He was often breathless, frequently in pain, exaggerating the minor complaints of a fundamentally strong constitution by a hypochondriacal self-concern.[1] He had, indeed, though, much to worry him, apart from his health.

Nine years after his illegal marriage to Mrs Fitzherbert he had felt obliged, partly by the need for an heir, more, no doubt, by debts, which amounted to £400,000 in 1792, to marry again. His father had refused to increase his allowance until he chose a suitable wife; and the Prince of Wales, who clearly could not tell his father that he already had a wife, agreed to choose his cousin Princess Caroline of Brunswick, a short, coarse, highly-sexed, fair-haired woman who wore dirty underclothes and was, according to the diplomatist sent out to bring her back from Germany, consequently rather smelly.[2] The Prince married her with sulky desperation, caused his lovely mistress Lady Jersey – he had temporarily forsaken Mrs Fitzherbert – to become one of her ladies-in-waiting and took her to Windsor for the first part of their honeymoon.

By the time the summer came and they went on to Brighton they were already no longer sleeping together. Indeed, according to a journal purported to have been kept by the Princess, the Prince was so drunk 'the night he married that, when he came into her room, he was obliged to leave it again; and he remained away all night and did not return again till the morning; he then obliged her to remain in bed with him and that is the only time they were together as husband and wife'.[3]

'Judge what it was to have a drunken husband on one's wedding-day,' the Princess told Lady Charlotte Campbell, 'and one who passed the greatest part of his bridal-night under the grate, where he fell and where I left him. If anybody say to me at dis moment – will you pass your life over again, or be killed? I would choose death; for you know, a little sooner or later we must all die; but to live a life of wretchedness twice over, – oh! mine God, no!'[4]

Certainly the Prince, for his part, decided that he would rather see toads and vipers crawling over his 'victuals than sit at the same table with her'.[5] When Princess Charlotte was born, nine months less one day after the wedding, the Princess of Wales went to live in a different house.

She was an irritating, vulgar, vapid, unbalanced woman; but it was she who had the people's sympathy.

The Prince's fantastic extravagance, the fortunes he spent on his idiosyncratic house at Brighton and on Carlton House in London, the widespread reports of his vast losses at racing, his drinking bouts, his extravagant parties, his flippant friends, his unsavoury brothers whose publicised vices put emphasis upon his own, his taste for middle-aged grandmothers who would indulge his need to be fondled and fussed over like a child, the sight of his grease-painted face, of his bulging though corseted figure in its richly coloured clothes and of his yellow Berlin coursing, with purple blinds drawn down, to his mistress's house in Chelsea, were alike angrily condemned by a country at war with France and forced to pay for the cost of it all. The Whigs, infuriated by what they took to be his betrayal of their support after he became Prince Regent, added their antagonism to that of the people at large, while viciously satirical poets and lampoonists portrayed him to the disgusted public as a blubbering, monstrous, drink-swilling lecher without taste or feeling.

Nor were his wife and the public all that the Regent had to worry him. His daughter Charlotte who had grown up into a high-spirited, capricious, rather rowdy, fat and clumsy girl, passionately attached to her friend Miss Mercer Elphinstone yet provocatively flirtatious with most presentable young men,[5] much preferred her mother's *outré* household to the stifling atmosphere at Windsor where visits with her aunts — the 'Sisterhood' as her father compassionately described them — to her grandmother's house at Frogmore, were rare breaks in the long, dull days spent in the company of her governesses in the school-room. At her mother's, life was much more exciting. Apart from the far from respectable guests who so often stayed in the house, there were two intriguing children, William Austin and Edwardina Kent, who, Charlotte was convinced, were her mother's bastards. William Austin slept in her mother's bedroom and it was here that she was allowed to meet Captain Hesse of the Light Dragoons, supposedly an illegitimate son of her uncle the Duke of York, whom she had met while out driving in her carriage at Windsor. The affair with Captain Hesse lasted for several weeks until, at a party at Carlton House, she met Prince William of Orange, whom her father wished her to marry and of whom she became quite fond. In the summer of 1814, however, when for that one 'year of revelry' the war with Napoleon was over, she decided that Prince William was less attractive than most of the dashing young princes with whom London was filled and far less desirable than Prince Frederick William Henry Augustus of Prussia with whom she fell passionately in love.[6] She told her father that she would not marry the Prince of Orange after all. He was furious with her. She rushed out of the house and took a hackney-coach to her mother's. She was at length persuaded to return, and her father sent her down to Cranbourne Lodge at Windsor in the care of several ladies who might be relied on to ensure that she would not be left alone with the unsuitable Prussian Prince again.[7]

The newspapers and the public took the side of the young Princess against that of a tyrannical parent whose conduct was likened by a Member of Parliament to that of a 'Prussian Corporal'. Worse, though, was yet to come. In 1816 Charlotte married Prince Leopold of Saxe-Coburg, a handsome, ingratiating, ambitious, self-satisfied and somewhat unctuous man with no possessions and little money. Her father persuaded his Ministers to grant him an income of £50,000 a year and he gave the couple the beautiful house of Clare-mont as a wedding present. Here the following year Charlotte died, having given birth to a dead baby, and the shocked Regent who 'received the tidings of the death of his Beloved Daughter with the greatest grief', was once more reminded by the newspapers of his previous cruel treatment of an idolised heroine.[8]

Meanwhile the idol's mother, the public's other heroine, was providing Europe with a scandalous amusement which delighted her husband's enemies. Dressed in the most *louche* attire, she wandered from town to town accompanied by a crowd of excitable Italian attendants. At Genoa she was drawn through the streets in a gilt and mother-of-pearl phaeton; at Baden she appeared at the Opera in 'an enormous head-dress, as worn by the Oberlander peasants, and decorated with flying ribbons and glittering spangles'; on the way to Constantinople she spent her time in a tent on board ship with her Italian chamberlain, a lively young man, 'six feet high, with a magnificent head of black hair, pale complexion, mustachios which reach from here to London',[9] whom she made Grand Master of the Order of Caroline which she had created in Jerusalem; at Geneva she attended a dance, *en Venus*, naked to the waist, 'display-ing a bosom of more than ample proportions'.[10]

In 1819 the Prince Regent was told by his legal advisers that there was sufficient evidence for a divorce on the ground of adultery. The following year George III died and the new King began his reign under the shadow of the fear that his wife would return to England. She did so and was received with boisterous enthusiasm. The King felt that he could not but pick up the gauntlet of her defiance, and so she was brought before the House of Lords to answer a charge that her 'scandalous, disgraceful and vicious conduct' had made her unworthy of the title and rights of Queen Consort. She answered the accusation of adultery with the spirited reply that she had only once committed adultery and that was with the husband of Mrs Fitz-herbert. It was a response which found wide sympathy, and, after proceedings lasting almost three months, the Government realised that they would never get their Bill of Pains and Penalties through the House of Commons and so the charge was withdrawn. The celebrations were immediate and rapturous; for three nights flam-

148

beaux and lights were kept burning all night in London and those who refused to express their joy had their windows smashed by the mob. The King, more than ever an object of ridicule, retired to Windsor, lonely and depressed.

Here in the grounds of the Great Park, to the designs of John Nash, he had converted a small house, formerly occupied by the Deputy-Ranger, into a large Gothic *cottage orné*, (see plate 33), officially known later as the Royal Lodge. Its roof was thatched and its windows mullioned; it was beautifully decorated and furnished; it was surrounded by newly planted trees and shrubs, and it was estimated to have cost £200,000.[11] Everything inside was in faultless taste, and the dinner parties the King gave there after his delayed coronation were both lavish and amusing. For His Majesty was, by general if sometimes grudging consent, still an excellent host, attentive, entertaining and constitutionally generous. He had always been so, undeniably, but the worries of his middle age and the gloom of his recent career, had driven him to long moods of despondency and irritation, while the proceedings against the Queen had exhausted him. The coronation, though, had been a tonic. It was, in the first place, a magnificent and moving spectacle; and the King, gorgeously attired and looking unusually virile, was greeted with an enthusiasm which he had long since grown accustomed to believe was the prerogative of his enemies. Public memory is as short as public allegiance, and both, of course, are clouded and overcast by the emotions of the moment. As the cheers of the people rose above the boom of the guns, Queen Caroline who had unsuccessfully demanded to be crowned with her husband presented herself at Westminster Abbey and asked at least to be admitted. She was jeered derisively. She drove back to Piccadilly and the spectators shouted at her that she ought not to stop there but go on back to Italy. A few weeks later she was dead.

*　　*　　*

The King, released after twenty-five years from the humiliations of a disastrous marriage, and encouraged by triumphant visits to Ireland and Scotland, felt a resurgence of a youthful *joie de vivre*. His wonderful gift for mimicry was unimpaired, and the charm of his conversation, when too much drink had not made him excessively garrulous, remained fascinating. He had always taken great pains to make even the least brilliant of his guests feel at ease with him, and although he clearly preferred the conversation and company of such witty, worldly, scintillating men as Charles James Fox and Richard Brinsley Sheridan, of Beau Brummel and the Duke of Orléans, of amusing, vulgar women like Lady Lade and the Earl of Barrymore's swearing sister, 'Billingsgate', of cheeky jockeys, sprightly actresses and *jouisseurs*, his ability to disarm a man of Dr Burney's more staid character had never failed him. Dr Burney, indeed, was 'astonished to find him amidst such constant dissipation possessed of so much learning, wit, knowledge of books in general, discrimination of character, as well as original humour. . . . He may with truth be said to have as much wit as Charles II with much more learning.'[12] He spoke knowledgably about music for half an hour, and then for a further half-hour about Greek literature to Dr Burney's son.

It was not an affectation. He had a real interest books and music, as in architecture and painting, furniture and in objects of art. And his taste rarely faltered. His collection of pictures, chosen with great care and discrimination, might alone now be said to justify all his other inordinate extravagances, while his patronage of great artists like Gainsborough and Sir Thomas Lawrence, his encouragement of sculptors and architects and those writers like Sir Walter Scott and Jane Austen from whom political antagonism had not estranged him, went a long way to excuse the shortcomings of a man, who, as Dorothea de Lieven, the Russian Ambassador's wife said, while not bad in himself was 'capable of bad actions'. 'He was,' she added, 'full of vanity and could be flattered at will. Weary of all the joys of life, having only taste, not one true sentiment, he was hardly susceptible to attachment, and never I believe sincerely inspired anyone with it. . . . No one trusted him.' Yet, Dorothea de Lieven had 'never known a person like him, who was also affectionate, sympathetic and gallant'.[13] This fragmentation of his character, at once selfish and generous, vain yet sensitive, occasionally vindictive and heartless as well as sincerely good-natured and kind, was also commented upon by the Duke of Wellington. He was, the Duke said, the 'most extraordinary compound of talent, wit, buffoonery, obstinacy and good feeling – in short a medley of the most opposing qualities, with a great preponderance of good' that he had ever known in his life.[14] Thackeray confessed that he could see nothing of George IV behind the clothes, beyond the bow and the grin. 'There must be something behind, but what?'[15]

There *was* something, though, behind the clothes and the bow and the grin. His frustrated sisters adored him. His difficult mother forgave him and grew to love and respect him; and she died holding his hand. His tiresome brothers quarrelled with him from time to time, but the fault was theirs more than his own. His behaviour to his father was often cruel, but George III was not a father likely to inspire obedience or devotion in a high-spirited, sensual son; and the gulf between the two mutually antagonistic characters was not so deep that the son could not cry when he visited his father, old and frail, and saw him so pathetically and helplessly insane.[16] He fell out with Sheridan and Brummell. But he offered Sheridan an apartment in Carlton House and sent him £500 in his last illness; and Brummell was a highly provocative man. The King was unfaithful to his wife as well as to Mrs Fitzherbert, but he never suggested that he would remain faithful to Caroline and he died with Mrs Fitzherbert's picture round his neck. To his other mistresses he gave more loyalty and affection than they had any reason to expect; and it was not, in any case, an age in which fidelity was a common virtue, nor did he come from a family whose forbears had ever shown much inclination to faithfulness.

He was flamboyantly self-indulgent, of course; but he raised £50,000 so that his brother, the Duke of York, could settle his debts, and asked him never to refer to the gift as he wished the rest of their lives to be spent 'in uninterrupted friendship and the warmest affection'; and he gave £15,000 to Charles Arbuthnot to settle debts incurred as Ambassador at Constantinople, saying, 'Take this and never let the subject be mentioned again and, above all, do not let it cause any shyness or embarrassment between us.' It could not have been done, Mrs Arbuthnot decided, 'with more kindness and delicacy'. But then, the King was always 'kind and good-natured', when he acted upon his impulses and had 'no ill-natured person to check him'.[17]

This kindness and humanity is reflected in his sensitivity to the sufferings of animals in an age when they were tortured for sport,[18] his refusing to go to another boxing match after seeing a prize-fighter killed in the ring at Brighton,[19] and above all in the support he gave to the reform of the criminal code and in the numbers of death sentences he commuted. Often he would write to his Ministers insisting on his right to exercise his prerogative of mercy; once he sat up most of the night with his mistress trying to devise a way of saving a man from being hanged; and there is something both revealing and touching in the story of his sending for Peel in the middle of the night because the imminent execution of a criminal upset him so. Peel agreed to pardon him and the King excitedly kissed him; then, noticing the poor quality of the Home Secretary's dressing-gown, he said suddenly, 'Peel, where *did* you get that dressing-gown. I'll show you what a dressing-gown ought to be.' And he made Peel put on one of his own.[20]

His Ministers found him trivial and vain; and he had, indeed, where matters of State were concerned, an undeniably frivolous mind. Like many kings before and after him he set great store by the observance of what to outsiders seemed the absurd rigmarole of protocol and the petty rules of dress. Nothing appeared to upset him so much, when Caroline returned from the Continent, as that she rode in a carriage through the streets of London sitting next to 'that beast Wood', an alderman who was a chemist. And nothing appeared to upset him as much at a ball as that an officer should be improperly dressed. Once, seeing Lord Charles Russell without the regulation aiguillette, he called out in a loud voice, 'Good evening, sir. I suppose you are the regimental doctor.'[21]

His vanity was legendary, and one of its least distressing manifestations was his affected belief that he was to a considerable extent responsible for all the triumphs of the age which had been named after him, including the military and naval ones, victories that were attributable to his 'own original and indefatigable exertions'.[22] Roger Fulford, whose excellent biography of George IV provides a just and sympathetic portrait, describes as 'whimsically attractive and essentially human', as they certainly are, the particular interests of the King on the battlefield of Waterloo. While Wellington described in detail the dispositions of the armies and their tactical movements, and while the King's secretary spoke solemnly of the possibility that the blades of grass on which they stood formed 'part of some warrior's frame', the King was much more interested in poking about for Lord Anglesey's leg and in framing an inscription – GEORGIO AUGUSTO EUROPAE LIBERATORI – for a bench he proposed to make from the trunk of a battle-scarred tree.[23]

Far less attractive, though, is the King's blind indifference to practically all the aspirations of the country's more enlightened politicians. His only political objects were to avoid trouble, to indulge his own whims and prejudices, and to ensure the continuance of royal patronage. It was a selfish programme which might be said to justify his unpopularity. He handed on 'a great inheritance to his successor', as Professor Webster has said. But it was the monarchy, rather than the monarch, which had the deep reserves of power which enabled him to do so.

The youthful association with the Whigs that had enraged his father was more the result of personal predilections than political convictions. As Prince Regent he became an obstinate Tory, and as King he developed into a constitutional monarch, and all the time his opinions were a reflection of his friendships, prejudices and lazy selfishness.

He objected to George Canning succeeding to the Foreign Office when Lord Castlereagh cut his throat, partly because he thought Canning too liberal, partly because he did not approve of his views on Catholic emancipation, but mainly, it seems, because he had opposed the proceedings against Caroline, with whom, he believed, he had had an affair. Nor, when the King was obliged to accept Canning into the Cabinet, did he scruple to invite to the Royal Lodge the Princes Esterhazy and Polignac and Count Christopher Lieven, representatives of Austria, France and Russia, the most powerful reactionary governments in Europe.

The conversations he had there with them were not, however, as dangerous to the future of Europe as many liberals were inclined to suppose. For the amusement of her lover Prince Metternich, Countess Lieven recorded their extraordinary nature:

His Majesty: My dear I'm no ordinary man; and − as for you − you've more intelligence in your little finger than all my subjects put together. I said 'little finger' because I did not want to say 'thumb'. Now you, my dear, who are *so* intelligent, you must admit I am not a fool.
Myself: Indeed, Sir, I wish I could tell you what I think without descending to commonplace flattery. Obviously your Majesty is a very remarkable man.
His Majesty: That's true. You have no conception of the ideas which sometimes go through my head. I have seen everything in a flash. I'm no mystery-monger; but I am a philosopher. Nesselrode [Russian Secretary for Foreign Affairs] is an honest fellow; but Capo d'Istria [Russian statesman from Corfu and Nesselrode's colleague] is a rascal. . . . Lieven, I've just been saying that Capo d'Istria is a rascal; but (*sotto voce to me*) one of these days soon I shall be sending the Emperor a certain document − something really memorable − quite unprecedented − a document that will make a tremendous effect. I composed it myself; but I shall not tell you what it is. No good making those charming eyes at me. You won't discover. My dear, if I had a difficult negotiation on hand, I should entrust it to you in preference to anybody else. (*To the Princess Augusta*) Sister, I drink to your health. Long live wine. I say, Long live women. 'Long live wine, long live men', you will retort. Gentlemen (*addressing the whole company*), the finest supporter of the throne, the one man . . . (*Here the King stops short, joins his hands, lifts his eyes to Heaven and moves his lips as if he were reciting a prayer. Then to Princess Esterhazy*) My dear child, do you know the story of the tailor who was

perpetually dropping his wife into the Seine? Very well, I'm the tailor. You don't understand me, but Madame de Lieven does – I can see that from the corner of her mouth.
Myself: I understand the moral of the story, Sir. (*What story or what moral, I had no idea. But it didn't matter; he had no more idea than I had.*)[24]

On another occasion, the King was 'in a more talkative mood than ever', Countess Lieven said.

I wish I could remember his ideas and the order in which he gave them. I know that three times I bit my lip so as not to laugh, and that I ended up by eating all the orange peel I could find, so as to give my mouth something to do to hide its twitching if the danger grew too great. . . . We had Poland, mystery-mongers, M. de la Harpe, the Don Cossaks, a great deal about gold, my wit, the Hanoverian Sappers who wear green aprons with gold fringes, Benjamin Constant and Madame de Deken, the Hungarian infantry and the prophecies of the King in 1814, Jesus Christ and the Emperor Alexander. . . . The whole speech was addressed to me; but in a tone of voice which obliged everyone close to listen in silence. We should still be there, if Admiral Nagle had not begun to snore so loudly that the King lost his patience and broke up the meeting.[25]

Eventually the King promised Canning that the 'continental gossipings' at the Royal Lodge would come to an end. But here again, he was not so much influenced by a change of heart as by the knowledge that Canning's policy had improved his own prestige in Europe, by the recognition of Canning as a man with much of Fox's wit and charm, and by gratitude for his having appointed as his Under Secretary one of the sons of the woman with whom he shared the last years of his life, and for having despatched her tiresome lover on a diplomatic mission to South America.[26]

* * *

This woman was Lady Conyngham, with whom he fell in love so helplessly that to many observers he seemed not merely embarrassing but even disgusting in his mawkish sentimentality. Both he and his new companion were over fifty and yet he behaved towards this far from beautiful, far from amusing, rather fat, kindly but rapacious mother of five grown-up children, as if he had been a boy again and she a brilliant beauty. Mrs Arbuthnot, the highly intelligent but somewhat priggish High Tory friend of the Duke of Wellington, thought it was all 'very ridiculous', and thoroughly indecent. She recorded with distaste in her diary that at a ball in the summer of 1821, the

King made a complete fool of himself, remaining by Lady Conyngham's side all evening and at last shutting himself up in a room with
her and placing a page outside the door with instructions to let no
one in.[27] He made no secret of his passion, which was reported to all
the foreign Chancelleries of Europe where these matters receive that
proper importance which is considered improper in England.[28]
Dorothea de Lieven told the Duke of Wellington that she had sat
next to the King while Lady Conyngham sat on his other side. The
King had said to Madame de Lieven that 'he had never known what
it was to be in love before, that he was himself quite surprised at the
degree to which he was in love, that he did nothing from morning
till night but think what he could do to please Lady Conyngham and
make her happy, that he would do anything upon earth for her . . .
and that she was an angel sent from Heaven for him. He cried, Lady
Conyngham cried, and Madame de Lieven said later, being nervous
and easily agitated, she had cried also; and all this passed in a crowded
Drawing-Room'.[29]

A few weeks later to Mrs Arbuthnot's horror, the King drove
down from Carlton House to the Royal Lodge at Windsor with Lady
Conyngham '*tête-à-tête* in his carriage' to spend a day alone with her
there. Mrs Arbuthnot could 'hardly believe this', when the Duke of
Wellington told her, but he assured her it was true. 'Lady Conyngham has no sense of shame about her connection with the King,' Mrs
Arbuthnot went on, 'she continually boasts of her influence over
him.'[30]

The influence was certainly considerable. And in time she 'gained
the summit of her ambition', according to a correspondent quoted in
the memoirs of Lady Charlotte Bury (who did not like her any more
than Mrs Arbuthnot did) and she had 'all the honours paid to her as
a royal mistress'.[31]

Her whole family came to Court. Her husband was made a Marquess and, on Lord Hertford's retirement, the King wanted to make
him Lord Chamberlain as well. This, however, Lord Liverpool, the
Prime Minister, would not consider, despite the King's protestation
that 'Whatever appointments the King may think proper to make in
his own family, they are to be considered as quite independent of the
control of any Minister whatever.'[32] As a result of Lord Liverpool's
refusal to agree to Lord Conyngham's appointment as Lord Chamberlain, the King demanded that he should be appointed Master of the
Horse. Again Lord Liverpool objected. Already the Conynghams
used the horses and carriages from the royal stables whenever they

liked,[33] and the idea of driving them about in the royal liveries was unthinkable. Obviously, though, some appointment must be found for him. 'After all,' as the Duke of Wellington sensibly observed to Lady Conyngham herself, 'you are going abroad with the King; and depend upon it, the first remark at all the courts you go to will be, "Who the Devil's Lady Conyngham? What post does she hold? What business has she with the King?" All of which would be easily answered if Lord Conyngham was in the Household.'[34] It was an argument which Lord Liverpool could not overlook, and so he agreed to Conyngham's being appointed Lord Steward of the Household.

His children benefited from his wife's position, too. One of his sons, 'a very good boy', in the King's opinion, although there was 'nothing in him',[35] became Master of the Robes and later Under Secretary for Foreign Affairs; another son, through the King's influence, was offered the command of the Clare Militia; his eldest daughter, whom the King himself was rumoured as wanting for a wife,[36] for he generally took her into dinner with her mother 'and divided his presents between them',[37] married Lord Strathavon from the Royal Lodge. Even the sons' tutor, the Rev. Charles Richard Sumner, who had, to the grateful Lady Conyngham's relief, married a Swiss girl with whom her eldest son had fallen unsuitably in love, was appointed a bishop when Lord Liverpool refused to sanction the King's offer to him of a canonry at Windsor.[38]

It did not appear, however, that Lady Conyngham's new life at Windsor and the favours which it enabled her to bestow upon her family, made her happy. Charles Greville, the accomplished, observant and fastidious Clerk-in-Ordinary to the Privy Council, whose diary is one of the most entertaining and revealing of the nineteenth century, says that at a party which he attended at the Royal Lodge she looked 'bored to death'. The King, delighted with some Tyrolean singers and dancers that his friend Prince Paul Esterhazy had brought down to entertain him, was obviously enjoying himself immensely. The women kissed his cheek, the men kissed his hand and he, speaking to them in German and to his guests in English, never stopped talking. Lady Conyngham, however, never spoke at all.[39]

It was her own fault, though, people believed, if she were bored, since she had succeeded in excluding from Windsor most of the King's former gay friends. The Duke of Wellington told her, when she confessed to him that she found life so tedious she felt she could no longer stay with the King at Windsor, that the blame was entirely hers. She could have a hundred people there every day if she wanted to; and to suggest that she was 'afraid of her character', as she had begun to do, was surely a little late in the day.[40]

Her frustrations drove her, the Duke noticed, to behaviour which was 'really quite shocking'. The King was still most attentive to her, but she 'shrugged her shoulders at him and seemed quite to loathe him, so much so that everybody observed it. She told the Duke that the whole thing bored her to death and that she would go away and have done with it. The Duke said to her, "If you had asked my advice in the beginning as to whether you should get into the scrape or not, I would have urged and advised you by all means to keep out of it; but, now that you are established here, that it has been entirely your own seeking, that you have driven out everybody who used to be here, for God Almighty's sake don't make a fresh scandal by leaving him."'[41] Sulkily she replied that the country should feel greatly indebted to her, for if she had not taken the King from Lady Hertford he would certainly have married her. But she had, so Mrs Arbuthnot believed, no real intention of leaving, anyway. She grew more and more 'wonderfully haughty and high and mighty'. She made less and less effort to disguise her boredom and her irritation with the King, but she would never leave him, continuing to content herself with the nursing of her grievances and ill-humour and continuing to accept all his presents.[42] 'She does not love him,' Madame de Lieven, writing from the Royal Lodge, told Prince Metternich, 'and she shows her distaste for him; he sees it, but although he thinks she is a fool, and has told her so a score of times, he feels he is too old to contract fresh habits; and a habit he must have. Wellington and I have been laughing together like children. This really is a madhouse.' The trouble with Lady Conyngham was, so Dorothea de Lieven concluded, that 'though she can do without sentiments, she can't do without diamonds'.[43]

The King, while remaining for the time being patient and loving in the face of all Lady Conyngham's exasperating provocations, did not, however, preserve this tolerant demeanour with the other person whose influence with him was greater even than her own. The equivocal relationship between this person, Sir William Knighton, and the King has never been satisfactorily explained.

Knighton had begun life as an apothecary in Plymouth and had earned a high reputation as an *accoucheur*, in which capacity he attended the mistress of Lord Wellesley, 'the Epicurean brother of the Spartan general', described very well by the King as 'a Spanish grandee grafted on an Irish potato'.[44] Wellesley recommended Knighton to the King, whose passion for gossip, so it was said, was gratified by a man who entertained him with details of 'all the complaints of all the ladies that consult him'.[45] It was not, though, because Knighton was supposedly a skilful doctor that the King took him into his Household, nor because he was in a position to provide him with physiological tittle-tattle.

Charles Greville thought, from what Lady Conyngham's son, Lord Mount Charles, told him, that there was 'some secret chain' which bound them together, which compelled the King to submit to the presence of a man he detested and which induced Knighton to remain in spite of so much hatred and ill-usage. Greville could not make out exactly what that secret chain was, but he could not otherwise account for the King's behaviour. According to Mount Charles, the King abhorred Knighton with 'a detestation that could hardly be described'. He was afraid of him and that was the reason why he hated him so bitterly. He delighted in saying the most mortifying and disagreeable things to him. Once he cried out, 'I wish to God somebody would assassinate Knighton';[46] and Greville himself once heard the King say at an unusually boisterous party, 'I would give ten guineas to see Knighton walk into the room now.'[47]

Thomas Bachelor, who had for many years been the Duke of York's valet and who was later appointed Page of the Back Stairs to George IV, confirmed Mount Charles's opinion. Bachelor spoke about Knighton to Greville, whose enjoyment of backstairs gossip was as great as the King's, with 'a sort of mysterious awe, mixed with dislike, which was curious'. Talking 'as if the walls had ears', Bachelor confirmed that the King hated Knighton but that his influence was without any limit, 'that he could do anything and without him nothing could be done; that after him Lady Conyngham was all-powerful, but in entire subservience to him; that she did not dare have anyone dine there without previously ascertaining that Knighton would not disapprove of it'.[48]

Charles Arbuthnot, who as Joint Secretary to the Treasury and Patronage Secretary was often at Windsor, believed that the King feared and hated Knighton 'as a madman hates his keeper'. He was 'perpetually talking at him' and at dinner one day 'jeered at him for not understanding French, which nettled Knighton extremely'.[49] And yet the King in a letter to Lord Liverpool supported Knighton's claims to be made a Privy Councillor with a scarcely less than vehement determination. 'You are already acquainted with my feelings relative to the admission of my invaluable friend Sir Wm Knighton into the Privy Council. The thing is so proper and so just that I wish to have no conversation on the subject.'⁵⁰ Lord Liverpool, however, refused to consider the appointment, and yet the King, Knighton complained to Arbuthnot, seemed not in the least annoyed about the refusal – 'on the contrary was rather pleased'.⁵¹ Knighton, on another occasion it seems, 'abused the King, called him a great beast who liked nothing so much as indecent conversation and that, in that respect, Lady Conyngham managed him well for he dared not do it in her presence. He said he had no regard for anybody but himself and did not care a pin whether he was in the Privy Council or not.'⁵²

On the same day as Knighton relieved his feelings by this outburst, the King revealed to Arbuthnot his version of the reason for the curious relationship between himself and 'a fellow who fifteen years ago' (the comment is Mrs Arbuthnot's) 'carried phials and pill boxes about the town of Plymouth'.

Some time after his secretary Colonel McMahon died, the King said, Knighton asked for an audience. He was received and he immediately asked whether McMahon had ever mentioned him. 'The King said, Yes, he had heard McMahom mention him as a friend but nothing particular. Upon which Knighton said, "Your Royal Highness is not aware that I have done the business of Mr McMahon for some years and that I am the depository of all your Royal Highness's most secret affairs, and perfectly acquainted with every part of your concerns."' The King went on to tell Arbuthnot that he had given Knighton £25,000 which the doctor had said was not enough and so had been obliged to give him £25,000 more. Even this was not sufficient. For there was apparently 'a place in the Duchy of Cornwall' which Knighton wanted to be taken from McMahon's successor, Benjamin Bloomfield, and given to him. This cost the King a further £12,000 in compensation to Bloomfield, 'making altogether £62,000'. Knighton was certainly very clever, the King admitted, and when Bloomfield became a Methodist and hung a great white placard outside his door with the words 'At Prayer' written on it and showed other signs of oddity – apart from a very ill temper – and was dismissed, Knighton succeeded him, managing everything 'excessively well'. He was, though, 'very absurd'. 'He fancies that being in the Privy Council will raise him in society, and that the foreign Ministers and people who come here will show him more respect when they know he is a Privy Councillor,' the King concluded. 'He is very much mistaken. He does not know how to behave himself in good company, and he will never be the least raised by honours and titles.'⁵³

It was certainly true that Knighton was ambitious. When he realised how little he might expect from Lord Liverpool, he began to cultivate George Canning, at that time Foreign Secretary and the most influential member of the more liberal-minded section of the Tory administration. Canning was responsive. He let Knighton know, through his Under-Secretary, Lord Francis Conyngham, that he personally regretted that the Prime Minister had not agreed to his becoming a Privy Councillor and when Knighton, whom the King had already created a Knight Grand Cross of his Royal Guelphic Order, asked to be made one of the Vice-Chancellors of the Duchy of Lancaster, with a salary and fees amounting to £1,500 a year, Canning gave his support. Lord Liverpool once more, however, gave an immediate refusal to the King's importunate secretary; and the King, to Knighton's renewed anger, appeared indifferent.

He was, in fact, becoming increasingly indifferent by now to most things. And it was this indifference and laziness that made Knighton so indispensable to him. Despite all that he said against the strange doctor and all that others believed about him, Knighton was, though ambitious, irritating, pompous and affected, a good and conscientious servant. His position naturally made him the object of suspicion and jealousy, and inevitably the centre of intrigue. But, as Charles Greville noticed, he was 'the only man who could prevail upon the King to sign papers, etc.'. There was, nevertheless, something more than necessity that bound the two men together. Their relationship resembled more that of exasperated father and wayward son than master and servant. They quarrelled; Knighton complained of the King's ingratitude, the King insulted Knighton and told lies about him; the secretary went away to sulk; but he returned in the end with a Bible in his hand to lay by the royal bed.

When Knighton was away, the King became more wayward than ever.

His greatest delight [Greville angrily complained] is to make those who have business to transact with him, or to lay papers before him, wait for hours in the ante-room while he is lounging with Mount Charles or anybody, talking of horses or any trivial matter; and when Mount Charles has said, 'Sir, there is Watson waiting, etc,' he replied, 'Damn Watson, let him wait.' He does it on purpose and likes it. . . . A more contemptible cowardly, selfish, unfeeling dog does not exist than the King, on whom much flattery is constantly lavished. He has a sort of capricious good nature, arising, however, out of no good principle or good feeling, but which is of use to him, as it cancels often in a moment and at small cost a long score of misconduct.

23. Frogmore
from the engraving by W. J. Bennett after C. Wild in W. H. Pyne,
History of the Royal Residences, 1819

24. The Dining Room at Frogmore
from the engraving by T. Sutherland after C. Wild in W. H. Pyne,
History of the Royal Residences, 1819

25. George IV
from the engraving by E. Scriven after George Atkinson

Princes have only to behave with common decency and prudence, and they are sure to be popular, for there is a great and general disposition to pay court to them. I do not know of anybody who is proof against their seductions when they think fit to use them in the shape of civility or condescension. . . . There have been good and wise kings, but not many of them. Take them one with another, they are of an inferior character, and this I believe to be one of the worst of the kind. . . . There never was such a man or behaviour so atrocious as his — a mixture of narrow-mindedness, selfishness, truckling, blustering, and duplicity with no objects but self, his own ease and the gratification of his own fancies and prejudices.[54]

This harsh and aggravated judgment was one which found wide acceptance; for the King, who hated to be unpopular, whose character was unsuited to bear dislike without loss of self-esteem, took little trouble to make himself admired or respected. He shut himself away at Windsor to escape the attention of a people who, since the brief spell of popularity that had surrounded his coronation and despite the cheers that greeted his appearances at the theatre or at Ascot races, seemed once more to have turned against him. And the further he retired into seclusion the less he was liked. People gossiped about the trouble he took not to be seen when he went for a ride in the Park, how the ponies' heads would be turned sharply round if anyone was sighted on the road, how he always used private roads when he could, how he was constantly planting new avenues 'from which the public were wholly excluded', how furious he became when workmen or maid-servants stared at him when he drove out of the Lodge or Castle to Sandpit-gate Lodge (see plate 32), where he liked to visit the animals in his menagerie and then come back to sit in his pony chaise with his favourite cockatoo on his arm and a glass of cherry-gin ('which was always kept in preparation for him') in his hand.[55]

He was fatter than ever since he had abandoned the diet that his love for Lady Conyngham had imposed upon his vanity, and this distressed him. And after the autumn of 1822, when he became ill again and his legs began to swell and he showed symptoms of dropsy and was constantly sweating, he became more and more depressed and disinclined to show himself.

Madame de Lieven during a visit to the Royal Lodge in 1823 described the extraordinary life that was now led there. It was raining in torrents and field mice came in from the garden and ran about the rooms; the King was limping and often in tears; and one night he began to sing and 'in order to produce the sole musical sound of which his throat is capable he closed his eyes, shed tears'. Madame de

Lieven got up at nine, went out into the garden, went into luncheon with the King between eleven o'clock and one, went out for a drive or on the river between two and four and then came back for dinner.

After dinner the piano [she told Prince Metternich]. After the piano, *écarté*, and at twelve to bed. Occasionally, the conversation is interesting; but usually, it is so stupid that one begins to doubt one's own intelligence. I look into my mind and, honestly, I find nothing in it; if you were to beat me you would not get a sensible idea out of me.* I was reflecting yesterday that there were better ways of spending an evening, and I remembered Verona. At this moment I looked up: the King was gazing at Lady Conyngham with an expression in which commonsense battled against love: Lady Conyngham was gazing at a beautiful emerald on her arm; her daughter was toying with a ruby laying round her neck. . . . I was very close to tears.

The following day, unable to control herself any longer, she was seized with a fit of laughter during grace 'after the first glass of sherry, when everyone is supposed to be silent'.

The daughter who is always ready to laugh, caught it from me [she said], and old Admiral Nagle could not contain himself. Fortunately, he upset a bottle, which gave us an excellent excuse to go on laughing, and even get worse. The King was angry. He thought we were laughing at him. I did not mind; for the moment I was beyond caring. He could not scold me, so he scolded the daughter. Afterwards, we played fourteen games of *écarté* and thirty-three games of patience.[57]

To overcome his depression and alleviate his boredom, the King began to drink heavily. According to the Duke of Wellington 'the quantity of Cherry brandy he drank was not to be believed' and without it he could not bring himself to eat anything. As the months passed it became more and more difficult for his Ministers to get him to concentrate on matters of State. He was 'extraordinarily ingenious in turning the conversation from any subject he did not like', so Wellington said, and it was often impossible to discover what his true feelings about it were.

There were, however, two matters upon which the strength of his

* Chateaubriand believed that there never were any sensible ideas in her anyway. 'She was thought to have wit,' he wrote, 'because her husband was supposed to have none, which was not true. . . . Madame de Lieven . . . with sharp, unprepossessing features, is a commonplace, wearisome, arid woman, who has only one style of conversation: vulgar politics; for the rest, she knows nothing and she hides the dearth of her ideas under the abundance of her words: when she finds herself with people of merit, her sterility is silent; she invests her nullity with a superior air of boredom, as though she had the right to be bored.'[56] It should be added in her defence, though, that Metternich and Guizot, as well as George IV, found her much more entertaining.

feelings was never in doubt. One was Roman Catholic emancipation, a reform which, encouraged by his brother the Duke of Cumberland, he opposed with all the vehemence of his father, becoming so heated about it that Mount Charles 'verily believed he would go mad', as, once he got on to the subject, there was 'no stopping him'.[58] The other was the necessity of transforming Windsor Castle into a palace suitable for the kings of the greatest country in Europe.

[iv]

GEORGE IV – THE GOTHIC CASTLE

For the first few years of his reign he had lived always at the Royal Lodge, staying at Carlton House when he had to be in London and occasionally visiting Brighton. But the Royal Lodge was, in Greville's words, although a 'delightful place to live in', too small 'for very large parties'. And so in the summer of 1823 the King decided to close the terraces of the Castle – except on Sundays – and to stop the people of Windsor walking and playing in the Home Park. In the autumn, having given orders for the demolition of Queen's Lodge, he moved into the Castle for two months to see what living there was like, choosing to occupy the rooms that his mother and sisters had used rather than the gloomier north front which his father had occupied and which was for the future to be reserved as State Apartments for distinguished visitors. Neither front, however, seemed to the King sufficiently splendid and dignified, and Parliament was asked to vote money for the extensive rebuilding which was considered necessary.

The scheme was approved and James Wyatt's nephew, Jeffrey Wyatt, was chosen as architect in charge of the reconstruction. Wyatt, a man of 'low stature and inelegant personal form, redeemed by liveliness of expression and sincerity of manner',[1] immediately moved into the Castle, to be ready to direct the labours of over five hundred workmen who were soon to start work on the Upper Ward. In August 1824 the King drove up from the Royal Lodge to lay the foundation stone of a new archway which was to bear his name and was met by Mr Wyatt, described now as 'a busy, bustling, vain little

163

man',[2] who asked him if he might change his name to Wyatville, to avoid confusion with other members of his family some of whom were mere builders. 'Ville or mutton,' the King is said to have replied cheerfully, 'call yourself what you like.'*[3]

Wyatville was soon in difficulties. His original estimate, submitted in competition with Robert Smirke and John Nash – John Sloane was also asked to compete but declined – was for £122,500. This figure seems to have been arrived at in a curiously unorthodox way. Before he was invited to submit his estimate by the commissioners appointed to supervise the work, Wyatville was asked by the King personally to draw up some designs. Later, so he said, the Chancellor of the Exchequer, one of the commissioners, told him that the Government could afford £150,000; and so he adjusted his estimate accordingly.[4]

From the beginning it was clear that this sum was completely inadequate. A further £150,000 was voted by Parliament and when it was obvious that even £300,000 was far from sufficient and had been greatly exceeded, Members began to show their alarm. They remembered the cost of the Pavilion at Brighton, 'a squanderous and lavish profusion which in a certain quarter resembled more the pomp and magnificence of a Persian satrap seated in all the splendour of Oriental state than the sober dignity of a British Prince'.[5] There was the cost, too, of reconstructing Buckingham House, a cost far from being covered by pulling down Carlton House and building private houses on its site and in its garden. Within a few years the cost of the works at Windsor rose to £800,000; and when they were asked to vote an additional £100,000, Parliament rebelled. Who could say, protested one Member, whether there would be any 'limit to such extravagance.' It was all very well for Henry Goulburn, the Chancellor of the Exchequer, to say that leaving the building unfinished would be 'a disgrace to the country'; but might not there be another demand next year for £300,000 or £400,000? Daniel O'Connell – who seemed to the King at least one very good reason for keeping Roman Catholics out of the House of Commons to which they had at last been admitted – said that he thought £100,000 would come in very useful in Ireland and there was 'abundant reason for opposing such profligate expenditure' at Windsor.[6]

---

* The morning after the change of name was announced the following verses appeared in a newspaper:
> Let George whose restlessness leaves nothing quiet
> Change, if he must, the good old name of Wyatt;
> But let us hope that their united skill
> Will not make Windsor Castle, 'Wyatt-ville.'

The Chancellor of the Exchequer was obliged to withdraw his motion and the Duke of Wellington, spelling the Chancellor's name with disdainful inaccuracy, reported his failure to Windsor. 'The question is a bad one,' Wellington continued. 'We are in the wrong for bringing forward for the third or fourth time a vote for a fresh grant without an estimate of the whole expense.'[7]

The rest of the Government was constrained to agree with him and a Select Committee was appointed to try to discover the likely amount of this expense. The original estimate was made, Wyatville reported to this Committee:

when the King was residing at the Castle. I could not go and strip the apartments to see the walls and timbers when the King was there, and therefore they were calculated, as any person might do, a probable expense. When the King retired, and I stripped the walls, the timbers were all found rotten, and necessarily the whole of the floors were removed . . . and the roof was in an equally bad state, and obliged to be taken off also, and many of the walls were cracked through, and many holes had been cut in, the Castle having been divided into different residences; it was very much dilapidated by each inhabitant cutting closets and cutting through the walls with out any regard to the destruction of it. Then when the roof was removed, as there was not sufficient room for the King's servants, advantage was taken to put the roof higher, and make another storey over, which of course would increase the estimate.

The Committee took Wyatville's point and as a large part of the £100,000 which was requested had, in fact, already been spent, they could not but recommend (while deploring the evident disregard of economy) that 'the complete repair of this ancient and Royal Residence', being an 'object of national concern', should be provided for. They also recommended 'for the sake of uniformity of character and design' that the works – of which, incidentally, they entertained 'a favourable opinion' – should be completed under the same direction.

Their favourable opinion of the works was not, however, shared by everyone who visited the Castle during the years of its reconstruction, and Wyatville's alterations and embellishments have been severely criticised since. No one could complain about the completion of the Long Walk, the beautiful elm-lined avenue which Charles II had begun in 1685 and which by the demolition of Queen's Lodge could now be taken through the new George IV Gate up into the Quadrangle. No one could complain, either, about the magnificent Grand Corridor which, providing a much needed covered way between the north front and the east, would have saved George III many a cold walk across the Quadrangle when he went to see his wife and daughters. No one should blame Wyatville – as he has often been blamed – for filling in the medieval ditch round the Castle, for this was done in the 1770s. But it was possible to complain about the somewhat arch manner in which Wyatville continued, on a much more ambitious and grandiose scale, the Gothicisation of the Castle which his uncle had begun in 1800, going so far as to introduce excessively picturesque machicolations to overhang the summit of his new towers, although examples of this architectural contrivance – originally designed for the medieval warrior so that he could accurately pour molten lead on his enemies from between the corbels – had hitherto been unknown at Windsor and were, in the nineteenth century, it was to be hoped, no longer of practical use.

Wyatville might also be criticised for his architectural *blague*. He inserted bogus portcullis-grooves in his gates; he cut long, straight indentations in his freestone blocks and filled them with mortar and flint chippings to give an impression of regularity at once improbable and unsightly; he increased the height of the Round Tower by providing a stone crown thirty feet higher than the former structure, and while this structure had already been much altered over the centuries, its original proportions were now destroyed for ever.

It can, however, be argued that while most of Wyatville's architectural deceits are inexcusable, an essentially Gothic structure demands Gothic treatment and even those to whom the Gothic taste does not appeal might agree that the drawing printed in plate 28 shows that Wyatville's work has successfully imparted to the Castle that appearance of solid grandeur which has made it one of the most distinctive monuments in the world.

Beset as he was with many difficulties both financial and structural, Wyatville achieved a great work [Sir Owen Morshead, Windsor Castle's most recent, learned and sympathetic historian has written] despite his natural limitations and the taste of the generation which his style reflects. When we admire Windsor from a distance it is Wyatville's Windsor that we see. He found a workhouse and he left a palace. He found 'the coldest house, rooms and passages that ever existed'; he left a warm, dry, comfortable, well-appointed house. He did his job so well, in fact, that nothing has needed to be done to it since.*[8]

* Sir Owen Morshead wrote this in 1951. The Ministry of Public Buildings and Works has spent £126,000 on the Castle in 1963–64. Most of this sum, however, has been spent in improving the internal fittings, and in installing a new central heating system to replace a defective one which was over a hundred years old.

Many of Wyatville's contemporaries thought that it was not, however, nearly grand enough despite the sumptuously gilded woodwork and plaster of the private apartments, the richly brocaded walls and the fine doors from Carlton House. Charles Greville decided that not enough had been 'effected for the enormous sums expended' when he went all over it in the summer of 1827. Although it was a 'fine house' it was still far from being a palace 'like Versailles, St Cloud and the other palaces in France'.[9] Nine months later John Wilson Croker walked round and thought the new work 'handsome and not inconvenient', but he, too, was expecting something far more imposing. 'After all, the rooms are by no means what they ought to be', he wrote. 'They are very handsome and even noble but they are neither in number and size what might have been produced for much less expense.'[10]

Thomas Creevey thought so, too. 'Went in the carriage yesterday to see all that is going on at Windsor,' he told his step-daughter, 'and Mr Wyat-*Ville* himself did us the honour of conducting us thro' all the new apartments and showing us all the projected improvements. All the New Living Rooms make a very good Gentleman's or Nobleman's house, Nothing more.' But he thought the Grand Corridor, '16 feet wide and 560 feet in length, above all price'.[11]

And once the Corridor was decorated and furnished, there were few who disagreed with him. Indeed, the resplendent decorations of the Castle as a whole, which reflected the King's taste more than Wyatville's, were almost universally admired, even though, as Croker said, they were perhaps more in the style of Louis XIV than accorded with the general character of Windsor. Wyatville, also, thought them too 'Frenchy' and was often persuaded with difficulty to incorporate some finely wrought door or fireplace from Carlton House in his designs. 'Wyatville hummed and hawed at first a good deal', when asked to incorporate some painted glass from Carlton House in the walls of a staircase, the King told Knighton. 'However, I brought him at last to say that he thought "he cud pleace soom of't to adwantage, though' e 'ad not joust thin fix'd where."'[12]

*　　*　　*

As well as collaborating on the reconstruction and redecoration of the Castle, George IV and Wyatville worked together on improving its surroundings. The East Terrace was laid out with a central pool surrounded by lawns, flower beds and groups of vases and statuary; the Moat Garden, south and west of the base of the Round Tower was cleared and improved and some miles across the Great Park to the south-east, ornamental temples were built to decorate the shores of a lovely artificial lake. (See plate 34).

This lake, known as Virginia Water, had been made by the King's great-uncle, the Duke of Cumberland ('Billy the Butcher' of Culloden) who for all his faults was a man of aesthetic sensibility. He had been made Ranger of Windsor Great Park after his return from Holland in 1758 and had given employment to as many discharged soldiers as he could find work for in building roads and planting trees and lawns. He lived at Cranbourne Lodge, the house which Nell Gwynn's grandson, the Duke of St Albans, had occupied as Lord-Warden of Windsor Forest; and his Deputy Ranger, Thomas Sandby, lived in the smaller house which the Regent had converted into the Royal Lodge. Sandby, the brother of the painter Paul Sandby, who shared the house with him and one of whose beautiful water colours of Windsor can be seen in plate 17, was responsible for the operations at Virginia Water, which were carried out with more artistry than practicability. In order to make the lake, he dammed the small rivulets with soft banks of sand and clay which during a heavy thunderstorm in 1768 were washed away by floods 'causing £9,000 worth of damage'.[13]

After the dams were rebuilt, a Chinese temple was put up on an island in the middle of the lake, and it was this that gave George IV the idea of building other ornamental temples around its shores. Wyatville helped him design a fishing temple, also a folly which was to be built out of various classical remains that had for some time been kept in a courtyard of the British Museum and which was to be decorated with Greek statues captured in a French frigate during the Napoleonic wars.

On warm days in the summer the King liked to drive down in his phaeton to Virginia Water followed by guests in landaus. When he reached the landing stage, his band seated in a boat moored in the lake, would strike up 'God Save the King' and he and his guests would step into a barge to spend an afternoon fishing or go aboard the junk, *The Mandarin*, which had been brought to Virginia Water by the Duke of Cumberland. Sometimes there were tents on the shore and the King's guests would have dinner in them while the band went on playing; and afterwards they would stroll on the lawns by the water's edge.[14]

Once the little Princess Victoria went with her uncle across the lake in his barge. It was in 1826 and she was seven and he asked her to kiss him, and more than half a century later she remembered it as being 'too disgusting because his face was covered in grease paint'. But he was kind and she had liked him then. She was staying at Cumberland Lodge, where most of his guests usually stayed, with her aunt the Duchess of Gloucester who took her over to the Royal Lodge.

'When we arrived,' she remembered, 'the King took me by the hand saying "Give me your little paw." He was large and gouty but with a wonderful dignity and charm of manner. He wore the wig which was so much worn in those days. Then he said he would give me something to wear, and that was his picture set in diamonds, which was worn by the Princesses as an order to a blue ribbon on the left shoulder. I was very proud of this — and Lady Conyngham pinned it on my shoulder.' The next day she went for a drive with her mother and they met the King who was driving his sister, the Duchess of Gloucester, to Virginia Water in his phaeton. 'And he said, "Pop her in" and I was lifted in and placed between him and aunt Gloucester who held me round the waist. (Mamma was much frightened.) I was greatly pleased.'

She was taken fishing; she was taken to see the King's menagerie at Sandpit Gate and she looked at the wapitis and chamois and gazelles; and in the evening she was allowed to go to listen to the band, which was playing in the conservatory by the light of coloured lamps. But best of all she liked going in the phaeton with her uncle and her aunt Gloucester.[15]

The King was sixty-three then and had only four more years to live; and these trips in his phaeton to Virginia Water were becoming more and more rare.

Most days at Windsor during the rest of his life were, in fact, spent indoors wearing flamboyant and not always very clean dressing gowns and turbans in stuffy, overheated rooms, reading, drinking cherry brandy and punch, dosing himself with laudanum, eating strange meals with quantities of pastry and vegetables at irregular times, talking to his pages and *valets de chambre*, to his stud groom, Jack Redford, or to O'Reilly, Surgeon to the Household.

Mount Charles told Greville that he led 'a most extraordinary life'. The curtains of his room were opened between six and seven. He had breakfast in bed and then 'read every newspaper quite through'. Occasionally he read a novel and was always pleased when a new book by Walter Scott came out. The rest of the morning was spent dozing. He rarely got up before six or seven o'clock in the evening, and when he felt too ill to get up at all, Lady Conyngham would visit him in his room. But otherwise she never entered it and he went to hers for an

hour or so[16] – not to make love, for 'he sought affection rather than
sensual delight';[17] and perhaps he never had made love to her, even in
the beginning. She still sometimes talked of leaving him, although
she remained incapable of doing so; and for hours on end when he
seemed really unwell she would devote herself to prayer. Once,
although like Mrs Fitzherbert she knew that 'he always wished everyone to think him dangerously ill when there was little the matter with
him',[18] she burst into tears on being told he was 'very ill'.[19] She and
Knighton were on better terms now and this, Greville thought, was
because the calculating Knighton opposed every kind of expense
except that which was 'lavished on her'. The amount she had accumulated by savings and presents must have been 'enormous'.[20] The
malicious Lady Anne Hamilton said she had been 'very credibly informed' that the total sum was more than £500,000.[21] Certainly
Lady Conyngham's servants and those of her husband were all found
situations in the Royal Household so that they did not have to pay
their wages themselves, and even in London when the Conynghams
gave a dinner at Hamilton Place the food was cooked at St James's
and brought over by hackney coach in machines specially made for
this purpose.[22]

The Conynghams, nevertheless, were one of the least of the King's
extravagances. Apart from the cost of decorating and furnishing the
new rooms in the Castle – where the whole of the length of the
Corridor alone was furnished with the 'luxury of a drawing room, and
full of fine busts and bronzes, and entertaining pictures, portraits and
antiquities'[23] – the expenses incurred by the various departments of
the Household in the first half of 1829 were far in excess of the income. In the Master of the Robes's department alone there was an
excess of about £10,000, for the King loved his clothes and could not
be persuaded to economise on them. He thought nothing of spending
£800 on a cloak or £300 on a plain coat. 'This, of course, included
several journeys of the master tailor and his men backwards and forwards to Windsor, and they almost lived on the road.'[24] One of his
first acts on being made Prince Regent was to promote himself Field
Marshal and when he wore the uniform people noticed that even the
seams of the coat were heavily embroidered. It must have cost and
weighed, someone said, two hundred pounds.[25] For less formal occasions he had an immense variety of suits and coats, boots and breeches,
gloves and hats, some of which he designed himself. He could
rarely bring himself to part with any of them and after he was dead,
amongst the volumes of love letters (including copies of his own 'des-

criptive of the most furious passion') amongst the 'five hundred pocket-books of different dates, and in every one of them money', amongst the quantities of women's gloves, the 'vast number of wigs', the trinkets, the dirty handkerchiefs, the faded nosegays, the locks of women's hair 'of all colours and lengths, some having the powder and pomatum yet sticking to them', were found all the coats he had ever had for fifty years, scores of waistcoats, three hundred whips, 'canes without number, every sort of uniform, the costumes of all the orders in Europe, splendid furs, pelisses, etc., hunting coats and breeches', and, among many other things, a dozen pairs of new corduroy riding-breeches ordered from his tailor long after he had given up riding.[26]

His pages said that he could remember all these clothes and that he developed an old man's habit of asking for coats and trousers he had worn many years before.[27] He developed, too, the habit of pretending that he had taken part in events or shared feelings which were entirely outside his experience. He once said with a quite passionate sincerity that Lord Chesterfield had told him, 'Sir, you are the fourth Prince of Wales I have known, and I must give Your Royal Highness a piece of advice: stick to your father; as long as you adhere to your father you will be a great and happy man, but if you separate yourself from him, you will be nothing and an unhappy one. And by God, I never forgot that advice and acted upon it all my life.'[28]

In the last years he even liked to pretend that he had fought at Waterloo, won the Battle of Salamanca by leading a splendid charge with his Dragoons, and ridden Fleur-de-Lis for the Goodwood Cup.[29] Often when recalling these stirring events the tears would start to his eyes, and no one was quite sure that he had not persuaded himself that he had actually participated in them.

He had always been excessively emotional and as he grew older he became more and more maudlin, frequently bursting into tears, kissing envelopes and writing letters of grotesque sentimentality, especially when he was drunk.

The death of his favourite brother, the Duke of York, upset him profoundly. Even Charles Greville admitted that he 'showed great feeling about his brother and exceeding kindness in providing for his servants. . . . He gave £6,000 to pay immediate expenses and took many of the old servants into his own service.'[30]

He decided that the funeral, which was to be held at Windsor, should be a fitting tribute to the Duke's services. It was, in fact, a disaster. At least the undertaker's men were not 'unmistakably

171

drunk' as they had been at Princess Charlotte's funeral at Windsor, ten years before,[31] but the Chapel was bitterly cold and draughty and there was no matting or carpeting in the aisle, where for almost an hour several members of the Royal Family and most of the Cabinet waited shivering in the gloom. Peel advised old Lord Eldon, the Lord Chancellor, to stand on his cocked hat, which he did. The Dukes of Wellington, Sussex and Montrose all caught severe colds. Canning, who presumed that 'whoever filched the cloth or matting' from under their feet in the aisle had bets against the lives of the Cabinet,[32] contracted rheumatic fever. And the Bishop of Lincoln died. 'According to the gossips the common soldiers (who had no doubt been paraded for hours before) died at the rate of half a dozen a day.'[33]

And this was not all that the gossips said. But the rumours that were spread concerning the effects of the appalling inefficiency of the King's arrangements were harmless in comparison with those that went about some time later concerning the deceased Duke's younger brother, Ernest Augustus, Duke of Cumberland, the strange death of whose valet Sellis had so distressed George III.

It appeared that a Captain Thomas Garth of Melton Mowbray had filed an affidavit in Chancery maintaining that he had come into possession of certain documents which Sir Herbert Taylor, formerly George III's private secretary, had agreed to buy from him in exchange for an annuity of £3,000 a year and an undertaking to settle all his debts. Taylor, Garth contended, was trying to get these documents removed from the bank where they had been deposited, without fulfilling his part of the bargain. What these documents were was naturally the subject of excited speculation. The most persistent rumour was that they proved that Thomas Garth was the child of an incestuous relationship between the Duke of Cumberland and his sister, Princess Sophia. It was 'notorious', according to Greville, 'that the old Queen forbade the Duke access to the apartments of the Princess'.[34] This, however, may well have been due to the influence which the Queen thought the mysterious and reprobate Duke might have on a sister of whom, as his letters to the King when Prince Regent show, he was extremely fond and for whose welfare amidst the dreary 'constant scene of Windsor' he was obviously concerned.[35]

Greville, in any case, did not give credit to this rumour, preferring to believe another story that Garth was the Princess's son by 'some inferior person' in the Royal Household – the most commonly suggested person being Christopher Papendiek – and that the secret of his birth had been entrusted to General Thomas Garth, one of

George III's equerries, whose name he bore. It was Lady Caroline Thynne's more credible belief that General Garth himself was undoubtedly the father. As Mistress of the Robes to Queen Charlotte Lady Caroline was at Windsor when Princess Sophia, being ill, had been removed from the Lower Lodge to Queen's Lodge where she was put in a bedroom beneath General Garth's. 'Nine months from that time she was brought to bed.' The secret of her pregnancy was kept from the old King, who was told she was dropsical and, after the birth, that she had been cured by roast beef. 'This he swallowed and used to tell it to people, all of whom knew the truth, as "a very extraordinary thing".' People had doubted that Garth could be the father as he was so ugly and had a great claret mark on his face but this, Greville decided when he heard the story and believed that it satisfactorily contradicted his misapprehension about Papendiek, was 'no argument at all, for women fall in love with anything'. Certainly, as Lady Caroline knew, Princess Sophia, lonely and passionate, was very much in love with the old General, whom Sir Herbert Taylor had no doubt was the father.[36]

Even if the Duke had been shown to have been his sister's lover, though, the Garth scandal could scarcely have provided gossip more damaging to the Royal Family. And the King was said to be 'horribly annoyed by the business'. This in addition to the Catholic problem and followed by the suicide of Lord Graves, Comptroller of the Household to the Duke of Sussex, who cut his throat when he could no longer bear the thought of his wife (the mother of his ten children), having a well-publicised affair with his master's infamous brother, Cumberland, reduced the King to an almost constant state of nervousness and irritation.

He began to sleep very badly and seemed in permanent need of company and reassurance during the night, ringing his bell several times every hour to ask what the time was or to tell a valet to pour him out a glass of water, although there was a jug by his bed. He was frightened that there was something seriously wrong with his bladder, which gave him so much discomfort that he took far more laudanum than he should have done.[37] He had been drinking too much of it, in fact, for years and sometimes, so Mrs Arbuthnot said, passed 'the greater part of the twenty-four hours in a state of stupor'.[38] The Duke of Wellington, Mrs Arbuthnot's informant, said that he had been known to take two hundred drops in a single night. Frequently Ministers called to discuss business with him and found him incapacitated by the drug or by alcohol from doing so.

* * *

His doctors were far from being in agreement as to how the King should be treated and were on the worst possible terms with each other. Knighton, it was said, detested O'Reilly and distrusted his other colleague, Sir Henry Halford. The King, apparently, did not put much trust in either of them, always sending for Knighton when he was frightened; but Halford prescribed the opium and O'Reilly, although in his patient's opinion 'the damnedest liar in the world', brought him the gossip that he still longed to hear. When they both joined forces in advocating the use of a *bougie* for the King's urethral complaint, Knighton was furious, and justifiably so, for the *bougie* made the irritation worse than ever.

The King was a difficult patient, combining a nervous apprehension as to his condition with a refusal to adopt a way of life which might improve it. On occasions he would alarm his doctors by going almost black in the face as he tried to get his breath and, afraid that he was going to have a heart attack, they would give him a large glass of brandy, which made him feel so much better he would suddenly decide to go for a long ride in his carriage.

His mode of living during these last months of his life was 'really beyond belief', Mrs Arbuthnot thought:

One day [in the middle of April 1830], at the hour of the servants' dinner, he called the Page in and said, 'Now you are going to dinner. Go downstairs and cut me off just such a piece of beef as you would like to have yourself, cut from the part you like the best yourself, and bring it me up.' The Page accordingly went and fetched him an enormous quantity of roast beef, all of which he ate, and then slept for five hours.

One night he drank two glasses of hot ale and toast, three glasses of claret, some strawberries!!! and a glass of brandy. Last night they gave him some physic and, after it, he drank three glasses of port wine and a glass of brandy. No wonder he is likely to die! But they say he will have all these things and nobody can prevent him. I dare say the wine would not hurt him, for with the Evil (which all the Royal Family have) it is necessary, I believe, to have a great deal of high food, but the mixture of ale and strawberries is enough to kill a horse.[39]

He affected to believe that he would die at any minute, but after saying one day with a sort of reckless cheerfulness, 'You know, I shall be dead by Saturday,' he began to discuss the horses he wanted to buy for Ascot races. And when Halford told him that he was, indeed, going to die soon, he refused to accept the dismal verdict and replied that he was sure to recover.[40] On some days, though, he obviously doubted it. On 17 May 1830 Peel visited him and 'in the minds of both men was the thought that it would be their final inter-view, and all past animosities were put away'.[41] He had been very angry when Peel and the Duke of Wellington had resigned on Lord Liverpool's death thus forcing Canning to form a Government which included no sound Tories; and he had been angry, too, when after Canning's death Peel had come into office again as Home Secretary in the Duke of Wellington's government to support the Roman Catholic Relief Bill. But now all this was forgiven, and the two men spoke as friends. The King asked Peel to push his chair to the window and said, with characteristic self-dramatisation, that it was the last time he would be able to look out into the garden. 'You are just returned from your father's funeral,' he added, 'you will soon have to pay the like ceremony to me.'[42] Ten days later he made a similar remark to the Duke of Wellington.[43]

There was, indeed, little hope now for his recovery. His legs were scarified to take away the water, but they soon swelled up again. He continued to find it difficult to get his breath; and a Bill had to be passed – for he had begun to grow blind – to enable his signature to be fixed to documents by means of a stamp.

Momentarily he improved. On 9 June he was sitting up in bed talking with Knighton as though he were quite well and young again; and on 12 June the Duke of Wellington found him looking much better and stronger. He decided the following day that he was well enough to take the sacrament which Lady Conyngham and Sir William Knighton had between them managed to persuade him was of a deeper significance than he had formerly supposed. But he got better only to relapse again. He was so enormously fat now, 'like a feather bed', the Duchess of Gloucester said, and his heart was grow-ing weaker every day. When the Bishop of Chichester knelt by his bed and said the prayer for his recovery which was to be read in all churches the King said fervently, 'Amen! Amen! Amen!' and then added the touchingly predictable comment: 'It is in very good taste.'[44]

At about half-past three in the early morning of 26 June he sud-denly called out, 'Good God, what is this?' His page, Thomas Bachelor, ran towards the easy chair in which he had spent the night, his head resting on his hands across a table, for the palpitations of his heart prevented him from lying down. 'My boy,' he said, clutch-ing Bachelor's hand, 'my boy, this is death.'[45]

[v]

WILLIAM IV – THE RESPECTABLE OLD ADMIRAL

Before the King was buried Lady Conyngham had left the Castle, taking – so everyone in London believed although no one in Windsor seems actually to have seen her – wagonloads of treasure and, as Mrs Arbuthnot predicted, no sooner had she gone than she was scarcely ever 'thought of or heard of more'. 'Good riddance, say, I,' Miss Margaretta Brown, the sister-in-law of one of the Windsor canons, wrote emphatically in her diary, underlining each word with heavy strokes. 'I am glad we are going to have a Queen.'[1]

There were many, though, who welcomed the departure of Lady Conyngham without looking forward to the arrival of her successor. Queen Adelaide was 'frightful', Charles Greville thought, 'very ugly with a horrid complexion.' It was not an exceptional verdict. 'The Queen is even worse than I thought,' a woman told a friend after seeing her for the first time, 'a little insignificant person as ever I saw. She was dressed, as perhaps you will see by the papers "exceedingly plain", in bombazine, with a little shabby muslin collar, dyed Leghorn hat and leather shoes.'[2] The new King had married this unprepossessing daughter of the Duke of Saxe-Meiningen in 1818, seven years after breaking with Mrs Dorothea Jordan, a motherly actress, who had borne him ten illegitimate children. These children all came to live at Windsor with their wives and husbands so that by the summer of 1831 the Castle was 'quite full with *toute la bâtardise*'.[3] They were frequently quarrelling amongst themselves and with the King, to whom the sons were constantly appealing for more money and better titles. He gave them all £30,000 in addition to their allowances,[4] but this did not, apparently, prevent one of them, Lord Frederick FitzClarence, sending him a bill for £12,000 and 'flouncing off with 8 or 10 of the King's horses, half a dozen servants and 3 carriages without a word of notice' when the King refused to pay it.[5] Another son, George, created Earl of Munster in 1831, replied that he saw no use in having his picture 'when it was very probable that in less than three years it would be in a pawnbroker's shop', after the King had offered to sit for a portrait for him.[6] A son-in-law, Lord Errol, who had married Elizabeth FitzClarence and was accordingly

176

26. The East Front in 1824 before the alterations by Wyatville
from an original drawing in the Royal Library, Windsor Castle

27. The East Front and "Sunken Garden" in 1830
from a drawing on stone by C. Basebee

28. The North Front of the Upper Ward before and after the alterations by Wyatville from an original drawing in the Royal Library, Windsor Castle

made a Lord of the Bedchamber, Master of the Buckhounds and Master of the Horse, refused to have his official accounts inspected and, when this was insisted upon, he threatened to resign. The Queen pleaded with him to stay but he 'abused her so violently she threw herself on a sofa in his room in a flood of tears'. At dinner she put a bon-bon on his plate as a peace offering; but he threw it back on to hers.

The King himself did his best to keep out of the family quarrels. He was a good-natured man; and as soon as his brother died 'began immediately to do good-natured things'. One of his first acts was to invite Mrs Fitzherbert to Windsor where he 'treated her with the greatest respect, gave her permission to clothe her servants in the royal livery, placed implicit reliance in all her statements, and having sanctioned an arrangement by which all private papers were to be destroyed – with a few exceptions that were placed under seal at Coutts's banking-house – settled upon her an income of £6,000 a year'.[8]

William IV clearly loved being King and his excitement, enthusiasm and energy during the first few weeks of his reign were touchingly boyish. Without any conception of protocol he walked about London quite alone, nodding, brusquely yet cheerfully, to left and right, and one day in St James's Street the mob followed him and 'one of the common women threw her arms round him and kissed him'.[9] At George IV's funeral at Windsor he strode briskly into St George's Hall, shook Lord Strathavon (Lady Conyngham's son-in-law) heartily by the hand, repeatedly nodding to the other mourners. He talked 'all sorts of nonsense' to Prince George, the young son of his brother the Duke of Cumberland, the 'most mischievous child that ever was born', and then invited himself to dinner with the Duke of Wellington.[10]

The following week he was due to dine with the Duke again and, having taken the King of Württemberg down to Windsor, forgot all about it. At the hour the Duke was expecting him at Apsley House he was seen in an open carriage with the King of Württemberg, both of them covered in dust and being rattled along by sweating, panting horses to Grillon's Hotel.[11] The next morning he was back at Windsor, making preparations for a dinner to be held there in August. His 'chief gratification', the Duke of Buckingham said, 'was playing the hospitable host' and he entertained on an average two thousand persons a week.[12] Over a hundred guests were invited to dine in St George's Hall on his first birthday as king and three thousand in the Long Walk; and Charles Arbuthnot, who was one of them, thought it 'the finest thing he ever saw'. The King was in the highest spirits and made a 'very good speech'.[13] He was extremely fond of making speeches, but they were rarely as successful as this one apparently was, for his congenital lack of tact was preposterous.

One characteristic after-dinner speech has been recorded by Charles Greville. It was made during the Queen of Portugal's visit to Windsor, and, although the King did not approve of her having come to England, he was resolved to receive her with the greatest honours as he believed her to have been badly treated by Louis Phillipe, and he hated Louis Phillipe, as he did all Frenchmen, 'with a sort of Jack Tar animosity'. Having already made a 'panel of foolish speeches', in a more or less anti-French vein, he praised the Peninsular exploits of one of the regiments at Windsor and went on: 'Talking of France, I must say that whether at peace or at war with that country, I shall always consider her as our natural enemy, and whoever may be her King or *ruler*, I shall keep a watchful eye for the purpose of repressing her ambitious encroachments.' If 'He was not such an ass that nobody does anything but laugh at what he says,' Greville thought, 'this would be very important. Such as he is, it is nothing. "What can you expect" (as I forget who said) "from a man with a head like a pineapple?" His head is just of that shape.'[14]

Even when proposing a toast to a dinner guest in the Castle he could be extremely embarrassing. And Lady Bedingfield, woman of the Bedchamber to Queen Adelaide, recorded how 'terribly embarrassed' the Duke of Argyll was on one such occasion. The King for once, evidently, realised he was making his guest feel uncomfortable and quickly called out 'Doors!' which was the signal for the Queen and her Ladies to leave the dining-room.[15]

So far as practical politics were concerned, however, he seemed obligingly ready to follow his Ministers' advice.[16] It did not appear that he had any strong ambitions as a monarch and concerned himself happily with details as his father might more profitably have done. Immediately on his accession he announced, for instance, that he would 'change the uniform of the Guards and put all the cavalry into scarlet except the Blues'.[17] But while he shared his father's passion for the details of military uniforms, he did not seem at all anxious to insist that his ideas even about these should be put into effect. He was quite content to present himself as a bluff, simple, patriotic sailor without dangerous ambitions or aggravating pretensions; and to a large extent he succeeded. The Duke of Wellington, who thought, with good cause, that when, as Duke of Clarence, he had been Lord High Admiral, he had been 'a very bad head of the Navy' (the insult was turned and Wellington was called 'a lucky sergeant') now expressed himself as delighted with the King who behaved like a 'respectable old Admiral'. And certainly his people were prepared to welcome him if only for this small virtue of respectability. He had little 'information and strong prejudices', so the *Spectator* wrote of him when he was dead. 'A weak, ignorant, common-place sort of person . . . sufficiently conceited and strong-willed,' he was nevertheless 'to the last a popular sovereign'.[18]

To the people of Windsor he seemed a delightful one after George IV. Within a few weeks of his accession he threw the terraces and the drives in the Home Park once more open to the public, who were permitted to go anywhere they liked provided they did not walk immediately under the windows of the private apartments. 'Their majesties are accessible at all hours,' a visitor happily wrote, 'the apartments are open to everybody; there is no seclusion, no mystery, nothing to conceal.'[19] As well as demonstrating that he was less of a selfish recluse than his brother, the new King also showed his people that he was less extravagant. He pruned the Castle staff and dismissed the French cooks; he had the recently fitted but uneconomical gas installation pulled out; he replaced the German band by a smaller English one; he pulled down most of the Royal Lodge, leaving only the great saloon that Wyatville had added to Nash's original design as a sad folly to exercise the imagination of the congregation in the nearby Chapel Royal; he sent the expensive animals in the menagerie to the London Zoo; he made over a miscellaneous collection of treasures and objects of art to the nation.[20] His brother had been fond of such knicknackery, he explained, when looking at some of his pictures, but he couldn't see much in them himself. Aye, they might be pretty. 'Damned expensive taste, though.'[21]

He had no such tastes. Wyatville's work in the Castle was completed, and the Waterloo Chamber (see plate 29) was built by roofing over an interior courtyard known as Horn Court to house George IV's magnificent collection of paintings — mostly by Lawrence — of distinguished men who had contributed to Napoleon's downfall. But both William IV and Queen Adelaide appeared to take more interest in the model cottages which were going up in the Park than they did in the Castle. The Queen visited these cottages on Sunday afternoons and 'when she appeared all the children came running out to her and she talked to them and patted their heads'.[22]

Neither she nor the King liked racing. She took her woolwork to Ascot and he, when asked which horses to enter for a particular race, gaily replied, 'Take the whole fleet. I suppose some of them will win.'[23]

He settled down at Windsor to a life of quiet domesticity not unlike that of his father. He slept in the same room as the Queen, a kind and admirable wife, not at all the frightful creature that Greville had described, and he got up every morning at ten minutes to eight, exactly five minutes after his valet knocked on the door. Immediately he put on his trousers and a flannel dressing-gown and took no notice of anyone until he had been to the lavatory. Despite his brisk start to the day, however, he did not sit down to breakfast until half-past nine, for he dressed extremely slowly, rarely taking less than an hour and a half. After breakfast he read *The Times* and *The Morning Post*, occasionally breaking out with an angry comment such as 'That's a damned lie!' Having finished the papers, he transacted business with his secretary until two o'clock, when he had his luncheon, which usually consisted of cutlets and a couple of glasses of sherry. In the evening while the Queen sat knitting he went to sleep in his chair, 'occasionally waking up for the purpose of saying, "Exactly so, Ma'am"' and then sleeping again.[24] After dinner, while the band played, he went back to sleep once more. He ate moderately and did not drink much, although he did not like people who did not drink at all. And once at dinner in the Castle he called across the table to his niece's husband Prince Leopold of Saxe-Coburg, whom he detested, 'What's that you're drinking, sir? Water, sir! God damn it! Why don't you drink wine! I never allow anybody to drink water at my table.'[25]

When this scene took place he was within a few months of his death. He was seventy-one and had aged quickly since he had come to the throne six years before. His early energy had soon wilted and his bonhomie had degenerated into bluster. His Ministers, since the disputes over the Reform Bill, no longer found him tolerant and pliable and he in turn shut the doors of the Castle against them. When one of his sons told him that he really ought to give a dinner during the Ascot week of 1835, he burst out angrily, 'You know I cannot give a dinner. I cannot give any dinners without inviting the Ministers and I would rather see the Devil than any of them in my house.'[26] As his brother had given offence by refusing to ask certain

Whigs to Windsor, so William IV gave offence by only having Tories as his guests there. The sight of Peel in the Royal Stand at Ascot had prompted George IV to remark sardonically that he would 'have as soon expected to see a pig in church' as him at a race.[27] Six years later William IV was making quite as 'extraordinary speeches' at Ascot about Melbourne.[28]

The most extraordinary speech he ever made, however, was made in the Castle at a dinner party during the late summer of 1836. The circumstances were these: The King had invited his sister-in-law, the Duchess of Kent, and her daughter Princess Victoria to Windsor for the Queen's birthday on 13 August, and he had asked them to stay on at the Castle until his own birthday which was to be held privately on 21 August and publicly the following day. The Duchess, ignoring the invitation for the Queen's birthday, said she would come to Windsor on 20 August. The King, having to be in London that day, called at Kensington Palace to discover that his sister-in-law had appropriated a set of seventeen apartments which she had applied for the previous year and been refused.

The King returned to Windsor at ten o'clock and immediately on entering the drawing room took both Princess Victoria's hands in his own and told her how sorry he was he did not see her more often. Then, turning to her mother and bowing low, he announced that a 'most unwarrantable liberty' had been taken with one of his palaces; he neither understood nor would endure conduct so disrespectful to him.

The following day at dinner he elaborated his complaint. Standing up, with the Duchess of Kent by his side and Princess Victoria opposite him, he declared with mounting anger:

I trust in God that my life may be spared for nine months longer, after which period, in the event of my death, no Regency would take place. I should then have the satisfaction of leaving the royal authority to the personal exercise of that Young Lady (pointing to the Princess), the Heiress presumptive to the Crown, and not in the hands of a person, now near me, who is surrounded by evil advisers and who is herself incompetent to act with propriety in the station in which she would be placed. I have no hesitation in saying that I have been insulted – grossly and continually insulted – by that person, but I am determined to endure no longer a course of behaviour so disrespectful to me. Amongst many other things I have particularly to complain of the manner in which that young lady has been kept away from my Court; she has been repeatedly kept from my drawing-rooms, at which she ought always to have been present, but I am fully resolved that this will not happen again. I would have her know that I am King, and that I am determined to make my authority respected, and for the future I shall insist and command that the Princess do upon all occasions appear at my Court, as it is her duty to do.

The King ended his alarming speech on a quieter note, referring with avuncular affection to Victoria and her future reign. But the damage was done. The Princess was already in tears; Queen Adelaide appeared in 'deep distress'; and as soon as dinner was over the Duchess of Kent announced her immediate departure.[29]

It seemed doubtful by the end of the year that the King's prayer that he would live long enough for there to be no regency would be answered. And many of those who did not believe that he would die, thought that he might at least go mad. 'His habitual state of excitement,' Charles Greville thought, would 'probably bring on sooner or later the malady of his family.' Constantly excited, he was frequently unable to control his temper and one of his lords of the bedchamber, Lord Torrington, was publicly humiliated more than once by the King's savage and uncontrolled anger. 'Hold your tongue, sir!' he snapped at him on one of these occasions when Torrington had announced a guest as a deputy-governor and been unable satisfactorily to answer the question, 'Deputy-Governor of what?' (there being no further information on the man's card). 'Hold your tongue, sir. You had better go home and learn to read.'[30]

The King retained his sanity, however, and he held on to life until Victoria reached her eighteenth birthday. Less than four weeks after that birthday, however, he lay dead in the Blue Room at Windsor.

His thoughts during his last illness were often with his niece. He felt sure she would be 'a good woman and a good Queen'. 'It will touch every sailor's heart to have a girl queen to fight for,' he added with characteristic pride in the service in which his birth and incapacity had denied him fulfilment. 'They'll be tattooing her face on their arms, and I'll be bound they'll all think she was christened after Nelson's ship.'[31]

5

Victorians

[i]

VICTORIA – THE YOUNG QUEEN

Charles Creevey was standing outside the Castle gate when Victoria rode in as Queen. Her mother was with her and her uncle Leopold, now King of the Belgians, and the 'Boss King very gallantly held his horse in a little to let his Queen niece be first.' 'I was quite delighted with Vicky in every way,' Creevey told Miss Ord. 'She looks infinitely better on horseback than in any other way; she was dressed so nicely too, and her manner *quite perfect.*'¹

During these first few months of her reign, there was scarcely anyone who did not agree with Creevey that the little Queen was delightful. From the very hour when Lord Conyngham, as Master of the Household, and the Archbishop of Canterbury, having ridden through the night from Windsor to Kensington Palace, told her that she was Queen and knelt before her to kiss her hand, she had behaved with a quiet grace and simple dignity. Later on that morning she received the Privy Council, and Charles Greville, who had described her eight years before as a 'short, vulgar-looking child', thought that 'there never was anything like the first Impression she produced'. She appeared to 'act with every sort of good taste and feeling'. A little bewildered, occasionally looking at Lord Melbourne for instruction when she had any doubt what to do, 'which hardly ever occurred', she remained calm, self-possessed, graceful and modest.² Her voice was soft and, if a little high and thin, beautifully clear.

Those who knew her best were well aware, however, that behind her attractive manner was a spirit far tougher than could at first be imagined. She was uncompromisingly truthful and direct, obstinately accurate and tenacious, capable and conscientious, nervous yet insensitive. She had many firmly held prejudices. She attached great importance to the observation of forms and precedents and had a respect for detail which she never lost. On going down to Windsor to offer her sympathy to the Queen Dowager on King William's death, she realised that the flag on the Round Tower would be flying at half-mast. She suggested to Lord Melbourne who was with her that a message should be sent on ahead of them that the flag should not be raised in honour of her arrival. Melbourne confessed that he 'had never thought of the flag or knew anything about it.'³

Her mind was not subtle and her knowledge was very fragmentary, so that, as she confessed herself, she often felt 'conscious of saying stupid things in conversation'. She was particularly apprehensive of appearing stupid, for despite the accomplishments of her public performances and her determined self-confidence, she was innately shy and to the end of her life found official engagements unusually tiring as they not only bored her but made her nervous and often she restrained herself with difficulty from giggling. She had little cause, though, to be unsure of herself in the presence of great and clever men, for she had many talents of her own. She had – it is an invaluable attribute for a queen – an astonishing memory. She wrote extremely well; she had a good ear for music; she could draw with an almost professional skill; she danced with enviable grace. She may have had a limited intellect, but she played the part of Queen with an instinctive and formidable distinction.

Her life at Windsor was energetic and she was as happy as she had ever been. She worked quite hard, allowing herself to be guided by Lord Melbourne, while anxious to understand the complexities of government herself. But she spent many hours every day enjoying herself and was often still dancing at three o'clock in the morning singing the tune or nodding her head in time with the music.[4]

She had not liked the Castle at first. It always, so she wrote to her 'dearest, best Uncle', appeared very melancholy to her; but soon she grew to love it[5] and to feel a deep respect for what her Private Secretary was later to describe as its 'dignified feudalism'.[6]

Sometimes she got up early, but more often, and always after a late night, she would lie in bed, feeling vaguely guilty, before having breakfast in her room. For three or four hours every morning she devoted herself to business, reading all the despatches and having 'every matter of interest and importance in every department laid before her'. Between eleven and twelve o'clock Lord Melbourne came to see her and they would talk about business or gossip; and after luncheon she would go riding in the Great Park, 'the greater part of the time at full gallop', accompanied by several equerries and ladies-in-waiting. Later in the afternoon there was music and singing and if there were any children staying in the Castle – 'and she is so fond of them,' Creevey said, 'that she generally contrives to have some there' – the Queen would play and romp with them. On Sunday evenings, after having been twice to church during the day, the ladies would accompany the Queen for a stroll on the Terrace and around the great parterre, watched by crowds of men and women and Eton boys whom the gentlemen of the Household tapped out of the way as she got close to them. The band played; the standard on the Round Tower flapped in the wind or drooped against the white pole; and the fountain splashed its water high into the air.[7]

At half-past seven the guests assembled for dinner and the men were told by the lord-in-waiting whom to take in with them. A little before eight o'clock the Queen came into the room, preceded by the gentlemen of the Household and followed by her mother and her ladies. She spoke a few words to every woman who was there, bowed to every man, and then went immediately into dinner, with the man of the highest rank in the room or a foreign ambassador on her right, and Lord Melbourne on her left.[8]

The men were not permitted to remain long after the ladies had retired and were usually back in the drawing room drinking coffee within a quarter of an hour. The Queen, who did not sit down until they had returned, spoke a few words of a 'trivial nature, all however very civil and cordial in manner and expression', to each of them.

Charles Greville recorded this as a typical conversation the Queen once had with him:

'Have you been riding to-day, Mr Greville?'
'No, Madam, I have not.'
'It was a fine day.'
'Yes, Madam, a very fine day.'
'It was rather cold, though.'
'It *was* rather cold, Madam.'
'Your sister, Lady Frances Egerton, rides, I think, doesn't she?'
'She does ride sometimes, Madam.'
A pause.
'Has Your Majesty been riding to-day?'
'Oh, yes, a very long ride.'
'Has your Majesty got a nice horse?'
'Oh, yes, a very nice horse.'[9]

When the series of little conversations was over, the band struck up again, chairs were brought up to the Duchess of Kent's whist table, and the Queen sat down with Melbourne at a large round table with those guests who were not playing cards, to indulge in two hours of further and often as wearying conversation.

Melbourne was nearly always there. At first it was through a sense of duty, but he was not a man 'to carry out a duty so rigorously,

187

if it went against his inclinations. As a matter of fact, all his inclinations were in its favour; and what had begun as a duty very soon turned into an intense pleasure.'[10]

Men who had known him well in the past were amazed at the change in him. 'Never was such a revolution seen in anybody's occupations and habits.' Instead of sprawling about in his chair, talking, laughing and swearing, as he had been used to do at Holland House, he sat bolt upright and his conversation was 'carefully guarded and regulated by the strictest propriety'.[11] He was clearly extremely fond of his young Queen, 'passionately fond of her as he might be of his daughter if he had one', Greville observed, 'and the more because he is a man with capacity for loving without having anything in the world to love'.[12] Some observers, while acknowledging the Prime Minister's duty to instruct so young a monarch in the business of government, thought that it was wrong of him to be so constantly at her side at Windsor. He had no precedence, the Duke of Wellington complained, 'and ought not to be placed in the post of honor to the exclusion of those of higher rank than himself'.[13] When he was with her, Princess Lieven reported, he looked respectful and loving but 'a little pleased with himself'.[14] People even made jokes about an early marriage.[15]

His influence for good could not, though, be denied. The Queen needed such a man. She was, after all, very young and her lonely upbringing had given her a curiously naïve outlook on the world. She was often shrewd but her judgments were never tentative, never in doubt. It was not merely that she was incapable of dissembling or lying, but that she was incapable of understanding that there were degrees of reprehensibility. A thing was right or it was wrong; a person was good or bad; and once her own mind was made up she had absolute confidence in her opinion. The presence of a man like Melbourne to help her form these opinions was essential, and it was essential, too, that the man should be, as Melbourne was, one who could interest her emotions and arouse her innocent love.

There were occasions, however, when the Queen's strength of character and innate prejudices were too powerful to be restrained or guided by the elderly, handsome and distinguished man she so obviously worshipped. The most notorious of these occasions in her early career was one which temporarily threatened all the goodwill that had surrounded her from the day of her accession. The origins of this sad affair went back to the days of her frustrating childhood.

*   *   *

The atmosphere at Kensington Palace was stifling and clouded with intrigue. The Duchess of Kent, 'a short, stout, foolish woman, rustling self-importantly about in velvet and ostrich plumes',[16] was intoxicated by the thought that she was mother of the future Queen. She distrusted nearly all her late husband's relations and, as William IV had so vehemently complained, rarely permitted Victoria to see them. Her brother Leopold was allowed to exercise a deeper influence, but even he was not entirely to be trusted. Victoria was consequently rarely left alone. Her nights she spent in her mother's bedroom; her days were carefully regulated by Baroness Lehzen, the strict, narrow-minded, vigilant daughter of a Hanoverian clergyman who was her 'Lady Attendant', in fact her governess.

Victoria was rather frightened of this plain, yellow-skinned woman with her rasping voice and her passion for caraway seeds, just as she was frightened of her mother, who once made her pin a sprig of holly to the neck of her dress to make her sit erect at table; but she also, as she later admitted herself, adored the Baroness and the Baroness in turn adored her pupil, who had been in her care from the age of five. She protected her jealously from those who hoped to profit by their closeness to her and in particular from the Duchess of Kent's confidential secretary, the equivocal, pompous and scheming Sir John Conroy, formerly the Duke's equerry. Few people liked Conroy but Louise Lehzen hated him, and Victoria shared her hatred. It was said that the Princess had once discovered her mother in his arms and that they were lovers; and it was also believed, with better cause, that they had plotted together to have Victoria's coming of age delayed so that the Duchess might become Regent with Conroy as her principal adviser. What at least was certain was that soon after she became Queen, Victoria dismissed Conroy with an annuity and broke the close bonds that had formerly tied her to her mother.

Immediately upon her accession she gave orders that her bed should be removed at once from the Duchess's room; she had her meals by herself; and she recorded with pride and relief in her journal, underlining the important words, that on the day of William IV's death she saw the Lord Chamberlain, the Archbishop of Canterbury and the Prime Minister 'of course quite alone'. The Duchess came with her to Windsor, but she was never allowed to regain control over her daughter's life or Household, all the details of which the Queen now regulated herself with the help of Melbourne and Baroness Lehzen.

There remained, however, one unwelcome link with the past and that was the Duchess of Kent's lady-in-waiting, Lady Flora Hastings. Lady Flora returned to the Castle at the beginning of 1839 from a holiday in Scotland, and it was rumoured that she had shared a carriage as far as London with the detested Conroy whose plots, hatched at Kensington Palace, she had apparently helped to further. A month or so after her return Lady Flora's stomach began to swell and when they discovered that the Court physician, Sir James Clark, shared their suspicions, neither the Queen nor Baroness Lehzen had any doubt that Lady Flora was pregnant and that, as the Queen wrote in her journal, the horrid cause of the pregnancy was that 'monster and demon incarnate' whose name she forbore to mention. Lady Flora was asked to submit to a medical examination which revealed that she was not pregnant at all. Her distended stomach was due to an enlarged liver. Melbourne with characteristic sound sense had advised against taking any action which would complicate what might turn out to be an extremely awkward situation. He was constantly, if often by implication, advising the Queen to be more tolerant, to curb the excesses of her youthful morality, not to expect perfection in anyone; and although he was anxious that nothing should be done to compromise the dignity of the Crown or Court – he forbade, for instance, the ladies-in-waiting to walk unchaperoned on the terrace at Windsor for fear of causing offence in the town, and he advised Lady Holland, distinguished old friend that she was, against coming to Court as she was a divorcée – Melbourne was also anxious that the Queen should not appear unduly censorious. But there was always this difficulty of making her see that 'you cannot always go straight forward, that you must go round about sometimes'.[17] By insisting that Lady Flora should be medically examined, by refusing to do more in the face of Lady Flora's brother's angry protests than apologise coldly and in private, the Queen appeared not merely censorious but vindictive.

The matter might have died quietly down had not the justifiably indignant Hastings family published their correspondence with the Court, a correspondence which the newspapers and disaffected politicians made the most of. Eventually the Duke of Wellington, who loved 'being consulted and mixed up in messes',[18] lent his great reputation to a pacification of the whole affair. But the damage had been done. 'In the space of a week or two, the Queen's early popularity had vanished.'[19]

At Ascot that year she was hissed as she drove down the course;[20]

and as she came out on to the balcony a man shouted out, 'Mrs Melbourne'.[21] Always deeply distressed and furiously indignant when she was criticised, she complained to Melbourne that this sort of disrespect to the Sovereign ought to be stopped by law. 'Those two abominable women', the Duchess of Montrose and Lady Sarah Ingestre who had expressed their disapproval of her conduct in a most humiliating way, 'ought to be flogged.' Then, in the summer, Lady Flora became seriously ill. The Queen at first refused to believe that she might be dying, but Melbourne persuaded her that she was and that she ought to visit her. Reluctantly she consented and the sight of the sick woman's haggard, fevered face upset her profoundly. 'Poor Lady Flora! Poor Lady Flora!' she kept repeating and ten days later when Lady Flora died, the Queen burst into a flood of tears. She sent a carriage to follow the funeral procession to the station. And the police had to guard it from being wrecked.[22]

In this same year the Queen's troubles were further increased by what became known as the Bedchamber Plot, an affair which confirmed the distrust with which most Tory politicians regarded her.

In May 1839 the Whig government was clearly collapsing and the Queen was faced with the dreaded possibility of losing Lord Melbourne. She begged him 'not to forsake her'; but he told her that there was no avoiding it and advised her to send for the Duke of Wellington who said, in his turn, that he was too old and suggested she asked Sir Robert Peel instead. The Queen disliked Peel. She found him uncouth, cold and clumsy, without grace or charm, and she was determined not to have him as her Prime Minister if she could possibly retain her beloved Melbourne. Peel's insistence that she should replace some of her ladies – who being chosen by Melbourne were all the wives or daughters of Whigs – by others with a Tory background, gave her her opportunity. She adamantly refused to change any of her ladies; she had become devoted to them; admittedly Lady Normanby, Mistress of the Robes, was the wife of a Whig Minister but there was 'no significance in that as she never discussed politics with any of her ladies', either at Windsor or elsewhere; certainly there were a number of Pagets amongst them but there was no significance in that either – she was very fond of them. 'The Queen maintains all her Ladies,' she insisted. And she did maintain them. Melbourne, who had advised her to give way to Peel, realised she would never do so and agreed, with a pleasure clouded by apprehension, to stay in office.

The delighted Queen gave a ball for the Grand Duke Alexander of Russia the night she brought the Bedchamber Plot to this dangerously triumphant conclusion, and she danced happily till a quarter-past three in the morning. The Red Drawing Room at Windsor shone with the glittering light of hundreds of candles and the Queen's eyes sparkled with excitement as the handsome figures in their splendid uniforms swirled around her dancing the Mazurka and a new German dance, the *Gross Vater*. The young Grand Duke was delightful. Indeed, she confessed in her diary, she was a little in love with him. She was 'talking jokingly', of course; but a young person like her, who hated 'a Sunday face' 'must *sometimes* have *young* people to laugh with'. She said as much to Lord Melbourne. 'Nothing so natural,' he replied and there were tears in his eyes. [23]

Later on that year another handsome young man came to Windsor and after two days in his company she had decided that she was in love, not 'jokingly' this time but truly and deeply. It was providential that she was so, for an early marriage and an heir were essential if the country were to be saved from the danger of the Duke of Cumberland inheriting the Crown.

Prince Albert of Saxe-Coburg-Gotha, her Uncle Leopold's nephew and her own cousin, was 'fascinating' and '*beautiful*'. On the fourth day she made up her mind to marry him; and on the fifth day, having decided, as she told her Aunt Gloucester later, that Albert 'would never have presumed to take such a liberty to propose to the Queen of England', she sent for him to come to her little blue boudoir and there, trembling as she spoke, she told him that he had gained her whole heart and that he would make her intensely happy if he would make the sacrifice of sharing his life with her. [24]

He accepted her proposal graciously, but his letters reveal his reluctance to abandon the quiet, studious life he preferred for the frivolities and superficiality of an unintellectual court. He danced well but he hated late nights; he enjoyed serious conversation but he detested gossip.

Although he was far more attracted by the Queen than Lytton Strachey suggests, he wrote of marriage as if he were going into battle. 'I will not let my courage fail,' he assured his tutor in that stilted, portentous style which characterised most of his writings. 'With firm resolution and true zeal on my part, I cannot fail to continue noble, manly and princely in all things.' 'Oh, the future,' he sighed to his grandmother. 'Life has its thorns in every position,' he told his stepmother, 'and the consciousness of having used one's

29. The Upper Ward as reconstructed by Wyatville from the engraving by W. F. Starling after Benjamin Baud in *Illustrations of Windsor Castle* by the late Sir Jeffrey Wyatville, 1841

30. King George IV gate in 1827
from a drawing on stone by W. Westall

31. King Henry VIII gate *c.* 1840
from the engraving by Sands after T. Allom

powers and endeavours for an object so great as that of promoting the good of so many, will surely be sufficient to support me.'²⁵

The sentiments may have a sadly priggish and sanctimonious ring for a young man of twenty, but they were unquestionably sincere. Prince Albert was an honest and good, a profoundly dutiful and a devoutly conscientious man. And it was, indeed, these almost oppressive virtues, unrelieved by any frailty except a certain hesitancy and deviousness, a bigoted outlook on religion and sex, an occasional nervous irritability and a tendency to 'allow himself opinions', as Duke Ernest of Coburg said of him, 'which are wont to arise from contempt of mankind in the abstract', which led to his being accepted by Englishmen with ill-concealed reluctance. He clothed his shyness with a veneer of stiff formality. He seemed, on occasions, excessively critical and condemnatory, even harsh. His fine features and clear blue eyes were often overcast by a disquieting expression, distant and lugubrious. One evening at Windsor shortly before his wedding he was playing a letter game with Melbourne who was given the word 'pleasure' to guess. Offering the Prime Minister a hint, the Prince said forlornly, 'It is not a *common* thing.'²⁶

*　*　*

The honeymoon took place at Windsor and Charles Greville thought it 'a very curious affair'. Very early on the first morning the bridegroom and his wife were up and dressed and walking in the garden, and Greville remarked to Lady Palmerston that this was not the way to provide the country with a Prince of Wales. Lady Palmerston, for her part, was much irritated by the whole business. The honeymoon was practically public. An immense party of guests was staying in the Castle, where a dance was given three days after the wedding, to which, incidentally, scarcely any Tories had been invited. Lady Palmerston was much vexed that the Queen, whose 'prejudices and antipathies were deep and strong' and whose disposition was 'very inflexible', should have nobody about her to tell her that this was 'not becoming and would appear indelicate. But she has nobody that dares tell her, or she will not endure to hear such truths.'²⁷

She had not yet fallen as completely as she was later to do under the Prince's benign yet overwhelming influence; and, although she wished him to be made King Consort by Act of Parliament or, at least, accorded the first place of precedence in the country after herself, she did not intend to forget that *she* was Queen and must maintain her position and dignity. She did not want him to take any part in political business, allowing him to do little more than 'help with the blotting paper', as she herself ingenuously put it in her journal, and she organised his official life to such an extent that she chose all the officers of his Household, including his confidential secretary. He protested mildly at first and then almost despairingly, but the Queen calmly and firmly assured him that he could 'perfectly rely on her'.[28] And he gave way. He was a patient as well as an unselfish man.

He had his own way, however, with regard to London, which the Queen had loved and from which he always longed to escape. Within six months he had succeeded in transforming the Queen's tastes to accord with his own. She who had once delighted in court ceremonies, etiquette and trivial formalities – as the Prince long before their marriage had complained to a friend – who enjoyed staying up late at night, sleeping late into the day, and who took not the slightest interest in nature, now began to share his love of the country and of a peaceful life. She eventually agreed that to come to the Castle from London was like being 'freed from some dungeon'.[29]

The Prince himself was delighted with Windsor. 'I feel as if in Paradise in this fine fresh air,' he told his brother, and there was so much to do that interested him.[30] The Park and gardens were neglected, many paths overgrown, much farmland in waste. He set to work to improve the estate with an industry which no one could but admire. He planted trees, laid out new paths, supervised the stables, reorganised the Home, Norfolk and Flemish Farms – which extended in all to nearly two thousand acres – until they were making a profit. He saved the remains of George iv's Royal Lodge and the fishing temple at Virginia Water from destruction. Inside the Castle he inspected with an expert eye the treasures of centuries which hung on the walls, which stood scarcely noticed on out of the way tables or lay disregarded on cupboard shelves; and he soon had librarians and indexers at work sorting out the vast muddle of the Queen's papers.[31]

He was helped and encouraged in this work by Baron Stockmar, a shrewd little doctor who had been his Uncle Leopold's confidential adviser and his own tutor. Gladstone thought that Stockmar was a 'mischievous old prig' and there were many others who believed his influence over the Prince and the Queen was, in some curious and undefined way, far-reaching and sinister. In fact, he was, as his son wrote in a panegyric no more exaggerated than such filial compilations may be expected to be, a man who 'to a straightforward under-standing which simplified all questions presented to it, a sober habit of mind and great objectivity of apprehension, united deep feel-ing, good nature and love of mankind'.[32] He was also moody, sar-donic, hypochondriacal, inflexibly and obsessively moral, loyal and tenacious. He liked to think of himself as an indispensable adviser; and at Windsor, where he stayed for months on end, he was as familiar a sight as that other old family friend who shared his middle-class German background, Baroness Lehzen. Permitted to ignore many of the rules of court etiquette, he could be seen in the morning walking about the Castle in his dressing-gown and slippers and in the evening going in to dine without decorations and wearing ordinary trousers instead of the regulation court breeches. After dinner, he was allowed to go straight through the drawing-room back to his own apartments.[33] Here in his studiously thorough way he conducted his voluminous correspondence and prepared his immense memoranda, indulging his 'harmless foible of thinking that he directed and controlled his old pupil'.[34]

*　　*　　*

If Stockmar's foible was harmless and his advice generally beneficial, it was impossible to view the prejudices and activities of Baroness Lehzen in the same light. She had always been more anxious to stir up trouble between Victoria and her mother than to settle their differences, and once the Prince Consort had succeeded in ending the estrangement between his wife and the Duchess of Kent, the Queen began to learn that 'dear Lehzen' had not always taken her part for the right reasons. The more successful the marriage between Victoria and Albert promised to be, the more jealous and interfering the Baroness became; and no one could have expected her not to be, for she felt unwanted and lonely, cut out of a life over which she had formerly held such a dominating influence.

As the Queen's personal private secretary during the early years of her reign, with unquestionable authority in all the affairs of the Household, she had formed one of what Roger Fulford has aptly described as a 'cosy triumvirate' and had been even more concerned than her fellow members, Victoria and Melbourne, to exclude from this triumvirate 'a new-comer who was certain to ask questions and to raise objections'.[35]

Before the Prince brought his more far-seeing mind to bear on the affairs of the Household she had not only been in the habit of padding

195

about the Castle, giving orders and making inspections, but she had also been largely responsible for the explosively provocative appointments to its senior posts, all of which were held by Whigs, and so many of them by Pagets that newspapers had referred to the Castle as the Paget Club House.[36] Lord Conyngham, the husband of a Paget, was allowed to remain as Lord Chamberlain after he had obtained a court appointment for his mistress who, on at least one occasion, was discovered in her lover's arms;[37] and the Lord Steward, another Paget – and one, incidentally, who was particularly antagonistic to the Prince – also established his mistress at Court.[38]

The Prince, who confessed to his secretary that 'he had never feared temptation with regard to women because he had no inclinations in that respect and that that species of vice disgusted him,'[39] naturally found such appointments not only inexcusable on moral grounds, but unforgivable on political grounds as endangering the position of the monarchy. And when Baroness Lehzen spent £15,000 of the Queen's money on behalf of the Whig Party,[40] the Prince was 'alarmed and horrified' and protested to Melbourne. The Baroness, however, was undeterred. She replied to the Prince's exasperated attempt to dismiss her from Court that 'he had not the power' to turn her out of the Queen's house.[41]

Prince Albert had won the battle in the end, though, and by the summer of 1841 the moon was, in his own words, 'on the wane'.[42] He had not had the courage to approach the Queen directly about the Baroness, but eventually he succeeded in making her accept the advisability of her departure. In October 1842 Baroness Lehzen left Windsor never to return. After she had gone the Prince told the Queen the history of his quarrels with her. 'I blame myself for my blindness,' the Queen wrote contritely in her diary. 'I shudder to think what my beloved Albert had to go through.'[43]

*   *   *

Soon after Baroness Lehzen left the Castle, the Prince began to consider the complete re-organisation of the Household, the archaic administration of which Baron Stockmar had outlined in one of his memoranda.

In this memorandum the Baron explained the difficulties of running the Castle when its daily life was ruled by three separate departments – those of the Lord Steward, the Lord Chamberlain, and the Master of the Horse – which changed with every Ministry. The heads of these departments no longer lived at Court but delegated their authority to 'servants very inferior in rank', none of whom was sure how far they might trespass upon the customary preserves of another department and all of whom went through an elaborate procedure before anything important was done. It was known for certain that the housekeepers, pages and housemaids were under the authority of the Lord Chamberlain; that the footmen, livery-porters and under-butlers were, by the strangest anomaly, under that of the Master of the Horse, at whose office they were clothed and paid, and that the rest of the servants were under the jurisdiction of the Lord Steward. But as only the Lord Steward had a responsible official – the Master of the Household – actually living in the Castle, two-thirds of the servants were left without a master and 'if smoking, drinking and other irregularities' occurred in the dormitories, where the footmen slept ten and twelve in a room, no one could help it.

When guests arrived no one was prepared to show them to or from their apartments. There was often, in fact, no one to be found who knew what or where these apartments were, so that it frequently happened that visitors to the Castle were unable to find the drawing-room and at night if they happened to forget the right entrance from the corridors they wandered for an hour helpless and unassisted. Once a visitor got lost on his way to bed and was forced to spend the night on a sofa in the State gallery adjoining the Waterloo gallery where a housemaid found him and supposing him to be drunk fetched a policeman.[44] And when Guizot got lost one night, 'he spent nearly an hour wandering about the corridors to try and identify his bedroom'. At length he opened a door which he imagined led to it and came upon the Queen having her hair brushed by a maid.[45] Even when a man could be found to perform an unexpected duty, there was frequently an argument as to whether the duty could properly be performed by his department. On a celebrated occasion Stockmar complained to the Master of the Household that the dining-room was always cold. 'But you see,' that official replied, 'properly speaking, it is not our fault; for the Lord Steward lays the fire only, and the Lord Chamberlain lights it.'

There were similar problems with repairs. If, for instance, a pane of glass required replacing in the kitchen or a cupboard door mending, a requisition had to be prepared and signed by the chief cook; it had then to be counter-signed by the Clerk of the Kitchen; then taken to be signed by the Master of the Household; then taken to the Lord Chamberlain's office, where it was authorised and passed on to the

Clerk of the Works who was responsible to the Department of Woods and Forests. The consequence of this rigmarole was that many a window and cupboard remained broken for months.[46] The reason for this and other procedures no less complicated was, of course, the necessity to keep some check upon the immense expenditure entailed in the maintenance of the Castle and the other royal palaces. At Windsor, for instance, in a single quarter – and the accounts for preceding and subsequent quarters contain similar figures – no less than 184 brushes, brooms and mops were purchased by the Lord Chamberlain's department, including forty-three scrubbing brushes, thirty blacklead brushes and fifteen carpet brooms, not to mention (among many other items) twenty-four pairs of housemaid's gloves, twenty-four chamois leathers and ninety-six packing mats.[47] As in each year about seven hundred brushes of different kinds had to be bought for the Castle, it was a natural assumption that the forty housemaids were either peculiarly vigorous or that they, their supervisors, or those responsible for the purchase were not entirely honest. Certainly the housemaids were suspected of being very careless with their dusters, between three and four hundred dozen of which, according to the Housekeeper, were 'in constant use, scattered all over the Castle'; and the Master of the Household was forced to suggest that 'they should be *printed all over* with a distinctive mark such as 'V.R. Windsor Castle'.[48]

It was not that the housemaids were poorly paid. In the first year of the Queen's reign when money was worth perhaps six or seven times its present value and domestic servants' wages were always far from generous, the lowest of the four grades into which housemaids were divided received £15 15s. 0d. a year, the highest £45 10s. 0d. And these wages were increased twenty years later by the Queen, who, however severely she might deal with those whose lapses she considered inexcusable because of their education or upbringing, was a tolerant and generous mistress to her domestic servants. Nor were these wages all that the housemaids received, for they were paid, in addition, two shillings a day board wages, and when they became too old or ill to perform their duties they might expect a pension which in 1837 was between £30 and £40 a year for twenty years' service. Apart from their regular emoluments they were often also given tips by foreign visitors to the Castle and these were usually liberal. In 1842, for example, the King of Prussia left £500 for distribution and the share of a housemaid of the First Class was £5 15s. 0d.[49] The Tsar Nicholas I left £2,000, gave the

198

housekeepr a diamond parure worth another thousand pounds, and 'freely bestowed rings, watches and brooches'.[50]

The more senior servants were paid salaries on a proportionately generous scale. The First Page of the Backstairs received £320 a year and even the Fourth Page of the Presence, Second Class, had £140 a year. The Housekeeper's salary of £112 a year does not, perhaps, appear to compare favourably with the Mistress of the Robes's £500 a year or the Resident Bedchamber Woman's £300, but at that time it was an excellent salary, and she had many under-servants to assist her, including linen women at £60 a year.

The annual expenses in salaries alone were, then, considerable and it distressed the practical, methodical and somewhat parsimon-ious minds of Stockmar and Prince Albert to discover how ill organised the Household was. They had no cause to complain of the way the specialists amongst the 445 persons under the authority of the Lord Chamberlain (£2,000 a year) performed their duties. The Rat Killer (£80 a year), the Chimney Sweep (£111), the Chemist and Druggist to the Person (£50), the four Physicians to the Person (£214 each), the two Sergeant Surgeons (£283 each), the Physician, Surgeon and Apothecary to the Household (£200, £400 and £414 respectively), the Dentist (£100), the Poet Laureate (£72), the Principal Painter (£59)[51] all performed their duties, no doubt, with more or less distinction. But housemaids who were paid by the year when they only worked for half of it, candles (still an official perquisite) newly installed every day in the public rooms, an under-butler who received £1 15s. 0d. a week for 'Red Room Wine' – a legacy from the days when officers on guard in George III's time were allowed this sum for wine served in a room hung in red – were extravagances which could no longer be tolerated. They were all stopped on Prince Albert's orders; and the running of the Household was made more efficient by making the Master of the Household responsible for the co-ordination of the activities of all the separate departments involved.

*   *   *

Naturally the activities of the Prince Consort did nothing to make him better liked. Caricatures of him were drawn depicting him ferreting for candle-ends at Windsor where, it was said, he had given instructions that the servants must provide themselves not only with their own soap but with their own tea, mops and brushes.[52] Servants in the royal service had grown accustomed to their perquisites, official and assumed, and guests did not take kindly to being allowed only two candles in their rooms and on ringing for more being told by the maid, as Madame Titiens was when she was summoned to Windsor to sing to the Queen, 'that the allowance to each room was just two candles and no more. "But," added the maid considerately, "there is no regulation which would prevent you cutting those two candles in halves and making four."'[53]

In the town of Windsor the Prince was, it seems, particularly unpopular. His profits on the royal farms were said to be the result of unfair competition; his improvements of the parks and his diversion of footpaths were said to have been done without regard to the feelings and, indeed, the rights of local people; his reverence for the Game Laws was said to be absolute and anachronistic; and when a firm of architects prepared a fantastic scheme for removing the town and placing it a more suitable distance from the Castle as a preliminary step in overcoming royal objections to the Great Western Railway line being brought further south-west from Slough (Stephenson's *North Star* did the journey from there to Paddington in less than half an hour in 1838) it was all said to be his idea.[54]

To the Prince Consort, though, the fulfilment of duty was more important than the attainment of popularity. And he could never be popular. He was so serious, so high-minded, so aloofly reserved. He was also so German. By blood the Queen was, too, for she had only the merest trace of British blood, derived from the Electress Sophia, grand-daughter of James I, the mother of George I and her own great-great-great-grandmother; but her husband was German both by birth, education and temperament. And it was clear that he wanted to remain so, that he resisted Anglicisation as if it were in some way degrading, that he did not much care for English people. In the way he talked, in the way he wore his clothes, in the way he rode a horse and shook hands, there was something unmistakably, and, so it seemed, determinedly, even arrogantly foreign. His English was slow to improve and he usually spoke German with his wife. When shaking hands he kept his elbow tucked well into his side in the German manner. His clothes were almost aggressively strange, and although the 'black velvet jacket without a cravat' that he wore on his honeymoon seemed 'youthfully manly and perfect' to his bride,[55] and although the long boots of scarlet leather he wore out shooting at Windsor were described by her as 'very picturesque',[56] they appeared to others in a different light. He was, it had to be admitted, a good shot; but his liking for a *battue*, conducted on the lines of a military operation in which hundreds of animals were killed, his insistence on breaking off for a hot luncheon, and the evident difficulty he experienced in concealing his 'chagrin if he shot badly, combined to give the impression that he was not a sportsman in the English sense'.[57] If he had always shot badly much might have been forgiven him; but his skill with a gun, like his enterprise when hunting with the Belvoir, and his graceful accomplishments as a tennis player, a swimmer and a fearless and vigorous ice-hockey player, all seemed vaguely suspect.

Even those who knew him well and esteemed him highly, could not fail to be conscious of the unfortunate effect he had on his wife's insular-minded people. 'One heard them say, "He is an excellent, clever, able fellow, but look at the cut of his coat, or look at the way in which he shakes hands."'[58] With women he was especially ill at ease and they found it difficult to forgive him because he was so obviously unmoved by their charm. In the Park at Windsor he would ride by with his equerry or walk across their path with his adored greyhound Eos and he would scarcely glance at them. In the drawing-room his dignity was frigid.

Formal as the Court had been – despite the extra-curricular activities of some of its senior officers – before the Queen's marriage, it became and remained far more so afterwards. No man was thenceforward permitted to sit in the Queen's presence except at dinner; none of her maids-of-honour was allowed to sit in the Prince Consort's presence, or to speak to him unless first addressed. When presented to the Queen a gentleman was expected to go down on one knee and raise his right arm, with the back of the hand uppermost. The Queen would then lay her hand on his, and the gentleman would 'barely touch' it with his lips. He must not speak. After rising he must bow, first to the Queen and then to the Prince Consort. Ladies on approaching the Sovereign's presence had to drop their trains – these were to be at least three-and-a-quarter yards in length – which were spread out for them by attendants armed with wands.[59] And although the Queen no longer sat on a raised throne so that those presented to her had to walk backwards down the steps without falling over their skirts, they still had to retreat several paces backwards holding their trains over their arms.[60]

The Queen, who ultimately became even more inflexible than the Prince regarding the procedure to be observed at presentations, was inflexible, too, over the clothes to be worn. Married ladies wore lappets; unmarried ladies wore veils; both wore a headdress of three white feathers. Anyone who wanted, for reasons of health, to wear a dress cut higher in the neck than was customary had to obtain permission to do so from the Lord Chamberlain. The permission was usually granted but the Queen insisted on the veils, lappets and feathers. A Mrs Sebastian Gassiot who, being unable to fasten her plumes in the usual way because ill-health had obliged her 'to have all her hair cut quite short', wanted to know whether she might appear in a 'Dolly Varden cap with the plumes and lappets fastened to it', was told that the Queen, who had been 'much amused' by the request, had replied to it – 'decidedly no.'[61]

Gentlemen, if they were not entitled to wear a uniform had to appear in court dress with a claret-coloured coat, knee breeches, long white stockings, buckled shoes and sword, although later on in her reign old men were allowed to wear breeches which came down to the ankle and buttoned there. They were meant to 'give the same impression as stockings. In most cases they fitted so badly that they resembled the more ancient peg-topped trousers. Lord Salisbury, who as Prime Minister constantly came down to dine and sleep at Windsor, had such ill-fitting breeches that they looked like ordinary trousers.'[62]

The problem facing American ministers abroad was settled by William Marcy, Secretary of State, who ruled that they should appear 'in the simple dress of an American citizen'. At that time the American Ambassador in London was James Buchanan, who later became President. Sir Edward Cust, the Queen's Master of the Ceremonies, told Buchanan that although the Queen would no doubt receive him whatever he wore, an ordinary suit would be disagreeable to her, so he appeared in a black coat and pantaloons, white waistcoat and cravat. The Queen greeted him with an 'arch but benevolent smile'.[63]

If the Queen's views on court dress called forth a good deal of satirical comment in the Press, her views on the uses and scope of the *Court Circular* aroused much more. Every day, in the most ponderous and humourless way, her activities and those of her family were recorded under this heading in the newspapers. Every time the Queen left Windsor for 'the Paddington Terminus of the Great Western Railway', every time she and the Prince 'promenaded in the pleasure grounds adjacent to the Castle', every time he went 'shooting in the royal preserves', every time she invited an honoured guest to 'partake of a collation', the facts were recorded and detailed until Thackeray promised to subscribe to any daily paper which came out without such 'trash – were it the *Morning Herald* it-self'.[64]

'The Marmosets, pretty little dears, are in good health', an apposite parody ran in a comic journal. 'The severe frost has not in any way injured the turtle-doves in the new dovecote. The tailless cats have been slightly affected owing to their having been indulged with a tête-à-tête on the Castle walls.'[65] Sometimes there was no need of parody. Once 'Her Majesty was most graciously pleased during her stay at Windsor to enjoy most excellent health and spirits.' And later 'Her Majesty, attended by Viscountess Jocelyn, went riding in the Park on two ponies.'[66]

Thackeray would not have complained, he said, if the activities so painstakingly and eccentrically recorded had occasionally contained some suggestion of excitement or originality. But there was little chance of this, for since the Prince had turned the Queen into a country lover their life was not dramatic.

I don't know why [one of the Queen's maids-of-honour wrote home to her father in 1849], but the dullness of our evenings is a thing impossible to describe. The Queen and Ladies sit at the round table and make conversation; and Flora and I sit at our own table and work; and the Prince generally stays in the other room talking with the Gentlemen till near bed-time; then he comes in with one or two big-wigs who sit at the Queen's table, where they sit till she gives the move at half-past ten, then the other gentlemen make a rush, from the whist table or from the other room, and we gladly bundle up our work, and all is over.[67]

Visitors to Windsor Castle frequently complained of the lack of 'sociability which makes the agreeableness of an English country house'. There was no room in which the guests could 'assemble, sit lounge, and talk as they please'. The billiard room was so inaccessible it might as well have been in the town of Windsor; the library, 'although well stocked with books', was cold, and unfurnished, 'offering none of the comforts of a habitable room'.[68] If the 'most agreeable people in the world' were 'invited one hardly' saw them as the 'chacun chez soi system' was the fashion of the place.[69]

Some guests, of course, preferred to be left on their own, to do as they pleased throughout the day until dinner time; and Lord Clarendon told the Duchess of Manchester that he always liked Windsor better than any other country house because 'one is left to one's own devices and nobody does anything to *amuse* one'.[70] But, for most, the lack of even the pretence of gaiety, the need to observe 'a continual air of deference and respect', was depressing and enervating.

At dinner, when the guests met for the first time during the day, a military band usually 'covered the talk', as Lord Macaulay discovered on a visit in 1851, 'with a succession of sonorous tunes'. He found himself next to a 'foreign woman who could hardly speak English intelligibly'.[71] And this was not at all uncommon. Lord Ashley found that the band was very necessary to fill up the long 'pauses of conversation'.[72] Even during Ascot races when a splendid banquet was given in St George's Hall, which appeared 'very magnificent, blazing with gold plate and light', it was, Charles Greville thought, despite the splendour, all 'very tiresome'.[73]

After dinner there was sometimes a concert by the Castle band or by a distinguished musician invited to Windsor for this purpose.* Occasionally there was an opera, the performers and orchestra being brought down to Windsor by special train and sent back afterwards. The performance was given in the Waterloo gallery where the acoustics were not very good and where Francisco Tamagno, not having arrived in time to try out his voice there, once let himself go with such force that the Queen, who was as usual sitting in the front row, almost had her cap blown off.[77] Occasionally, too, there was a play – after the Prince's death the Queen did not enter a public theatre again, believing that for a widow it was not seemly – with a cast brought down from the West End. More often the play was performed, rather nervously, by members of the Household or by the royal children, and sometimes there was a presentation of tableaux in which all the members of the Royal Family joined and this was 'very wearying for the audience, who had to sit for two and a half hours with very long intervals between the tableaux'.[78]

But boring as these performances usually were, it was better to have something to do after dinner, Charles Greville decided, having sat through a series of declamations by Rachel in French which he could not understand, for otherwise there was nothing at all with which to occupy the evening. And getting through the evening was always the 'great difficulty in Royal society'.[79]

* The Queen's taste for music was the one artistic pleasure she shared with her husband. She had no deep interest in literature – although after her Highland Journal was published her conversation took on a much more literary flavour[74] – believing to the end of her life that Marie Corelli would rank as one of the greatest writers of her time. She read a number of books every year but after Prince Albert's death they were mostly romantic novels.[75] The only paintings she liked were those that reproduced their subject with photographic accuracy. She treated the work of the Impressionists as a joke in rather bad taste.[76]

The Prince Consort, himself, confessed that he got bored in the evenings[80] and told his brother that he sometimes wished he were back at Coburg 'in a small house' instead of living the life that his sense of duty had imposed upon him.[81] He was constantly disappointed that he had not been able to fulfil his ambition and bring scientific and literary people about the Court, to make it a more general reflection of the life of the country.[82]

There were times, though, when he seemed relaxed and content. Children were born and he watched them grow with fond concern. 'He romps with them so delightfully,' the Queen wrote, 'and manages them so beautifully and firmly.'[83] And when they had gone to bed there were evenings when he could enjoy himself with his games of double chess and when he evidently derived deep pleasure from his organ which he played with 'such master skill', so a lady-in-waiting said, 'modulating so learnedly, winding through every kind of bass and chord'.[84] There were times, too, when he could indulge his taste for interior decoration by changing the appearance of a room in the Castle, re-hanging the Gainsboroughs and the Winterhalters, finding new places for the prints and etchings long since forgotten in the library drawers. *

Sometimes the Prince was even cheerful. His humour was generally limited to making puns and inventing riddles, and catching the unwary out on April Fool's Day.[86] But he was far from being as incapable of laughter as many of his contemporaries supposed. He was even capable of laughing at himself and had a large collection of caricatures, some of which lampooned him mercilessly.[87] One evening after dinner he showed the Queen and her ladies some caricatures, 'running from one to the other, and standing over us to see how we laughed,' the widowed Lady Lyttelton told her daughter, 'and laughing so loud himself as to be quite noisy and boyish. But' – and there was so often this '*but*' – 'his voice! It is sadly disenchanting.'[88]

The Queen without doubt still worshipped him. He was, she wrote in her journal, her 'inestimable husband and friend', her 'all in all'.[89] She could not disguise her pleasure at his 'utter indifference to the attraction of all ladies', nor could she disguise her jealousy of 'his talking much even to men',[90] for she was so afraid that he might develop other interests in which she could not join. But there

---

* He was not always very successful, although no room was made as forbidding as the drawing-room at Osborne which Roseberry once said he thought the ugliest in the world until he saw the one at Balmoral.[85]

was no fear of this. He was in that sense as in so many others a perfect husband for her. From the beginning he set himself the task of forming her mind, drawing out her natural talents and powers which had been only partially developed by her education, selflessly guiding her in the creation of a new English monarchical tradition.[91] He taught her to bear with more understanding and less resentment the actions and opinions of those she took to be her enemies, and he was so wise and unselfish, wary and discreet, that she was soon not only trusting him absolutely, allowing him to step on to the very throne of England, but expressing her belief that women were not fit to govern.[92] People began to refer to her, noticing the change, as Queen Albertine. She could disregard the scorn. To her it seemed a compliment. 'It is you,' she said to him, 'who have entirely formed me.' And she was proud and happy that it was so. She and the Prince were reading Hallam's *Constitutional History of England* 'together most carefully,' the royal children's governess noticed in the winter of 1842, 'and for a light book, *St Simon's Memoirs*. It was very pleasant to find him reading aloud to her while she waited, doing her cross-stitch, for one of her ladies to come in to dress her for dinner. Oh, what a blessing it was that love ruled the court!'[93]

The conversation at dinner on informal occasions began to be less trivial. 'Many bits of information, and naval matters, and scientific subjects come up, and are talked of very pleasantly,' Lady Lyttelton said. 'The Prince, of course, encourages such subjects.' He was always a 'nice neighbour', she thought, and the Baron was always 'comfortable and easy'. Indeed, dinner at the Castle was far less of an ordeal now. Sometimes when the Duke of Wellington came it was rather exhausting to have to sit next to him for he was so fearfully deaf and shouted so. '*Very good-looking man*,' he once bawled in Lady Lyttelton's ear, referring to the Tsar Nicholas i who sat immediately opposite and understood English perfectly. 'Always was so – scarcely altered since I saw him last – rather browner – no other change – very handsome man now – *don't you think so?*' And she felt compelled to scream out her answer, 'Yes, very handsome, indeed!' But usually it was just 'a great joke' to hear him talking 'as loud as thunder' about some 'matter of such serious and critical and difficult State importance that it ought only to have been alluded to in cabinet' and to see the Queen blushing 'over and over' and at last succeeding in 'screaming out upon some other subject'.[94]

After dinner it was sometimes almost gay in the drawing room now that Baroness Lehzen had gone. Occasionally the Prince, who nearly always left the dining-table before the other men, sang a duet with the Queen; and one evening the whole Court 'took to playing spillikins and puzzling with alphabets'; another evening they 'learnt a new round game', and they 'all grew quite noisy over it' – it was called *main jaune* and they liked it better than *mouche*. When they played *vingt-et-un* or Pope Joan the stakes were never high, and it was rather tiresome always to have to remember to carry new coins so that court etiquette should not be broken by passing used money to the Sovereign, but the maids of honour, all wearing their badge of the Queen's picture surrounded with brilliants on a red bow, looked so cheerful when they were gambling and a haul of even threepence excited them.[95] Quite often there was a children's dance or a children's charade and the little Prince of Wales did his 'highland fling, a sort of difficult and athletic hornpipe'. And then there were the balls when the reels and Scottish jigs, the 'wildest and merriest dances', were performed with such spirit and grace. And one evening they danced the reel 'con amore: it was very amusing and made the Queen laugh heartily'.[96] And on another evening the minuet broke down because the band could never learn the tune, so they danced 'quadrilles and Sir Roger de Coverley; and then the Queen issued her commands that every one should dance the country dance who could dance at all! The obedience was like the effect of a magical horn . . . Lord Aberdeen who looked more like a scarecrow than ever, quite as stiff as timber, and Sir Robert Peel, so mincing with his legs and feet, and his countenance full of the funniest attempt to look unconcerned and "matter of course", while he was evidently, very naturally, both shy and cross.'[97]

At Christmas, which was always spent at Windsor, the chandeliers were taken down in the Queen's private sitting room and big Christmas trees hung with candles and toffees took their place; and the dining-room tables were piled high with food and on the sideboard stood an immense baron of beef; and in the Oak Room there was another Christmas tree surrounded by presents for the members of the Household, and on each present was a card written by the Queen.[98] Everything, so the Prince told his brother, was 'totally German and *gemütlich*'.[99] Sometimes the lake at Frogmore would freeze over, and the family would walk down to the ice and the Prince would skate 'so picturesquely before them, the snowflakes from the trees caught in his hair'.[100]

*   *   *

The years passed and the Queen's devotion to her husband deepened. 'She is certainly an odd woman,' Charles Greville noted in his diary with more than a hint of scorn. 'Her devotion and submission seem to know no bounds.' She hated to be away from the Prince. Even to part from him for a day when he went shooting at Windsor caused her unhappiness,[101] and when he spent four days in Germany without her, she complained that his prolonged absence was *very* trying'. 'Four days absence!' Greville commented derisively, 'Her Majesty thinks nothing of taking her Ladies from their husbands and families for a month together.'[102]

She delighted in being alone with the Prince and was never more contented than when she was at Osborne, the small estate on the Isle of Wight which they had bought soon after their marriage so that they could have a place to do with as they liked, or when at Balmoral, the Scottish castle in the Highlands that they both loved, and when she could forget the Chartists and all those other tiresome people at home and abroad who were trying to disturb the settled and satisfactory structure of the world.

She would watch him as he sat at his desk, growing bald now and, despite his nervous energy, rather fat, writing with his sharp quill pen, drafting letters for her, thinking, planning, putting his sound common sense to a hundred different uses.

They were both called at seven o'clock by a wardrobe-maid and he got up almost immediately and went to his desk in his dressing-gown. He felt the cold and wore a wig indoors and he usually had a fire lit, although the Queen disapproved of this except in winter,[103] and even then she would only approve of beech-wood fires as she had the 'same rooted objection to coal as to gas'.[104] He dressed before breakfast, often putting on one of those gaily coloured waistcoats that his mother-in-law gave him at Christmas and always wearing the ribbon of the Garter under it.[105] At breakfast he read *The Times* and did not like to be disturbed, and sometimes he showed his irritation if his children or the Queen interrupted his concentration.[106]

Usually he was patient with the Queen, though. He was tolerant of her sometimes cloying admiration, for, after all, he did love her; he was tolerant, too, of her moods of gloomy depression, her self-indulgent lamentations when someone she loved died, her outbursts of irritation, her sudden and (except to him) engaging bouts of giggling. And there were those, of course, who thought that he was frightened of her.

At Windsor when the clocks struck eleven and it was time to go

32. George IV in his pony-chaise riding past Sandpit Gate Lodge

33. The King's Lodge

34. Virginia Water
from engravings by Melville in Robert Huish, *Memoirs of George IV*, 1830

35. Queen Victoria as a
young woman
from the miniature by Robert
Thorburn in the Royal Library, Windsor Castle

36. Queen Victoria in old
age
from a previously unpub-
lished photograph in the
Royal Portrait Albums
Windsor Castle

to bed, the Queen's voice could be heard: 'Tell Lord Alfred to let the Prince know that it is eleven o'clock. Tell him the Prince should merely be told the hour. The Prince wishes to be told, I know. He does not see the clock'.[107] And so the game was finished and the Prince obeyed his summons.

Greville believed, from what Lord Clarendon told him of conversations he had had with Baron Stockmar on the subject of the children's strict upbringing, that the 'Prince could do nothing; that he was completely cowed, and the Queen so excitable that the Prince lived in perpetual terror of bringing on the hereditary malady'. That he did not approve of the 'aggressive system' which the Queen adopted towards her children, but that he had 'always been embarrassed by the alarm he felt lest the Queen's mind should be excited by any opposition to her will'.[108]

Certainly the Queen was a selfish and sadly unimaginative, almost — despite her consciousness of her own inadequacies — an unfeeling mother, determined that her daughters should marry men who would not upset the rhythm of her life and that her sons should be treated with the most rigid severity, for they would have no one else to be strict with them unless their parents were. When they were small, their governess said she was *'exigeante'* and was always complaining that they were making insufficient progress or were too naughty.[109] And as they grew up she often spoke slightingly of them, wishing, for instance, that the Princess Royal was better looking, or that the Prince of Wales was more like his father. This was his trouble, of course, and everyone else's. No one compared well with the Prince. And she, for her part, needed no one else in her life, neither children nor intimate friends. She believed with an 'instinctive certainty' that God would *never* part them and that He would allow them to grow old together. But when on the evening of 1 December 1861 she came to bed and found him shivering with cold and unable to sleep, she felt at once that he was seriously ill.

He got up the next morning, however, and lay on a sofa while the Queen read to him. Sir James Clark was called and reassured her that he was suffering from a 'feverish sort of influenza'. 'I think that everything so far is satisfactory,' he said.[110] But he had been wrong about Lady Flora Hastings and he was wrong now. Dr William Jenner was asked for his opinion and he diagnosed typhoid fever.

For months the Prince, worn out by work and worry, had been suffering from a growing lassitude. 'I am tired, I am tired,' he had complained continuously as he looked out of the Castle windows across the Park to the stark shapes of the leafless chestnuts.[111] That year the Duchess of Kent had died at Frogmore and the Queen recorded with her sure eye for every vivid evocative detail, how a cock crowed and a dog barked in the distance and how a large watch in a tortoiseshell-case struck each quarter of an hour, bringing back all the recollections of her childhood, for she used to hear it at night at Kensington. The Prince 'melted into tears . . . unusual for him' when they realised that the faint breathing had stopped and he clasped the Queen in his arms and led her into the sitting-room where a 'little canary bird which *she* was so fond of' was singing.[112]

'I do not cling to life,' the Prince had told the Queen. 'If I had a severe illness, I should give up at once.'[113]

For a fortnight in December 1861 he lay dying in the Castle; and the Castle itself was, no doubt, the cause of his death.

Work had begun only fifteen years before on an adequate system of drainage, but only the main drains had been constructed and 'nothing had been done,' so the Lord Chamberlain reported, 'to improve the drains in connection with the various water closets, sinks, etc., within the Castle. The noxious effluvia which escapes from the old drains and the numerous cesspools still remaining, is frequently so exceedingly offensive as to render many parts of the Castle almost uninhabitable.'[114]

The Queen had suffered from typhoid fever many years before, the Prince of Wales was later to have an almost fatal attack, and now the Prince Consort was dying of it, and he knew that he was.

There was something else, though, the Queen thought, apart from the Castle drains, which was responsible for her husband's illness. A fortnight before that evening when she had come to bed to find him shivering feverishly, he had had a telegram to tell him that one of his favourite cousins, King Pedro of Portugal, had died of typhoid fever in Lisbon. The following day he was told something which, in the Queen's words, broke her Angel's heart: the Prince of Wales, at the age of nineteen, had got into trouble over a woman. The Prince Consort's reactions might seem abnormal, but he could not accept such information with a normal mind. Obsessively concerned with the reputation of monarchy, he was at the same time incapable of viewing sexual behaviour outside marriage with anything but horror and disgust. The Queen did not doubt that worry over their son was hurrying her husband to his grave. She refused to ask the Prince of Wales to come to Windsor, although she could not but be sure now that Albert was dying; and eventually he had to be summoned to the Castle by his sister without their mother's knowledge.[115]

*   *   *

Early on the morning of 14 December the Queen went into her husband's room, the Blue Room, in which her uncles George IV and William IV had both died. 'It was a bright morning, the sun just rising and shining brightly,' she remembered. 'The room had the sad look of night-watching, the candles burnt down to their sockets, the doctors looked anxious. I went in, and never can I forget how beautiful my darling looked.'[116]

She never did forget. At first she 'thought she was going mad' with grief. During his illness, while she watched over him as he lay on his bed moaning when she kissed him as if he felt that she was leaving him, she had not once cried; but every hour or so she had gone into the next room and given way to 'a terrible burst of misery'.[117] Nor when she knew that he was dead had she cried out, but had kissed him on the forehead and, dropping to her knees, had 'called him by every endearing name',[118] before being helped from the room. But now she kept tapping her forehead and repeating 'My reason, my reason.'[119] Dr Jenner prescribed the comforting presence of her four-year-old daughter Beatrice, who was brought down to her bedroom every morning as soon as she woke up;[120] but the close warmth of the child did little to alleviate her mother's loneliness, and a change of scene seemed essential. The Queen took her uncle's advice and, so as not to be at Windsor while the funeral was taking place in St George's Chapel, she left the Castle for Osborne, wearing the widow's clothes she never discarded.*

She was only forty-two, but it was as if she were already an old woman. The Prince had said of her that she lived 'much in the past and in the future, perhaps more than in the present'.[122] When he died she abandoned herself to the past and to her memories of him with a passionate intensity. It was selfish and hysterical, but it was predictable. She could not forget him: no one else must. Everyone at Court had to wear mourning on all social occasions until the end of 1862; and after 1864, although her ladies were allowed to wear grey, violet, lilac or white, the Lady-in-Waiting was obliged to

---

* She had always had an excessive, almost hysterical predilection for mourning and a deep concern for its correct observance. She had caused 'IMMEDIATE search to be made for Precedents as to the Court going or not going into mourning for a sovereign with whom at the time of his decease England was at war' when the Tsar died during the course of the Crimean War.[121]

continue to wear mourning as deep as the Queen's own.[123] Even the Castle servants had to wear 'a black crape band upon their left arm for at least eight years'.[124]

She gave orders that at Windsor and elsewhere, her husband's rooms were to remain exactly as he had left them, and she had cards fixed to the doors, not only of his rooms but of her own boudoir, which informed the curious that everything within had been arranged by the Prince.[125] No clothes, no papers were to be touched. Lytton Strachey recorded, on the evidence of 'private information' – 'gossip' a Lord-in-Waiting, Lord Ribblesdale called it, 'which even in my time [the 1880s] nobody believed',[126] although it was in fact quite true – that each evening at Windsor a manservant placed a jug of hot water in his dressing-room and laid out fresh clothes on his bed.[127] It has also been recorded that before she signed a document of State she would look up at the Prince's marble effigy and ask him softly if he approved,[128] and that the glass from which he had taken his last dose of medicine was kept by his bedside in the Blue Room and that it remained there for forty years.[129] And almost every day she strewed fresh flowers on his bed and took more to St George's Chapel.[130]

It was expected that he would be buried at Windsor in the chapel which Henry VII had begun in 1494 as a tombhouse for himself and Henry VI and which Wolsey, who had been a canon at Windsor between 1511 and 1514, had also hoped to occupy when he was dead. The Queen had its walls lined with marble and its roof crowned with copper, and on the sarcophagus the wings of four bronze angels supported the Prince's marble effigy. The tombhouse was renamed the Albert Memorial Chapel.

She had never intended, however, that he should be buried there, but, in accordance with the 'Prince's own inclinations', in a more pastoral setting.[131] And so, a year after his death, his body was removed from St George's Chapel, where it had lain in the entrance to the royal vault, and taken to a mausoleum at Frogmore, near the mausoleum where his mother-in-law the Duchess of Kent lay buried. And it was to Frogmore that the Queen herself was to be taken when the century was past.

[ii]

VICTORIA – THE WIDOW AT WINDSOR

The Queen lived on as a widow for forty years. In the beginning she shut herself away with her family and Household, seeing her Cabinet Ministers as rarely as she could. When she came to Windsor or left it, the railway station had to be cleared of other passengers as if she were in *purdah*. She had only been able to tolerate her duties as Queen, the ceremonial functions of monarchy, she explained, because of the support of her husband. Now that he was gone, they could not expect her to carry on as before.

When the Prince of Wales was married in St George's Chapel in March 1863 to Princess Alexandra, daughter of Prince Christian of Schleswig-Holstein-Sonderburg-Glucksburg and niece of the King of Denmark, the Queen looked down upon the tiaras from the high oak closet on the north side of the altar that Henry VIII had built so that Catherine of Aragon could watch the ceremonies of the Order of the Garter. She was wearing the black streamers of widowhood and a long white veil, and her only concession to the happy splendour of the occasion was a badge of the Order of the Garter that her 'beloved one had worn'. She had 'felt very low and nervous *before*,' Lady Augusta Bruce recorded. 'All seemed so lost without him to organise and arrange everything, and all were there with their Husbands. Where was Hers?'[1] And now in the Chapel she was 'agitated and restless, moving her chair, putting back her long streamers, asking questions of the Duchess of Sutherland. Her expression was profoundly melancholy.'[2] When the organ played the first anthem, to 'his' music, and Jenny Lind sang in the chorale she sat 'as if transfixed'. She looked across at the new East Window and reredos that the Dean and Canons had erected in his memory (in place of Benjamin West's Resurrection which Fanny Burney had found so 'earthly'[3]) and she suffered 'indescribably'. 'Not a gleam of joy at her son's marriage illumined her desolation.'[4]

Yet the wedding was, in Disraeli's opinion, 'a fine affair, a thing to remember'; and Bishop Wilberforce thought it 'the most moving sight' he ever saw. The only unpleasant moments were when the bridegroom's four-year-old nephew, the future Kaiser William II, tried to throw the cairngorm from the head of his dirk across the choir and, his uncles Prince Alfred and Prince Leopold restraining

213

him, he 'showed his displeasure by biting them hard on the legs';[5] and when the Eton boys, who had been given a holiday, rushed at the bridal carriage on its way to the railway station.

Nothing stood before us [one of these excited boys, Lord Randolph Churchill, told his father]. The policemen charged in a body, but they were knocked down. There was a chain put across the road, but we broke that; several old *genteel* ladies tried to stop me, but I snapped my fingers in their face and cried, 'Hurrah!' and 'What larks!' I frightened some of them horribly. There was a wooden palisade put up at the station but we broke it down. . . . I got right down to the door of the carriage where the Prince of Wales was, wildly shouting 'Hurrah!' He bowed to me, I am perfectly certain; but I shrieked louder. I am sure, if the Princess did not possess very strong nerves, she would have been frightened; but all she did was to smile blandly.[6]

The Queen, meanwhile, was performing her duty to her nine hundred guests; and as soon as she had done so, she went down the path to Frogmore to give way to her tears alone in the Prince Consort's mausoleum.[7]

As the years passed and she showed little inclination to come out of her lugubrious seclusion, her people began to grumble and the newspapers took up their complaint.

There were malicious rumours, too, about her relationship with one of her Scottish servants, the gillie John Brown, who had been sent down from Balmoral to Osborne with her favourite pony when she refused to leave her rooms in the early agonies of her bereavement, as it was hoped that the sight of them would tempt her to take some exercise. Brown, faithful, honest and blunt, had already been a servant for twelve years then and the Queen, so obviously in need of a link with her dead husband that it was said in London that Brown acted as a medium at seances, became excessively fond of him, allowing him to say things to her which she would not have permitted in anyone else. He put whisky in her picnic hamper, he criticised her clothes, he even, on occasions, called her 'woman'. He was appallingly disrespectful not only to her but to the members of her Household and her Ministers whom he would slap on the back. Gladstone detested this 'moor-cock turned peacock' as Ivor Brown has aptly described him,[8] but Disraeli was astute enough to come to terms with him.[9] It was as well to do so, for Brown, in the Queen's own words, was 'groom, footman, page and maid'. He came to Windsor when she came, sleeping in a room not far from hers, and she grew to depend upon him 'in a manner both touching and ludicrous'.[10] She was undoubtedly attracted by him as a man, but no one close to them seems to have believed that their relationship was anything more than that of employer and devoted, if tiresome and objectionable, retainer. The lives that kings and queens are constrained to lead makes them liable, of course, to particularly close relationships with servants who do not have the same sort of ambitions that courtiers and politicians have; and Queen Victoria was peculiarly susceptible to such influences. She was always indulgent with her servants — except with housemaids who put things back in their wrong places — and she could never bring herself to feel the indignation of her informants when told of the pilfering and tippling that went on below stairs at Windsor. 'It always distresses one to see so much of it,' Lady Lytton, one of her ladies-in-waiting, recorded in her journal;[11] but the Queen did not seem to mind. When a drunken footman fell over and dropped a lighted lamp in the Castle, her only recorded comment was, 'Poor man!'[12]

With Scottish servants she was especially indulgent — for most things Scottish she had a high regard, and one of her favourite statues of Albert was one which portrayed him in the dress of a Highlander — and with Brown she was so indulgent that stories of a criminally irresponsible liaison, given a quasi-authentic air by such publications as *Mrs John Brown*, were widely accepted as true.

Brown's behaviour at the servant's ball at Windsor has been amusingly described by Lord Ribblesdale, a lord-in-waiting:

Mr John Brown acted as Master of the Ceremonies in the Evening tartan of the Stuarts. The Queen, a terpsichore of the first order in her younger days – at least, so Mr Strachey tells us – followed the evolutions of the dancers with a benevolent but critical eye. Deference was paid to the Highland character and preferences of the Mistress and Household. We had what seemed to be incessant reels, Highland schottisches, and a complicated sustained measure called the 'Flowers of Edinburgh'. Even with proficiency this dance requires constant attention, if not actual presence of mind, to be in the right place at the right moment – anyhow, more than I possessed in the mazy labyrinth. I was suddenly impelled almost into the Queen's lap with a push in the back and 'Where are you coming to?' It was Mr John Brown exercising his legitimate office as M.C. After a good many Caledonians, Mr Brown came to ask the Queen, 'Now what's you Majesty for?' Mindful of her English subjects the Queen suggested a country dance. This did not find favour. 'A country dance,' he repeated, turning angrily on his heels.[13]

When Brown died in 1883 she erected a monument to his memory; she had numerous statuettes of him made; and every Sunday at

Windsor she had placed on her luncheon table where she could see them two silver salt cellars, in the shape of shells supported by mermaids, which he had given her.[14] She would have written a third journal of her life in the Highlands, which would have been all about John Brown, had not the Dean of Windsor, Randall Davidson, advised her strongly against it. She was very cross and Davidson felt obliged to offer his resignation,[15] but in the end she agreed that Volume 3 should not be written and Davidson ultimately became Archbishop of Canterbury.

The damage, however, had already been done. Queen Albertine, formerly Mrs Melbourne, was now – and the insinuation was far more damaging in late nineteenth-century society – Mrs Brown.

* * *

A republican feeling had already grown up in England. Charles Bradlaugh, the Radical atheist, made speeches condemning the Royal Family; numerous republican clubs were inaugurated all over the country; G. O. Trevelyan in a widely read pamphlet entitled *What does she do with it?* condemned the Queen's parsimony and her hoarding of money; and Charles Dilke, who estimated the cost of the Royal Family to the nation at £1,000,000 a year, suggested in a loudly cheered and much praised speech at Newcastle that this enormous expenditure was 'chiefly not waste but mischief'.[16] When, referring to the extravagant numbers of officials at Court, Dilke said that one of them was a court undertaker, a man in the crowded audience called out that it was a pity there was not more work for him to do.[17]

It was felt, too, that despite the great cost of maintaining the Royal Family, foreign rulers and other important people were not being received during their visits in the way that they ought to have been received.

Before the Prince's death, in a single year (in 1841) altogether 113,000 people had dinner at Windsor.[18] But since he had died the Queen seemed to have given up entertaining almost entirely. Queen Emma of the Sandwich Islands who came to England in 1865 was asked, for instance, to come to Windsor at half-past three in the afternoon so that the Queen would not have to have luncheon with her.[19]

Comparisons were made with the splendid receptions formerly given to the Tsar Nicholas I, the King of Saxony, Prince William of Prussia, King Louis Philippe, the King of Sardinia, Napoleon III and the Empress Eugénie, all of which had been very popular in the country: 'The Queen was being magnificent in her entertainment of the Kings of the earth (and that is what a Queen should be).'[20] People could feel proud that in the magnificent Waterloo banqueting hall at Windsor, their Queen 'the little *Hausfrau*', in Lytton Strachey's evocative words, 'who had spent the day before walking out with her children, inspecting her livestock, practising scales at the piano, and filling up her journal with adoring descriptions of her husband, suddenly shone forth, without art, without effort, by a spontaneous and natural transition, the very culmination of Majesty'.[21]

It had not mattered that the Tsar, according to Greville, had been 'excessively disgusted with the dullness of the Court' at Windsor, nor that, as Lady Lyttelton said, his suite were 'one more hideous than the other', nor that the suite of Louis Philippe seemed grave and bored, nor that the King of Sardinia appeared to be 'frightful in his person, a great, strong, burly, athletic man, brusque in his manners, unrefined in his conversation, very loose in his conduct, very eccentric in his habits', the only Knight of the Garter that the Duchess of Sutherland had ever seen 'who looked as if he would have the best of it with the dragon'.[22] Nor had it mattered that the Queen had put up her face to be kissed 'for ever so long before the King of Sardinia consented to touch it' nor that when eventually he had kissed her face, 'he began upon her hand, and bestowed upon it three kisses that resounded through the room'. It had not even mattered that when he was installed as a Knight of the Garter, he had put forward one leg, then the other until 'at last he said to the Queen in his loud, short, voice, "*laquelle?*". She nearly let fall the Garter from laughing, the Prince was in fits and all the K.G.'s at the table began to titter.'[23]

Nor had it been of much consequence that the Prince Consort did not – as was well known – approve of the morals of Napoleon III who 'struck everybody', so Charles Greville said, as a 'mean and diminutive figure' of vulgar appearance. And it had only been a momentary embarrassment when the Prince seemed to take 'longer than usual' to tie the Garter buckle round the leg of the Emperor, who afterwards put his wrong arm through the ribbon.[24] For the visits were all, on the whole, as successful as such visits could ever hope to be. Indeed, the success of Napoleon III's visit had been 'complete'. Elaborate preparations had been 'put in hand', as Raymond Mortimer explains in his introduction to the Queen's own subsequently published account of the visit; 'new carpets and silks were bought for the suite to be occupied by the imperial couple; the furniture was regilded; the Waterloo Chamber was tactfully renamed.' The Queen had decided that the Emperor was entrancing, 'so very quiet, good natured and unassuming and natural'. And with the King of Sardinia she had been 'wonderfully cordial and attentive' and had got up at four o'clock in the morning to see him depart.[25]

Of course, it was often difficult for a woman of the Queen's temperament to tolerate the eccentricities of some of these visiting monarchs without the support of her husband.

When the Tsar had come to Windsor his first action was to send to the stables for a bundle of straw on which to sleep, and he had spent a large part of the next day making eyes at all the pretty women he saw. And when King Louis Philippe came to the Castle – the first time a French King had visited England since 1356, when John II had been brought there after the battle of Poitiers – he was preceded by an alarming letter from his daughter who said that he must on no account be allowed to come down to breakfast as he would certainly eat something if he did and this was dangerous before he had his chicken broth a little later on, that he must have a hard bed with a horse-hair mattress, laid, if possible, on a plank, and that he must never be allowed to ride the horses which he was having sent over from France.[26] These instructions did not worry her unduly, however, for Albert was there. But now that he was there no longer, the arrangements that had to be made for such potentates as the Sultan of Turkey and the Shah of Persia were excessively tiresome and worrying to her. A report about the Shah's behaviour and entourage that reached Windsor from Berlin was, for instance, peculiarly distressing: 'His Majesty generally dines alone, and when so, prefers to have his meals on the carpet. For that purpose a moveable carpet should be kept ready whereupon *his* servants will put the dishes etc. brought to the door by the English servants . . . The Shah does not like to have cut up his meats. Rice, lamb, mutton, fowls are favourite dishes. The cuisine should be somewhat *relevée.'* According to the British ambassador in Berlin nobody had ever dared venture to tell the Shah that he should not put his arm round the Queen's chair at dinner, 'or put his fingers into dishes, or take food out of his mouth again to look at it after it has been chewed, or fling it under the table if it does not suit his taste', and that he should not make such embarassing attempts to console himself for the absence of his harem.[27]

The Queen could not perhaps be blamed then for being so 'fidgety', as her Secretary, Sir Henry Ponsonby, described her, before the Shah's visit to Windsor and for asking crossly why he was called 'Imperial'. 'Because he is the Shah in Shah', Ponsonby replied. 'Well, that's no reason!' she snapped; and the title was removed from the programme.[28] But she *could* be blamed, it was generally agreed, for twice changing her mind about the date of the Military Review to be held in his honour in the Park, and for declining to come down from Balmoral a single day early for the Sultan's visit when, as the Prime Minister put it, English influence was just now paramount at Constantinople and might well be damaged if the Sultan were received less royally and graciously at Windsor than in Paris or Berlin.[29] And she *could* be blamed for refusing to return the hospitality of the Tsar, who had entertained the Prince of Wales for three weeks, because she was 'UTTERLY *incapable* of entertaining any Royal personage as she would wish to do, except those who are very nearly related to her, and for whom she need not alter her mode of life'.[30]

Eventually she gave in, though. Having made her vehement protests, she entertained the Tsar, just as, after overcoming her gloomy and hypochondriacal apprehension, she consented to put herself out for the Sultan and the Shah. Indeed, she quite enjoyed their visits. The Sultan was so obviously delighted with Windsor and with the Order of the Garter which the Prince of Wales persuaded his mother to give him, although a Moslem. And the Shah turned out to be a far less formidable person than she had feared, 'fairly tall and not fat', with a 'fine countenance and very animated'. She received him in full state at Windsor, wearing her large pearls, and she sat next to him in the middle of the White Drawing Room, surrounded by Persian and English Princes and Princesses, conscious of the absurd figure she must have cut and feeling 'very shy'. But he behaved most decorously and was so impressively attired with huge rubies as buttons in his diamond-studded coat, and epaulettes of diamonds and emeralds. She invested him with the Garter and, having kissed her hand, he gave her two Orders in return and the Grand Vizier helped to save her hat from falling off.

At luncheon in the Oak Room, bagpipers marched up and down and the Shah told her that he had had her *Leaves from the Journal of a Life in the Highlands* translated into Persian so that he could read it. He had little to eat but fruit, so that he had no opportunity of transgressing western decorum as he had on another occasion when he threw an unwanted quail bone under the table,[31] and he drank quantities of iced water and afterwards he went for a rest attended by his Pipe-bearer and Cup-bearer. When he appeared again he had taken the aigrette of diamonds out of his astrakhan hat and put on his spectacles. The Queen was so pleased with him that she conducted him all over the Castle herself, and when he left it he showed the crowd a miniature of Her Majesty 'set in diamonds, which she had given him, and kissed it with reverence'.[32]

*   *   *

These days of pleasure were rare now. The Queen had outgrown the worst of her grief; but there was always this insistent conscious-ness of bereavement and widowhood.

Her general mode of life was still severe as well as withdrawn. And it continued to be severe after the Prince of Wales's recovery from typhoid fever in 1871 and her own survival of attempts on her life in 1872, after the hectoring, rough affection of the faithful John Brown and the amusing society of the chivalrous Disraeli – so welcome a relief from the critical Gladstone and the rudely self-opinionated although ultimately acceptable Palmerston – and after the profoundly beneficial effect of the publication of her warm and human *Highland Journals*, had all contributed to restore to the Queen her lost popularity and to bring her out from the black shrouds of her self-enforced seclusion.

It was still an austere life, for she remained for ever conscious of her widowhood and the influence of the long dead Prince. She might smile sometimes, even laugh; she began once more to record incidents in her diary that had amused her; her letters became more cheerful; she brought herself to play nostalgic tunes on her piano, and she began to dance again – she was still dancing ('like a pot' a German prince whose English was not strong enough for the com-pliment informed her) at Windsor when she was seventy – she told funny stories about herself and was fond of relating how one clear and starlit night she had opened her bedroom window to look out into the dark sky and a sentry at the foot of the Castle wall, thinking she must be a housemaid, 'began to address her in most affectionate and endearing terms. The Queen at once drew her curtains but was simply delighted at what had happened.'[33] She was still capable of exercising an undoubted charm, which a Dean of Windsor described as 'irresistible'.[34]

There was no relaxation, though, in the prudery that the memory of Albert's strict moral sense had emphasised. At meal times she would suddenly change the conversation if it took an unsuitable turn, and when she overheard what she believed to be excessive eagerness in conversation or a lack of delicacy in laughter at the other end of the table she would ask what the subject of discussion was, and if she did not think it was a proper one she would indicate her disapproval and thereafter the meal continued in embarrassing silence. This was not, however, always considered a disadvantage, for at least it ensured that the members of the Household could keep their eyes on their plates and concentrate on eating rather than on whispered exchanges with a neighbour. This was important, as the Queen ate quickly and the servants, according to Lord Ribblesdale, had 'a menial trick of depriving us of our plates as soon as she had finished'. The lords-in-waiting, being 'mostly of the deferential breed', did not complain and were, therefore, all the more astounded when one evening a guest did complain. This was Lord Hartington who was in the middle of enjoying some mutton and green peas.

'The Queen could dispose of peas with marvellous skill and dexterity [Lord Ribblesdale said], and had got into conversation with Lord Hartington, thus delaying his own operations. They got on very well together. Though Lord Hartington, like Peel and the Duke of Wellington, had neither small talk nor manners, yet he seemed to me less shy with the Queen than with his neighbours. This may be accounted for, perhaps, by their both being absolutely natural and their both being in no sort of doubt about their positions.

'Well, anyhow, in the full current of their conversation the mutton was taken away from him. He stopped in the middle of a sentence in time to arrest the scarlet-clad marauder: "Here bring that back!"'

The members of the Household held their breath, but when Lord Ribblesdale looked up at the Queen he saw that she was both amused and pleased. 'I knew this,' he said, 'by one of the rare smiles, as different as possible to the civil variety which, overtired, uninterested or thinking about something else, she contributed to the conventional observations of her visitors.'[35]

Lord Ribblesdale had to admit, though, that for the most part the Queen's own observations were conventional in the extreme. 'One way or another,' he wrote in his memoirs, 'I must have dined a great many times at the Queen's dinner party, and I personally never heard her say anything at dinner which I remembered next morning. Her manners were not affable; she spoke very little at meals; and she ate fast and very seldom laughed. To the dishes she rejected she made a peevish *moue* with crumpled brow more eloquent than words.'[36]

Even when she entertained guests she had not previously met, she did not, apparently, make any noticeable effort to entertain them. The young and beautiful American heiress Consuelo Vanderbilt, who had married the Duke of Marlborough, came to Windsor to be presented in 1896 and found the old Queen 'so severe and sombre'. 'It seemed to me,' she wrote years later, 'that it was her deliberate intention to emphasize the dignity of her rank and person, and I felt that any warmth she might have possessed must have been buried with the Prince Consort.' Dinner was a 'most depressing function. Conversation was carried on in whispers, for the Queen's stern personality imposed restraint'.[37]

Sometimes, however, those who sat next to the Queen when she was in a more lively mood were surprised to find that, despite her habit of turning a conversation into a rigorous cross-examination, she was a less forbidding personage than they had been led to expect. Aga Khan, for instance, who was a guest at Windsor two years after the Duchess of Marlborough, found the 'facility and clarity' of her conversation 'astonishing'. 'She had an odd accent,' he thought, 'a mixture of Scotch and German' with 'the German conversational trick of interjecting "so" – pronounced "tzo" – into her remarks.' She wore on her wrist – as she always did[38] – a large diamond bracelet, in the centre of which was a miniature of the Prince Consort and a lock of his hair, and her appetite was wonderful.

The dinner was long and elaborate [Aga Khan remembered]. Course after course, three or four choices of meat, a hot pudding and an iced pudding, a savoury and all kinds of hothouse fruit – slow and stately in its serving. We sat down at a quarter past nine, and it must have been a quarter to eleven before it was all over. The Queen, in spite of her age, ate and drank heartily – every kind of wine that was offered,* and every course, including both the hot and iced pudding.[39]

The Hon. Reginald Brett, who had been a guest at Windsor the year before, and Lady Ribblesdale had also both noticed how excellent was the Queen's appetite. She preferred plain food, such as boiled chicken and roast beef, haggis and potatoes, to anything more

---

* This was unusual. Although the immense wine cellars at Windsor, thanks to George IV who made the most of his right to import wine duty free, were extraordinarily well-stocked with what Lord Ribblesdale considered 'superlative' wines, the Queen generally preferred a glass of the Scotch whisky which was distilled expressly for her by John Begge. She drank it with Apollinaris, soda or lithia water.

exotic; but she liked a good helping and she liked her brown Windsor soup made no longer simply, with ham and calves' feet as served to her children in the nursery, but including game, madeira wine and shell-fish; and she loved her puddings, her cranberry tarts and cream, her chocolate cakes and chocolate biscuits, her 'stodgy trifle of jam and sponge cakes'.[40]

Gold plate, and beautiful Sevres [Brett recorded in his journal], Indian servants behind the Queen. A Highlander to pour out the wine. The Queen ate everything. No 'courses'. Dinner is served straight on, and when you finish one dish you get the next, without a pause for breath. Everyone talked as at any other dinner, only in subdued tones. The Queen was in excellent humour. After dinner the Queen rose and we stood back against the wall. She went out and we followed. Immediately to the left of the doorway in the Corridor was placed a chair, and in front of it a little table. There the Queen seated herself. We stood in a circle at a considerable distance away from her. The coffee was brought and liqueurs. The Queen sipped her coffee while a page held the saucer on a small waiter. Then the princess spoke to the Queen for a few minutes, and afterwards moved to Nellie [Mrs Brett]. The Queen talked a while to Lady Downe, who was sent to fetch Nellie. Meanwhile the circle whispered discreetly.[41]

The Queen demanded impeccable discretion in conduct as well as in conversation. She found it difficult to forget – and the Prince perhaps had found it impossible to forgive – the conduct of Palmerston, who, 'always enterprising and audacious with women', had once, years before, at Windsor gone into the room of one of her ladies in the unfulfilled hope of seducing her.[42] George Anson, the Prince's secretary, putting a slightly different interpretation on Palmerston's visit, recorded that he had been accustomed to sleeping with another lady in that bedroom and 'probably from force of habit floundered in'.[43]

Nor could the Queen forget how badly Lady Augusta Somerset, eldest daughter of the Duke of Beaufort, had behaved with her cousin Prince George of Cambridge and how when there were rumours that she had become pregnant by him she had been brought to the Castle, so it seemed, to get rid of the scandal. Albert had said that as Prince George had given him his word of honour that the story was untrue they must believe it was so, and the Queen herself had written to the Beauforts to say that, as she was now entirely satisfied, she begged there might be no further discussion on the subject.[44] But the unpleasant memory of suspicion lingered. To satisfy the Queen, people whose birth or duties brought them into her presence must not merely be innocent, they must never have appeared to be guilty.

They must also conform to those rules of conduct she established for her Household. It was well known, for instance, that she did not approve of any of its younger members, of either sex, getting married. The maids-of-honour, in fact, had never been allowed to receive any man, even their brother, in their own rooms, and they had had to entertain them as best they could in the waiting-room downstairs. When Sir James Reid, her Resident Physician and a particular favourite of hers, being both a Scot and a German scholar, had the audacity to become engaged to one of her maids-of-honour, Susan Baring, Lord Revelstoke's daughter and Maurice Baring's sister, the Queen was so cross she refused to see Reid for three days and only forgave him when he amused her by promising 'never to do it again'.[45]

It was also well known that there must be no smoking in any room she might enter. Nor were her secretaries allowed to smoke when handling papers she might have to touch.[46] Before she was persuaded – apparently by John Brown – that a little tobacco smoke was 'no bad thing to have about a hoose', cards were framed and hung upon the walls of the Castle calling attention to the prohibition against smoking;[47] and visitors to Windsor waited until the Queen went to bed and they could go along to the billiard-room, the only place where smoking was tolerated.[48]   Once Count Hatzfeldt, who could not be bothered to make the long journey to the billiard-room, yet 'could not live without a cigar', was reduced to lying on his bedroom floor and blowing the smoke up the chimney.[49] The King of Saxony was less discreet and profoundly shocked the Court by having the audacity to walk up the grand staircase with a cigar in his mouth.*[50] Courtiers who smoked secretly took to carrying peppermints in their pockets, for there was no telling when a summons to the Queen might come; and even to be in church was no excuse for being late in answering it.†[52]

* The Queen herself was apparently capable of smoking out of doors. Lord Churchill told Lord Mersey in 1931 that he could remember, as a small boy, being taken on a picnic by his mother, who was one of the Queen's ladies-in-waiting. The flies were 'very tiresome, so the Queen lit a cigarette and puffed the smoke very delicately at them'.[51]

† The Queen had never herself been a convinced churchwoman, and was a tireless critic of church dignitaries. Her journal contains many references to 'terribly long services'; and she had always detested long sermons, of which she grew increasingly intolerant in her old age. The Duke of Portland recorded that A. V. Baillie, later to be Dean of Windsor, but then a young curate, once asked Sir Henry Ponsonby for his advice about a sermon

37. Queen Victoria and Prince Albert on the East Terrace
from the engraving by T. A. Prior after T. Allom

38. The Queen and Prince Albert after the Prince's return from shooting from the painting by Landseer in the Royal Collection

The duties of a courtier were rendered even more tiresome by the rule that all communications with the Queen had to be in writing and the letters, which had to be sealed with an official seal, had also to be couched in the most formal terms. As the Queen's eyesight became very bad during the last years of her life it was necessary to make each word big and unmistakably legible, and Frederick Ponsonby, who was appointed Assistant Private Secretary in 1895, was constrained to buy some copy-books published for girls' schools and 'some special ink like boot varnish' and to develop a completely new handwriting. It was unfortunately so large and black, though, that it showed through on the other side of the paper and he was compelled to write on one side only, and, as the Queen kept all the important papers in a case in her room, this did not suit her, for in a short time they became so bulky. He was told to revert to his former method. He ordered a much thicker paper which would carry the writing on both sides; but this did not suit the Queen either. He went back to ordinary paper and ordinary ink, and was told to write blacker because she couldn't read his writing. Ponsonby 'grasped that it was hopeless' and consulted Sir James Reid who told him that explanations would be useless.[54]

It was not only, as Reid knew, that the Queen would not have accepted the explanation, but that she might well have been cross with Reid and Ponsonby for bringing the unpalatable fact of her failing sight into discussion. Ponsonby himself had had experience of this problem. While his father was alive and acting as Private Secretary, Frederick Ponsonby was serving in the Army in India and the Queen had sent him a telegram asking him to go and see the father of her favourite Indian servant whom she had recently promoted from Khidmutgar to Munshi, destroying all photographs of him handing dishes to her and giving him permission to enter the billiard-room and even the dining-room as though he were one of her secretaries.[55] The Munshi was (like John Brown) a man whom the rest of the Household found disconcertingly pretentious. He went everywhere with the Queen, giving her daily lessons in Hindustani, and he was soon an object of jealousy and hatred. His father, so he said, was a Surgeon-General in the Indian Army. Ponsonby did as he was asked, sought the man out in India and discovered that he was, in fact, an apothecary in the gaol at Agra. Ponsonby told the Queen

he was to preach in the Queen's presence. 'It doesn't matter much *what* you say,' Ponsonby told him, 'because Her Majesty is too deaf to hear, and will probably go to sleep; but on no account let it last for more than five minutes.'[53]

this when he came to Windsor to take up his Household appointment and for a year she did not ask him to dinner.[56]

Thereafter he acted with extreme caution in his dealings with her. One of his duties was to write out the details of certain public occasions to enable her to enter them accurately in her diary; and when in 1897 she reviewed the Colonial troops and it was reported in the newspapers that she had spoken to the Indian officers in Hindustani, which he knew she had not done, he did not know whether to add this item or not. He decided to do so, but when the Queen had Ponsonby's account read out to her she commented, 'That's not true. I did not speak in Hindustani but in English.' Should that part be crossed out? she was asked. 'No,' she said, 'you can leave it, for I could have done so had I wished.'[57]

More and more imperious, cantankerous and forthright as she became old, she let it be known that she did not want anyone to meet her in the Park when she went out for a drive in her pony chair. The very sight of this carriage was enough to make men jump out of sight behind trees and bushes, and once when the Chancellor of the Exchequer found himself in danger with no suitable cover in sight – for he was six feet four inches tall – he was advised to turn back.*[58] New servants were not permitted to look her in the face, for, although she loved to have her photograph taken, she hated to be stared at by strangers, and when receiving orders they had to look at the ground by her feet. If she by chance met one of them in a corridor of the Castle as she passed by in her wheel-chair or hobbled along with the help of a stick and an Indian attendant, she would look straight ahead as if he were not there.[60]

Her closest attendants in these years were her Indians – 'rather second-rate servants', Aga Khan thought them.[61] When they were not required to serve her with food, they stood motionless behind her chair, dressed in scarlet and gold in winter, in white in summer, their hands clasped in front of their sashes, their beards so startlingly black against the pale, spotless cloth. They were there at

---

* It was sometimes as difficult to keep visitors out of each other's sight as out of the Queen's. One day Frederick Ponsonby was told to ensure that two Spanish diplomatists did not meet, for if they did they would certainly spit at each other. To avoid this, Ponsonby was obliged suddenly to push one of the incompatible diplomatists into a nearby room and shut the door, telling him that there was a picture he was most anxious for him to see. Ponsonby pointed to one and said, for want of anything better to say, 'We have never been able to find out for certain who it was of and who it was by.'

The Spaniard looked at the picture which had the artist's name displayed beneath it in large letters. 'I see clearly the name Winterhalter,' he said.

'Ah!' Ponsonby replied, desperately. 'But is it by Winterhalter? *That* is the point.'[59]

breakfast, which she had in the oak dining room in the middle of the corridor (see plate 29) with a gold breakfast service on the table and her egg in a golden cup; they were there at luncheon, and they were there at dinner and they rarely seemed to move. Neither at breakfast, nor at luncheon were there any members of her Household at her table. The ladies of the Household had these meals in the big dining room with the lord-in-waiting; the gentlemen had theirs in a downstairs room adjoining the equerries' room. In the evening those members not invited to the royal table all dined together and were afterwards occasionally invited to the White Drawing Room after dinner where they stood 'for an hour; but the usual routine was that those who were not wanted by the Queen remained in the Red Drawing Room until a page came in and announced in sepulchral tones that the Queen had gone to bed.' It was usually cold there, as the Queen had a horror of overheated rooms – and saw to it that there was a thermometer on the mantelpiece of every room in the Castle.[62] 'Sometimes whist would be played, and candles had to be sent for. After much trouble a card table with candles and cards was prepared. Usually the pack was one card short.'[63] As the Queen disliked changes in her Household, most of its members were very old – some of them were over eighty – and consequently the few young ones did not enjoy their evenings much. 'As no one had the least knowledge of whist, I cannot say it was amusing,' Frederick Ponsonby commented sadly. 'Lord Stafford, who was an equerry, had always been told that the danger of card-playing was that unscrupulous people looked over one's hand, and therefore held his hands so tightly under his chin that it took him nearly two whole minutes to find a card. Of course no smoking was allowed.'[64]

The Queen, perhaps, understood little of their boredom. She did not often see them, except at dinner, and spent most of her free time with her ladies and with her youngest daughter Beatrice, Princess Henry of Battenberg – whose husband and four children lived with the Queen – and with those numerous relatives who came frequently to visit her.

It was an honour to come, for she was Europe's matriarch. Understanding this and that the strange, often irritable, old 'Widow at Windsor' in her shapeless but expensive black clothes, her widow's cap occasionally enlivened by diamond stars at a dinner-party, her several lockets containing strands of hair or miniature portraits of her innumerable relations, knowing that this little woman was the ruler also of an immense Empire (with which Disraeli had so skilfully identified her), her own people, too, felt proud that she belonged to them. She might have some curious ideas and many outrageously provocative opinions. She might be 'Coburgised from head to foot' and take the part of foolish foreign royalties with extraordinary zeal; she might believe that education ruined the health of the 'higher classes uselessly' and rendered 'the working classes unfitted for good servants and labourers',[65] that the campaign for women's suffrage was 'a mad, wicked folly', and that Lady Amberley who supported it 'ought to get a good whipping'.[66] But she was an admired and respected institution as well as a reactionary, and she had, after all, been on the greatest throne in the world for more than half a century.

Young relatives who came to see her at the Castle in these last years found a solemn but benevolent old lady, demanding yet kind, impatient of humbug but often surprisingly tolerant. She felt more at ease with these young relatives, particularly with her grand-children, than she had ever felt with her own children, and would allow them liberties that surprised those who believed her to be so uncompromisingly severe. She liked to have them near her when she was watching a game of tennis or a display by an Indian servant of acrobatic riding; and she liked to bring performing bears to the Castle for them and Punch and Judy shows; and once Buffalo Bill and his troupe came to put on their show below the East Terrace. And another day a man with a barrel organ and a monkey was summoned to the Quadrangle for the Little Princess Ena who had seen them in the town, and the 'Queen was much amused when the monkey climbed the portico and tried to find a way into the Castle through the dining-room windows'.[67]

'She wore a white tulle cap, black satin dress and shiny black boots with elastic sides,' one of her forty grandchildren remembered. 'What fascinated me about "Gangan" was her habit of taking breakfast in little revolving huts mounted on turntables, so that they could be faced away from the wind.' She would ride to the huts in her carriage to be served with steaming hot porridge by her Khidmutgars and then she would send for her Private Secretary and begin the business of the day.[68]

The Queen was still even now often shy with young people and would sometimes giggle apprehensively or give a diffident little shrug of her shoulders as she cross-examined them. But the affection of those who succeeded in penetrating beyond the crust of her nervous reserve was undoubtedly genuine. 'Grandmama so kind and dear as usual,' Princess Victoria of Prussia told her mother, describing in her letters home[69] the quiet summer days at Windsor, the green grass in the Park – 'no one knows what grass is until they come to England' – and the rhododendrons – 'like a dream' – the Queen making a speech, 'so well and without hesitation' as she gives away new colours to a regiment in the courtyard, the drives to Frogmore and the picnic teas with the nurses in their long, rustling dresses running after children down the slopes, the Queen working so conscientiously at her papers in the shade of an immense cedar tree, the games of tennis on the courts below the East Terrace, the Eton boys rowing on the river in the evening and Uncle Bertie, charming and pleasingly raffish, coming to dinner and talking of a different world.

Queen Victoria's world was already dying, and she clung with characteristic tenacity to her memories of the past, remembering with distressing accuracy the anniversaries of the deaths of nearly all the members of her family and refusing to perform any public duties which interfered with their proper observance. It was characteristic of her attitude, for instance, that she refused to have her Jubilee on 20 May as planned because her 'Uncle William IV had died that day'.[70]

The four rooms she used at Windsor contained almost two hundred and fifty pictures as well as the many photographs that were carried from Balmoral and Osborne every time she moved. They covered the green silk walls of her bedroom and the rich crimson flock of her sitting-room; they stood on her desk and on tables by the heavy damask curtains; and her servants often found her looking round at them as she played patience in the evenings by the light of the wax candles in the huge chandeliers. In the daytime, too, she was often to be seen pottering about amongst her treasures, picking them over with her chubby, heavily beringed fingers, looking at bundles of letters, sheets of music, paper weights, ink stands, old penknives, dead flowers, turning the pages of her ever-expanding inventories or of her Birthday Book, full of the signatures of her visitors, that she took with her wherever she went so that it was sometimes mistaken for a Bible.[71]

The century drew close to its ending and the Boer War began and she went to the barracks at Windsor to inspect the troops before they embarked for South Africa. Thirty-five years before she had inspected others of her soldiers before they sailed for the Crimea and they were wearing scarlet then. Their uniforms were khaki now and it seemed a curiously symbolic change as well as a practical one. In May 1900

Mafeking was relieved and the boys from Eton gathered in the upper quadrangle of the Castle to sing patriotic songs to her and she leant out of her window and said 'Thank you, thank you', repeating the words many times. And as she listened to the last song, the Eton boys were astonished to see an Indian servant appear at her side and hand her a Scotch and soda. [72]

She was sleeping badly now, and her eyesight and rheumatic pains were getting worse. But she went on working until the end, although she could hardly see the papers she signed.

She died in January 1901, like a great three-decker ship sinking, the Duke of Argyll said, now rallying, now failing. For two-and-a-half hours the Kaiser, kneeling down by the bed, supported her with his arm; but the last coherent word she spoke was 'Bertie'. [73]

A few moments later Bertie was King and the Edwardian Age had begun and, as if to herald its beginning, the Kaiser, the King of the Belgians, and the King of Portugal, while waiting for the funeral of the Queen to start, stood by a fireplace in a corridor in the Castle, smoking cigars. [74]

6
Edwardians

[i]

EDWARD VII – 'A VERY BAD BOY'

There is no position in the world more difficult to fill than that of Heir-Apparent to the throne. It is beset by more than all the temptations of actual royalty, while the weight of counteracting responsibility is much less directly felt. It must be with a feeling akin to hopelessness, that a man in that position offers up the familiar prayer, 'Lead us not into temptation'.[1]

As the readers of *The Times* knew very well when they read this comment, the new King, as Prince of Wales, had succumbed to temptation often enough. It was, though, as was generally admitted, not altogether his fault. His upbringing as a boy at Windsor had not been as severe, perhaps, as that of the Prince Regent and his brothers, one of whom was flogged for contracting asthma;[2] but it was quite as severe as any education a boy in his position might expect to have in the middle of the nineteenth century. And after his father's death, his mother, who could never forget what she took to be the Prince of Wales's responsibility for her widowhood, had been determined that her eldest son should not exercise any power or influence or enjoy any privileges that might have been exercised or enjoyed by her husband, and had continued a régime that she believed her 'Angel' would have approved.

He was a far from clever boy and although he had a good memory and an alert mind he did not take kindly to his lessons. Even English came with difficulty to him, and in his bilingual nursery he preferred to speak German and never in after life lost the faint traces of a German accent. His lessons were drawn up by his father and mother, with the help and advice of Baron Stockmar, into a regular and demanding curriculum. As soon as he was seven, half an hour had to be devoted every day to each of the following subjects: writing, music, drawing, geography, calculating, and religion, and a full hour had to be spent in learning French, English, and German.[3] But the longer he spent with his books, the less profit he seemed to derive from them.

He was considered not only rather stupid but, despite his cheerful and lively nature, lazy and obstinate. As his tutor, a kind and tolerant Eton master with the inappropriate name of Birch, was unsuccessful with him, it was decided that his father should administer a sound whipping.[4] This proved useless and a phrenologist was consulted who reported upon the Prince's 'nervous excitability, extreme obstinacy and passionate nature'.[5] His next tutor, a severe barrister named Gibbs whose strict moral sense was more to Baron Stockmar's liking than the tolerance of Henry Birch, had no more success with the Prince than his predecessor had had. 'A very bad boy,' he wrote in his diary, making a sad entry which had regrettably been paralleled on several earlier pages. 'The P. of W. has been like a person half silly. I could not gain his attention. He was very rude, particularly in the afternoon, throwing stones in my face. During his lesson in the morning he was running first in one place, then in another. He made faces, and spat. Dr Becher complained of his great naughtiness. There was a great deal of bad words.'[6]

The Queen did not disguise her opinion of her eldest son. 'With the Prince of Wales,' she told Major Howard Elphinstone, a member of her Household, 'one had to contend with an unhappy temper, incapacity of concentrating his mind and defective mental qualities.'[7]

He was certainly always longing to escape from the schoolroom, but while 'sport and amusement of a sober kind were permitted to him' (provided they were 'strictly rationed and supervised') he was kept aloof from companions of his own age, lest they lead him astray, as his great-uncles had been led astray. Freedom in any relation in life was, in fact, to be 'sternly denied him'.[8] On the rare occasions when suitable companions were summoned to the Castle to play games with him, they dreaded the invitation, for the Prince was likely to spend most of the time bullying them.[9] He was, in any case, never very successful with his outdoor pursuits even when he was not fighting.

He rode hard, he played fives in the courts at Eton, he practised his croquet shots, he went out with the royal buckhounds at Windsor, and shot regularly from his thirteenth year over the Windsor coverts, but he never managed to become as good a shot as his father (although sometimes he appeared to be so since he never fired at a difficult bird), and he never became more than an average performer at any ball game. It was obvious that he enjoyed games as a boy only as a means of escape from his lessons and his early wish to become a soldier, despite the difficulty he had had restraining his tears when as a little boy he had watched the military reviews in the Park and heard the boom of the cannon, seemed to stem more from his interest in uniforms and his desire for travel and independence than in any taste for military glory.

The Prince Consort, however, persisted in trying to make a scholar out of him. He was provided with appropriately accomplished friends who were in no sense companionable; he was brought into touch with scientists, historians, professors and bishops who could impart nothing to him; he was sent to Edinburgh University as well as to Oxford and Cambridge without obtaining much benefit from his short courses at any of them except a softening of his German accent. His father, who felt that the only use for Oxford was that it was 'a place for study',[10] wrote to him and trusted that he understood that 'the Balls etc., etc., which he visited were not visited by him for his own amusement but to give pleasure to others'.[11] There was something profoundly pathetic in these repeated entreaties made to him by his father in his determination to raise his son's mind and character up to the level of his own; and there is something quite as pathetic in the son's inability to profit by them or even to attend to them, for in the admiration and respect he felt for his father there was a depth of love he did not fully recognise until it was too late to show him that it existed.

He had been able to share few of his father's interests. Music — except French and Viennese light operas — meant little to him; painting and literature bored him. As a child he had enjoyed the Christmas plays in the Castle when Charles Kean had been the director of performances; but his happiest memories were of conjurers — Papa knew how all the tricks were done, he proudly confided to a guest — of circuses, and the antics of Wombwell's menagerie which he had seen perform in the Quadrangle.[12] And in later life he preferred light plays and musical comedies which did not exert undue strain upon his limited intellectual strength or upon his somewhat narrow imaginative faculties. When he was given a book he would say how much he was looking forward to reading it, but he rarely got beyond the first few pages and often did not attempt even those.[13] Clothes and decorations interested him, of course, and his collection of uniforms and helmets, of the robes of various Orders of Chivalry and Masonic regalia was immense. His insistence on all the regulations concerning dress was in later life to be such a 'conspicuous foible' that he would 'rebuke with a freezing inattentiveness or a biting scorn the least neglect of sartorial convention'.[14] One of his secretaries — who said that he 'adored uniforms and decorations' and that if there was one thing he liked doing 'it was presenting medals' — has recalled several occasions upon which he was excessively put out when people appeared in his presence in the wrong clothes or wearing their orders the wrong way round. An English girl who came to an official luncheon in Algiers wearing 'flannels' and a squash hat, a groom-in-waiting who intended going to a wedding in a black waistcoat – 'My dear fellow, where is your *white* waistcoat? Is it possible you are going to a *wedding* in a *black* waistcoat?'[15] – an unconcerned Lord Rosebery who went aboard the royal yacht wearing a Yacht Squadron mess jacket and a white tie and at Windsor came to a banquet in evening clothes instead of uniform – 'I see you belong to the American Embassy'[16] – a careless Lord Haldane whose hat 'looked as though it had been inherited from Goethe',[17] all upset him profoundly. To see a decoration worn incorrectly caused him even greater pain, and he once sent Benjamin Constant a Garter ribbon to show him that the colour he had painted it in a portrait of Queen Victoria was the wrong shade of blue.*

Edward himself never made a mistake and was always faultlessly attired. Today his overcoats might be considered a trifle too tight and his large tie-pin faintly vulgar, but they did not offend his fashionable contemporaries, whose ambition was to dress as he did and know as much about clothes as he did. He even had a special dress for visiting picture galleries: country clothes being too informal and a frock coat too formal, he went in a short black coat and a top hat. And he even knew what the answer was when the Russian ambassador asked him if it would be proper for him to attend race-meetings when he was in mourning: 'To Newmarket, yes, because it means a bowler hat, but not to the Derby because of the top hat.'[19]

Like his father he did not often linger at the dinner-table, but this was not because he did not enjoy male conversation and ribald stories, drinking brandy and smoking cigars, but because he preferred the company of women; and it was, in fact, his reputation as a *donnaiuolo* that lay behind much of the solemnly censorious and understandably apprehensive comment that surrounded his accession.

* * *

While his mother had been living out the last years of her life at Balmoral, Osborne and Windsor, the Prince of Wales had been entertaining her subjects with the reports of his adventures at Marlborough House in Pall Mall, at his country estate, Sandringham, in Norfolk which had been bought for him in 1861 for £220,000, and at

---

* Benjamin Constant, who received the ribbon without a covering letter, thought that he had been made a Knight of the Garter. When he discovered that he had not, he 'absolutely refused' to alter the picture.[18]

various other places up and down the country and abroad where his activities as a gambler, *bon viveur* and *paillard*, a patron of cockpits, of race-courses, casinos and brothels were assiduously discussed with some exaggeration and a great deal of conjecture.

Partly no doubt from an unwillingness to share the power and privileges of her position but also because she had so little faith in his capacity, the Queen continued to try to keep him excluded from even the feeling of responsibility. He succeeded in learning much of affairs of State from her Ministers and from foreign ambassadors, of course, but he did not obtain a key to Cabinet boxes until seven or eight years before she died.[20] 'He had no intellectual grasp, no balance or stability; he seemed to think that the correct wearing of an order or decoration was of greater moment than the merit that had won it. It was ludicrous, absolutely laughable, to imagine that, while his mind was still so unformed, his judgment, his views on great issues could be of value; and with his unguarded tongue, secret negotiations and lines of policy would soon be known to the Rothschilds who were such friends of his.'[21]

It might have been gratifying to the Queen, perhaps, that he was an arbiter of fashion, had the fields in which he gave the lead not been those in which she would have been happier to see him less at home. There was little harm, no doubt, in the fashions he set. He had always followed her advice, given many years ago, never to be '*extravagant*' or '*slang*'. The waistcoat did possibly look better with its bottom button undone, even if the fashion was inspired, as were others, by his own comfort; and the soft felt hat he brought back from Homburg was perhaps acceptable despite its rakishly curling brim; and, after all, he could not be blamed for the new way of shaking hands with the elbow held stiffly to the side, for he had been obliged to shake hands like that because of the rheumatism in his elbow; and neither he nor his wife could be blamed for the 'Alexandra limp' which became such a fashionable way of walking when the Princess of Wales developed a limp after an attack of rheumatic fever. But the bad habit of smoking cigarettes, and the even worse habit of smoking cigars directly after dinner, were entirely his responsibility. And he had even invented a 'Cocktail' of whisky, Angostura bitters, maraschino, champagne, pineapple, lemon peel and powdered sugar,[22] which was, she must have felt sure, reprehensible in every way.

Then there were the scandals over the Tranby Croft baccarat case and the Mordaunt divorce and all the stories about his gay and irresponsible life and – despite an income of more than £100,000 a year – his constant debts, which fixed the Queen's determination to contradict the rumours that she might abdicate.

It was too late now to wonder whether it had been wise to bring him up so strictly and under so careful a surveillance until his marriage, and then allow him his freedom as a rich young man of twenty-two. Hearing about his activities at 'Mott's' and the 'Cremona', his visits to young women from *cinq à sept*, his wild parties at the houses of his extravagant friends and his enjoyment of all the careless pleasures of the mid-Victorian 'epidemic of *nostalgie de la boue*',[23] there were many who agreed with the Queen that, when her son succeeded her, the monarchy would enter a phase as dangerous as the one that her uncles had precipitated.

It was all very well for the Prince to show that he was regal as well as *roué*, or coldly to inform a man who had gone too far by calling across the billiard-table after a bad shot, 'Pull yourself together, Wales,' that his carriage was at the door; but it is not always easy to understand that it was not so much that he was pompous as because he had a passionate belief that royalty must be accorded a special respect. Nor was it always easy to understand that when brandy was poured over Christopher Sykes's head this was not only to indulge in his regrettable pleasure in practical jokes – they must never be played on him – but also to make his friends laugh with him at Sykes's complaisantly lugubrious, inimitably long-suffering, 'As your Royal Highness pleases'.[24] And it was all very well for him to show, with such evident expectations of compliment, how fond and proud of his beautiful wife he was, and how well he had demonstrated that he was, in at least one sense, a family man by ensuring that she had several healthy children, when every one of his mother's subjects knew that being a proud and virile husband was only one of the requirements of an heir to the throne.

[ii]

EDWARD VII – 'L'ONCLE DE L'EUROPE

The Prince of Wales was already in his sixtieth year when his mother died; his beard was grey; he had become very portly; and, although a lotion was vigorously applied to his scalp twice a day, he was nearly bald. The death of his eldest son – the lethargic and dissipated Prince Eddie – in 1891 had been a profound shock to him; and his heavy smoking had exacerbated his bronchitic tendency.

While making no secret of his disappointment that his honours had come to him so late in life, he nevertheless undertook his duties as king with his habitual energy and a deep consciousness of the importance of his vocation. He was anxious to learn quickly. Lord Esher, the Deputy Constable and Lieutenant-Governor of Windsor Castle, who was later to exercise so much influence over him, described how he would ask question after question, interrupt the answers with his quick, 'Yes . . . yes . . . yes', give orders, scribble notes on bits of paper in his scarcely legible writing, and then stand in front of the fire with one of his immense cigars between his teeth, 'looking wonderfully like Henry VIII, only better tempered'. The impression he gave Lord Esher was 'that of a man, who, after long years of pent-up action, had suddenly been freed from restraint and revelled in his liberty'. He insisted on having all his letters 'brought to him unopened, about 400 a day', and sorted them by himself. 'He tried at first to open them all but found that impossible.'[1]

When he came to the Castle for the first time as King with what Sir Sidney Lee called his 'charming circle of cavaliers' it was much as though, so one of his grandsons was given to understand, 'a Viennese hussar had suddenly burst into an English vicarage'.[2] Soon motor cars were rattling unsteadily through the arches, and his own Daimler and Mercedes were garaged in the converted coach houses; plumbers were installing new bathrooms and ventilation; telephone engineers were trailing their equipment over the carpeted corridors, extending a system first introduced in 1896; and inventory clerks were listing the muddled accumulations of half a century: the thousands of mementoes, the innumerable photographs, the ornaments and pieces of bric-à-brac, the elephant tusks and boxes of armour and statuettes of gillies, the ornamental dinner services, the gold plate and horse harnesses, the treasures of a distant childhood, the quantities of marble busts, the silver dishes for roasted chestnuts in the form of table napkins, and the countless relics of a dead age which lay, stored in improbable places or exposed to unwilling view, amidst the remains of George IV's magnificent collections.[3]

The King strode through the Castle, supervising all the redecorations, for the new Queen had little interest in such things, 'with a pot hat on, and his stick and his dog . . . as if he were out for a walk'.[4] He went to the library one day 'and ransacked every kind of bookcase and picture cupboard. He got rid of an enormous number of rubbishy old coloured photographs and things'.[5] 'I do not know much about Arrt,' he would say, rolling his r's, 'but I think I know something about Arr-r-angement.'[6]

He rearranged and repainted almost everything; but he felt compelled to leave the heavy carpets and curtains untouched for they were, although so unbecoming, as good as new.*

The ceremonious Lord Esher was doubtful at first that all the changes were for the better. 'It may be my imagination,' he confided to his journal, 'but sanctity of the throne has disappeared. The King is kind and debonnair, and not undignified – but too *human!*'[9] All the atmosphere of the Castle had changed. The Indians wandered about 'like uneasy spirits, no longer immobile and statuesque'. In the evening the King came unannounced into the Green Drawing Room with his daughters and his sister, and the 'the quiet impressive entrance of the Queen into the corridor' was 'as obsolete as Queen Elizabeth'. The dinner was 'like an ordinary party. None of the "hush" of the Queen's dinners. Afterwards we left "arm-in-arm" as we entered.' Later the etiquette 'stiffened up very much' but it was never as formal as before, and Esher could not help but 'regret the mystery and awe of the old Court'.[10]

All the old members of Queen Victoria's Household and all her servants were permitted to retain their places and salaries for six months, however, including the Indians who continued to occupy their rooms in King John's Tower. But before their departure, secretaries, equerries and servants who had been with the King as Prince of Wales were found employment too, for Edward VII was determined to change immediately the whole ambience of the Court.

*　　*　　*

Queen Victoria, who considered that the English aristocracy, 'apart from a righteous remnant', had 'no other aim in life save pleasure-

---

* Some of them *were*, in fact, new, for Queen Victoria, unable to part with anything that she and Prince Albert had shared, had had the furnishings accurately copied when it became necessary to replace them. 'The occasional redecorating of the Queen's private apartments has to be done with the greatest care,' one of her servants had written, 'in order that Her Majesty shall not even perceive that they have been more than cleaned. On one occasion while the Queen was away from Windsor an armchair in her private sitting-room was re-stuffed and re-covered. Her Majesty at once ordered it out of her sight on her return, saying it was "too smart".[7] She passed the same verdict on the gates and railings which divide Castle Hill from the South Terrace, when their tops were gilded in her absence. An army of painters was summoned, and by the time the Queen left the Castle for her afternoon drive all traces of the garish display had been removed.'[8]

39. The Queen's Sitting Room
from the lithograph by Joseph Nash

40. The White Drawing Room

seeking or dissipation', had frequently reproached her son for his appalling taste in friends; and he, although his views on social liberalism were much more generous than hers, and although he was and remained on friendly terms with men like Charles Dilke and Joseph Chamberlain, believed that there should be preserved a class between the Crown and the proletariat. In a letter to his mother he expressed the opinion that

in every country a great proportion of the Aristocracy will be idle and fond of amusement and have always been so, but I think in no country more than ours do the Higher Classes occupy themselves, which is certainly not much the case in other countries. We have always been an Aristocratic Country, and I hope we shall always remain so, as they are the mainstay of this country, unless we become so Americanised that they are swept away, and then the state of things will be quite according to Mr Bright's views, who wishes only for the Sovereign and the People, and no class between.[11]

But the Queen had been distressed, of course, not only by the numbers of apparently idle aristocrats amongst her son's friends, but also by the terms of familiarity upon which he lived with other socially unacceptable people who, after her death, entered the rooms at Windsor and altered their whole atmosphere. Tradesmen, financiers, Jews and actresses were accepted into a Court where unhealthy prejudices about race and colour were not tolerated, where intelligence and wit and money and a knowledge of fashionable scandals were more dearly prized than Coburg blood. In addition to Americans, of whom he had always been fond – although he could not bear their clothes – and in addition to men in public life like Lord Fisher whose personality and views he admired, parties at Windsor often included such apparently disparate guests as the Marquis de Soveral (the clever, ugly and loquacious Portuguese diplomatist – 'a sort of Cyrano,' Lord Esher called him, 'very ugly but hyper-smart' – whose monocle and fierce black moustache interfered in no way with his easy charm), Sir Ernest Cassel, son of a Cologne banker,* reserved but masterful, rich and generous, Sir Marcus Lipton, also rich and far less reserved, Eduardo de Martino, a Neapolitan who had served in the Italian Navy and had been a Marine Painter-in-Ordinary to Queen Victoria and was now 'a sort of Court Jester, a butt for the King's jokes' to which he would reply with 'quaint remarks in very

* His strong similarity to the King was predictably ascribed to a common ancestry. Rumours were revived about Prince Albert's Jewish blood, derived, so it was said, from a Jewish Court chamberlain with whom his mother had been in love, although the affair was not in fact begun until after Albert was born.

bad English',[12] Sir Felix Semon, a nose and throat specialist of German descent, who was a witty *raconteur* and an excellent bridge player, and the Sassoon brothers, rich and charming descendants of Jews from the Middle East.

It seemed, then, entirely appropriate that at a magnificent ball held in the Waterloo Chamber at Windsor in 1903, the first ball held in the Castle for half a century, Prince Adolphus of Teck and Princess Victoria should fall flat on their backs, when the Prince's spurs caught in the 'awfully long gown' of Mrs George Keppel, the King's vivacious mistress.[13]

*　　*　　*

King Edward was fond of his wife and children but a quiet family life bored him and he liked to fill Windsor with rich, amusing and worldly guests and to make the Castle as much like a rich man's country house as possible. 'He was always accessible and friendly,' the American Duchess of Marlborough said, 'and knew how to discard ceremony.'[14] But he never allowed behaviour or conversation at Windsor which he thought might detract from his dignity. Even if it were obviously inadvertent, a *faux pas* was inexcusable; and one poor woman had her name struck off the Court list for falling over in front of the King and Queen because she could not manage her train.*

Abroad the King enjoyed a reputation for gay familiarity. He would cheerfully tolerate La Goulue who shouted at him one night in Paris when she caught sight of him in the middle of her 'quadrille in delirium', 'Allo, Wales. *Est-ce que tu vas payer mon champagne?*' He smiled at the black-stockinged leg thrust out at him through an expanse of billowing petticoats, and he bought her a bottle.[17] But when an Englishwoman, who he felt should have known better than to have been so arch with him, offered him a cup of tea at a charity fair at the Albert Hall and, having taken a sip of it herself, said that the charge had consequently gone up from its already very high price to five guineas, he looked at her with cold distaste, gave her the five guineas and said sharply, 'Will you please give me a clean cup.'[18]

The Queen, too, carefree as she usually was, insisted on being

---

* Almost any behaviour, of course, was excusable in kings and princes, for they were a class apart. The King would happily throw asparagus stalks over his shoulder so as not to embarrass an Indian prince who was disposing of them in this way at a dinner party.[15] And he did not hesitate to insist that King Kalakua of the Cannibal Islands should take precedence over the Crown Prince of Germany. When the Germans objected, the King replied, 'Either the brute is a king or else he is an ordinary black nigger, and if he is not a king, why is he here?'[16]

treated with the formal respect which the King liked her to receive. Lord Ormathwaite confessed that he could never forget his first waiting at Windsor.

We were standing about the drawing-room after dinner listening to one of the Guards' bands which happened to be playing some of the loudest passages from Lohengrin [he wrote in his memoirs]. Quite forgetting that Queen Alexandra [who was already rather deaf] always heard best when the noise was loudest, I said incautiously to my neighbour: 'Are we never going to sit down to-night?'

To my horror the Queen turned round and I realised that my remark had been overheard and nearly died of shame – but worse was to come. The Queen, moving away to the wall against which large gilt and scarlet brocade arm-chairs were arranged, seized hold of one of these and, declining the assistance of the gentlemen standing about the room, pushed it up to me. 'Sit down', she commanded. I demurred, but she repeated the words, and then said to the assembled company: 'Poor thing, he is so tired.' Wishing that the floor would open and swallow me up, I wondered when my deliverance would come. To my relief the King entered the room, and I perforce had to stand up. . . . The next morning, the Queen, with a smile expressed the hope that I had slept well and was rested, and I realised that my lapse had been forgiven.[19]

The King insisted that his women guests should wear tiaras at dinner every night at Windsor and that the men should wear court costume and their decorations. Nor did he permit any woman to go to bed before the Queen went, which was rarely before midnight, or any man to go before he went, which was between one o'clock and half-past. Everyone had to spend the evening doing something which appeared to him enjoyable, and this was as much a duty for his guests as for his Household. One evening he went on a tour of inspection, counting the number of men in the drawing-rooms and, finding one short, he rang for a page and told him to go and fetch back the absentee who, he imagined, was one of the younger guests. It turned out to be General Sir Dighton Probyn, v.c., the seventy-five-year-old Keeper of the Privy Purse, who had gone to bed because he was not feeling well. The King 'was very much amused at this, but Sir Dighton was not'.[20]

But although an exacting host and an exacting master, King Edward was far more considerate with members of his Household than his mother had been, 'always thinking of small acts of kindness and often, without being asked, suggesting to some married man that he should go away and spend the week with his family'.[21] He was considerate with his domestic servants, too. He often gave them orders himself in his sharp, intimidating voice,[22] but he made sure they were well looked after and had comfortable quarters. A French visitor to Windsor noticed how pleasant their rooms had been made since the Queen's death and how many bathrooms they had.[23]

As well as being considerate the King was also very businesslike. All the departments of the Household were modernised and the abuses that had grown up in the day of his mother, who hated all change, were swept away. The economies did not go far enough for Henry Labouchère, the fiery Radical proprietor of *Truth*, whose antagonism the King could never understand;[24] but there could be no doubt that the Household was a much more efficient organisation than it had ever been since Prince Albert's death; nor could there be any doubt that the Castle was a much more pleasant place in which to spend the night than it had been for years. 'The whole arrangements here are extraordinarily comfortable,' Lord Haldane told his mother at the beginning of 1905. 'They could not be more so.'[25]

The Lord Chamberlain's office was also reorganised and the old afternoon receptions or 'Drawing-rooms' became the new evening 'Presentation Courts', while the times of levees, which had previously prevented those who attended them from having any luncheon, were altered to a convenient hour.

Being very business-like, the King liked every one to be punctual, and the Queen, who was usually late for everything – even, so it was said, for her own coronation – tried him sorely. She was rarely less than twenty minutes late for dinner at Windsor and the King would wait for her 'with the face of a Christian martyr'. He had long since accepted her unpunctuality 'as inevitable and never attempted to remonstrate with her'.[26]

He would get extremely cross with anyone else who kept him waiting, however, and once when Herbert Asquith was late in arriving to join a party in the Castle courtyard, the King 'looked first at his watch and then at the Castle clock, and fussed crossly about the yard'. He had told Asquith and his wife to join himself and the Queen at four o'clock 'to motor first to the gardens and then to Virginia Water for tea'. But Asquith was late. Once before he had forgotten about an invitation to Windsor altogether and had gone abroad on holiday instead. It looked as though he had forgotten this appointment, too. The King 'angrily turned to his gentlemen-in-waiting, Harry Stonor and Seymour Fortescue, and demanded, "What have you done? Where have you looked for him? Did you not

give him my command?"' Mrs Asquith suggested that they should
start without him, but the King snapped 'Certainly not!' So she went
to the Queen and said that she 'feared there had been a scandal at
Court and that Herbert must have eloped with one of the maids-of-
honour'. She begged the Queen to save her blushes 'by commanding
the King to proceed, at which she walked up to him with her amazing
grace, and her charming way, tapping him firmly on the arm pointed
with a sweeping gesture to his motor and invited Gracie Raincliffe
(the Countess of Londesborough) and Alice Keppel to accompany
him; at which they all drove off.'[27]

The Queen could manage him better than anyone else. She was a
delightful and remarkable woman, possessively devoted to her children and loyal to her wayward husband. She was ill-educated, without
intellectual curiosity or any artistic taste except a liking for music,
which in her later years she could not hear any more. Gay and lively,
beautiful, graceful, recklessly generous and painfully insensitive, with
large deep blue sympathetic eyes and a delightful accent, she had an
'almost childish interest in everything',[28] a lively sense of the
ridiculous – which included, it has unfortunately to be admitted, her
husband's fondness for practical jokes – and a refreshing irreverence
for convention. She once appeared to the King's appalled consternation, wearing 'the famous Koh-i-noor as well as the fabulous Cullinan
diamonds', with her Garter star on the wrong side because, so she
said, it clashed with her other jewels.[29]

Sir Frederick Ponsonby has described her curious views on golf.
The King, who was very fond of the game, had a course made at
Windsor in the grounds below the East Terrace, but the Queen
seemed to confuse the game with hockey and was 'under the impression that one had to prevent the opponent putting the ball in the hole.
This usually ended by a scrimmage on the green. She also thought that
the person who got into the hole first won it, and she asked me to
hurry up and run between my strokes. It was very good fun, and we
all laughed. Francis Knollys (the King's Private Secretary) always
played in a square-shaped billycock hat and a London tail coat, and
hit so hard that his hat almost invariably fell off.'[30]

The Queen's hockey-golf was, of course, very hard on the balls,
which she managed, when playing with her daughter Victoria, to
batter into crooked pyramids. The King, finding a pair of these
curious shapes on the first tee one afternoon, thought that his
opponent was 'trying to be funny',[31] and was extremely cross until
he learned that his wife was responsible.

Although extremely indulgent with the Queen's caprices, the King was capable of outbursts of alarming anger if anyone else irritated him. He would swear furiously if his golfing partner played badly; and once, playing croquet with Frederick Ponsonby, Harry Chaplin, his old Oxford friend, and the beautiful Madame Letellier, he got so cross with Ponsonby (who kept knocking the King's ball to the other end of the ground because he did not like the game and did not want to be asked to play again) that Madame Letellier begged him 'with tears in her eyes not to make the King so angry'.[32] At bridge, though he did not play at all well, he did not hesitate to criticise all his partner's mistakes and he would say crossly 'This is becoming a very expensive evening.' But the anger generally died down as quickly as it had risen, and then would come that 'kindly and merry laugh, and he lit another enormous cigar which made him cough.'[33]

It was 'usual with the King after he had let himself go and cursed someone,' one of his equerries said, 'to smooth matters by being especially nice to them afterwards'.[34] 'If the King assailed you, as he sometimes assailed me,' Lord Esher said, 'it was almost certain that within an hour or two he would send for you, or dispatch a few lines on a slip of paper, on some wholly different subject, in the friendliest manner, with no allusion to what had passed.'[35]

For despite a peppery temper, a caustic tongue, moods in which he indulged his taste for what the Duchess of Teck called 'odious chaffing', and despite a domineering manner that made even his best friends frightened of him sometimes, he was an essentially and obviously warm-hearted man. 'He was naturally and genuinely kind-hearted,' Winston Churchill decided, remembering an occasion when, as a young subaltern, he had kept the King waiting twenty minutes for supper, been reprimanded severely and then, almost immediately, forgiven.[36] Lord Esher found him the 'kindest and most considerate' master and friend that a man could have. 'Jealousy was a word he could not understand. . . . If he gave his confidence it was given absolutely.'[37] Esher had, of course, as Lord Mersey said, 'a flatterer's tongue',[38] but these compliments were not undeserved.

In many respects, though, King Edward's was a childish nature. He rarely dissembled; he refused to try to understand problems that did not interest him; he worked quite hard at being a King but this was mainly, perhaps, because he enjoyed the work. 'It's all so interesting,' he once explained to Lord Redesdale when settling down at midnight to great boxfuls of papers. He never grew tired of giving presents and decorations. He was sulky when he lost a bet and paid his debt as though he were making a presentation. He was fecklessly and unconsciously extravagant and thought nothing of bringing an immense cast of West End actors and actresses to perform for a few friends at Windsor or of asking an expensive veterinary surgeon to come out to Marienbad at a fee of £200 when his adored dog Caesar was ill.[39]

Caesar, a curiously scruffy fox terrier, was as devoted to the King as he to him and would jump up at his legs whenever he saw him and the King would pat him and say, 'Do you like your old master then?' The little dog walked proudly round Biarritz and Paris and through the corridors at Windsor bearing on his collar the legend: 'I am Caesar, the King's dog'.[40] If he was ill, the King decided, of course he must have the best man sent from England to look after him. It did not occur to the King that he was being extravagant - he had a generous mind, not a sensitive one. He did not much care what the provident thought of him. His actions were governed more by instinct than by calculation. He indulged himself certainly, but his concern with the alleviation of pain, the care of the sick, and his interest in cancer research, went far deeper than the superficialities of royal patronage. He was prepared to spend £200 on his terrier but he was also prepared to spend £30,000 on giving dinner to the London poor.[41] He was 'good old Teddy!' to them. Not many of them objected to his cigars and his racehorses or to the genial and generous, witty but discreet Mrs Keppel, whose pretty face smiling under her enormous hats was so often at his side. He was a popular king because he was so obviously a human one. 'He is loved,' Lord Granville said, 'because he has all the faults of which the Englishman is accused.'[42]

*　　*　　*

Englishmen saw much more of him than they had seen of his mother. His restlessness ensured that he was often abroad, and every year he felt in need of a cure at a watering-place to offset the effects of his *gourmandise*. But when he was at home he was constantly on the move, going with perfect regularity to all the principal race meetings and visiting the country houses of his numerous friends, who can be seen with him in a hundred different photographs staring fixedly, bewhiskered, self-confident and strangely menacing into the camera's lens.

He was accompanied to these country houses by a large train of servants, including his own footman to wait upon him at meals, and his Austrian valet, Meidinger, to get him out of bed early in the morning. But although he was so coddled and so practised a guest, he was not always an easy one. He liked to know who all his fellow guests would be, and was known not only to cross off names he did not like on the lists submitted to him by his hosts, but also to add other names to them. He was superstitious and hated to sit down to dinner when there were thirteen at table – he once comforted himself with the knowledge that on one occasion when he had appeared to tempt providence in this way he had not in fact done so because one of the thirteen guests (Princess Frederick Charles of Hesse) was pregnant[43] – and it was even said that he disliked having two knives laid in front of him at once in case they became crossed. He preferred, as a dedicated *gourmet*, to leave his mind free to concentrate on his food and to leave conversation to the intervals between the courses.[44] He was not a 'great talker', Sir Sydney Lee said, nor did he compare as a raconteur with most of his friends. He was a pleasant enough neighbour, though. He was a good listener and liked to be told gossip by pretty women.

He had an excellent appetite like his mother, and, although he did not drink much, he could 'eat with impunity a wonderful quantity and mixture of dishes'. He could enjoy several dozen oysters at a sitting and he set the good example of eating them with brown bread and butter. He loved lamb and chicken and turkey and trout and eggs in aspic and strawberries; and with his dessert he always like to drink champagne, preferably Duminy *extra sec*, 1883, decanted – another fashion set – into a glass jug from which he helped himself.

He did not eat much before luncheon but at Windsor, when he had a morning's work ahead of him, he would have a 'true country break-fast'; and after luncheon (which was served at half-past two) and before dinner (the time of which varied according to the evening's arrangements) he was ready for a good tea at five o'clock with sand-wiches, cake and biscuits.[45] Dinner was served in the State dining-room and afterwards the King liked to play bridge in the White Drawing Room, or to walk about ensuring that all his guests were enjoying themselves, or to watch, with one of his immense Corona y Corona cigars in his mouth, the impromptu dancing in the Crimson Drawing Room where the band played every night.[46]

This was the life he loved, and the rich were the people whose company was essential to his happiness. He never got on very well with the professional classes or the gentry, whose lack of wealth kept them from Court, or with intellectuals. He did not always succeed with women, and Margot Asquith decided after a week-end at Windsor that 'if you don't keep a firm grasp on yourself on the rare occasions when you are with Kings and Princes, you notice little, enjoy nothing and lose your individuality. Royal persons are divorced from the opinions of people that count, and are almost always condemned to take safe and commonplace views. To them clever men are "Prigs"; clever women "too advanced"; Liberals are "Socialists"; the uninteresting "Pleasant"; the interesting "Intriguers"; and the imaginative "Mad".'[47]

The King always found it difficult to carry on a conversation with a man or woman who did not share at least some of his tastes. On one occasion, finding a conversation with a bishop appallingly heavy-going, he switched in despair from one subject to another without arousing the least response. At length, catching sight of a photograph of himself on a side table, he thought he would try that. What did the bishop think of the likeness? 'Yes, yes,' the bishop replied, having put on his spectacles, 'yes, yes, poor old Buller!'[48] And there was another occasion when he was talking to a young woman who was 'esteemed for her many good works' but who seemed on this occasion to be very nervous. 'I want to have a long chat with you,' he told her, hoping to put her at her ease, 'but if I should unfortunately bore you pray tell me so.' The King 'who was an adroit cross-examiner, wished to ascertain the young lady's age, which she had no intention of divulging, 'You have already told me where you were born,' he said. 'May I ask in what year?' 'You bore me, sir', she said.[49]

It was rarely, though, that he had such little success. He had the good manners, rare in kings, to display an apparently absorbed interest in the people to whom he was talking, and he took the trouble — as all of his successors on the throne were also to do — to find out all he could about them, storing the information in an exceptionally retentive memory. Above all he was, when he wished to be, captivatingly charming. Had he not been so he could never have become l'Oncle de l'Europe.

It took more than charm, of course, to become that, to make Europeans believe, as millions of them did believe, that he was 'the arbiter of their fate', 'Edward the Peacemaker'. It took moral courage and common sense and his sort of intuitive tact. It took an ability to make men realise that there was a purposeful seriousness behind the gaiety, that the milieux of Lily Langtry and the Professional Beauties, of Lady Warwick and the Palais Royal, of Yvette Guilbert and the Moulin Rouge, of Harry Chaplin and the Turf Club were not the only interests he had. He could persuade Gambetta that although he had no real power it was far from being a waste of time to talk to him. And by becoming a distinguished European figure he could help to bring about the dream of his youth, an *entente cordiale* with France.

As he moved about Europe from Paris to Hamburg, Carlsbad to Cannes, to Biarritz and Marienbad, setting fashions and earning the sort of popular adulation that made women collect cigar stubs that had touched his lips and enabled men to sell bones that had been left on his plate,[50] he gained a personal though sometimes overrated influence in European affairs that his conceited and jealous nephew the Kaiser William II was never able to rival, except through the power of Germany.

When he returned to England he was able at Windsor to impress his guests by a return of hospitality on a scale that had been unknown there since the 1850's. Visiting emperors, kings and presidents were dazzled by its splendour. King Alfonso might hold his stomach with hunger 'as he waited for luncheon, at the awful hour of half-past two, while King Edward displayed the treasures of his ancestral house to the Master of the Escurial'.[51] And the genial, red-faced President Loubet might become exhausted by his long walks down the halls and galleries, but neither he nor the Spanish King could fail to be impressed by what they saw. Even the disliked and distrusted Kaiser was overwhelmed when he found himself the principal guest at a magnificent luncheon in the Castle with twenty-three other royalties. His War Minister suffered agonies from the tight black pumps that he was obliged to wear with his court costume until Haldane, the English War Minister, told him that it was 'the custom in Windsor Castle' when the King had gone to bed for the others to kick their shoes off, and so they both did so. And Haldane himself got lost when trying to find his way back to the Lancaster Tower.[52] But the visit went off without any serious mishap and the Castle 'turned the Kaiser into a rhapsodist'.[53]

The Kaiser's visit took place in the autumn of 1907 and the King was showing signs of increasing ill-health. His bronchitis was now a matter of serious concern, yet he would not give up smoking and sometimes the paroxysms of his breathlessness and coughing were alarming. He was more and more subject to fits of almost savage ill-temper, and although he quickly recovered and quickly apologised with a laugh 'like the sound of tearing linen',[54] it was clear that his physical health and emotional stability were being affected. He was

subject now to long moods of depression in which he saw republicanism as an irresistible force and his efforts to compose the quarrels
of Europe leading to tragic failure. He had done his best to show his
sympathy with social reform by identifying the monarchy with the
awakening conscience of his people; but he had no time for socialists
and never succeeded in understanding their ideals. He was 'a strong
Conservative,' Sir Charles Dilke said of him, 'and a still stronger
Jingo,' and he feared that 'continental socialism' was threatening all
that he held most dear. He had been careful never to flout the Constitution, as his mother had done, but he went to his death believing
that his son would be the last king of England.[55]

7
Windsors

GEORGE V

'A terrible day for us all. We hardly left him all day, he knew us and talked to us between his attacks up till 4.30. The last thing he understood was when I told him his horse Witch of the Air had won at Kempton to-day and he said he was pleased. . . . At 11.45 beloved Papa passed peacefully away and I have lost my best friend and the best of fathers. I never had a word with him in my life. I am heartbroken and overwhelmed with grief but God will help me in my great responsibilities and darling May will be my comfort as she always has been. May God give me strength and guidance in the heavy task which has fallen upon me.'[1]

The new King, who wrote these characteristic entries in his diary on the evening his father died, was well aware how much strength and guidance he would need. For 'it was plain,' as Sir Arthur Bryant has said, 'that a time of uncertainty, strife and rapid and probably violent change was about to take place. In such a maelstrom, with the House of Lords and the ownership of the soil already threatened, what hope was there that the crown could survive, unless it was worn by a man possessed of the most exceptional powers of judgment, understanding and moral integrity.'[2]

The new King appeared, indeed, to have few qualifications for his office and his consciousness of his own inadequacies seemed justified. He had lived in the shadow of a domineering father whom he had unquestioningly admired, whose advice he had always sought and followed, and whose word he had always accepted as law.

As Edward vii had come to the throne in the face of openly expressed doubts as to his capacity, so did George v. There were the same sort of malicious rumours, too: that at the time of his marriage to Princess May, daughter of the Duke and Duchess of Teck, he was already morganatically married to an Admiral's daughter whom he had met while serving in the Royal Navy at Malta; and that, in addition to this, he was an excessively heavy drinker. Both these rumours were ill-founded, but it was felt necessary publicly to contradict the one and wait a long time before the other died of its own accord.[3]

Often it did seem, in fact, to a distant observer, that the King *was* drunk, for – apart from a blotchy complexion which never returned to a normal colour after a serious attack of typhoid fever – he had an extremely hearty laugh and an alarmingly loud voice. He had, indeed, developed the sort of character which is commonly supposed to accompany these idiosyncrasies.

As Duke of York and later, after his brother's death, as Prince of Wales, he had lived at York Cottage, Sandringham – 'a glum little villa', as Sir Harold Nicolson has aptly described it – the life of a young Norfolk squire 'to whom money was no object, and business duties but an interlude of no grievous length'.[4] He was not well educated, having gone to sea at an early age after the Rev John Neale Dalton, his tutor, had advised his parents that neither he nor his brother would be able to keep up to the standard of their contemporaries at a public school; and he had no deeper intellectual curiosity or more fully formed artistic tastes than his father had had. Indeed, although in later life he read more than Edward VII had ever done, 'almost the only criticism of his father to be found in the length and breadth' of his correspondence with his mother is of an arbitrary decision to convert the bowling alley at Sandringham into a library.[5]

He had been perfectly happy leading a regular, quiet, even placid country life, helping with the management of the estate, shooting – he was a fast and very accurate shot – dabbling in gardening, going to bed early after watching his children have their bath, and then playing a game of billiards with an equerry or reading aloud to his wife. He liked babies and animals, and he loved his wife and his mother – at the age of twenty-five he was still signing his letters to 'darling Motherdear', 'your loving little Georgy'. In fact he was the epitome of the contented family man.

He wanted little else from life. He 'preferred recognition to surprise,' as Sir Harold Nicolson has said, 'the familiar to the strange'. He could not talk easily to many of his father's friends, particularly the beautiful and witty women and the foreign men, for he was conscious that his mind though shrewd enough was far from subtle. He did not altogether trust foreigners, anyway, and he detested travelling abroad. 'England is good enough for me,' he once said. 'I like my own country best, climate or no, and I'm staying in it. I'm not like my father. There's nothing of the cosmopolitan in me. I'm afraid I'm insular.'[6]

He could never master German and his French accent was atrocious. Nearly all his own friends were simple, honest, well-born men like himself. In later life both he and his wife 'felt more at ease with British working people than they ever did with members of London society or with foreign royalties'.[7]

41. The arrival of Napoleon III at Windsor Castle in 1855 from the water-colour by G. H. Thomas in the Royal Collection

42. Edward VII and Queen Alexandra with a group of friends in
the Great Park in 1905
from a photograph in the Royal Photograph Albums, Windsor Castle

He liked to have a down-to-earth conversation, blunt and direct; and once he had settled down to talk he was nearly always voluble as well as noisy, often indiscreet and sometimes so emphatic that he would bang on the table with his fist. His humour was predictably broad and simple and, like most men who compensate for an innate diffidence by a boisterous gusto, he enjoyed practical jokes, provided they were limited to the family circle. Rude banter always amused him and he loved to tell the story of how one day when he was making his usual morning telephone call to his sister, Princess Victoria, she picked up the receiver at the regular time and said, '"Hullo, you old fool!" And the voice of the operator broke in, "Beg pardon, Your Royal Highness, His Majesty is not yet on the line."'[8]

He confounded all his critics, though, by proving an exceptionally skilful king, just as he had been an exceptionally able naval officer. He never pretended to understand the complexities of the more abstruse political or diplomatic questions of his day, but he worked hard and conscientiously to grasp the fundamental problems that faced his governments, never contenting himself with summaries as his father had done, and reading his papers, as he read his books, with a slow, thorough, tenacious mind. Had that mind been more subtle and devious he could never have achieved the success he did achieve in establishing the central position and constitutional importance of the Monarchy.

He was a Conservative at heart, but when a Labour Ministry came into power and a member of his entourage, 'whose roots were firmly planted in the Edwardian age', attempted to commiserate with him on his having to deal with these 'tiresome' people, he turned his back on the would-be sympathiser and would not answer him.[9] He had shown in the Navy that he was not only intensely loyal and balanced but also quite without snobbishness or pretension, and he showed these qualities as a king. It helped him, of course, to be so English, to be quite without the German accent of all his Hanoverian predecessors, to have married a girl who, despite her German origins, had been brought up in England and seemed as English as himself, to combine with his father's interest in yachting and shooting, and other sports considered to be more or less those of a gentleman, an interest in football and in cup-tie finals at the Crystal Palace.

'He was a symbol but he was a person as well. The symbol inspired awe, and he never did anything which could mar his symbolic dignity; but only the person could inspire affection, and we liked to think of him as a very homely person. Mr Page, the American ambassador and no admirer of the king species, was delighted and half surprised to find that King George and he could "chat like two human beings".'[10]

Being 'a very homely person', he at first preferred Sandringham and Balmoral to Windsor, which he associated with ceremonial and large-scale entertainment; and he and the Queen did all they could to make the Castle as domestic as possible. Lord Esher was clearly delighted with the change. 'Nothing can be quieter or more domestic than the Castle,' he wrote in his journal in April 1911. 'We have reverted to the ways of Queen Victoria. Dinner in the Oak Room, sitting in the Corridor till tea, when all go to their avocations – the King to his work and early to bed. We wear short coats in the daytime! Instead of frock coats! It is all very home-like and simple . . . How the King loves to renew his grandmother's habits in all things.' 'You have no idea of the change that has come over this place,' he continued the following day in a letter to the Duchess of Sutherland. 'We are back in Victorian times. Everything is so peaceful and domestic. Early rides at 8.30! The King sits mostly in a tent below the East Terrace. He works in his room all the morning. Curious vicissitudes we have gone through in the last twenty years under the shadow of this old castle.'[11]

Gradually the Castle began to exercise over the King 'the same impelling attraction which almost without exception has captured and held all sovereigns who have lived there'.[12] His sitting room was the Blue Room where his grandfather had died, and just as his grandmother had wished to leave it as her beloved husband had left it, so George V wished to keep it just as his father had furnished it. Nothing must be changed, not the red leather chairs, nor the stiff sofa, nor the mahogany bookcase nor any of the pictures. Once when it was changed by a new housemaid who 'put everything back wrong', the King flew into one of his sudden rages. He rang for the housekeeper, who watched apprehensively as the slight, bearded figure of her master strode up and down across the carpet, asking furiously and repeatedly why the girl should have done such a thing.

'Well, Your Majesty,' the housekeeper said at last, 'be sure it will never be wrong again.' And then she added with sudden inspiration, 'I'll get the room photographed.' The original idea so impressed the King that he fell suddenly silent; and the room *was* photographed.[13]*

---

* In his later years the King seems to have changed his views about the inviolability of their private museums within the Castle. 'Here I am now,' he complained to the Dean of

3

3333

Although nothing in his sitting-room was changed, however, much else in the Castle was; for the new Queen was a museum director *manquée*. She was frequently to be found walking about the Castle giving orders for the removal or replacement of pieces of furniture, objects of art or of vertu, and of souvenirs and relics in the lace room. She was interested more in royal iconography than in art, and her reputation as an infallible connoisseur is certainly unjustified;[15] but she did train herself to be something of an expert on antique furniture and china and was a determined, indeed an avaricious, collector, diligently pursuing items dispersed from the royal homes by Queen Victoria, who had allowed members of her family to borrow freely from them, and even soliciting gifts from houses whose owners were by no means willing to part with them. She kept details of her private possessions and those of her husband and his family in little notebooks, and delighted in conducting guests round the Windsor collections of which she liked to think of herself as 'custodian for the nation'.[16]

The Queen's pride and interest and some crumbs of her knowledge 'were eventually absorbed by the King, but although he had a good memory like his wife and could recite the history of many of their possessions with the fluency of a museum guide', sometimes 'flaming "howlers" crept into the text of his discourse', and he was therefore usually content, if the Queen were with him, to turn to her and say with his hearty laugh, 'May: now you know all about this.'[17]

In fact, he enjoyed himself more outside the Castle than in it. He got up early, did some work before breakfast, which he ate every morning punctually at nine o'clock, walking into the room as the clock was chiming. After reading *The Times* he went out, tapping the barometer on his way, with a cigarette – in a holder – in his mouth, his parrot, Charlotte, on his wrist and a dog at his heels, to see what the weather was like. If it was fine and his work permitted it, he might go for a walk round the farms or the garden at Frogmore, or visit the new gardens which were being made in the Park, always returning between eleven o'clock and twelve for a bowl of soup. Or he might go shooting at Flemish Farm or Cranbourne Tower, play a game of golf, pick some flowers on the Castle slopes, or set out for a slow and gentle ride in the Park with a close friend like Lord Revelstoke, or with his children.[18]

Windsor, 'with one room in which my father slept, kept with a dressing-gown over the chair, and my brother's room with his toothpaste undisturbed. If it went on you'd never have any rooms left to live in.'[14]

Occasionally in the afternoons he would go out into the Park with his wife for a picnic tea. The place they usually chose was Adelaide Cottage, which William IV's Queen had built from fragments of the partially demolished Royal Lodge. His mother, too, had often had picnics here and had built on to the end of Wyatville's great saloon (which William IV's demolition men had spared) a charming octagonal room hung inside with chintz like a marquee. She and Edward VII had taken Lord Haldane and his sister to tea there one day and the 'Queen made tea herself and spilt it plentifully'.[19]

Queen Mary was more practical than her mother-in-law, but one day when she made tea there for Lord Esher there were other problems. 'As there was only one servant in attendance, the Queen and Princess Mary laid the table,' Lord Esher wrote in his diary. 'There was apparently a shortage of silver as well as of servants, for when it came to the making of the tea there was no urn. But the King would not allow the tea to be made in the kitchen, and, to the obvious indignation of the servant, he was made to bring up a very heavy and dirty tea-kettle from which the tea-pot was regularly filled.'[20]

*   *   *

To his children the King appeared as a stern, demanding and intimidating figure. The bluff, quarter-deck, insistently jovial manner in which he addressed them in his less severe moments was both aggravating and embarrassing to sensitive children. Neither the eldest son David nor his younger brother, who in the words of his biographer was 'easily rebuffed and prone to take his weaknesses and mistakes too seriously',[21] ever felt completely at ease in his company. Nor did his favourite child, Mary, who blushed scarlet whenever he teased her, which was often. He was emotional and susceptible himself, yet he did not have the imagination to understand how these same characteristics affected the personalities and attitudes of his children.

'I have often felt,' his eldest son wrote later, 'that despite his undoubted affection for all of us, my father preferred children in the abstract, and that his notion of a small boy's place in a grown-up world was summed up in the phrase, "Children should be seen, not heard." It was once said of him that his naval training had caused him to look upon his own children much as he regarded noisy midshipmen when he was captain of a cruiser – as young nuisances in constant need of correction.' No words that the Prince ever heard in later life were 'so disconcerting to the spirit' as the summons, usually delivered by a footman, that the King wanted to see him in the library.

A 'perfect expression of the Victorian and Edwardian eras', strict, demanding, rigidly courteous, with an adamantine sense of probity, and with a habit, adopted on the advice of his mother, of reading his Bible every day, the King believed 'implicitly in God, in the invincibility of the Royal Navy, and the essential rightness of whatever was British'.[22]

He believed, too, not only that his sons should be compelled to share these beliefs, but that the rising generation of his subjects, many of whom clearly did not share them, were in danger of perdition. They had behaved well in the War, to be sure, and he had set them a predictably fine example, behaving well and courageously in public, undertaking all his duties with an almost passionate conscientiousness, and leading a rigorously abstemious private life in which alcohol – at the prompting of Lloyd George – was banned at his tables, in which his cellars were locked, and those who were not in the dining room as soon as the echoes of the gong had died away sometimes got nothing to eat at all. Once, indeed, an equerry who had been kept talking on the telephone arrived for breakfast after everyone else had sat down, to find that there was no food left on the table. He rang the bell and asked for a boiled egg. 'If he had ordered a dozen turkeys he could not have made a bigger stir. The King accused him of being a slave to his inside, of . . . unpatriotic behaviour, and even went so far as to hint that we should lose the war on account of his gluttony.'[23]

The King did not observe his own rules too strictly, however. His guests were handed a list of soft drinks at dinner – Lord Rosebery, who reluctantly chose ginger ale which seemed to him the nearest thing to alcohol he was likely to get, suffered a fearful attack of hiccups[24] – but the Queen's jug of fruitcup was well spiced with champagne, and the King himself, when the meal was over, retired to his study 'to attend to a small matter of business. The matter in question was tacitly assumed to be a small glass of port, and this no one would grudge him.'[25]

It was, after all, the public example that was important and no one could criticise the King in this respect. Beneath his study windows the lawns of the Castle 'had been ruthlessly dug up for growing vegetables, and in the Drawing-room the Queen was knitting hard amongst her Ladies'.[26] The King showed Lady Curzon his potato patch one morning. Did he do all the work himself, she asked him. 'Of course I do,' he told her, indignant at her doubt. 'I dug it all – just look at my hands.'[27]

Always very susceptible to criticism, whether justified or not, the

King was constantly anxious that his people should know the energetic part he was playing in the conduct of the War. And so when it was whispered that he could not be doing much to win it, as he must be pro-German for he had a German name, 'he started and grew pale'.[28]

In fact no one in his family was quite sure what their surname was, and when the College of Heralds was consulted, Mr Farnham Burke had to admit that he could not be sure either. It was not Stewart; Mr Burke doubted if it were Guelph; it might be Wipper, but there again it might be Wettin. The King resolved that the problem must be solved by the adoption of a name which was unmistakably British, or at least obviously not German. The Duke of Connaught suggested Tudor or Stewart. Other suggestions were York, Lancaster, Plantagenet, England, Fitzroy, or even D'Este. The proposal of the King's Private Secretary, however, seemed the best. He thought that as Edward III had been known as Edward of Windsor, they need look no further for a name at once undoubtedly English and undeniably appropriate. The suggestion was adopted[29] – and the Kaiser, so it was said, retaliated by ordering a performance of the Merry Wives of Saxe-Coburg and Gotha.[30]

It was also agreed that those members of the Royal Family who had foreign titles should relinquish them and be given new ones instead. So the Duke of Teck, the King's brother-in-law, became the Marquess of Cambridge; Prince Alexander of Teck became the Earl of Athlone; the King's two cousins, Prince Louis of Battenberg and Prince Alexander of Battenberg, became the Marquess of Milford Haven and the Marquess of Carisbrooke with the family name of Mountbatten.[31]

The King's shock when he heard that people were hinting that he was pro-German was all the more painful because not only was he extremely sensitive to criticism but he was also, as his Assistant Private Secretary said, 'so accustomed to people agreeing with him' that he grew to dislike those who ventured to express opinions contrary to his own. Consequently such opinions rarely were expressed. It was no doubt true that he hated all insincerity and flattery, but his staff soon learned that he did not like the 'candid friend business' either, and they acted accordingly.[32]

He hated to be argued with or interrupted, and when an intrepid member of the Household suggested a different course of action from one he had decided upon, he would refuse to listen to his arguments and snap, 'Go on and do it, you obstinate devil.' He was not blindly stubborn, though, and a few days later he would sometimes ask, 'Well, have you done it?' 'No, Sir, I thought I'd let it cool.' 'Well, well, perhaps you're right.'[33] He was far less hasty and indiscreet in action than he was in word, and as Roger Fulford suggests, while always saying exactly what was in his mind, he did not perhaps believe that he would be taken entirely seriously.

He could never, however, overcome his obstinate prejudices against the activities and attitudes of those whom he thought of with perplexed distaste as the Younger Generation. His wife could become 'ragingly angry' with a young woman who appeared at Court with a dress slit 'almost to the knee';[34] but she, despite her often formidable expression, had much more sympathy with the young than he had. And he himself was not, after all, nearly so sternly dignified and disapproving as he sometimes appeared. He enjoyed *La Vie Parisienne* and seaside postcards as much as the next man; he was even once heard singing *Yes, We Have No Bananas* to shock a particularly staid member of the Household;[35] and when during his serious illness the unmarried daughter of one of his servants became pregnant he was often heard to murmur in his semi-delirium that the father 'must show mercy for her', that he must be told to 'treat the girl gently'.[36]

Nevertheless, the King was constantly shocked, particularly after the War, by the young. New ways of dancing, American drinks and jazz, Soviet Russia, painted finger-nails, going away for the week-end, girls who smoked in public or rode horses astride, men who rode in jodhpurs and polo-neck sweaters, all excited a wrath which he did not hesitate to advertise in front of his servants and Household in the most pungently acrimonious or disdainful terms. If his favourite expression was 'keep your hair on', picked up in his Navy days and never abandoned, he was almost as often heard to say, 'Well we never did *that* in the olden days.'[37]

He himself never forsook the fashions of his youth, continuing throughout his life to wear stiff collars, hard hats and cloth-topped boots – all, incidentally, like his every other possession, of the most expensive quality. Even in the mid-1930s he was still wearing trousers with side creases, and his letters to the obsessively dress-conscious Prince of Wales are full of scornful criticisms of what he took to be laxness in some detail of dress that he had noticed in a photograph. Anyone who did not observe the conventions in dressing was a 'cad'; and the picture of his own son wearing 'a turned down collar in white uniform, with a collar and black tie' was acutely painful. 'Anything more unsmart' he never saw.[38] On another occasion, having rebuked the Prince for not wearing a top-hat on a visit to the Midlands, he only grudgingly accepted the excuse that a top-hat was not altogether suitable for a visit to a factory. Before the War, Guards officers were expected to wear a white tie in the evening for dining out, if the King were in London, and to wear a top-hat and morning-coat for walking in the streets in the daytime. After the War these regulations were necessarily relaxed, but the Prince was still expected to wear a morning-coat to visit his father; and he had to wear a white tie, tails and the Garter Star whenever he dined with him, even if there were no other guests. [39]

The sight of visitors to Windsor Castle walking about the grounds carelessly or outlandishly dressed always irritated the King, and one Easter Bank Holiday the Queen was obliged to call on him 'peremptorily to be silent' when she was embarrassed beyond endurance' by the loud comments and criticisms – 'Good God, *look* at those short skirts, *look* at that bobbed hair!' – which he delivered from an open window while looking down upon the visitors who passed along the Terrace below. [40]

*　　*　　*

With such a man at its head it was not to be expected, of course, that life in the Castle could be remotely gay. Meals were prompt and quickly served and usually very simple. The King hated exotic food and once when the Prince of Wales ordered him an avocado pear for a special treat he was horrified. 'What,' he asked, 'in heaven's name is this?' [41] After dinner was over – it rarely took more than half an hour – and the Queen had been followed out by the ladies, each of whom curtseyed to the King who bowed in return, he would remain talking to his male guests, whose company he preferred, drinking port.

The running of the Household in the later years of the reign was governed by rules laid down generations before. 'Everything had to be carried out according to precedent,' the King's nurse, Sister Catherine Black, discovered. 'Old forms and ceremonies that had been in use for centuries were scrupulously observed. The rules and conditions of service laid down for the Household in the reign of George III were still referred to when any doubt arose and "It has always been done that way" was considered the last word in any argument.' [42]

If there were no guests, and often there were not, the King would spend the evening by the fire with the Queen, looking at his stamps, or reading – biographies mostly, or books of adventure by John Buchan or Charles Kingsley, and 'he could enjoy a good detective story'.[43] He had enjoyed a game of whist occasionally, too, as a young man, but when bridge took its place he found the new game too difficult and took up poker instead. He did not often play, however, and when he did it was only for small stakes. Nor did he enjoy the wireless much, although he would occasionally listen to the news. He preferred the gramophone because he liked to have the same record, often a Gilbert and Sullivan song, put on time after time 'innocently regardless of the tastes of his audience. Indeed, he was suspicious of the "highbrow" (a word which had once puzzled him when he had believed that it was spelt "eyebrow")'[44] – he was always a bad speller and never became adept at either punctuation or syntax. Sometimes in later years there was a film. He liked adventure films best, such as *Lives of a Bengal Lancer*, or English comedies, particularly Tom Walls's. He went to bed at 11.10 p.m. precisely.[45]

When he felt obliged to have a house party in the Castle, few of the young guests – except those who still subscribed to some of his old-fashioned notions or otherwise deferred carefully to his opinions – looked forward to the event with pleasurable anticipation. The days were long past when Queen Mary might be seen, as she once had been, 'hopping in a green and white brocade dress round one of the drawing-rooms at Windsor to represent a grasshopper in a game of dumb crambo'.[46] After the War the parties, as a matter of course, would mainly consist of their Majesties' stodgy old friends who would disapprove of the dancing. And the ceremonial protocol was always exacting.

During Ascot week the ladies, each of whom had to have two new dresses for the mornings, four new *ensembles* for the races, and five new full evening dresses, were lined up in the Green Drawing Room before dinner by the Lady of the Bedchamber in a quarter circle, in strict order of precedence, while the men were lined up by the Master of the Household on the other side of the room. Promptly at half-past eight the King and Queen, and any other members of the Royal Family who were present, arrived at the Green Drawing Room door. The Master of the Household bowed and backed across the threshhold. The Queen shook hands with the curtseying women. Then the man who had been commanded to sit on the Queen's right bowed to her, offered her his arm and escorted her to the dinner table to the strains of 'God Save the King' played by a Guards string band concealed behind a grille in the dining-room.

At dinner, served on gilt or silver services by pages in blue livery and footmen in scarlet, the band continued to play. Within an hour the meal was over and the Queen caught her husband's eye as a signal that she was about to leave with the ladies, who curtsied in turn to him as they withdrew. The King, who, like his sons, a few close friends and members of the Household, was wearing the Windsor uniform, motioned to two men to take the empty chairs beside him. 'Over the port, coffee, and liqueurs the day's racing and current politics would be discussed,' the King's eldest son recalled years later. 'My father never sat more than twenty minutes – there was barely time to smoke even the shortest cigar. Abruptly, as if controlled by a hidden time-clock, he would rise and lead his guests back to the Green Drawing Room to join my mother.'[47]

The Queen meanwhile had taken up her crochet. This was a sign for the Lady of the Bedchamber to bring up the first of the ladies to whom she had previously expressed a wish to talk. The brief conversations were ended by the return of the King; and the guests then settled down to play cards.[48] At eleven o'clock 'as if by magic' the company would resume their places in the two quarter circles they had adopted before dinner. The Royal Family then bade their guests goodnight and the evening was over. Once the King's sons waited until their parents were safely in bed and then returned to the Green Drawing Room, rolled back the rugs and invited the younger guests to join them in dancing. 'The musicians, more familiar with classical music and martial airs, made an earnest attempt to cope with out-moded foxtrots, which were as close as they could come to jazz. But our efforts to be gay were a failure. The ancient walls seemed to exude disapproval. We never tried it again.'[49]

Each morning at a quarter-past eleven the open landaus, drawn by four horses with bewigged postilions in special Ascot livery – red jackets, black velvet hunting-caps, white buckskin breeches and top boots – were driven out to a rendezvous in the Park where they waited for the arrival of the Castle guests, who left by car at twenty minutes to one and transferred to the carriages for the last part of their journey to the Course. Each car took two men and two women and was left in the Park to await the return of the guests in the carriages. This procedure was followed every year and on each day of the Royal Meeting except the last day when the guests returned all the way to the Castle in the carriages.

On the last evening of their visit the guests assembled outside the royal apartments to take leave of their hosts, and on their return home they had to write a letter of thanks which was to arrive not later than the following Monday.

The list of guests varied almost as little as the routine. The King's sons complained of their father's unalterable habits, but he refused to change anything or to strike any guest however tiresome off his list. 'No one has the exciting feeling that if they strive they will be asked again next summer,' Lady Airlie complained. 'They know they will be automatically as long as they are alive. Traditionalism is all very well, but too much of it leads to dry rot.'[50]

*   *   *

The King's insistence on the meticulous observance of traditional forms, his rigid conservatism, made his happy relationship with his Labour Ministers all the more remarkable to his friends. But to George v himself there was nothing remarkable about it. He had read his Bagehot carefully; he had always paid close attention to what his Private Secretary and intimate adviser, Lord Stamfordham, told him; he was not only consistently faithful to his ideal of the Monarchy as something 'sacramental, mystic and ordained', but he was also consistently faithful to the Constitution of which it formed a part. His Ministers might be Socialists and had, therefore, ideas very different from his, but 'I must say,' he admitted, having met them in turn in February 1924, 'they all seem to be very intelligent and they take things very seriously. . . . They ought to be given a chance and ought to be treated fairly.'[51]

He did treat them fairly. To the surprise of some of them, they liked him and grew to admire a character so straight and honest, so uncompromising and yet on occasions so considerate; and he discovered that he liked most of them. Ramsay MacDonald impressed him 'very much' and he grew particularly fond of J. H. Thomas, who made him laugh – once in 1929 after an operation on his chest, so heartily that he burst an abscess below his ribs[52] – and who, during a visit to Windsor, after the King's slow recovery in 1929, surprised the Household by saying bluntly that he attributed the recovery to the old man's 'bloody guts'.[53]

The King did all he could to put his new Ministers at their ease and to gain their confidence; and so complete was his success that, without being pressed to do so by him but under some pressure from MacDonald who had no personal adversion to the practice, they were induced to accede to the King's known wishes with regard to their clothes.

He did not expect them to provide themselves with full court uniform, but he hoped that they would make some concessions to

tradition, as American envoys had been prepared to do.* Lord
Stamfordham told the Chief Government Whip that it was obviously
too much to expect that the Labour Ministers should patronise the
principal court tailor whose charge for a levee dress, for instance, was
£73 2s. 6d., but he thought that they might have recourse to
Messrs Moss Bros. which was, he believed, 'a well-known and
dependable firm'.[55]

The question of dress had been given an added significance by the
problem of filling court appointments with Labour nominees. Mac-
Donald wanted to escape this predicament by leaving the King free to
fill the vacancies as he wished, but the King realised the danger of
laying himself open to the accusation that he was surrounded by
personal friends. Eventually it was agreed to compromise: the Lord
Chamberlain, the Lord Steward, the Master of the Horse, the
Captain of the Gentlemen at Arms, and the Captain of the Yeomen of
the Guard, and three Lords in Waiting were to be appointed by the
Sovereign, subject to their taking no part in Parliamentary votes and
proceedings; while three other Lords in Waiting, the Treasurer of
the Household, the Comptroller and the Vice-Chamberlain were to be
appointed upon the advice of the Prime Minister.[56]

The sight of Mr Tom Griffiths, who had once earned fourpence a
day in a tinplate works and was now appointed Treasurer of the
Household, wearing levee dress complete with a plumed hat,
naturally earned a good deal of satirical comment from both Right
and Left, but to King George v it seemed perfectly in order and very
gratifying. He had got his own way not so much by tact, for he was
not a tactful man, but by the force of an utterly honest personality.

* In 1929, however, the problem of knee-breeches for American ambassadors again
became a difficult one when President Hoover sent Brigadier-General Charles G. Dawes
as Ambassador to London. General Dawes, an outspoken Chicago banker, had assured an
anxious press conference before his departure that he would not wear knee-breeches at the
English Court. The King, convalescing at Windsor, was, in the words of Lord Cromer,
the Lord Chamberlain, 'extremely upset'. The Prince of Wales, who knew the General,
was asked to help to overcome the difficulty and he suggested that he should be advised to
wear his ordinary trousers over the top of the knee-breeches to satisfy the reporters who
were certain to be watching his departure from the American Embassy. Before entering
the presence of the Queen, who was deputising for her ill husband, he could take his
trousers off and hand them to an equerry. The Prince of Wales, being unwilling to propose
this ingenious solution himself, however, as he did not want to spoil the goodwill he had
built up for himself in America, and no one else being prepared to propose it, General
Dawes came to Court in trousers. 'Papa will not be pleased,' the Queen murmured
apprehensively. 'What a pity such a distinguished man should be so difficult.'[54] Eventually
the Ambassador's blunt charm and capacity overcame the prejudice that his unconventional attire aroused, and when Joseph Kennedy came to the London Embassy a new
tradition for American ambassadors had been established.

The longer he lived, the more deeply his people became aware of the admirable qualities of this personality, so stable, old-fashioned and reassuring in an almost hysterical world. He had played a more important part in the conduct of their affairs than they knew, perhaps; for he had made good use of what Walter Bagehot had called the Sovereign's 'right to be consulted', his 'right to encourage' and his 'right to warn'. 'It's not for me to have opinions, or to interfere,' he would say, passing his right hand across his body in a well-known and deprecatory gesture;[57] but he saw to it that his opinions *were* known well enough, and they were not always opinions of which his people would have approved. But they knew little of this.

In 1932, when he eventually overcame his reluctance to use a new invention and made his first broadcast, his bluff yet kindly voice enchanted them. Already the War had made them think of him as the Father of his People,[58] now he was far less remote a figure. At his Jubilee in 1935 the unmistakably enthusiastic acclamations made him realise, as if for the first time, how really loved he and his wife had become. 'I'd no idea they felt like that about me,' he told Sister Black when he returned from a visit to the East End during which he had been vociferously cheered. 'I am beginning to think they must really like me for myself'.[59] He made a speech afterwards, and at the end his voice failed him when he made a reference to the Queen. He had known it would and when preparing the draft had told his Secretary to put that part at the end. 'I can't trust myself to speak of the Queen when I think of all I owe her.'[60]

They had grown up together and together they had tried to overcome their disabilities. She had been a shy and very reserved girl, and as Princess of Wales 'her shyness had so crystallised that only in moments of intimacy could she be herself. The hard core of inhibition which gradually closed over her, hiding the warmth and tenderness of her own personality, was already starting to form.'[61]

Overshadowed in her early years both by her mother, an expansive, stout and talkative woman, and by her mother-in-law, whose spontaneous gaiety was often unnerving and whose apparent indifference to Princess May's need for more stimulating occupations than child-bearing was always stultifying, she had grown particularly vulnerable to criticism and, although when she became Queen her confidence increased, she was still far from being the imperious, prudish and self-assertive woman of popular imagination. 'Before her, scandal sits dumb: she has a quiet but inflexible power of silencing everything which seems likely to approach ill-natured gossip,' Augustus Hare wrote of her in the 1890s. But immediately after she had shown evidence of her disapproval she gave such 'a genial kindly look and word to the silenced one as prevents any feeling of mortification'.[62]

She had, as her biographer James Pope-Hennessy says, 'no comprehension of the flippant'; and, being a traditionalist like her husband, she had never been able to accustom herself to the activities of her father-in-law's friends. '*Je n'aime pas leurs* "goings-on",' she confessed to her old governess;[63] and she told Lady Airlie that Edwardian society suffered from a 'surfeit of gold plate and orchids'.[64] Yet she was always far more sympathetic towards those whose tastes differed from her own, particularly the young, than the King could ever bring himself to be, and she was never aggressively censorious. Open-minded and curious, she once asked a member of the Household to teach her some of the new dance-steps of the period; but the lesson was interrupted by the King 'who expressed himself so violently' that she never attempted to repeat the experiment.[65]

She was 'almost Victorian in her attitude to her husband', Lady Airlie thought. 'She had more originality of mind than he, and their views on current topics often differed widely, but when he contradicted her she never argued with him.'[66] She suppressed her feelings in other ways, too. She felt it was her duty to continue to keep out of her expression in public all her inner grief when her eldest brother, her 'beloved Dolly', died;[67] and she continued to smile, if rather transfixedly, when excited people shouted in her ear, acutely sensitive though she was to any loud and sudden noise. And although she was capable of fainting when a footman cut his finger, her insistent sense of social responsibility made her visit the badly wounded during the War with an almost masochistic determination, insisting on seeing the worst cases.[68] 'It was indescribable,' she said, having spent a long time talking and looking into what remained of the face of a sailor, most of whose features had been burned away. 'I thought I could not do it; but then, of course, there is simply nothing one can't do.'[69]

She was, as well as being an extremely conscientious woman, a very competent one; and her interest in Windsor Castle, that 'dear glorious old castle so full of historical associations'[70] of which she was 'passionately fond',[71] went far beyond its artistic treasures. The plans for new cottages for the estate workers came to her for approval before building began. She was responsible for many new decorative schemes, and the cream-and-gold walls and rose-coloured hangings in her own private sitting-room were a characteristically elegant background for her beautiful eighteenth-century French and English furniture. She was responsible, too, for many improvements in the grounds, for the planting of new shrubs and trees, and for clearing away the tangled undergrowth on the slopes beneath the North Terrace.

She was, as her servants well knew, a mistress not to be trifled with, and her investigation of departments and her inspection of store-rooms which had previously been left to the Housekeeper, surprised and often alarmed the senior members of the Castle staff. She made a habit of inspecting rooms at Windsor after the servants had finished preparing them for her guests;[72] and she was quite capable of inspecting other people's houses as well as her own; and once, having inspected every corner of her second son's house and 'opened every cupboard', she pronounced herself satisfied that it was 'very clean'.[73]

When she discovered incompetence, laziness or disrespect, she could, although her nature was not in the least passionate, be as furiously angry as her husband. But her anger, like his, soon cooled and was rarely resented.[74]

She seemed to share his taste in clothes as well as his tendency to outbursts of anger and his sensitivity to criticism. The style of her clothes, however, was dictated more by her husband's taste than her own, for she believed that everyone, herself included, should bow to his will. Once she thought that she would like to shorten her skirts in accordance with current fashion, as she had attractive legs and ankles, and she accepted the offer of one of her ladies who suggested that she act as a guinea-pig to test the reactions of the King. The King did not at all approve of the lady-in-waiting's appearance, and the Queen's idea of becoming fashionable was immediately abandoned.*[75] Also, because her husband did not like them, she gave up wearing picture hats in the summer when these came into fashion after the First World War.[77] She remained, in fact, with her long, voluminous skirts, as if rooted in the past; and the distressing toques that covered her grey hair, and the folds of pale blue and mauve brocade and the silk and

---

* The King declared his taste with equal emphasis to guests at the Castle. Once, soon after her marriage, Lady Curzon was asked to dinner. Having embarrassed her during the meal by telling her more than once in his loud voice, which was certainly audible to every-one else at the table, what a wonderful showman her husband was, he turned her attention afterwards to her dress. It was a highly fashionable black dress, which she had recently bought in Paris. 'It was rather short in front,' she remembered, 'and had a long pointed train. This made the King laugh very much. I was made to turn round in front of him, and he laughed and said, "How ridiculous! Off the ground in front, and all that trailing behind on the floor!" However, His Majesty was kind enough to assure me that I looked charming in it.'[76]

lace that concealed her stately bosom, were accepted as essential and entirely appropriate parts of the *persona* that she had become.

Of the King's devotion to her no one could doubt, and he felt sure, listening to the continuous cheers that so pleased and astonished him that Jubilee Day in 1935, that they were cheering her as much as him. For he, after all, as he told the Archbishop of Canterbury, was 'a very ordinary fellow'.[78] That was his triumph, of course. He *was* an ordinary fellow and yet he was the King; and there were few Englishmen who did not feel moved when he died.

At his last Privy Council Meeting, he sat in his bedroom in his dressing-gown, small and frail and looking very old, and took the pen from Lord Dawson, his doctor, and attempted to trace his childlike signature at the bottom of an Order appointing a Council of State. But he could not grasp the pen properly and as he struggled to write Dawson whispered to him to try to write with his left hand. Making his last, bad joke, he said, 'Why? Do you want me to sign with both hands?' He did change the pen to his other hand, though, but still he could not sign and as he fumbled he looked up at the Council and said pathetically, 'I am sorry to keep you waiting, gentlemen, but I find it difficult to concentrate.' He would not let anyone guide his hand and he would not give up trying to sign the paper, on which at last he managed to scrawl two 'barely recognisable marks. When he had dismissed them with his charming smile and they came out, it was noted that most of them were in tears.'[79]

Earlier that morning he had seen Lord Wigram, who heard the King's feebly whispered question, 'Empire?' Wigram replied, 'It is all absolutely right, Sir.' The King smiled and went back to sleep. Later the Archbishop of Canterbury came and asked if he might give him his blessing. 'Yes, do please give me your blessing,' the King had said, and having received it he had tried to repeat the Lord's Prayer but he had gone to sleep in the middle.

He was still asleep that night when Lord Dawson was asked to give his wording for the nine o'clock bulletin. 'I think the time is past for details,' Dawson said, and he wrote on the back of a card the message that was soon afterwards broadcast to millions of waiting people: 'The King's life is moving peacefully towards its close.'[80]

Eight days later, on 28 January 1936, he was buried in St George's Chapel, Windsor. His eldest son scattered earth over the coffin from a silver bowl and then came out into the cold sunless air, his 'grey face sad and frightening'.[81]

. George V, Queen Mary and the
Prince of Wales

m photographs in the Royal Photograph Albums, Windsor Castle

44. George V and Queen Mary in 1909

45. The York children in 1905

46. An aerial photograph of the Castle today

EDWARD VIII

The Prince of Wales had been told of his father's illness while out shooting with friends in the Great Park. A few years before he had moved into a 'Grace and Favour' house six miles from the Castle – Fort Belvedere, 'a castellated conglomeration', as the Prince himself described it, which, begun by William, Duke of Cumberland, had been enlarged by Wyatville on George IV's instructions. And it was while modernising the house and clearing its tangled grounds that the Prince had discovered the 'true charm of Windsor Castle'.[1]

Until then it had seemed more of a 'museum than the residence for the Sovereign', but now that he had come to live nearby and grew to know it better he began to 'revere it not only for its treasures but also for its tranquillity'.[2] He had spent part of his boyhood at Frogmore when his father was Prince of Wales and had enjoyed riding in the Great Park, going for trips with his mother in a big electric launch upriver to Maidenhead and downstream to Staines, exploring the roof of the Castle – 'all the more desirable because it was forbidden ground' – playing hide-and-seek amongst the marble busts in George IV's long corridor, wheeling his brothers about on the tall ladders in the library.[3] Although Frogmore itself, with its single bathroom on the ground floor, its innumerable marble busts and memorials to the dead, was more of a family necropolis than a house, this did not worry the royal children as they pedalled furiously on their bicycles around the rhododendrons, past the mausoleums where their great-great-grandmother, the Duchess of Kent, and their great-grandparents lay buried.[4]

When their father returned from his shooting in the north, the carefree games were played with more restraint. His children were once more, as his eldest son David, the future Edward VIII, put it, 'on parade'. Stockings were pulled up over the knees to the thighs, starched Eton collars encircled their necks, the pockets of their sailor suits were sown up so they could not put their hands in them. A lanyard a fraction of an inch out of place or a sporran slightly awry would earn a parental reprimand of terrifying vehemence.

Their father, as a child, had sometimes felt afraid of *his* father, but this was less because Edward VII was an intentionally intimidating figure than because he was almost a stranger to his sons, both of

T

whom were shy and nervous with those they did not know well. Indeed, Edward VII's relatively liberal and – despite his habit of teasing his children to the point of bullying them – his generally sensible behaviour as a parent was due to a determination not to make the same mistakes as his parents had done. '*We* were perhaps a little too much spoken to and at,' he once told Lady Augusta Stanley.[5] Nor did George V's self-confessed childhood fear of his father have any very noticeable effect on his own, noisy, rough, sometimes hot-tempered and often naughty behaviour. There is a pleasant story that he was once ordered under the table as a punishment. After a few minutes he said he was good and was told that he could come out again. His reappearance caused 'fearful consternation' for to shock his grandmother, Queen Victoria, he had taken off all his clothes.[6]

None of George V's sons would have dared, perhaps, to make so provocative and rebellious a gesture; for George V believed that it was necessary for a parent to be frightening. 'My father was frightened of his mother,' he once apparently said to Lord Derby, 'I was frightened of my father, and I am damned well going to see to it that my children are frightened of me.'[7]

He *did* see to it, and they *were* frightened of him, and although their mother was there to intercede with him on their behalf when he was angry with them, she, too, as James Pope-Hennessy has said, 'never possessed the knack of winning the confidence of her sons in their boyhood'.[8]

Their grandfather, a more remote but more indulgent figure than their father, seemed to David to be 'bathed in perpetual sunlight'.[9] His clever and raffish friends with their beautiful, laughing women driving up to the Castle gates in noisy cars, surrounded by an aura of cigar smoke and scent, showed the impressionable boy a brief glimpse of another world, less restrained and far more exciting. He was not afraid of his grandfather, even if his father had been, and was even capable, on one occasion at least, of interrupting his conversation at table. He was reprimanded, of course, and sat in silence until given permission to speak. 'It's too late now, grandpa,' David said, 'it was a caterpillar on your lettuce, but you've eaten it.'[10]

David grew up young for his years, but 'a most captivating, strange, intelligent boy with a remarkable vocabulary, sad – with the sadness of the world's burdens',[11] and perpetually conscious of the gulf that separated his father from himself. He tried to be obedient, he did his best to carry out his duties conscientiously, but there was always the shadow of his father behind him, demanding, anxious and critical. There was cause, of course, for the father's concern; but frequent chastening served only to make his son 'secretive, stubborn and more self-willed than ever . . . he came to look upon his father, the Archbishop and some of the older Ministers as a critical and unsympathetic company, designed to frustrate his natural eagerness. He therefore made his own life as he wished.'[12]

Restless, impatient, impulsive, frustrated, emotional, affectionate, unstable and indiscreet, he earned as Prince of Wales much popularity and some respect. He had far more charm than talent, far more capacity for feeling than for thought. His sudden enthusiasms, his discordant ambitions, were likely to die as quickly as they had been born. His longing to fight in the war, his insistence on learning to fly, his reckless steeplechasing, his carefree friends, can all be seen as a revolt against his upbringing or as a reflection of his passionate wish to be accepted as an ordinary human being.

It was his tragedy that he never entirely succeeded in reconciling, as his grandfather had been ultimately able to do, his love of life with his position and responsibilities. To spend all evening dancing with the same girl on one of his frequent foreign travels delighted the newspapers but it could not fail to embarrass his official hosts.[13] And when his friend Major 'Fruity' Metcalfe, who called him 'The Little Man', struck a match on the sole of his boot in the hunting field it 'amused and delighted' him,[14] but it could not fail to shock those spectators who had been brought up to believe that even the boot of a Prince of Wales was sacrosanct.

What might have been overlooked in a boy was less excusable in a young man of thirty. In 1918 when the Prince visited the United States for the first time, for instance, all his faults were forgiven. His reception was tumultuous, and most newspapers shared their readers' unalloyed enthusiasm over the 'bewildered, delighted boy'. But in 1924, when most of the stories printed about him concerned his pleasures, there was open criticism. 'He managed, by his choice of friends and diversions,' one newspaper wrote, 'to provoke an exhibition of social climbing on the part of a few Americans which has added nothing to his prestige nor to the prestige of royalty in general.'[15]

At home his father was aghast at the reports about him; and when the son returned, he found the King's desk littered with newspaper clippings.

'Did you see this when you were in New York?' the King asked him, holding up one headline: '*Prince gets In with Milkman.*'

Other clippings were produced from the pile:

'Here He Is Girls – The Most Eligible Bachelor Yet Uncaught.'
'Oh! Who'll Ask H.R.H. What He Wears Asleep?'
'Prince of Wales has 'em guessing in the Wee Hours.'[16]

It was to be expected, of course, that the King would be shocked; but other less harsh critics were shocked, too. Already it seemed, to many observers, that the Prince's public duties were being performed in the intervals left in a life devoted to pleasure. Soon it was being said that the effects of his early life and training, his rushing about the world, the intoxication of his easy popularity, his lack of any close friends who could be expected to offer him any important advice, and his disinclination to listen to any advice at all, were in danger of undermining his character. 'He became increasingly stubborn and conceited over his popularity,' his biographer Hector Bolitho has said. 'Every incident of fifteen years of his life had contributed to the weakness of self-centredness, and his fantastic vanity over his own capacity was a matter for disappointment rather than blame. His natural graces, his charm, his kindliness, the serious and compassionate note which used to come to his voice when he spoke to suffering people, and the promises he had made, all seemed to turn sour within him.'[17]

He became irritable and morose. His servants, to whom he had always behaved with exceptional consideration, began to find him thoughtless and even petty. For days on end he would not attempt to do any work before noon, and frequently men summoned for interview would be sent away without having seen him. Often excited and even exhilarated, he rarely seemed happy. The only place where he appeared to be content was at Fort Belvedere, on which he had spent so much time and energy. And it was at Fort Belvedere that the Prince entertained, at several week-end parties during the last months of his father's life, Mr and Mrs Ernest Simpson.

He had first met Wallis Simpson, a handsome, well-dressed, ambitious, intelligent, good-natured but independent and determined woman with a pronounced Baltimore accent, at Melton Mowbray in 1931. Both she and her husband had been married before and were then living in London at a flat in Bryanston Square where the Prince was soon a regular visitor. By the time of George v's death it had been widely suggested abroad, although not yet by English papers, that the Prince was in love with Mrs Simpson and wanted to make her his Queen. His widowed mother, of course, was horrified. Her life had been ruled by 'one single abstract passion' – her passion for the

British Monarchy;[18] and her son's determination not to put his duty as King before his love for a woman caused her, so she confessed, a deeper distress and humiliation than any other event in the whole of her life.[19]

*　　*　　*

He was King for less than a year. During that time 'harassed, unreasonable and vain,' so Hector Bolitho describes him, 'he continued to play the rôle of a popular monarch.'[20] He did not neglect his duties, but without any political crisis to inspire him and without any encouragement from his Ministers to devote himself personally, as he would have liked, to the problems of the poor and the unemployed, he spent many weeks of his short reign on holiday. 'He has it in him,' Lord Wigram, who had been Lord Stamfordham's successor as George v's private secretary, told Aga Khan, 'to be the greatest King in the history of our country.'[21] And in spite of all that had been said against him, much of it biased and some of it untrue, it was not an unjustified verdict. But the King did not feel he could achieve this distinction, or any sort of distinction, without the support of the woman he loved.

She was more important to him than anything and he would not put her out of his life because he had become a king. 'The King unchanged in manners and love,' Lady Diana Cooper told her friend Conrad Russell, writing from Fort Belvedere in February 1936. 'Wallis tore her nail and said "Oh!" and forgot about it, but he needs must disappear and arrive back in two minutes, panting, with two little emery-boards for her to file the offending nail.'

Diana Cooper had stayed at Fort Belvedere the previous year in a 'pink bedroom, pink-sheeted, pink Venetian-blinded, pink soaped, white-telephoned and pink-and-white maided'. The food 'at dinner staggers and gluts', she had told Conrad Russell. '*Par contra* there is little or nothing for lunch, and that foraged for by oneself American-style (therefore favoured, bless him). We arrived after midnight (perhaps as chaperones). Jabber and beer and bed was the order.' After dinner the following night the Prince of Wales had dressed in a kilt and played the pipes round the table wearing a Scottish bonnet.[22]

The next year, when Diana Cooper was again a guest and the Prince was King, he 'donned his wee bonnet' again and marched round the table, 'his stalwart piper behind him, playing "Over the sea to Skye" and also a composition of his own. He suggested on

Sunday that we should all go over to Windsor Castle and see the library there. "No one ever sees it," he said, "I know Wallis hasn't. It's a bit off the beaten track. There's an awfully good fellow there called Mr Morshead. He's most awfully nice. He told me the other day to go over any time I like."'

The 'glorious stationery' was new, Diana Cooper said, and frock-coats were 'outmoded almost by law' and the servants were 'a bit hobbledehoy'. But although everything was expected to change, nothing much else was different at Windsor.[23]

It was clear, though, that the King would himself change his whole life soon. At a dinner party held in the Castle at the end of March 1936, the King, clinging 'to his secret and private life with a kind of desperation', Lady Hardinge recorded, spoke at length about George IV and Mrs Fitzherbert.[24]

On 10 December 1936 the King announced his decision to abdicate. The following evening he left Fort Belvedere for the Royal Lodge, where his three brothers and his sister and mother were waiting to dine with him. While they were still at dinner his friend Walter Monckton came to drive him to the Castle. 'The great quadrangle was dark and deserted as we entered,' he wrote later. 'I mounted the Gothic staircase to my old rooms in the Augusta Tower.' Here Sir John Reith, Director of the B.B.C., met him and asked him to read a paragraph from a newspaper to test his voice. Then Reith announced in his deep voice, 'This is Windsor Castle. His Royal Highness, Prince Edward.'

Prince Edward's voice, 'thick and tired', read the message, short, sincere and pathetic, which Winston Churchill, who had parted from him with tears in his eyes that afternoon at Fort Belvedere,[25] had helped him write.

Whether or not 'the writers of the future will write upon the romantic theme of a King who gave up his throne for love' or upon the theme 'of a man of promise who came to disaster through the slow disintegration of his character: disintegration which was hastened by the perpetual frustration which he suffered',[26] it was impossible as he spoke to deny him sympathy, just as it is impossible now to believe that he did not deserve it.

When the broadcast was over he left immediately for the Royal Lodge where his brothers were waiting to say goodbye to him. 'Dickie, this is absolutely terrible,' the eldest of them had said earlier to Lord Louis Mountbatten. 'I never wanted this to happen; I'm quite unprepared for it. David has been trained for this all his life.

I've never even seen a State Paper. I'm only a naval officer; it's the only thing I know about.'[27]

But the naval officer had already become a king, and as Prince Edward left the Royal Lodge that night, he bowed to him in the doorway, and their younger brother, the Duke of Kent, 'shook his head and cried almost fiercely, "It isn't possible! It isn't happening!"'[28]

[iii]

GEORGE VI

The Duke of Windsor regarded George v's life as a 'stubborn rearguard action against the acceptance of the march of his own times'.[1] The views of his brother, the Duke of York, who now succeeded him as George vi, were much more sympathetic to those of their father. George vi's opinions were more progressive than George v's had been, but he was far from being a revolutionary or an iconoclast; and he had always been prepared to listen to his father's advice: 'very different to dear David'.[2] If change were to come, he believed that it must come slowly and moderately. He was to be a faithfully constitutional monarch, but his own tastes and beliefs were always to remain innately and fundamentally conservative.

The régime of his childhood had had as marked an effect upon him as upon his brother, but the effect was ultimately a quite different one. Forced to write with his right hand when he was naturally inclined to be left-handed; obliged to wear splints for part of the day and even, for a time, in bed at night to straighten his knock-kneed legs; wanting desperately to satisfy his father but frequently being made to understand that he did not, he became liable to outbursts of anger and to moods of silent depression. By the time he was eight he had developed the stammer which, despite his determined and life-long struggle against it, was never entirely overcome.[3] Yet he never broke out into open defiance or rebellion, for it was his nature to accept discipline, to understand and eventually to share his father's views on behaviour, duty and restraint.

As a shy naval cadet at Osborne, and later at Dartmouth, he was conscientious, patient, painstaking and thorough. He was neither a clever nor an entertaining boy, and he played games with more diligence than skill. But of his application and his courage there could be no doubt. He was roughly treated by the other cadets, who called him 'Bat Lugs' because of his big ears, who pricked him with pins to see if he had blue blood and who kicked him so that they could say they had kicked the son of the King of England.[4] And when he went to sea he was appallingly sea-sick. He persisted in his career, however, as his father wished him to do.

His character, indeed, as it developed, grew more and more to resemble his father's. It was seen that they shared the same ideals; that they had similar faults and similar prejudices; that they were equally emotional. And as the son's self-confidence increased, he became capable of the father's abrupt displays of cantankerous criticism, sometimes made more wounding by a persistent and disdainful sarcasm. He was not at ease, as his father had never been at ease, with clever and brightly amusing or highly imaginative people. He preferred the company of sailors whose experiences he had shared, of men in positions of high responsibility whom he could question about their work, of men like gardeners whose interests were his interests and whose conversation was unlikely to stray into territory where he might lose himself. He was, in fact – again like his father – an unambitious, conservative country gentleman at heart and a king *malgré lui*. When he married in 1923, characteristically he chose a wife whose name was unfamiliar to most of his countrymen.

Modest, appealing and kind, Lady Elizabeth Bowes-Lyon was, though, more than a characteristic choice: she was an ideal one. More responsive and less shy than her husband, instinctively gracious and unemphatically good-looking, 'pretty and engaging and natural' as her mother-in-law said, she had no personal enemies and has made none. George v adored his son's 'dear little wife' and could even find it in his heart to forgive her when she was late for a meal. 'You are not late, my dear,' he was once, to the astonishment of everyone present, heard to say in reply to her apology. 'I think we must have sat down two minutes too early.'[5]

Towards the end of 1931 the Duchess of York came with her husband to live in the Royal Lodge in the Great Park. 'It is too kind of you to have offered us Royal Lodge,' the Duke told his father, who replied that he was pleased that they liked it but who hoped that they would call it '*the* Royal Lodge, by which name it has been known ever since George iv built it'.[6]

The Yorks took possession of the Royal Lodge at a difficult time. The crisis which had led to the creation of a National Government was not yet passed; and George v had felt it necessary to inform his new Government that the Civil List should be considerably reduced so long as the emergency lasted. He also wrote to the Duke of York to tell him that he was going to give up shooting in Windsor Park. 'I can't afford it,' he told him. 'I am sorry, as the birds fly so well there.'[7]

It was, then, some time before the Duke and Duchess could spend enough money on the Royal Lodge to make it into the home they wanted. By 1936, however, it had grown into a very large and comfortable house with well-furnished rooms and a fine garden in which the Duke took as great an interest as he was later to take in the gardens of the Castle.

The life lived there by the 'sweet young couple', as Duff Cooper called them,[8] was as domestic as their father's, and when they moved into the Castle as King and Queen the atmosphere that Lord Esher had welcomed twenty-five years before settled over it once again.

The extreme formality of George v's time did not, though, return. Sometimes guests were asked to bring knee-breeches but more often trousers were permitted for evening wear. On a visit in 1937 Diana Cooper found the company relatively relaxed.

She discovered that dinner was at 8.30 and usually took about an hour. The ladies left the dining-room with the gentlemen; but 'gentlemen don't stop,' she told Conrad Russell, 'they walk straight through us to the lu and talk and drinks. Girls gossip until 10.15 when the men reappear flushed but relieved, and at 10.30 it's "Good night" . . . through dinner they had what I thought was an inferior make of loud gramophone playing airs from *Our Miss Gibbs* and *The Bing Boys*, but from seeing a red-uniformed band playing after dinner I suppose it was them, muffled.'[9]

The King seemed to enjoy these evenings. He was far less shy now; far more ready not only to laugh at other people's jokes and stories, but to make jokes himself and to tell stories himself – they were sometimes bawdy and not very witty stories but most of them seemed amusing at the time – and he appeared far less overwhelmed by his responsibilities than he had been at the beginning of his reign.

He loved his wife and he was devoted to his two pretty daughters. He found it difficult to relax, however, for he was a man with an exhausting regard for the particularities of life, and eventually, as Sir John Wheeler-Bennett has said, he 'wore himself out with his care for detail'.[10] He could become excessively angry over trifling annoyances and, although his anger soon cooled, as his father's had done, his servants dreaded arousing it and being confronted by the King when they had offended him and having to listen to his angry voice and to see the muscles twitching in his cheek.[11]

His sporting life was almost his only relaxation; and in this life shooting provided his greatest pleasure. The pattern of 'royal sport', as his great-grandfather and grandfather had known it, was already almost destroyed when he became King. The grandeur and stage-management of the *grand battue* and the wholesale slaughter of driven birds, followed by a fine luncheon served by numerous retainers in a tent, had had to give way to a more exacting and less comfortable sport in which men had to shoot instead of simply firing their guns. And this was the sort of shooting that appealed to the King's nature. To him, being a good shot was more than being able to fire a gun accurately. He did fire accurately for he had a quick eye and 'his footwork was faultless', but he also understood his quarry; and he was patient and thorough.[12]

The qualities that made his fellow sportsmen revere him were the qualities that caused him to meet the challenge of the War with such effect. While Mr Churchill, in his own phrase, was answering the call to provide the lion with a roar, the King set an example, on a necessarily more muted note, which was felt to be at once unselfish and inspiring. It became his habit to come up from Windsor each morning to work at Buckingham Palace or to inspect the damage done in recent air raids. And one morning the Palace was bombed while the King and Queen were in it. 'I'm glad we've been bombed,' the Queen said; 'It makes me feel I can look the East End in the face.'[13] She and her husband continued their tours of inspection as long as the raids lasted so that, as Mr Churchill told them with understandable enthusiasm, the throne and the people were drawn 'more closely together than was ever before recorded' and Their Majesties were 'more beloved by all classes and conditions than all the princes of the past'.[14]

It was clear when the War ended, however, that the King's health, which had never been strong, had been irreparably damaged. He had never hesitated to do whatever his Ministers had suggested he should do, and his scrupulous, not to say obsessive, regard for detail had made his activities far more exhausting than they need have been. Indeed, his meticulousness was so pronounced as to be an eccentricity even in a king who, so George v told Aga Khan, is inevitably inclined to look upon a man with an improperly worn order with the same distaste as one of his subjects would regard a man who walked about with his shirt tails hanging out.

No sartorial eccentricity, however slight, failed to escape George VI's notice and he 'never failed to comment upon it'. The sight of a young fellow-king wearing a thin gold watch chain threaded through the two upper pockets of the tunic of his uniform once upset him profoundly. 'Is it part of the uniform?' he asked him coldly.

'No.'

'Then take it off. It looks damned silly and damned sloppy.'[15]

Irregularities in the wearing of uniform were, in fact, particularly distasteful to him; and one of his first acts on returning home after the wedding of his daughter, Princess Elizabeth, was to enquire why a certain admiral had not been wearing a sword.[16]

His knowledge of correct forms of dress was as profound as his eye was sharp, and having made a hobby of the study of decorations, and having his own large collection of ribbons and medals, he was even more of an expert in this esoteric field than his grandfather, Edward VII. Looking at the numerous medals on the chest of Lord Gowrie, V.C., one day at Windsor, he noticed that one of the five rows included both the China Medal for the Relief of the Peking Legations and Queen Victoria's Medal for the first part of the South African War. 'Have you ever known another case of a man's holding both these medals?' he asked someone later. 'I never have. How on earth did he get from China to South Africa in time?'[17]

It was natural, having these interests, that the King should be a keen student of the ceremonials of Freemasonry and of the Order of the Garter. His devotion to both these institutions went deeper, of course, than the trappings of their ceremonial and regalia, and his conviction that the Garter should be a non-political honour in the sole gift of the sovereign was, indeed, part of 'his strong belief in the *mystique* of monarchy'.[18]

He had intended to raise the matter with Neville Chamberlain in 1939, and would have done so but for the war. By 1945 there were seven vacancies in an Order which bore little resemblance to that exclusive and Christian fellowship founded by Edward III.

Charles II had freely bestowed the Garter upon his illegitimate children; in the reign of George I it became a political honour; and George III decided that the number of Knights which the original statutes permitted should be increased so that 'the said Most Noble Order', as his statute of 1786 put it 'shall in future consist of the Sovereign, and twenty-five Knights or Companions, together with such of the sons of us, or our successors, as have been elected, or shall be elected into the Order'.[19]

By the nineteenth century it was little coveted; and Lord Melbourne's contention that he liked the Garter well enough because there was 'no damned merit in it' was considered a fair summary of universal opinion. Once the Shah and the Sultan had been created Knights there had seemed no reason for withholding the Garter from other Eastern rulers and it had, accordingly, been bestowed upon the Emperor of Japan. Most Knights, however, were English and Scottish noblemen of very slender talents or distinction; and there seemed in 1945 no reason to disbelieve the contention that Lord Melbourne's verdict was still justified.

George VI was determined to rescue the Garter from further deterioration in public esteem. He did not take too seriously – as perhaps he was not intended to – Mr Winston Churchill's romantic suggestion that he should revert to the principles of Edward III and knight 'young paladins'; but he did believe that those appointed to the Order would have to be distinguished men who had performed some great service for the country. He spoke to Mr Clement Attlee, the new Prime Minister, who told him that he had no objection to allowing the Order to be in the King's gift. His people were 'against accepting honours', anyway, as the King noted in his diary, so that 'most recipients would have to be of the other party'.[20]

In fact, as was appropriate, only two of the seven new Knights were political nominations and these were nicely counterbalanced – Lord Cranbourne as the Conservative Opposition Leader in the House of Lords being knighted at the same time as Lord Addison, the Labour Leader of the Upper House. The other Knights were the soldiers Alanbrooke, Alexander and Montgomery, the sailor Mountbatten and the airman Portal. *

This early example set by the King in making the Order a reward of merit and service to the State was unfortunately not followed even by himself. When, on the six hundredth anniversary of the Order's foundation, his daughter Elizabeth was invested at Windsor with the insignia of a Lady of the Most Noble Order and her husband, Prince Philip, became a Knight Companion, the historical precedents for such pleasant and popular investitures were unquestionable. But their companions – the Duke of Portland, Lord Harlech, the Earl of Scarborough and Lord Cranworth – while having distinguished themselves in a variety of ways as became their high birth, were not men whom the country as a whole had any particular reason to revere. Nor were

* Winston Churchill was offered the Garter but refused. He accepted it eight years later from Queen Elizabeth II.

several of their predecessors, one of whom, Lord Middleton, confessed himself to be 'dumbfounded' when selected for this high honour. It appears that Mr J. A. Frere is wrong in suggesting that the Garter was a reward for the discreet manner in which Lord Middleton's forebears manipulated the Tranby Croft scandal for the sake of Edward vii in 1890,[21] but Lord Middleton's name is so little known outside Yorkshire that the allegation was widely accepted.

Of the other British Knights,* excluding those already mentioned and the Duke of Cornwall, only the Earl of Avon and Earl Attlee, the Marquess of Salisbury, Viscount Slim, Lord Ismay and Sir Gerald Templer may be said to have reached a distinction in life in any way comparable to that of the men elected to the Order in 1945.

George vi would not himself, of course, have risen to greatness through his own merits, which he well knew were limited. He had ascended the throne reluctantly and with trepidation. Never having been allowed by his father to be initiated even into the everyday working of government, he had 'stood appalled at the volume and the nature of the business which emerged day by day from those leather-clad despatch boxes which inexorably dog the life of every British Sovereign', Sir John Wheeler-Bennett has written. 'He was, moreover, more than ever conscious of his own physical disability and of what he believed to be his inferiority in comparison with his brother'.[22]

This belief in his own inferiority never completely left him; and in his later years his nervousness in the presence of strangers was sometimes marked by an almost aggressively domineering manner wholly alien to his true nature.

A former subaltern in the Royal Horse Guards, whose duties earned him invitations to dine in the Castle, describes how ill at ease he was made to feel.

Being the most junior guest [he says] the Monarch called me to sit next to him after the ladies had left the dining-room. The conversation took the form of a rather bawdy, bullying banter. . . .

When we left the dining-room I sat on a sofa with the Monarch whilst he scrutinised his guests for any sartorial indiscretions. He had a remarkable eye for detail. It was not, of course, permissible to guide the conversation

* In addition to the twenty-six British Knights Companion, there are eight extra Knights – the Kings of Denmark, Sweden and Norway, King Leopold iii, the Emperor of Ethiopia, Prince Paul of Yugoslavia, King Paul of the Hellenes and King Baudouin of the Belgians, – four royal Knights and two Ladies of the Order – the Queen Mother and the Queen of the Netherlands. Queen Elizabeth was a Lady of the Garter as Princess Elizabeth but upon her accession she automatically became Sovereign of the Order.

and this became a series of comments upon which complete agreement appeared to be essential. . . . Several topics were discussed and I remember that he asked me whether or not I shot. I told him that I didn't and this seemed to irritate him. We discussed the pheasants in the Park and I knew something of their number through riding there each morning. I mentioned a book which I had read a few days before by Ian Niall. He asked me about this book and I told him that Niall had written about the art of poaching. His only reply was, 'How very stupid of him'.[23]

While the unfortunate experiences of this young man were not unique, few guests at Windsor were unfortunate enough to find the King in so mortifying a mood. There were men and women, of course, whom the King could not bring himself to like, and with whom all the repressions of his nature found unattractive outlets. And no doubt this young, amusing, intelligent, tactless and self-confident officer was one of them. But for the most part the King's guests found him pleasant and, provided they shared his tastes and outlook, companionable.

'I was impressed by the easy manner of the King, dressed during the day in tweed jacket and slacks like a country squire relaxing at the week-end,' Eleanor Roosevelt wrote after a visit to the Castle during which the atmosphere of contented family life had been particularly apparent. 'Meg,' the King had complained, 'like any other father', one day when entering a room where his younger daughter was playing 'pop' records to her friends, 'Meg, the music's too loud. Will you please turn it down.'

One evening [Mrs Roosevelt went on], we played The Game – a form of charades which is also popular in America. Queen Elizabeth acted as a kind of master of ceremonies and chose the words that the rest of us were called upon to act out in such a way that they could be guessed. She puzzled for some time over various words and occasionally turned to Mr Churchill for assistance, but without success. The former Prime Minister, with a decoration on the bosom of his stiff, white shirt and a cigar in his hand, sat glumly aside and would have nothing to do with The Game which he obviously regarded as inane and a waste of time for adults. Not even the Queen's pleas for advice could move him to take a small part in the activities. He just kept on being glum.[24]

The Queen could have moved him, Mrs Roosevelt thought, if anyone could. For most people found her charm irresistible. Mrs Roosevelt's son James had certainly done so when he had visited Windsor on another occasion.

Feeling a 'real hick', so he told his father, he got lost in the Castle, as so many visitors had done before him, and when he was introduced to the King and Queen, instead of bowing low as he had been told to do and keeping his hands by his side, he offered to shake hands. The Queen rescued him, however, by affecting not to notice this breach of protocol and took his hand in her own. Again at dinner, although he was told that he must eat everything that was put before him before his plate was cleared away, he forgot his instructions and let his soup go cold while he carried on an animated conversation with his neighbour. 'Suddenly I realised everybody else had had their fish,' he wrote later, 'while the cold soup was still before me. Again the Queen rescued me with a signal to the butlers, and by eating fast I almost got co-ordinated by the time the meat course arrived.'[25]

He was made to feel at home in other ways, too, as his mother had been. And he was made to feel aware that while the King's manner was less spontaneously easy than the Queen's and that he did not share her capacity for polite small talk, he was extremely knowledgeable about matters of importance. Other Americans formed similar opinions.

'I was impressed with the King as a good man,' President Truman says; 'I found him to be well informed on all that was taking place.'[26]

'I found him to be completely informed on the day to day progress of the armed forces,' wrote the American Ambassador, John Winant, who dined at Windsor during the War, 'and on any other subject that concerned his people.'[27]

And it was, indeed, this undoubted and sincere concern for his countrymen that earned him their fond regard and enabled his elder daughter to say with conviction when he was dead that the 'friendliness and simplicity which so endeared him to his peoples during the trials of war were the fruit of a lifelong interest in his fellow men'.[28]

George VI's career may not have had any deep political or constitutional significance, his personality may not have been striking, but, despite his limitations and his frailties, Roger Fulford may well be right in believing that his character 'is likely to command both the attention and admiration of historians'.[29]

ELIZABETH II

Princess Elizabeth was fourteen when she came to Windsor in 1940 to spend the rest of her childhood there.

Already the Castle had taken on the aspect of a fortress. Air-raid shelters had been built and the dungeons had been made bomb-proof, flower-beds had been turned into vegetable gardens, anti-aircraft guns had been sited at the foot of the Castle slopes, black-out material hung in folds above hundreds of windows, stores contained food sufficient for several weeks of isolation, evacuees from London arrived to occupy houses in the Park, and troops practised their drill in the quadrangle and were instructed in their duties as escort in case it became necessary to take the Princesses away to a place of greater safety.* Queen Mary thought it sounded 'so depressing' that she decided to remain at Badminton;[2] so the two young girls were usually the only members of the Royal Family at Windsor during the day-time throughout most of the War. Occasionally their lessons would be interrupted by fire practice, or an hour of instruction in the art of bomb disposal, or a run across the East Terrace towards the cover of the slit trenches in the Park. At week-ends sometimes their parents would spend a day with them and they would go for a walk together; and their father, wearing the civilian clothes he never wore in London, would look less tired and tense. Each Christmas they helped to write a pantomime which was performed by themselves and the children of the Household and staff in the Waterloo Chamber, from which all the portraits had been removed; and one year they took part in a Nativity Play performed by the children of the Windsor tenants, and the King, overcome with emotion, confessed that he 'wept through most of it'.[3]

Princess Elizabeth was a happy, though serious and well-mannered child, less lively and more obedient than her sister Margaret Rose. She showed no marked intellectual capacity, nor any evidence of a strong or original imagination.[4] Her mother, who had planned and directed her education, and who had herself taught her to read, had

---

* It had been suggested, in fact, that the Princesses should be sent out of the country; but the plan was abandoned when their mother categorically said, 'The children won't leave without me; I won't leave without the King; and the King will never leave.'[1]

47. The Queen and Prince Philip on Garter Day

48. The Royal Family on the South Terrace

not, indeed, placed any particular emphasis on strictly intellectual disciplines or upon the development of a creative imagination. She had been content to see her daughter's academic studies play no greater part in her upbringing than other pursuits which she considered of equal or of greater importance. To spend as long as possible in the open air, to enjoy to the full the pleasures of the country, to be able to dance and draw and appreciate music, to 'acquire good manners and perfect deportment, and to cultivate all the distinctively feminine graces' were all activities and aspirations which the Duchess believed more essential to her daughters' education than mere book-learning. So that when it became apparent that Princess Elizabeth 'would never progress beyond the simplest elements of mathematics', for example, 'it did not worry the Duchess at all.'[5]

But although she never did master mathematics, Princess Elizabeth's academic attainments were not otherwise unduly disappointing. She showed no precocious enthusiasm for study; there were subjects – German was one of them – in which she could make no headway; but she had a good memory and a careful, orderly and conscientious mind. That it was a mind more receptive than creative was considered no disadvantage in a girl who one day soon might be Queen.

In so many ways like her father, who had told her so much about her future reponsibilities, she seemed most happy, as he had been, when out in the country. She was devoted to animals, particularly to horses, and she once told her riding-master that if she had not been who she was, she 'would like best to be a lady living in the country, with lots of horses and dogs'.[6] Almost every day towards the end of the war she went for a ride in the Great Park with her sister and the Crown Equerry;[7] and it is still her habit to do so at Windsor whenever she can. She has been described as an excellent horsewoman,[8] but she is far from being as good as she would like to be. She is, in fact, a 'competent rider, although not in the top flight';[9] for she is in no sense athletic. She has never played games with any skill and, despite her love of riding and racing, she has 'never acquired much taste for fox-hunting'.[10]

Were she to acquire a taste for this or any other sport, it is doubtful, indeed, that she would consider herself free to indulge it, for her sense of duty is so strong as to be overwhelming. She spends a great deal of time at race-meetings but racing is, after all, almost her only form of daytime relaxation; and an afternoon at the races does not preclude a morning at her desk. Even during the Ascot meeting the red leather-covered despatch boxes arrive daily at Windsor station, except on Monday, and their contents must be examined and approved. It is not difficult for her to be conscientious, though, for she enjoys her work and the satisfaction of being so privileged a spectator of the secret movements within the corridors of power.

She gets up early and after breakfast she looks at the newspapers – including the Royal Issue of *The Times* printed on special paper – which have been previously read by the Private Secretaries who have marked or cut out items likely to be of importance or interest to her. She reads these items with close attention and takes a 'rather mischievous pleasure in catching out her staff on matters relating to the day's news'.[11] If Parliament is sitting she then reads the report on the previous day's proceedings, which it is the duty of the Vice-Chamberlain of the Household to write for her; and she will also, if the occasion offers, enjoy catching out the Vice-Chamberlain on some item contained in his report or omitted from it.

There is then her correspondence to attend to. She receives an immense number of letters every day, most of them from complete strangers, and all of them are answered 'even those from manifest lunatics'. Those from friends and, when she has time, those from acquaintances, she answers herself in her neat hand, addressing the envelopes also, which accordingly have to be delivered by messenger or sent by registered post to avoid giving temptation to an acquisitive Post Office worker. After the letters have been answered, the work on the despatch boxes begins and when this has been done, she may – if she has no outside engagement – receive the first of her visitors or sit for one of those portraits which are constantly required by her subjects at home and abroad. Frequently an artist is staying at the Castle painting a picture commissioned for an embassy, a high commissioner's office, a governor-general's house, a service headquarters or a charitable institution under royal patronage; frequently a photographer arrives to satisfy the demand of an apparently insatiable public appetite for new pictures of the Queen; and frequently a dressmaker calls in an endeavour to ensure that Her Majesty's clothes are as discreetly fashionable and as varied as they are expected to be.[12]

So that she can spend as much time as possible with her children, her working days at Windsor are as carefully planned as those on which her public duties are performed. Having an orderly mind and a taste for regularity, she dislikes the unexpected. 'She is a planner,' one of her less fulsome biographers has written of her, 'a hard worker, sometimes a worrier . . . she is conscientious, perhaps even over-conscientious.'[13]

Her conception of the privileges, duties and responsibilities of queenship, as well as the inhibitions of an essentially shy and reserved nature, have made it difficult for her to make many intimate friendships or to feel at ease with people whom she does not know well. She has not, after all, had much opportunity of learning how to live or behave with people outside her own family or Household. Parties with the children of the Windsor staff and tenants, afternoons with Girl Guides, even an N.C.O.'s course at the Mechanical Training Centre at Aldershot at the end of the War when she was granted an honorary commission in the Auxiliary Territorial Service, cannot have taught her much about the lives and reactions, attitudes and behaviour of people who would have treated her as an ordinary woman rather than as a special Princess.

Sensitive to criticism, real, implied or imagined, she can appear both haughty and censorious when she is in fact merely unsure of herself or of her effect on others. She sets extremely high standards for her own conduct and expects high standards in those whose work brings them into contact with her. She has almost as inflexible notions of what is good and what is bad as her great-great-grandmother Queen Victoria had; and she is as capable as she was – and, for that matter, as her great-grandfather Edward vii, her grandfather George v and her father all were – of outbursts of sudden anger and moods of sulky irritation. But she is – and the verdict is inescapable, inevitable and undeniable – a good woman. She cannot, of course, be expected to have as much sympathy, understanding, consideration and tolerance as her more recklessly enthusiastic champions claim for her; but she does possess all these virtues in some degree and of her courage, determination, constancy, balance and sincerity there can be no doubt or argument. She is not a clever or a quick-witted woman; she does not pretend to any deep love of art; she prefers watching television to reading books, and gets her knowledge of the world from people; her vision is sometimes impeded by an inordinate regard for detail; she still speaks less impressively and walks less gracefully than is – however unfairly – demanded of one to whom speaking impressively and walking gracefully should ideally appear to be instinctive attributes. And yet, despite these limitations, she is a highly successful queen. Her popularity has inevitably dimmed since her coronation, when to millions of people she appeared surrounded by so mystical an air as to be scarcely human, but it remains immense and adamantine. And it remains so, although the English traditionally like their queens to be very young and innocent or very old and wise. It is true, of course, that this popularity owes much to the British view of monarchy itself.

For 'in its deeper meaning for the British peoples,' according to Dermot Morrah, that most learned and skilful of the Monarchy's apologists, 'it is scarcely a system of government at all. It is their way of life. As such it is necessarily popular. . . . Elizabeth II is just as fully a Queen as ever was Elizabeth I, though without a tithe of her predecessor's personal authority. She is Queen not because she governs England but because England would not be itself without her. . . . The Queen of England represents universally. She is the embodiment of the whole life of the people: she presides indeed over its political action, but only because politics are one of the necessary departments of life, and of all departments she is the head. . . . Her essential function is less to exercise power than to keep power in its proper proportion to the totality of life. It is a British characteristic to regard the worship of power as extremely vulgar. So the real possessors of power have to wield it under the eye of someone who is not herself powerful, but yet has to be treated with the utmost deference.'[41]

If all this is true, and it seems likely that it may be true, the Queen's dutiful and pleasantly unemphatic personality is perfectly suited to a calling which she herself believes to be an important, indeed an essential, service to her people.

Although republicanism in England is now virtually dead as a political force, there are those, of course, who would have the Monarchy change far more rapidly than it shows signs of being ready to do at present. According to Mr Morrah it is changing all the time. 'It is always changing,' he writes, 'and always the same; and it is always up to date.'[15] But there are many who would question the truth of this assertion; and it is certainly a fact, as Kingsley Martin has said, that 'thoughtful people have been disappointed by the failure of the young Queen and the Prince Consort to rejuvenate the Court and discard the stiff protocol with which it is traditionally surrounded', and that the Crown has failed to 'build harmonious relations with the press'.[16] It is also certainly true that this lack of harmonious relations is at least partly due to the attitude which the Duke of Edinburgh adopts towards the press, particularly the Beaverbrook newspapers which have consistently criticised various aspects of royal behaviour and of royal expenditure – whether by the Crown, the Government or local authorities – that are indeed open to criticism.

Public comment about the modernity of the Monarchy and the behaviour of its representatives still causes outcries of protest in the country. Feelings do not run so high as they did in the very recent past. When Lord Altrincham, a convinced Royalist and the son of a man who was once equerry to Edward VIII when he was Prince of Wales, suggested a few years ago that the Queen's personal staff were drawn from a single 'tweedy' social type and that her voice had been badly trained and sounded like a schoolgirl's, he was assaulted in the streets. And when Malcolm Muggeridge, one of the most acute and gifted journalists of his generation, complained that the Monarchy was being turned into a sort of snobbish soap opera, the B.B.C. cancelled his appearances in *Panorama* and, as he revealed later in *Encounter*, he was grotesquely insulted by many members of an outraged public.

Now, criticism of the Monarchy and of the public's attitude towards it, is far less wildly resented. The royal yacht, Princess Margaret's income, the activities of the Duke of Edinburgh as a Sunday polo player and as a stag hunter, are all considered suitable subjects for open discussion. Cartoons of the Queen and Prince Philip have begun to appear and jokes about them are at last being made in public.

Whether or not the criticisms are always justified or the cartoons and jokes always apposite, it is certainly difficult to believe that they are more harmful to the monarchical ideal than the blindly devoted loyalty to the Crown which has in recent years contrived to render anything other than emphatic admiration of the Monarch's character and way of life a kind of blasphemy. Damaged, as it is, by unctuous glorification, the Monarchy, Kingsley Martin believes, should break its traditional connection with the Establishment and model itself upon the far less expensive and somewhat less socially isolated monarchies of Scandinavia. And while it does not appear, however, that there is at present any widespread demand for so drastic a change as this, it is at least clear that the present uneasy compromise between the Court's attempts to present the Queen to her people as a real human being and its contradictory reluctance, in Walter Bagehot's phrase, to let light in upon magic, has resulted in her regular but fleeting appearances on the pages of the world's newspapers and magazines in the guise of a hybrid, never wholly real nor ever truly magical.

And yet her private life at Windsor is ordinary and sensible enough.

She is usually already awake when at half-past eight every morning, the Royal Pipe-Major marches up and down the East Terrace playing martial airs, and she is often out riding in the Park before nine o'clock. She does not like to be accompanied, as the young Queen Victoria did, by a large number of other riders and there are rarely, indeed, except during Ascot week and the Easter holidays, a large number of people staying in the Castle available to do so.

At these times when the Castle is relatively full, guests find the protocol neither strenuous nor intimidating. They are invited perhaps three or four weeks previously by the Master of the Household who usually advises them that 'dinner jackets will be worn'. They assemble in the Green Drawing Room before dinner and follow the Queen, 'in no particular order' into the white-and-gold panelled dining-room at half-past eight.[17]

The Queen herself, like her father, is not a gourmet and prefers plain, simple English cooking to any other.

It is the Queen's habit to have the chef's menu book sent up to her each day for her approval. If a suggestion does not please her she may cross it out and substitute another – she hates oysters, apparently, and she does not like grouse – but her amendments are not necessarily dictated by her own preferences for she will have a separate dish served to her if she does not like what her guests are to be given. She does not drink much – perhaps contenting herself with a single glass of champagne – although there is always a generous supply of bottles for those who do.[19]

After dinner the Queen enjoys taking her guests round the Castle and showing them its curiosities and treasures, and this tour of inspection 'generally occupies a considerable time'. When it is over the guests return to the drawing room where drinks are laid out. Conversation is often directed by Prince Philip, who has a 'useful talent for drawing opinions out of people', while the Queen listens and remembers. Neither of them likes to stay up late and the conversation is usually interrupted before midnight by their departure for bed. If the guests are leaving the next morning they are wished farewell that night, for they will have breakfast in their room – surrounded by pictures of various royalties, some recognisable, many unknown – and they will not see the Queen the next morning.

During Ascot week the evening's entertainment is sometimes extended by dancing, and an occasional added pleasure in the afternoon, after the return from the course at about five o'clock, is a strawberry and cream tea.

The entertainments, apart perhaps from the dinners held each year in the Waterloo Chamber on the anniversary of the Battle of Waterloo are, however, no longer lavish.

The ball held in the flood-lit Castle on 22 April 1963, two days before the wedding of Princess Alexandra to the Hon. Angus Ogilvy, was an exception. 'There has never, we believe, been a night quite like this in the Castle's 900-year history,' a member of the Household said. 'We have been preparing for twelve weeks.' After a banquet held in St George's Hall, almost two thousand guests, including between sixty and seventy European kings, queens, princes and princesses, were invited to dance in the Waterloo Chamber. The following day news about the ball and pictures of the guests filled column after column in the country's newspapers. The reports differed widely, particularly in regard to the amount of food and drink consumed – 1,600 bottles of champagne according to one paper, 1,120 bottles and 782 bottles of Scotch, 233 of vodka and 4,000 of beer according to another, both of which were wrong – but the papers agreed that it was 'the biggest thing of its kind this century'.[20]

It was, in fact, with the exception of the ball given by Edward VII in 1903, the most splendid entertainment provided at Windsor since the death of the Prince Consort. It was also the most expensive; and this once more drew attention to the finances of the Crown and the cost of running Windsor Castle and the other royal palaces.

*   *   *

The Queen's Civil List is fixed at £60,000 a year and she is granted, in addition, £306,000 for the salaries, pensions and expenses of her Household, which include the maintenance of Windsor as a royal home. As well as these two annual incomes, she receives a Royal Bounty of £13,200, which is given back to the people, and a Supplementary Provision of £95,000 to provide against serious inflation and to allow the Queen to make allowances to members of the Royal Family who do not have fixed incomes assigned to them by Parliament but are nevertheless considered to be precluded by their position from taking up paid employment. Any part of the annual Supplementary Provision which is not required is returned to the Treasury.

These sums, totalling £474,200, are granted each year in return for the Crown's traditional surrender of its own lands, which are managed by the Crown Estate Commissioners on behalf of the Government. Needless to say this Crown Estate would no longer exist had it been liable to death duties and its owners to income-tax; but it has been saved intact by the constitutional theory of taxation. It will be inherited by the Queen's heir who, in accordance with a tradition begun in the reign of William IV, will surrender it in turn to the Government on his accession.

The Queen does not, of course, have to rely for her income solely upon her Civil List. She is an extremely rich woman. Her personal fortune has been estimated as being between £50,000,000 and £60,000,000,[21] although this includes many millions of pounds worth of treasure, including hundreds of Old Masters and five tons of gold plate, which she could not very well sell even if she wanted to. She also has an income of about £90,000 from the Duchy of Lancaster which is a private property, not part of the Crown Estate; and the Prince of Wales, when he comes of age, will also receive about £90,000 a year from the Duchy of Cornwall. At present the Prince receives only a proportion of this income – £10,000 a year – for his maintenance, but when he is eighteen he will have £30,000 a year. Prince Philip receives a separate allowance of £40,000 a year. *

In view of his necessary commitments and the restraints imposed upon his undoubted talents this sum may, perhaps, be considered justified.

*   *   *

When he was a schoolboy Prince Philip's headmaster remarked upon his 'most noticeable' qualities of leadership, though these, he added, were 'marred at times by impatience and intolerance'.[22] These qualities and these limitations are still evident in his character now; and yet the limitations can be interpreted as virtues in the kind of public personality he has created for himself. He has an obvious 'enthusiasm for all that is energetic, progressive and masculine in the nation's life and work, especially in industry, technology and sport'.[23] He is outspoken, so self-confident that he is sometimes accused of arrogance, intelligent, adventurous and virile. He can be both rude and irritable, for he has no patience with people who do not interest him and with things which he believes should not interest others. A man of high and varied talents and of formidable vigour, he is at once a stimulus and a provocation.

---

* This is £10,000 a year more than Prince Albert received. Queen Victoria's Privy Purse was the same as her great-great-granddaughter's – £60,000 a year; and she received £2,240 less for Household expenses and salaries. With the fall in the value of money, however, the Monarchy may be said to be less generously treated than formerly.

'When he asks questions,' his cousin the former Queen of Yugo-slavia has written of him, 'and he asks questions everywhere, they are no longer the discreet, harmless little enquiries so long mur-mured by royalty, but questions both pointed and pertinent.'[24] They are also frequently and intentionally challenging, and an evasive or muddled answer may well be greeted with ill-concealed disdain. It can be said, though, that he has some right to show this disdain, for he takes the trouble to discover what questions will be most difficult to answer and most worthwhile considering. And although his emphatic opinions sometimes lead him to make assertions which are manifestly false, he usually briefs himself thoroughly and, having done so, he has the capacity to acquit himself well.

'Good God,' George v exclaimed when his eldest son told him he had accepted an invitation to talk to the British Association, 'you evidently don't seem to realise, my dear boy, what you've taken on. Don't you know who these people are. . . . Your audience will represent the most formidable brains in the country. The last member of the family, indeed the only one, who ever felt equal to the task was your great-grandfather, the Prince Consort, *and he was an intellec-tual.*'[25]

The Duke of Edinburgh would not, of course, care to consider himself an intellectual, but his address to the British Association was remarkably successful, and indicated well the sort of leadership which he, apparently, would like to see the Monarchy give. This leadership, he is given the credit of believing, cannot be achieved if the Royal Family is overwhelmed by the kind of adulation that began to threaten its whole existence ten years ago. And the steps, short and hesitant though they be, towards a more acceptable presentation of the Mon-archy are supposed to have been taken along a path mapped out in accordance with his suggestions.

Certainly the most recent of the numerous economies which are constantly being made in the running of the Household have been prompted by Prince Philip's enquiring, not to say inquisitive, mind. From the first he has made it his business to look into the workings of all the domestic departments of the Household and to investigate their weaknesses, a habit which, like his announcement in 1963 that their activities would be examined by a team of work-study experts, has caused a good deal of irritated consternation amongst the more self-indulgent members of the staff.

F. J. Corbitt, a former Deputy Comptroller of Supply, has recalled their annoyance when Sir Piers Legh had the whiskey decanters in the billiard-room placed in a locked tantalus so that their traditional custom of having a liberal night-cap on their way to bed had to be abruptly discontinued.[26] Prince Philip has ensured that there are now few such perquisites remaining.

There are few antiquated rules of procedure remaining either. Irritated by the difficulty which the Queen formerly experienced in obtaining, for instance, so simple a thing as a sandwich after a late return home, he has seen to it that the requirements of the Royal Family are far more simply and quickly met than has ever before been possible. For a time he even went so far as to cook his own breakfast on an electric frying pan until the Queen objected to the smell.[27] He gave up the experiment. But he does not, apparently, often give way.

'Certainly in domestic matters Philip is plainly in control.'[28] There are ways and means for a Queen to curb him, of course.

Lord Kinross says that the Queen once asked a friend, 'What do you do when your husband wants something badly and you don't want him to have it?'

'Well, Ma'am,' her friend replied, 'I try to reason with him and sometimes we reach a compromise.'

'Oh, that's not my method,' said the Queen. 'I tell Philip he shall have it and then make sure he doesn't get it.'[29]

Their marriage, nevertheless, and despite all the difficulties to which such royal marriages are bound to be subject, is far more satisfactory than is often suggested. Naturally they have their differences. They have few interests and few friends in common. He has been known to go to Ascot with a transistor wireless concealed in his top hat so that he can listen to the cricket commentaries; she has been known to look very bored while watching him play polo in Windsor Park; and when Princess Margaret and Lord Snowdon spend a weekend with the Queen Mother at the Royal Lodge, the Queen is sometimes a member of the party but Prince Philip rarely is.[30] But whatever their differences may be, they are not estranging ones.

And Windsor Castle, where both the Queen and the Prince feel happily at home and where they first fell in love,[31] is not the least important of the many links that bridge the gap between them. Here they can momentarily escape, as their predecessors tried to escape, some of the unwelcome attentions and most of the unpleasant duties of a curious and demanding world.

The Castle holds for them the same 'impelling attraction' it held for the Queen's grandfather. The Queen, like him and like her father, feels profoundly conscious there of the glory and responsibilities of their family's great inheritance. From her rooms in the Queen's Tower she can look south across the Home Park towards the Long Walk that Charles II planted, and east into the Sunken Garden made by George IV; and she can feel, and does feel, surrounded by memories of her own past and of those who lived in the Castle before her.

There are mementoes everywhere at Windsor. And it is impossible not to be moved by them – the stone figures of Edward III and the Black Prince in their niches beside the high arched window of the State Entrance, the exquisite iron gates in St George's Chapel behind which Edward IV lies buried, the oriel above them that Henry VIII built for Catherine of Aragon whose pomegranate badge it bears, the windows of so many periods overlooking the North Terrace where Queen Elizabeth I took her hurried walks, the French banner in the Queen's Guard Chamber still rendered annually by the Dukes of Marlborough as token rent for the royal park of Woodstock and the palace of Blenheim.

Each object, each picture, each room calls forth the past from its shadow. And seen again is Queen Anne sitting at the oriel window where she was given the news of the first Duke of Marlborough's great victory in 1704; and George III's good-looking daughters running across the garden of Queen's Lodge in their full, white dresses and their enormous hats; and their father trotting down Castle Hill with Colonel Goldsworthy panting after him; and their mother sitting in her room, worrying and frowning and sniffing snuff; and their eldest brother crying in his cups; and their other brother making his rambling speeches and going to sleep in his chair; and Queen Victoria dancing under the chandeliers and looking up happily into her husband's blue and anxious eyes, and hobbling, years later, down the long corridors in her black clothes and shiny black boots; and her eldest son marching up the stairs with Caesar at his heels, his pot hat on his head, a huge cigar in his mouth; and George V looking out of a window and criticising the behaviour of the young in his loud, alarming voice; and the Prince of Wales, in his starched Eton collar, wheeling his brothers about on the steps in the library; and George VI, pale and drawn, watching his daughters act their play with tears in his tired eyes. And behind them all and around them all is the Castle itself, warmed by the sun and washed by the rain, massive and immutable throughout the circling years.

ABBREVIATIONS

H.M.C.	Historical Manuscripts Commission
R.A.	Royal Archives
P.R.O.	Public Record Office
R.L.C.D.	Records of the Lord Chamberlain's Department
P.I.	Private Information

SOURCES

For full titles see the Bibliography on page 329 following

NORMANS AND PLANTAGENETS

[i] Fortress and Feasting Hall (pages 3–10)

1 *Giraldi Cambrensis Opera*, quoted Warren, 3
2 Norgate; Appleby: *Henry II*; Hall; Green, *passim*; Harvey, 41–42
3 Hall, iv
4 Peter of Blois, *Epistolae*, q. Morgan, 77
5 Eyton; *The Little Black Book of the Exchequer*; *The Red Book of the Exchequer*; Hall, 242–249; Thoms, 213–244
6 Warren, 136
7 Morshead, 5–10; Hope, i, 4–14
8 Hughes, 69, 402; Harwood, 58
9 Harwood, 159
10 Ibid., 37
11 Hope, i, 2; Morshead, 5; Barlow, 188; Freeman, iv, 356
12 Harwood, 203
13 Hope, i, 15–19; Morshead, 12–15
14 Hope, i, 26
15 Poole, ii, 621
16 Pyne, 55
17 Longman, ii, 261
18 Harwood, 87
19 Tighe, i, 124; Pipe Roll, 13 John, 109, xxii, q. Warren, 139
20 *County History*, 6; Tighe, 54
21 Warren, 259
22 Ibid., 2, 232–240; Appleby: *John*, 234–241; Painter, 285–348
23 *Histoire des Ducs de Normandie*, 177, q. Tighe, i, 56; *Rogeri de Wendover Flores Historiarum*, q. Hope, i, 26–27, Warren, 252
24 Hope, i, 27–32
25 Ibid., Tighe, i, 53–56
26 Powicke, 118
27 Harvey, 102
28 Sanders, 48
29 Tighe, i, 82
30 Ibid., i, 107–108

SOURCES

[ii] Knights of the Garter (pages 10–24)

1 F. J. C. Hearnshaw, *Chivalry and its place in History*, q. Coulton, 235
2 McKisack, 25
3 Froissart, q. Tighe, i, 139
4 Tighe, i, 139
5 *Adae Murimuth Continuatio Chronicarum*, q. Hope, i, 111–112
6 Lewinsohn, 135
7 Longman, i, 22
8 Couton, 249
9 Ibid., 142
10 Poole, ii, 623
11 Strutt, 129–143; Poole, ii, 622
12 Strutt, 143; Poole, ii, 623
13 Lewinsohn, 136
14 *Landsdowne Collection*, q. Harwood, 161
15 Poole, ii, 623
16 *Adae Murimuth*, q. Hope, i, 111
17 Ibid., q. Hope, i, 112
18 Sir Thomas Malory, *Le Morte D'Arthur*
19 *Adae Murimuth*, q. Hope, i, 112
20 Hope, i, 113
21 Ibid., i, 111–128; *The Impressment of Masons for Windsor Castle* in *Economic History*, iii (1937) (Knoop and Jones), 350–361
22 Walsingham, q. Hope, i, 128
23 Pote, 139; Tighe, i, 145
24 Tighe, i, 167
25 Walsingham, i, 272; Chandos Herald, 31, q. Vickers, 183
26 Longman, i, 295
27 Ashmole, 183
28 Heylin, i, 286
29 Ashmole, 180
30 Ibid., 183
31 Beltz, xlvii
32 Murray: *Divine King*, 18; Murray: *God of Witches*, 75
33 Ashmole, 108
34 Ibid., 181
35 Nicolas, i, lxxxiii
36 Galway, *passim*
37 Fellowes; Beltz; Ashmole
38 Ashmole, 202–227; Pote, 196
39 Ibid., 203
40 Ibid., 335
41 Ibid.
42 Pote, 336–343

43 Thoms, 162–165; Pote, 207–208
44 Ashmole, 621; Tighe, 484
45 Hudson Turner, *Domestic Architecture*, q. Harvey, 103
46 Tighe, i, 156; Morshead, 26; Hope, i, 129
47 Tighe, i, 521
48 Ibid.
49 Ashmole, 167–177; Tighe, i, 162–163
50 Tighe, i, 232
51 Bolitho: *Windsor*, 64
52 Anstis, i, 452; Tighe, i, 114–115, 283
53 Morshead, 36
54 Lambarde, *Topographical and Historial Dictionary*, q. Tighe, i, 428–429
55 Tighe, i, 426
56 Morshead, 33
57 Ibid., 37; Hope, i, 459
58 Tighe, i, 232
59 Ibid., i, 556
60 Burton, iv, 61–62

[iii] Knights for the Body (pages 24–32)

1 MacKinnon, 604
2 Vickers, 185
3 Oman, *passim*
4 37 Ed. III, c. 8, 14; Vickers, 250; Longman, i, 87–88
5 William of Malmesbury, Chron. IV, q. Morgan
6 Longman, i, 296–297
7 Holinshed, Chron. II, q. Morgan
8 Grosseteste, q. Poole, ii, 609; Coulton, 606–607
9 Poole, ii, 609; E. K. Chambers, ii, 262–264
10 Poole, ii, 606
11 Boorde, *passim*
12 Kendall, 161, 181
13 John Blacman, *Memoir of Henry VI*, q. Harvey, 184
14 Kendall, 162; Harvey, 184, 185
15 Myers, 6
16 Ibid., 3
17 *Babees Book*; R. W. Chambers, *passim*; Thornley, *passim*
18 *Black Book of the Exchequer*; Harleian MS. 293; Myers, *passim*
19 Vickers, 465
20 Kendall, 163
21 Kingsford, 386–388; Tighe, i, 368 *et seq.*
22 Hope, i, 129–219; Pote, 48; Morshead, 19–25
23 Hope, i, 178–219
24 Ibid., i, 221

SOURCES

25 Morshead, 28
26 Arundel MSS q. Tighe, i, 415

TUDORS

[i] The New Apollo and his Children (pages 35–44)

1 Sandford, 493–494; Stype, i; Tighe, i, 557–559
2 Salter, 81
3 Morris, 78
4 Tighe, i, 470
5 Cotton. MSS, q. Tighe, i, 470–482
6 Landsdowne MSS, q. Harwood, 241
7 Bagley, 16
8 Ibid., 123; Chapman, 30
9 Morris, 100
10 Bagley, 112, 135
11 Fuller, 254
12 Rowse: *Elizabeth*, 529
13 Prescott, 7
14 Ibid., 8
15 Nichols: *Ordinances*, 232; E. K. Chambers, i, 45–51
16 Goddard, 71; Doran, 134–138
17 Leland's *De Rebus Britannicis Collectanea*, q. Prescott, 8
18 Chapman, 107–8; Prescott, 9–10; Furnivall, *passim*
19 Morris, 106
20 Nichols: *Edward VI*, i, 131
21 Chapman, 285
22 Morris, 143
23 Prescott, 277
24 Ibid.
25 Morris, 144
26 *Venetian Calendar*, v, 532, q. Morris, 130
27 Prescott, 98–99, 179–181; Tighe, i, 507–509; Madden, *passim*

[ii] Queen Elizabeth I (pages 45–50)

1 Tighe, i, 632
2 Jenkins: *Elizabeth*, 28
3 Neale; Jenkins; Beckingsdale; Creighton, *passim*
4 Morris, 156, 157
5 Jenkins: *Elizabeth*, 314; Neale, 81
6 Jenkins: *Elizabeth*, 295
7 *Journal of de Maisse* (G. B. Harrison, Ed.), q. Jenkins, 299; Morris, 167
8 Neale, 218

304

9 Ibid., 222
10 *Aylmer*, John Strype, q. Jenkins, 217
11 Neale, 222
12 Ibid., 220
13 Morris, 39
14 Osborne, 236
15 Hentzner, 76
16 Jenkins: *Elizabeth*, 298
17 *County History*, iii, 13
18 Dutton, 34
19 Neale, 209–212
20 Tighe, i, 626
21 Ibid., i, 632
22 Stow, 14
23 Jenkins: *Elizabeth*, 228
24 Hentzner, 78
25 Jenkins: *Elizabeth*, 115
26 Ibid., 78, 99, 210–211; Neale, 87, 148
27 Jenkins: *Elizabeth*, 104

STUARTS

[i] James I (pages 53–62)

1 Willson; McElwee; Williams; Jesse; Weldon; Oglander, *passim*
2 McElwee, 42
3 Willson, 44
4 Ibid., 168
5 Ibid., 169, 196
6 Wotton, i, 314
7 Jesse, i, 68–69
8 Willson, 193
9 Harington; Kenyon, 51–52
10 Willson, 191
11 Jesse, i, 86; Tighe, ii, 71
12 Willson, 191
13 Dutton, 97
14 McElwee, 172
15 Francis Osborne, *Traditional Memoirs*, q. Turner: *St. James's*, 125
16 Rowse: *Elizabeth*, 388
17 Hope, i, 266–276; Tighe, i, 646
18 Neale, 332
19 Arthur Wilson, *The History of Great Britain*, q. Turner; *St James's*, 117
20 Jesse, i, 85
21 Turner: *St James's*, 130–131

22 Oglander, 197
23 Willson, 164
24 Ibid., 180–182
25 Oglander, 202
26 Jesse, i, 117
27 Kenyon, 67
28 Willson, 192
29 Weldon, 129
30 Kenyon, 58
31 Goodman, ii, 255–257
32 Ibid., ii, 290–291
33 Ibid., ii, 168
34 Jesse, i, 185–189
35 McElwee, 251
36 Weldon, 234
37 Ibid., 263
38 Goodman, ii, 409–410
39 Scaliger, q. Jesse, i, 87
40 Tighe, ii, 83
41 Willson, 184; Harwood, 36
42 Goodman, ii, 379
43 Jesse, i, 128–137
44 Williams, 297

[ii] Charles I (pages 62–68)

1 Gibbs, 21
2 Kenyon, 83
3 John; Belloc; Wedgwood; Bulstrode; Mathews; Gardiner; *passim*
4 Kenyon, 74
5 H.M.C. 11th Rep. App. i, 6
6 Wedgwood, 65
7 Burnet, i, 28
8 *Relazioni degli Ambasciatori Veneti*, ix, 393, q. Wedgwood, 74
9 Wedgwood, 69
10 Doran, 210
11 Turner: *St James's*, 145–146; Doran; Godard, 74
12 Hutchinson, 286
13 Clarendon; Gardiner
14 J. Heath, *Chronicle of the Late Intestine War* (1676)
15 *Exceeding True and Happy News from the Castle of Windsor* (1642)
16 *Joyful Tydings from Windsor*; Wilkinson, 105
17 *Lords Journals*, vi, 30
18 Morshead, 100–102
19 Tighe, ii, 182–183

20 Morshead, 103

21 Tighe, ii, 160–168; Harwood, 33–36

22 Tighe, ii, 178–223

23 Clarendon, v, 514

24 Rushworth, vi, 943, q. Tighe, ii, 218

25 Clarendon, v, 228

26 Tighe, ii, 229

27 *The Perfect Weekly Account*, 27 December 1648–3 January 1649

28 Belloc, 345–346; Bulstrode, 176

29 Henry, 12

30 Bolitho: *Windsor* 69–70

31 Clarendon, xi, 244; Tighe, ii, 233

32 Tighe, ii, 236

[iii] Charles II (pages 68–84)

1 Bryant: *Charles II*, 58

2 Ibid., 63

3 Brett, 148

4 Pepys, i, 357

5 Ibid., ii, 346

6 Evelyn, ii, 213–224

7 Bryant, 116

8 Kenyon, 128

9 Ibid.

10 Jesse, iv, 323

11 Bryant, 115; Jesse, iv, 324–327; Grammont, 109

12 Drinkwater, 258–259

13 Burnet, q. Jesse, iv, 342–343

14 Evelyn, ii, 18

15 Jesse, iv, 327

16 Bryant, 118

17 Burnet, 166

18 Grammont, 452

19 Pepys, ii, 246

20 Turner: *James II*, 237

21 Manchester, ii, 307–308

22 Thoms, 28

23 Jesse, iv, 252; Grammont, 449

24 Ailesbury, q. Crawford 24–25

25 Ibid, 23–24

26 Evelyn, 54

27 Hope, i, 295–302

28 Tighe, ii, 252

29 Hughes, 151

30 Tighe, ii, 254

31 Ashmole MSS q. Tighe, ii, 294

32 *Articles of Impeachment of Lord Mordaunt*, q. Tighe, ii, 336–337

33 Grammont, 269

34 Edinger, 278–281

35 Evelyn, ii, 54–55

36 Wren Society, XIII. 40, q. Morshead, 62

37 Pepys, i, 260

38 Evelyn, ii, 144

39 Morshead, 63

40 Evelyn, ii, 56–57, 180

41 Ibid., ii, 180

42 *London Gazette*, q. Tighe, ii, 389

43 Ibid.

44 Reresby, 194

45 *London Gazette*, q. Tighe, ii, 392

46 Hope, i, 326–329; Bryant, 272

47 Bryant, 198

48 Barillon, q. Brett, 278

49 Brett, 281

50 Bryant, 133

51 Ibid., 191

52 Jesse, vi, 148

53 Ibid., vi, 141

54 Drinkwater, 268

55 Bryant, 159

56 H.M.C. Reports, Duke of Rutland, ii, 27, q. Bryant, 196 (n)

57 Ashmole, 603–604

58 Ibid., 605

59 Ibid., 588–596

60 *Statutes of the Order of the Garter Reformed in a Chapter Holden at Windsor,* 17 *March* 1552

61 Goodman, i, 200

62 Ashmole, App. clxxx

63 Jesse, v, 188

64 Pepys, ii, 225

65 Evelyn, ii, 25

66 Pepys, ii, 17–18

[iv] James II (pages 84–87)

1 Jesse, iv, 246; Grammont, 448

2 Burnet, i, 168

3 Turner: *James II*, 60–61

4 *History To-day*, May 1963

5 Turner: *James II*, 234
6 Evelyn, ii, 96; *A True Description of the New-Erected Fort at Windsor* (1674)
7 Turner: *James II*, 237
8 Reresby, 459
9 Tighe, ii, 426
10 Bramston; Macaulay, ii, 920
11 Macaulay, ii, 1222

[v] William iii and Mary ii (pages 87–90)

1 Ogg, 8
2 Kenyon, 185
3 Jesse: *Continuation*, i, 221
4 Marlborough, 97; Jesse: *Continuation*, i, 196
5 Dutton, 168
6 *Supplement to Burnet's History* (Ed. H. C. Foxcroft, 1902), 192; Jesse: *Continuation*, i, 192
7 Petrie, 257
8 Marlborough, 129
9 Tighe, ii, 476
10 Burnet, q. Jesse: *Continuation*, i, 160, 222–224
11 Kenyon, 194
12 Jesse, vii, 180
13 Ibid., vii, 87
14 Ogg, 103

[vi] Queen Anne (pages 90–96)

1 Jesse: *Continuation*, i, 336
2 Ibid., *Continuation*, i, 331
3 Rowse: *Churchills*, 170
4 Fiennes, 358
5 Marlborough, 169
6 Rowse: *Churchills*, 282
7 Hughes, 73
8 *County History*, ii, 297, 305
9 Manchester, ii, 337
10 Marlborough, 172
11 Swift, ii, 328
12 Jesse, vii, 303
13 Ibid., vii, 297
14 Hope, i, 331–332
15 Poynter, 38
16 Tighe, ii, 454

17 Ibid., ii, 471
18 Hill, 102
19 Hopkinson, 351
20 Herbert M. Vaughan, 'King's Evil' in *Encyclopaedia Britannica*
21 Connell, 264
22 Bolitho: *Windsor*, 12

HANOVERIANS

[i] George III – The Royal Farmer (pages 99–124)

1 Walpole to George Montagu 25 October 1760
2 Jesse: *George III*, i, 29
3 Waldegrave, 201
4 Plumb, 116
5 Pote, 19; Morshead, 70; Hope, i, 347
6 Knight: *Varieties*, 69
7 *General Orders issued by the Duke of Montagu, Constable of Windsor Castle,* November 1781; Tighe, ii, 539–540; Knight: *Working Life*, i, 34–35
8 *Report of the Constable of Windsor Castle to the Lords of the Treasury* (1784)
9 Carolyn Powys, q. Bolitho: *Windsor*, 81–82
10 *Gentleman's Magazine* (letter from Francis Pigott), 20 June 1786
11 Tighe, ii, 465
12 Jesse: *George III*, i, 308
13 *George III, Letters*, iii, 373
14 Tighe, ii, 537
15 *George III, Letters*, iii, 482
16 Jesse: *George III*, iii, 304–311
17 Ibid., i, 136, 142, 146; Walpole: *George III*, 56; Vulliamy: *Royal George*, 119
18 Hervey, 329
19 Vulliamy: *Aspasia*, 246
20 More, ii, 97
21 Wraxall, v, 160
22 Delany, 2nd series, iii, 360
23 D'Arblay, ii, 370
24 Papendiek, i, 14
25 Lady Llanover (daughter of Georgina Mary Port, Mrs Delany's niece), editor of Mrs Delany's letters
26 Delany, 2nd series, iii, 361
27 Ibid.
28 D'Arblay, iii, 385–400; iv, 431–433
29 Walpole: *George III*, i, 56; Jesse, *George III*, i, 320
30 Melville: *Farmer George*, i, 133
31 Ibid., i, 208

32 Vulliamy: *Royal George*, 121
33 Jesse: *George III*, iv, 163; Melville, *George III*, i, 75
34 Joseph Taylor, 136; Jesse: *George III*, ii, 429
35 Joseph Taylor, 72
36 Vulliamy: *Royal George*, 181
37 Joseph Taylor, 155
38 Windsor: *Album*, 16–17; O. F. Morshead, 'The Windsor Uniform', *Connoisseur*, May 1935
39 Vulliamy: *Royal George*, 260
40 Hughes, 77
41 Ibid., 78
42 Holt, i, 295
43 Lord Carlisle, *Reminiscences*, q. Melville: *Farmer George*, 196–197
44 Joseph Taylor, 17
45 Melville: *Farmer George*, i, 179
46 Knight: *Working Life*, i, 37
47 Huish: *George III*, 392
48 Knight: *Working Life*, i, 39
49 Jesse: *George III*, ii, 401
50 Knight: *Working Life*, i, 39
51 Turner: *St James's*, 218–219
52 Ibid., 224
53 Joseph Taylor, 61
54 Ibid., 81–82
55 J. H. Rose, i, 74; Wraxall, ii, 66
56 Knight: *Working Life*, i, 38; Cobbin, 12
57 Melville: *Farmer George*, i, 172
58 Ibid., i, 168
59 Joseph Taylor, 152
60 Jesse: *George III*, ii, 406
61 Melville: *Farmer George*, i, 169
62 Wynn, 211
63 Jesse: *George III*, i, 334
64 Thackeray, 274
65 Wraxall, v, 158
66 D'Arblay, iii, 65–67
67 Jesse: *George III*, iii, 480
68 Molloy, ii, 131
69 Joseph Taylor, 149
70 Ibid., 150; Holt, ii, 108
71 D'Arblay, ii, 333, 340–341, 419, 435, 440; iii, 132, 331
72 Ibid., ii, 352
73 Holt, ii, 211
74 *The Rev. John Evans's Excursion to Windsor in 1810*; D'Arblay, ii, 431
75 D'Arblay, iii, 132

76 Melville: *Farmer George*, i, 186
77 D'Arblay, ii, 336–337; ii, 340–341
78 Jesse: *George III*, i, 154, 177, 183
79 D'Arblay, ii, 344
80 Thackeray, 282; Huish: *George III*, 351
81 D'Arblay, iv, 479
82 Nichols: *Recollections*, 301
83 Knight: *Working Life*, i, 46
84 Melville: *Farmer George*, i, 201
85 D'Arblay, ii, 314
86 Ibid., ii, 316–328
87 Ibid., ii, 431
88 Jesse: *George III*, iv, 170–172

[ii] George iii – The Royal Patient (pages 124–145)

1 Trench, 4
2 Withers, 17–18
3 D'Arblay, iv, 120
4 Ibid., iv, 122
5 Ibid.
6 Joseph Taylor, 34
7 Melville: *Farmer George*, ii, 209
8 Trench, 18
9 D'Arblay, iv, 129
10 Trench, 23
11 D'Arblay, iv, 129
12 Auckland, ii, 244
13 D'Arblay, iv, 147–154
14 Papendiek, ii, 15
15 Molloy, iv, 5–6
16 Holt, i, 313
17 Massey, q. Molloy, iv, 13–14
18 Trench, 60, 95
19 Ibid., 70
20 Papendiek, ii, 14–15
21 Papendiek, ii, 13
22 Vulliamy: *Royal George*, 200; Papendiek, ii, 12
23 Papendiek, ii, 19–20
24 Jesse: *George III*, iv, 265
25 Malmesbury, q. Melville, ii, 216–217
26 Papendiek, ii, 12
27 Ibid., ii, 24
28 D'Arblay, iv, 188–189; Papendiek, ii, 28
29 Fulke Greville, iii; Trench, 85–86

30 Papendiek, ii, 54
31 Molloy, iv, 24
32 Papendiek, ii, 62
33 Ibid., ii, 64
34 D'Arblay, ii, 338
35 Jesse: *George III*, iii, 367
36 Rose: *Diaries*, 94
37 D'Arblay, iv, 243–250
38 *Annual Register* (1789)
39 D'Arblay, iv, 287; Papendiek, ii, 112–116; Vulliamy: *Royal George*, 252–258
40 Turner: *St James's*, 232
41 Cobbin, 25
42 Pickering, 272
43 Boswell, i, 338
44 Jesse: *George III*, iv, 119–120; 454
45 Papendiek, ii, 259
46 D'Arblay, iv, 491
47 Melville: *Farmer George*, ii, 252
48 Knight: *Working Life*, i, 61
49 Malmesbury, 327
50 Eldon, 411
51 Plumb, 134
52 Malmesbury, Buckingham, Rose, Eldon, Auckland, Colchester, *passim*
53 *Taylor Papers*, 58
54 Auckland, q. Melville, 272
55 *Harcourt Papers*, vi, 83, q. Morshead, 82
56 *The Journal of One Day in the History of a Year*, q. Taylor, 51–52
57 Ibid.
58 Hope, i, 348
59 Ibid., i, 348; Morshead, 79
60 Goddard, 64–65
61 Knight: *Working Life*, i, 65
62 Vulliamy: *Royal George*, 288–289; Huish: *George III*, 656–657
63 Molloy, iv, 95–96; Fulford: *Dukes*, 203–209
64 *Sunday Telegraph*, 24 March 1963; P.I.
65 Fulford: *Dukes*, 209
66 Stuart, 377
67 Fulford: *Knight*, 85
68 Joseph Taylor, 54–55; Cobbin, 13
69 *Taylor Papers*, 59
70 Fulford: *Knight*, 86
71 Ibid., 341
72 Wynn, 212
73 Melville: *Farmer George*, ii, 287

74 Huish: *George III*, 690
75 Buckingham, q. Melville, ii, 287
76 Rose, Buckingham, Malmesbury, Colchester, *passim*
77 Stuart, 215
78 Papendiek, ii, 217
79 Melville: *Farmer George*, ii, 231
80 'Windsor was a Queen's "Little Paradise"' (Olwen Hedley), *The Times*
   30 April 1963
81 Melville: *Farmer George*, ii, 287
82 Joseph Taylor, 58
83 Cobbin, 74
84 Wynn, 212; Huish: *George III*, 697–700
85 Lord Carlisle, *Reminiscences*, q. Melville, ii, 287

[iii] George iv – The *Cottage Orné* (pages 145–163)

1 Malmesbury, iii, 201, 208
2 Arbuthnot, i, 81
3 Bury, i, 38–39
3 Bury, i, 38–39
4 Fulford: *George IV*, 55
5 *Princess Charlotte*, *passim*
6 Fulford: *Knight*, 167
7 Ibid., 181–189
8 Fulford: *George IV*, 112–115
9 Bury, i, 56
10 Fulford: *George IV*, 150–152
11 Harwood, 183
12 Burney, 124
13 Lieven, q. Fulford: *George IV*, 202
14 Fulford: *George IV*, 138–139
15 Thackeray, 320
16 Fulford: *George IV*, 44
17 Arbuthnot, i, 277
18 Leslie, 45
19 Ibid., 23
20 Fulford: *George IV*, 224
21 Ibid., 161, 195
22 *George IV, Letters*, 1032
23 Fulford: *George IV*, 190
24 Lieven, 96–97
25 Ibid., 116
26 Leslie, 144
27 Arbuthnot, i, 91
28 Leslie, 134

29 Ibid., 81
30 Arbuthnot, i, 102
31 Bury, i, 416
32 *George IV, Letters*, 946
33 Greville, i, 118
34 Arbuthnot, i, 111
35 Ibid., i, 232
36 Colchester, iii, 277; Creevey, ii, 58
37 Leslie, 137
38 Greville, i, 117–118
39 Ibid., i, 177
40 Arbuthnot, i, 242–243
41 Ibid., i, 270
42 Ibid., i, 335–336
43 Lieven, 271
44 Leslie, 82
45 Arbuthnot, i, 187
46 Greville, i, 236
47 Ibid., i, 178
48 Ibid., i, 273–274
49 Arbuthnot, i, 270
50 *George IV, Letters*, 1073
51 Arbuthnot, i, 256
52 Ibid., i, 270
53 Ibid.
54 Greville, i, 236–237, 262
55 Huish: *George IV*, ii, 360
56 Chateaubriand, iv, 74
57 Lieven, 228–229
58 Greville, i, 236

[iv] George IV – The Gothic Castle (pages 163–175)

1 Joseph Farington's diary, q. *History To-day*, June 1953
2 Frampton, 337
3 Morshead, 87
4 *Evidence before Select Committee of House of Commons* (1830)
5 *Letters, George IV*, ii, 158
6 *Hansard* xxiv (1830) cols 347–350
7 *Letters, George IV*, iii, 475
8 Morshead, 96
9 Greville, i, 181
10 Croker, i, 414
11 Creevey, 265
12 R.A., Georgian Papers 51308, q. Morshead, 92

13 Harwood, 46, 179; Tighe, ii, 524
14 Greville, ii, 31
15 *Victoria, Letters*, 1st Series, 1, 16–17
16 Greville, i, 273, 291
17 Plumb, 167
18 Leslie, 165
19 Arbuthnot, ii, 352
20 Greville, ii, 31
21 Hamilton, ii, 370
22 Greville, i, 291
23 Ibid., i, 376
24 Molloy, iv, 360
25 Fulford: *George IV*, 82
26 Greville, ii, 23
27 Huish: *George IV*, 400
28 Greville, i, 301
29 Leslie, 163
30 Greville, i, 167
31 Knight: *Working Life*, i, 173
32 Gash, 425
33 Ibid.
34 Greville, i, 270
35 *Letters, George IV*, i, 409
36 Greville, i, 270–271, 278–279; Arbuthnot, ii, 240; Iremonger, *passim*
37 Greville, i, 273, 290
38 Arbuthnot, ii, 48, 79; Parker, ii, 149
39 Arbuthnot, ii, 352
40 Ibid., ii, 362
41 Gash, 629
42 Ibid.
43 Arbuthnot, ii, 360
44 Fulford: *George IV*, 228
45 Leslie, 165; Fulford: *George IV*, 228; Arbuthnot, ii, 364

[v] William iv (pages 176–182)

1 Brown, 58
2 Fitzgerald, 224–225
3 Greville, ii, 150
4 *Taylor Papers*; Greville, iii, 127
5 Greville, iii, 127–128
6 Ibid., iii, 127
7 Ibid., iii, 128
8 Buckingham: *William IV*, i, 6–7
9 Arbuthnot, ii, 373

10 Greville, ii, 4; Arbuthnot, ii, 182, 370–371
11 Greville, ii, 13–14
12 Buckingham: *William IV*, i, 75
13 Arbuthnot, ii, 382–383
14 Greville, ii, 417
15 *Jerningham Letters*, ii, 372
16 Gash, 631
17 Arbuthnot, ii, 365
18 *Spectator*, q. Kingsley Martin, 26
19 Hopkirk, 86
20 Allen; Fitzgerald; Hopkirk, *passim*
21 Fulford: *George IV*, 197
22 Hopkirk, 91
23 Ibid.
24 Creevey; Greville, ii, 149
25 Greville, iii, 208, 311
26 Ibid., iii, 208
27 Arbuthnot, ii, 288
28 Greville, iii, 232
29 Ibid., iii, 309–310
30 Ibid., iii, 232
31 Fitzgerald, 382

VICTORIANS

[i] Victoria: The Young Queen (pages 185–212)

1 Creevey, 6 September, 1837
2 Greville, i, 293, iii, 373
3 Ibid., iii, 395
4 *Journal of Benjamin Moran*, q. Fulford, *Hanover to Windsor*, 75
5 *Victoria, Letters*, i, 85
6 Ponsonby: *Sidelights*, 1
7 Lyttelton, 282–283
8 Greville, iv, 108–109
9 Strachey, 62
10 Cecil, 269
11 Greville, iv, 110
12 Ibid., iv, 93
13 Ibid., iv, 109
14 Lieven, q. Cecil, 277
15 Creevey, q. Cecil, 277
16 Cecil, 272
17 Ibid., 277; 285–286; 299–301
18 Creevey, iv, 153

19 Cecil, 301
20 Ibid., 327
21 Ibid.
22 Benson: *Victoria*, 85–86; Cecil, 328
23 Cecil, 334
24 Benson: *Victoria*, 90; Bolitho: *Albert*, 56
25 Grey, 232, 238
26 Cecil, 340
27 Greville, iv, 241
28 Bolitho: *Albert*, 104
29 *Victoria, Letters*, i, 206
30 Theodore Martin, i, 93–94
31 Frederick Ponsonby, 67
32 Stockmar, i, xlviii
33 Ibid., i, lxxx
34 Benson: *Victoria*, 115
35 Fulford: *Consort*, 58
36 Ibid., 61
37 R.A., Fulford: *Consort*, 61
38 R.A., Fulford, 60
39 R.A., Fulford, 98
40 R.A., Fulford, 70
41 R.A., Fulford, 71
42 R.A., Fulford, 73
43 Queen Victoria's Journal, q. Fulford, 74; *Victoria, Letters*, 1st Series,
    iii, 435–439; Greville, v, 39
44 Frederick Ponsonby, 18
45 Tooley, 137–138
46 Stockmar, ii, 121–124
47 P.R.O. (R.L.C.D.), Watson, 94–95
48 Ibid., (R.L.C.D.), Watson, 238
49 Ibid. (R.L.C.D.), Watson, 129
50 Jerrold: *Married Life*, 185
51 P.R.O. (R.L.C.D.), Watson, 18
52 Benson: *Victoria*, 125; Jerrold: *Married Life*, 219
53 Jerrold: *Married Life*, 220
54 Harwood, 128–129; Jerrold: *Married Life*, 250–270
55 R.A., Fulford, 53
56 Queen Victoria's Journal, Fulford, 92
57 Fulford, 91
58 Stockmar, ii, 481
59 *Court Etiquette* (1849), q. Turner: *St James's*, 321
60 Tooley, 146
61 Watson, 234
62 Frederick Ponsonby, 16

63 G.T. Curtis, *James Buchanan*, q. Turner: *St James's*, 326–327
64 Turner: *St James's*, 318
65 Jerrold: *Married Life*, 253
66 Ibid.
67 Erskine, 176
68 Greville, iv, 108
69 *Dear Duchess* (*Manchester*), 131
70 Ibid., 32
71 Trevelyan, 548–549
72 Hodder, i, 236
73 Greville, iv, 383
74 Benson: *Victoria*, 23
75 Frederick Ponsonby, 51; *Private Life* (*Victoria*), 125–126; P.1.
76 Frederick Ponsonby, 52
77 Ibid., 50
78 Ibid, 51
79 Greville, iv, 383
80 *Memorandum by George Anson*, q. Bolitho: *Victoria*, 74
81 Bolitho: *Victoria*, 74
82 Fulford: *Consort*, 276
83 *Victoria, Letters*, i, 322
84 Lyttelton, 313
84 Frederick Ponsonby, 15
86 Fulford: *Consort*, 103, 243
87 Ibid., 242
88 Lyttelton, 307
89 Grey, 339
90 *Memorandum by George Anson*, q. Bolitho: *Victoria*, 74
91 Fulford: *Victoria*, 70
92 Benson: *Victoria*, 132
93 Lyttelton, 334–335
94 Ibid., 389
95 *Private Life* (*Victoria*), 83; Bloomfield, i, 130
96 Bloomfield, 125
97 Lyttelton, 357
98 Erskine, 155
99 Bolitho: *Albert*, 138
100 Ibid, 163
101 Ibid, 119
102 Greville, v, 59
103 R.A., Fulford: *Consort*, 234
104 *Private Life* (*Victoria*), 12
105 Fulford: *Consort*, 234
106 Theodore Martin, iv, 274
107 Lyttelton, 307

108 Greville, vii, 388
109 Lyttelton, 320
110 Theodore Martin, v, 435
111 Bolitho: *Victoria*, 176–177
112 Ibid., 178–179
113 Theodore Martin, v, 415
114 Watson, 97
115 R.A., Fulford: *Consort*, 264–272
116 Bolitho: *Victoria*, 186
117 Bolitho: *Albert*, 284
118 Stanley, 245; Fulford: *Hanover to Windsor*, 90
119 Villiers, 318
120 Duff, 39
121 Strachey, 257
122 R.A., Fulford: *Consort*, 247
123 Lytton, 16–17
124 Tooley, 204
125 *Private Life (Victoria)*, 66; Tooley, 205
126 Ribblesdale, 127
127 Strachey, 257; P.I.
128 Fulford: *Victoria*, 75
129 Benson: *Edward VII*, 55
130 *Dear Duchess (Manchester)*, 191
131 Article by Olwen Hedley in *The Times*, 4 June 1962

[ii] Victoria: The Widow at Windsor (pages 213–230)

1 Stanley, 282
2 Ibid., 307
3 D'Arblay, iii, 84
4 Benson: *Victoria*, 215; Bolitho: *Victoria*, 198–199; Hedley, 60; Lee, i, 159–160
5 Stanley, 286; Cowles, 66
6 Winston Churchill: *Randolph Churchill*, i, 10
7 *Victoria, Letters*, 2nd Series, ii, 58–77
8 Brown: *Balmoral*, 159
9 Benson: *Victoria*, 269
10 Ibid., 292
11 Lytton, 62
12 Bolitho: *Victoria*, 213
13 Ribblesdale, 126
14 *Private Life (Victoria)*, 65
15 Bell, 95; Benson: *Victoria*, 293
16 Jenkins: *Dilke*, 69
17 *The Times*, 24 November 1871, q. Bolitho: *Victoria*, 241

18 Bloomfield, 54
19 Watson, 170
20 Benson: *Victoria*, 137
21 Strachey, 110
22 Greville, vii, 175
23 Erskine, 303
24 *Victoria, Leaves*, 43
25 Greville, v, 179; vii, 129, 175; Lyttelton, 345, 349
26 *Victoria, Letters*, 1st Series, ii, 21–23
27 Watson, 221–222
28 Ibid., 219
29 Benson: *Victoria*, 232
30 *Victoria, Letters*, 2nd Series, 445, 446
31 Ponsonby: *Sidelights*, 122, 128
32 Benson: *Victoria*, 266; Bolitho: *Victoria*, 245; Watson, 223; *Victoria, Letters*, 2nd Series, ii, 258–261
33 Fulford: *Victoria*, 134
34 Bell, 77
35 Ribblesdale, 119–120
36 Ibid., 118
37 Balsan, 87
38 *Private Life (Victoria)*, 68
39 Aga Khan, 46–47
40 *Private Life (Victoria)*, 68; Ribblesdale, 131
41 Esher, i, 208–209
42 Greville, vi, 441
43 R.A., Fulford: *Consort*, 61
44 Greville, v, 50, 77, 79
45 Lytton, 147
46 Frederick Ponsonby, 16
47 Ibid.
48 Ibid., 17
49 Eckardstein, 43
50 Ibid., 44
51 Mersey, 359
52 Fulford: *Victoria*, 78
53 Portland, 125
54 Frederick Ponsonby, 57
55 *Henry Ponsonby*, 130–131
56 Frederick Ponsonby, 13–15
57 Ibid, 36
58 Ibid, 13
59 Ibid.
60 Turner: *St James's*, 334
61 Aga Khan, 46

62 *Private Life (Victoria)*, 7
63 Frederick Ponsonby, 24
64 Ibid, 25
65 Fulford: *Victoria*, 132
66 Martin: *Victoria*, 70
67 *Private Life (Victoria)*, 85–86
68 Windsor, 10
69 *Victoria of Prussia, passim*
70 Lytton, 59
71 Frederick Ponsonby, 36; Bolitho: *Victoria*, 285
72 Russell Thorndike: *Children of the Garter*, q. Bolitho: *Victoria*, 350
73 Frederick Ponsonby, 82; Bolitho: *Victoria*, 352
74 Frederick Ponsonby, 93

EDWARDIANS

[i] Edward VII – 'A Very Bad Boy' (pages 233–238)

1 *The Times*, 23 January 1901
2 Leslie, 19
3 Fulford: *Consort*, 255
4 R.A., Diary of Sir James Clark, q. Fulford: *Consort*, 256
5 Fulford: *Consort*, 256
6 *The Diaries of Frederick Weymouth Gibbs*, q. Cowles, 34
7 *Elphinstone*, 41
8 Lee, i, 17–28
9 Fulford: *Consort*, 260
10 Lee, i, 76
11 R.A., q. Fulford: *Consort*, 259
12 Lee, i, 18–22
13 Ibid., i, 569
14 Ibid., i, 172
15 Frederick Ponsonby, 202–203
16 *Rosebery*, ii, 640
17 Clowles, 229
18 Frederick Ponsonby, 139
19 André Maurois, *King Edward and His Times*; Frederick Ponsonby, 127, 139, 145, 202, 221, 224
20 Esher; *Cloud Capp'd Towers*, 173–174
21 Benson; *Edward VII*, 68
22 *Private Life (Edward VII)*, 272–273
23 Cowles, 78
24 Sykes, 27–29

[ii] Edward VII – *L'oncle de l'Europe* (Pages 238–251)

1 Esher, i, 291, 297; Esher: *Cloud Capp'd Towers*, 181
2 Windsor, 46
3 Benson: *Edward VII*, 216–218
4 Esher, ii, 139
5 Ibid.
6 Cust, 211
7 *Private Life (Victoria)*, 66
8 Ibid, 67
9 Esher, i, 280
10 Ibid., i, 291–292, 299
11 Lee, i, 170
12 Frederick Ponsonby, 149
13 Pope-Hennessy, 380; Esher, i, 413; Ormathwaite, 106
14 Balsan, 90
15 Cowles, 274, 272
16 Ibid., 159
17 Wortham, 69
18 *Private Life (Edward VII)*, 115
19 Ormathwaite, 114–115
20 Frederick Ponsonby, 201
21 Ibid., 124
22 *Private Life (Edward VII)*, 210
23 Legge, *Edward VII*, 386
24 Eckardstein, 50
25 Somner, 143
26 Frederick Ponsonby, 105
27 *Henry Asquith*, i, 242
28 Balsan, 92
29 Marie Louise, 173
30 Frederick Ponsonby, 137
31 Ibid, 138
32 Ibid., 244
33 Benson: *Edward VII*, 245; Frederick Ponsonby, 205
34 Frederick Ponsonby, 220
35 Esher: *Cloud Capp'd Towers*, 156–157
36 Winston Churchill: *Early Life*, 107–108
37 Esher, ii, 461
38 Mersey, xi
39 Frederick Ponsonby, 241
40 Lee, ii, 65
41 Turner: *St James's*, 348
42 Cowles, 210
43 Frederick Ponsonby, 109–110

44 *Private Life (Edward VII)*, 118, 120; Frederick Ponsonby, 109–110;
   Legge: *More About King Edward*, 229–230
45 *Private Life (Edward VII)*, 263–264; Legge: *Edward VII*, 285; Legge:
   More About King Edward, 316–317; Wortham, 61
46 Lee, ii, 70
47 Oxford, 240–241
48 *Felix Semon's Memoirs*, q. Lee, ii, 244
49 Legge: *More About King Edward*, 244–245
50 Legge: *Edward VII*, 299–300
51 Wortham, 140
52 Haldane, 222; Somner, 201
53 Wortham, 140
54 Pope-Hennessy, 359
55 Somner, 231

WINDSORS

[i] George v (pages 255–272)

1 Gore, 237
2 Bryant: *George V*, 53
3 Gore, 246
4 Ibid., 126
5 Ibid., 63
6 Black, 158
7 Pope-Hennessy, 473
8 Gore, 67, 76, 109, 118–119, 126–127, 331, 348, 426
9 Ibid., 345
10 Somervell, 45
11 Esher, iii, 48–49
12 Gore, 413
13 Ibid., 415
14 Bolitho: *Restless Years*, 150
15 Pope-Hennessy, 46, 409–414, 524–525
16 Woodward, 145
17 Ibid., 157; Gore, 414
18 Gore, 378, 415; Windsor, 6, 21; Frederick Ponsonby, 285
19 Somner, 226
20 Esher, iii, 256
21 Wheeler-Bennett, 27; Airlie, 112
22 Windsor, 25–27
23 Frederick Ponsonby, 329
24 Ormathwaite, 221
25 Windsor: *Album*, 54
26 Clynes, ii, 175–176; Woodward, 172

27 Curzon, 111
28 *Unpublished account of Lady Maud Warrender*, q. Nicolson, 309
29 Nicolson, 309
30 Arthur: *George V*, 351
31 Nicolson, 310
32 Frederick Ponsonby, 279
33 Gore, 360
34 Woodward, 129
35 Airlie, 147
36 Gore, 390–391
37 Windsor, 187
38 Windsor: *Album*, 13, 84
39 Ibid., 56, 58
40 Gore, 416; Windsor, 187
41 Corbitt, 200–201
42 Black, 156; Ormathwaite, 217
43 Black, 168
44 Gore, 378–379
45 Ibid., 73, 378, 441; Frederick Ponsonby, 356
46 Airlie, 147
47 Windsor, 185
48 Ibid., 185; Airlie, 158–161
49 Windsor, 186
50 Airlie, 158–163; Windosr, 184–186
51 Nicolson, 387
52 Windsor, 229
53 Airlie, 181; Gore, 344; Windsor, 229
54 Windsor, 233–234
55 Nicolson, 392
56 Ibid., 390–391
57 Aga Khan, 83
58 Gore, 270
59 Black, 170
60 Gore, 431
61 Airlie, 102
62 Hare, vi, 516
63 Pope-Hennessy, 314
64 Airlie, 106
65 Pope-Hennessy, 517
66 Airlie, 128
67 Arthur: *Mary*, 199
68 Pope-Hennessy, 498
69 Woodward, 10
70 Pope-Hennessy, 521
71 Airlie, 162

72 Cavendish, 231
73 Bolitho: *George VI*, 117
74 Woodward, 160–171, 269; Gore, 359
75 Airlie, 128–129
76 Curzon, 111
77 Pope-Hennessy, 431
78 Bryant: *George V*, 162
79 Gore, 442–443
80 Ibid., 443; Bryant: *George V*, 174–175
81 Bolitho: *Edward VIII*, 251

[ii] Edward VIII (Pages 273–279)

1 Windsor, 236–237
2 Ibid., 238
3 Ibid., 20–21; Windsor: *Album*, 5, 7
4 Windsor: *Album*, 9
5 Stanley, 247
6 *Private Life (Edward VII)*, 28; Bryant: *George V*, 16
7 Randolph Churchill: *Derby*, 159
8 Pope-Hennessy, 553
9 Windsor, 45
10 Bryant: *George V*, 33
11 Esher, iii, 108
12 Bolitho: *Edward VIII*, 210
13 Ibid., 226
14 Windsor: *Album*, 92
15 *New York World*, q. Bolitho, 227
16 Windsor, 201
17 Bolitho: *Edward VIII*, 237
18 Pope-Hennessy, 423
19 Ibid., 573
20 Bolitho: *Edward VIII*, 259
21 Aga Khan, 248
22 Cooper, 162
23 Ibid., 162–163
24 Hardinge, 181–182
25 Windsor, 409
26 Bolitho: *Edward VIII*, 284
27 Wheeler-Bennett, 294
28 Windsor, 414

[iii] George vɪ (pages279 –287)

1 Wheeler-Bennett, 270
2 Nicolson, 366
3 Wheeler-Bennett, 27–28
4 Frere, 114
5 Wheeler-Bennett, 151
6 Ibid., 259
7 Ibid., 258
8 Cooper, 73
9 Ibid., 192–193
10 Wheeler-Bennett, 739
11 Corbitt, 96, 112; P.1
12 Buxton, *passim*
13 Wheeler-Bennett, 470
14 R.A., Wheeler-Bennett, 467
15 Wheeler-Bennett, 737
16 Ibid., 736
17 Ibid.
18 Ibid., 756
19 Tighe, ii, 553
20 Wheeler-Bennett, 757
21 Frere, 70; P.I.
22 Wheeler-Bennett, 293
23 P.I.
24 Eleanor Roosevelt, 47
25 James Roosevelt, 288
26 Truman, 343
27 Winant, 19–20
28 Wheeler-Bennett, 804
29 *Spectator*, 31 May 1963

[iv] Elizabeth ɪɪ (Pages 288–299)

1 Morrah, 22
2 Pope-Hennessy, 605
3 Wheeler-Bennett, 741
4 Cynthia Asquith, 58
5 Morrah, 17
6 Horace Smith, *A Horseman Through Six Reigns*, q. Laird, 130
7 Randolph Churchill: *The Queen*, 42
8 Ibid.
9 Laird, 58
10 Morrah, 15
11 Ibid., 54

12 Ibid., 53–63
13 Laird, 36
14 Morrah, 37, 38, 41–42; P.I.
15 Ibid., 37
16 Kingsley Martin, 125, 126
17 Laird; P.I.
18 Corbitt, 64
19 Ibid., 62–67
20 National Press 23 April, 1963; P.I.
21 Kingsley Martin, 143
22 *Prince Philip*, 59
23 Morrah, 45
24 *Prince Philip*, 211
25 Windsor, 216
26 Corbitt, 66
27 Frere, 169; P.I.
28 *Time and Tide*, July 1963; P.I.
29 Ibid.
30 Frere, 251
31 Airlie, 214

BIBLIOGRAPHY

The dates are not always of the first editions but of those I have used.

AGA KHAN, *The Memoirs of Aga Khan* (1954)

AIRLIE, Mabel, Countess of, *Thatched with Gold*, Ed. Jennifer Ellis (1962)

ALLEN, W. Gore, *King William IV* (1960)

ANSTIS, John, *Register of the Order of the Garter* (1724)

APPLEBY, John T., *Henry II* (1962)

APPLEBY, John T., *John, King of England* (1959)

D'ARBLAY, Charlotte Barrett (Ed.), *Diary and Letters of Madame D'Arblay, 1778–1840* (1904)

ARBUTHNOT, Francis Bamford and the Duke of Wellington (Eds.), *The Journal of Mrs Arbuthnot* (1950)

ARTHUR, Sir George, *King George V* (1934)

ARTHUR, Sir George, *Queen Mary* (1935)

ASHMOLE, Elias, *The Institution, Laws and Ceremonies of the Most Noble Order of the Garter* (1672)

ASQUITH, Cynthia, *The Family Life of Her Majesty Queen Elizabeth* (n.d.)

ASQUITH, Cyril and Spender, J. A., *The Life of Herbert Henry Asquith* (1932)

AUCKLAND, William Eden, 1st Baron Auckland, *Journal and Correspondence* (1861–1862)

BABEES BOOK: F. J. Furnivall (Ed.), *The Babees Book* (1868)

BAGLEY, J. J., *Henry VIII* (1962)

BALSAN, Consuelo Vanderbilt, *The Glitter and the Gold* (1953)

BARLOW, Frank, *The Feudal Kingdom of England* (1961)

BECKINGSDALE, B. W., *Elizabeth I* (1963)

BELL, G. K. A., *Randall Davidson* (1955)

BELLOC, Hilaire, *Charles I* (1933)

BELTZ, G. F., *Memorials of the Order of the Garter* (1841)

BENSON, E. F., *King Edward VII* (1933)

BENSON, E. F., *Queen Victoria* (1935)

BLACK, Sister Catherine, *King's Nurse, Beggar's Nurse* (n.d.)

BLOOMFIELD, Georgiana, Baroness, *Reminiscences of Court and Diplomatic Life* (1883)

BOLITHO, Hector, *Albert the Good* (1932)

BOLITHO, Hector, *King Edward VIII* (1937)

BOLITHO, Hector, *George VI* (1937)

BOLITHO, Hector, *My Restless Years* (1962)

BOLITHO, Hector, *The Reign of Queen Victoria* (1949)

BOLITHO, Hector, *The Romance of Windsor Castle* (1947)

BOORDE, Andrew, *Scoggins Jests* (1626)
BOSWELL, James, *The Life of Samuel Johnson* (Everyman's Library, 1920)
BRAMSTON, *The Autobiography of Sir John Bramston* (1845)
BRETT, A. C. A., *Charles II and His Court* (1910)
BROOKE, Christopher, *The Saxon and Norman Kings* (1963)
BROWN, Ivor, *Balmoral* (1955)
BROWN, *The Diary of Miss Margaretta Brown* (Extracts printed in *Etoniana* and in *Report of the Society of the Friends of St George*, 1960 by Olwen Hedley in 'Court and Chapel 1760–1873')
BRYANT, Sir Arthur, *Charles II* (1955)
BRYANT, Sir Arthur, *George V* (1936)
BUCKINGHAM, Richard, Duke of Buckingham and Chandos, *Memoirs of the Courts and Cabinets of George III* (1853–1855)
BUCKINGHAM, Richard, Duke of Buckingham and Chandos, *Memoirs of the Courts and Cabinets of William IV and Victoria* (1861)
BULSTRODE, Sir Richard, *Memoirs and Recollections* (1721)
BURNET, Osmond Airy (Ed.), *Burnet's History of My Own Times* (1897)
BURNEY: Madame D'Arblay, *The Life of Charles Burney* (1832)
BURTON, *The Diary of Thomas Burton* (1828)
BURY, Lady Charlotte, *Diary of a Lady-in-Waiting* (1908)
BUXTON, Aubrey, *The King in His Country* (1955)

CAVENDISH, Mary Charlotte, *The Biography of Queen Mary* (1930)
CECIL, Lord David, *Melbourne* (Reprint Society, 1955)
CHAMBERS, E. K., *The Elizabethan Stage* (1923)
CHAMBERS, R. W., (Ed.), *A 15th Century Courtesy Book* (1914)
CHAPMAN, Hester W., *The Last Tudor King* (Readers' Union, 1961)
CHATEAUBRIAND, *Memoires D'outre Tombe* (1949)
CHURCHILL, Randolph, *They Serve the Queen* (1953)
CHURCHILL, Randolph, *Lord Derby, 'King of Lancashire'* (1960)
CHURCHILL, Winston S., *My Early Life* (1930)
CHURCHILL, Winston S., *Lord Randolph Churchill* (1906)
CLARENDON, Edward, Earl of, *The History of the Rebellion and Civil Wars in England* (1888)
CLYNES, J. R., *Memoirs* (1937)
COBBIN, Ingram, *Georgiana* (1820)
COLCHESTER, Charles, Lord (Ed.), *The Diary and Correspondence of Charles Abbot, Lord Colchester* (1861)
CONNELL, Neville, *Queen Anne* (1937)
COOPER, Diana, *The Light of Common Day* (1959)
CORBITT, F. J., *Fit for a King* (1956)
COULTON, G. G., *Medieval Panorama* (1947)
COUNTY HISTORY: P. H. Ditchfield and William Page (Eds.), *The Victoria History of the Counties of Britain*, Vol. 3 (1923)
COWLES, Virginia, *Edward VII and His Circle* (1956)

BIBLIOGRAPHY

CRAWFORD, Raymond, *The Last Days of Charles II* (1909)
CREEVEY, John Gore (Ed.), *Creevey* (John Murray, 1948)
CREIGHTON, Mandell, *Queen Elizabeth* (1896)
CROKER, Louis J. Jennings (Ed.), *The Croker Papers* (1885)
CURZON, The Marchioness Curzon of Kedleston, *Reminiscences* (1955)
CUST, Sir Lionel, *King Edward VII and his Court* (1930)

DELANY, Lady Llanover (Ed.), *The Autobiography and Correspondence of Mary Granville, Mrs Delany* (1862)
DORAN, John, *Court Fools* (1858)
DRINKWATER, John, *Mr Charles, King of England* (1926)
DUFF, David, *The Shy Princess* (1958)
DUTTON, Ralph, *English Court Life* (1963)

ECKARDSTEIN, Baron von, *Ten Years at the Court of St James's* (1921)
EDINGER, George, *Rupert of the Rhine* (1936)
EDWARD VII: *The Private Life of the King*. By One of His Majesty's Servants (1901)
ELDON: Horace Twiss, *The Public and Private Life of Lord Chancellor Eldon* (1844)
ELPHINSTONE: M. H. MacClintock, *The Queen Thanks Sir Howard* (1945)
ESHER, Maurice V. Brett (Ed.), *The Journals and Letters of Reginald, Viscount Esher* (1934)
ESHER, Reginald, Viscount, *Cloud Capp'd Towers* (1927)
ERSKINE, Mrs Steuart, (Ed.), *Twenty Years at Court: From the Correspondence of the Hon. Eleanor Stanley* (1916)
EVELYN, *The Diary of John Evelyn* (Everyman's Library, 1945)
EYTON, R. W., *Court, Houshold and Itinerary of Henry II* (1878)

FELLOWES, Edmund H., *The Knights of the Garter, 1348–1939* (n.d.)
FIENNES, Christopher Morris (Ed.), *The Journeys of Celia Fiennes* (1949)
FITZGERALD, Percy, *The Life and Times of William IV* (1884)
FRAMPTON, *The Journal of Mary Frampton* (1885)
FREEMAN, Edward A., *The History of the Norman Conquest of England* (1876)
FRERE, J. A., *The British Monarchy at Home* (1963)
FULFORD, Roger, *The Prince Consort* (1949)
FULFORD, Roger, *The Royal Dukes* (1933)
FULFORD, Roger, *George IV* (1949)
FULFORD, Roger, *Hanover to Windsor* (1960)
FULFORD, Roger, (Ed.), *The Autobiography of Miss Knight, Lady Companion to Princess Charlotte* (1960)
FULFORD, Roger, *Queen Victoria* (1951)
FULLER, Thomas, *Church-History of Britain* (1655)
FURNIVALL, F. J. (Ed.), *Manners and Meals in Olden Times* (1867)

GALWAY, Margaret, 'Joan of Kent and the Order of the Garter' (*University of Birmingham Historical Journal*, i, 1947, 13–51)

GARDINER, S. R., *History of England 1603–1642* (1883–4)

GASH, Norman, *Mr Secretary Peel* (1961)

GEORGE III, The Hon. Sir John Fortescue (Ed.), *The Correspondence of George III* (1928)

GEORGE IV, Arthur Aspinall (Ed.), *The Correspondence of King George IV* (1938)

GIBB, M. A., *Buckingham 1592–1628* (1939)

GODDARD, Arthur, *Windsor: The Castle of our Kings* (1911)

GOODMAN, Dr Godfrey, *The Court of King James I* (1839)

GORE, John, *King George V: A Personal Memoir* (1941)

GRAMMONT: Anthony Hamilton, *Memoirs of the Court of Charles II by Count Grammont* (1846)

GREEN, Mrs J. R., *Henry II* (1888)

GREVILLE, Lytton Strachey and Roger Fulford (Eds.), *The Greville Memoirs, 1814–1860* (1938)

GREVILLE, Fulke, F. McKno Bladon (Ed.), *The Diaries of Colonel the Hon. Fulke Greville* (1930)

GREY, General Charles, *The Early Years of the Prince Consort* (1867)

HALDANE, *Richard Burton, An Autobiography* (1929)

HALL, Hubert, *Court Life Under the Plantagenets* (1890)

HAMILTON, Lady Anne, *Secret History of the Court of England* (1903)

HARDINGE, Helen, *The Path of Kings* (1952)

HARE, Augustus, *The Story of My Life* (1896–1900)

HARINGTON, Thomas Park (Ed.), *Sir John Harington's Nugae Antiquae* (1804)

HARVEY, John, *The Plantagenets* (1948)

HARWOOD, T. Eustace, *Windsor Old and New* (1929)

HASSALL, W. O., *How They Lived* (1962)

HEDLEY, Olwen, 'Court and Chapel, 1760–1873', *Report of the Society of the Friends of St George* (1960)

HENRY, *Letters and Diaries of Philip Henry* (1882)

HENTZNER, Paul, *A Journey into England in the Year 1598* (1759)

HERVEY, Lord, *Some Materials for the Memoirs of the Reign of George II* Ed. Romney Sedgwick (1931)

HEYLIN, Peter, *Cosmographie and Historie of the Whole World* (1652)

HILL, B. J. W., *Windsor and Eton* (1957)

HODDER, Edwin, (Ed.), *The Life and Work of the 7th Earl of Shaftesbury* (1886)

HOLT, Edward, *The Public and Domestic Life of George III* (1820)

HOPE, W. H. St John, *Windsor Castle* (1913)

HOPKINSON, M. R., *Anne of England* (1934)

HOPKIRK, Mary, *Queen Adelaide* (1950)

HUGHES, G. M., *A History of Windsor Forest, Sunninghill and the Great Park* (1890)
HUISH, Robert, *Memoirs of George III* (1821)
HUISH, Robert, *Memoirs of George IV* (1830)
HUTCHINSON, Lucy, *Memoir of the Life of Colonel Hutchinson*, Ed. C. H. Firth (1896)

IREMONGER, Lucille, *Love and the Princess* (1958)

JENKINS, Roy, *Sir Charles Dilke* (1958)
JENKINS, Elizabeth, *Elizabeth The Great* (1958)
JERNINGHAM LETTERS: Egerton Castle (Ed.), *The Jerningham Letters* (1896)
JERROLD, Clare, *The Married Life of Queen Victoria* (1913)
JERROLD, Clare, *The Widowhood of Queen Victoria* (1916)
JESSE, J. H., *Memoirs of the Court of England during the Reign of the Stuarts* (1901)
JESSE, J. H., *Continuation of Memoirs of the Court of England from the Revolution in 1688 to the Death of George II* (1901)
JESSE, J. H., *Memoirs of the Life and Reign of King George III* (1901)
JOHN, Evan, *King Charles I* (1933)

KENDALL, Paul Murray, *The Yorkist Age* (1962)
KENYON, J. P., *The Stuarts* (1958)
KINGSFORD, R. L., *English Historical Literature* (1913)
KNIGHT, Charles, *A Volume of Varieties* (1844)
KNIGHT, Charles, *Passages of a Working Life* (1864)

LAIRD, Dorothy, *How the Queen Reigns* (1959)
LEE, Sir Sidney, *King Edward VII* (1925)
LEGGE, Edward, *King Edward in his True Colours* (1912)
LEGGE, Edward, *More About King Edward* (1913)
LESLIE, Sir Shane, *George IV* (1926)
LEWINSOHN, Richard, *A History of Sexual Customs* (1958)
LIEVEN, Peter Quennell (Ed.), *The Private Letters of Princess Lieven to Prince Metternich 1820–1826* (1948)
LONGMAN, William, *The History of the Life and Times of Edward III* (1869)
LYTTELTON, The Hon. Mrs Hugh Wyndham (Ed.), *The Correspondence of Sarah Spencer, Lady Lyttelton* (1912)
LYTTON, Mary Lutyens (Ed.), *Lady Lytton's Court Diary* (1961)

MACAULAY, Lord, *The History of England* (1914)
MACKINNON, James, *The History of Edward III* (1900)
MADDEN, Frederick, *Privy Purse Expenses of the Princess Mary* (1831)
MALMESBURY, 3rd Earl of, (Ed.), *The Diary and Correspondence of James Harris, 1st Earl of Malmesbury* (1844)

333

MANCHESTER, Duke of, (Ed.), *Court and Society from Elizabeth to Anne: From the Papers at Kimbolton* (1864)

MANCHESTER, A. L. Kennedy (Ed.), *'My Dear Duchess': Social and Political Letters to the Duchess of Manchester* (1956)

MARIE LOUISE, Princess, *My Memoirs of Six Reigns* (1956)

MARLBOROUGH, *An Account of the Conduct of the Duchess of Marlborough* (1742)

MARTIN, Kingsley, *The Crown and the Establishment* (1963)

MARTIN, Theodore, *The Life of H.R.H. The Prince Consort* (1875–1880)

MARTIN, Theodore, *Queen Victoria as I Knew Her* (1908)

MASSEY, William, *History of England during the Reign of George III* (1855–1863)

MATHEWS, David, *The Age of Charles I* (1951)

MCELWEE, William, *The Wisest Fool in Christendom* (1958)

MCKISACK, G. May, *The Fourteenth Century* (1959)

MELVILLE, Lewis, *Farmer George* (1907)

MERSEY, Viscount, *A Picture of Life 1872–1940* (1941)

MOLLOY, J. Fitzgerald, *Court Life Below Stairs or London under the First George, 1714–1760* (1882) *and under the Last Georges, 1760–1830* (1883)

MORE, *Hannah More's Memoirs* (1834)

MORGAN, E. B., (Ed.), *Readings in English Social History* (1923)

MORRAH, Dermot, *The Work of the Queen* (1958)

MORRIS, Christopher, *The Tudors* (1955)

MORSHEAD, Sir Owen, *Windsor Castle* (1957)

MURRAY, Margaret, *The Divine King in England* (1954)

MURRAY, Margaret, *The God of the Witches* (1952)

MYERS, A. R., *The Household of Edward IV* (1959)

NEALE, J. E., *Queen Elizabeth I* (1934)

NICHOLS, J. G., *The Literary Remains of Edward VI* (1859)

NICHOLS, John, *A Collection of Ordinances . . . from Edward III to William and Mary* (1790)

NICHOLS, John, *The Progresses and Public Travels of Queen Elizabeth* (1788)

NICHOLS, John, *Recollections and Reflections* (1822)

NICOLAS, Sir Harris, *History of the Orders of Knighthood* (1841–1842)

NICOLSON, Sir Harold, *King George V: His Life and Reign* (1952)

NORGATE, Kate, *England under the Angevin Kings* (1887)

OGG, David, *William III* (1956)

OGLANDER, *A Royalist's Notebook: The Commonplace Book of Sir John Oglander* (1936)

OMAN, Sir Charles, *The Great Revolt* (1906)

ORMATHWAITE, Lord, *When I was at Court* (1937)

OSBORNE, Francis, *Historical Memoires* (1658)

OXFORD: Margot Asquith, *More Memoirs* (1933)

BIBLIOGRAPHY

PAINTER, Sidney, *The Reign of King John* (1949)
PAPENDIEK, Mrs Vernon Delves Broughton (Ed.), *Court and Private Life in the Time of Queen Charlotte: The Journals of Mrs Papendiek* (1887)
PARKER, Charles Stuart, *Sir Robert Peel* (1899)
PEPYS, *Diary of Samuel Pepys* (Everyman's Library, 1923)
PETRIE, Sir Charles, *The Stuarts* (1958)
PICKERING, Anna Maria Wilhelmina, *Memoirs* (1903)
PLUMB, J. H., *The First Four Georges* (1956)
PONSONBY, Sir Frederick, *Recollections of Three Reigns* (1957)
PONSONBY, Arthur, *Henry Ponsonby: His Life from His Letters* (1942)
PONSONBY, Sir Frederick, *Sidelights on Queen Victoria* (1930)
POOLE, Austin Lane, (Ed.), *Medieval England* (1958)
POPE-HENNESSY, James, *Queen Mary 1867–1953* (1959)
PORTLAND, Duke of, *Men, Women and Things* (1937)
POTE, Joseph, *The History and Antiquities of Windsor Castle* (1749)
POWICKE, Sir Maurice, *The 13th Century* (1962)
POYNTER, Ambrose, 'An Essay on the History and Antiquities of Windsor Castle' in *Illustrations of Windsor Castle* by Sir Jeffrey Wyatville (1841)
PRESCOTT, H. F. M., *Mary Tudor* (1953)
PRINCE PHILIP: Her Majesty Queen Alexandra of Yugoslavia, *Prince Philip: A Family Portrait* (1960)
PRINCESS CHARLOTTE, Arthur Aspinall (Ed.), *Letters of Princess Charlotte* (1949)
PYNE, W. H., *The History of the Royal Residences* (1819)

RERESBY, Andrew Browning (Ed.), *Memoirs of Sir John Reresby* (1936)
RIBBLESDALE, Lord, *Impressions and Memoirs* (1927)
RICHARDSON, Joanna, *The Disastrous Marriage* (1960)
ROSE, George, *Diaries and Correspondence* (1860)
ROSE, J. H., *Life of Pitt* (1923)
ROSEBERY: The Marquess of Crewe, *Lord Rosebery* (1931)
ROOSEVELT, Eleanor, *On My Own* (1959)
ROOSEVELT, James and Sidney Shalett, *Affectionately F.D.R.* (1960)
ROPER, Lanning, *The Gardens in the Royal Park at Windsor* (1959)
ROWSE, A. L., *The Early Churchills* (1956)
ROWSE, A. L., *The England of Elizabeth* (1950)

SALTER, E. G., *Tudor England Through Venetian Eyes* (1930)
SANDERS, I. J., *Feudal Military Service in England* (1956)
SANDFORD, Francis, *Genealogical History* (1707)
SOMERVELL, D. C., *The Reign of King George V* (1935)
SOMNER, Dudley, *Haldane of Cloan: His Life and Times, 1856–1928* (1960)
STANLEY, The Dean of Windsor and Hector Bolitho (Eds.), *The Letters of Lady Augusta Stanley* (1927)
STOCKMAR, Baron E. von, *Memoirs of Baron Stockmar* (1872)

STRACHEY, Lytton, *Queen Victoria*, (Zephyr Books, 1945)

STRUTT, Joseph, *The Sports and Pastimes of the People of England* (1845)

STRYPE, *Ecclesiastical Memorials*(1721)

STUART, D. M., *The Daughters of George III* (1939)

SWIFT, Jonathan, *Journal to Stella*, Ed. Harold Williams (1948)

SYKES, Christopher, *Four Studies in Loyalty* (1946)

TAYLOR, Sir Herbert, *The Taylor Papers: Being a record of Certain Reminiscences, Letters and Journals* (1913)

TAYLOR, Joseph, *Relics of Royalty: Or Remarks, Anecdotes and Amusements of George III*(1820)

THACKERAY, W. M., *The Four Georges* (1861)

THOMS, William J., *The Book of The Court* (1838)

THORNLEY, Isobel D., *England Under the Yorkists* (1920)

TIGHE, Robert Richard and James Edward Davis, *Annals of Windsor, Being a History of the Castle and Town* (1858)

TOOLEY, Sarah A., *The Personal Life of Queen Victoria* (1901)

TRENCH, Charles Chenevix, *The Royal Malady* (1964)

TREVELYAN, Sir George Otto, *The Life and Letters of Lord Macaulay* (1908)

TRUMAN, Harry S., *Year of Decisions* (1955)

TURNER, F. C., *James II* (1948)

TURNER, E. S., *The Court of St James's* (1959)

VICKERS Kenneth H., *England in the Later Middle Ages* (1926)

VICTORIA: *The Private Life of the Queen.* By One of Her Majesty's Servants (1897)

VICTORIA, LEAVES: *Queen Victoria: Leaves from a Journal* with an introduction by Raymond Mortimer (1961)

VICTORIA, LETTERS: A. C. Benson and Viscount Esher (Eds.), *The Letters of Queen Victoria* (1908)

VICTORIA OF PRUSSIA: James Pope-Hennessy (Ed.), *Queen Victoria at Windsor and Balmoral: Letters from her grand-daughter* (1959)

VILLIERS, George, *A Vanished Victorian* (1938)

VULLIAMY, C. E., *Aspasia: The Life and Letters of Mary Granville, Mrs Delany, 1700–1788* (1935)

VULLIAMY, C. E., *Royal George* (1937)

WALDEGRAVE, James, Earl Waldegrave, *Memoirs from 1754–1758* (1821)

WALPOLE, Horace, *Memoirs of the Reign of George III* (1894)

WALPOLE, W. S. Lewis (Ed.), *Correspondence of Horace Walpole* (1937–)

WARREN, W. L., *King John* (1961)

WATSON, Vera, *The Queen at Home* (1952)

WEDGWOOD, C. V., *The King's Peace 1637–1641* (1955)

WELDON, Anthony, *The Court and Character of King James* (1651)

WHEELER-BENNETT, Sir John, *King George VI* (1958)

WILKINSON, Clennell, *Prince Rupert* (1934)

WILLIAMS, Charles, *James I* (1951)

WILLSON, D. Harris, *King James VI and I* (1956)

WINANT, John, *A Letter from Grosvenor Square* (1947)

WINDSOR, *A King's Story: The Memoirs of H.R.H. The Duke of Windsor* (1951)

WINDSOR, The Duke of Windsor, *A Family Album* (1960)

WITHERS, Philip, *History of the Royal Malady: Variety of Entertaining Anecdotes. By a Page of the Presence* (1789)

WOODWARD, Kathleen, *Queen Mary* (1927)

WORTHAM, H. E., *Edward VII* (1933)

WOTTON, L. Pearsall Smith, *Life and Letters of Sir Henry Wotton* (1907)

WRAXALL, H. B. Wheatley (Ed.), *The Historical and Posthumous Memoirs of Sir Nathaniel William Wraxall, 1772–1784* (1884)

WYNN, A. Hayward (Ed.), *Diaries of a Lady of Quality* (1864)

INDEX

Aberdeen, Lord (1784–1860), 207

Adam of Hartington, 32

Adams, John (1735–1826), 137

Adelaide, Queen of William IV (1792–1849), appearance, 176; and Windsor Park, 179–80, 185, 260; relations with William IV, 180, 182

Adolphus of Teck, Prince, 242

Adolphus Frederick, Duke of Cambridge (1774–1850), 143

Aga Khan, (1877–1957), 222, 226

Airlie, Lady, 267, 270

Albert of Saxe-Coburg-Gotha, Prince (1819–61), Consort of Victoria, and Victoria's proposal, 192–3; character, 193, 194, 200–1, 205; and Windsor, 194; gets rid of Baroness Lehzen, 195–6; organizes the Household, 196–200; his unpopularity, 199–200; as a husband, 205–7, 208–9; last illness and death, 209 –11; and Napoleon III, 217–18; and the Prince of Wales, 233–4, 235; alleged Jewish blood, 241n.; his allowance, 296n.

Alexandra, Princess (1844–1925), Queen of Edward VII, 237; her marriage, 213–14, 238; as Queen, 242–3; character, 244, 245, 269; and her husband, 245

Alfonso, King (1886–1941), 250

Altrincham, Lord, 293

Anthia, Princess (1783–1810), 123; her death, 142–3

Anne (1665–1714), 89; dislike of William III, 90; her children, 90–1, 93; character and appearance, 91, 93, 94; and her favourites, 91–2; love of hunting, 92–3; her Court, 93–4; and Windsor Castle, 94–5; her death, 95–6

Anne Boleyn (1507–36), 2nd Queen of Henry VIII, 39

Anne, Queen of Bohemia (1366–94), Queen of Richard II, 25–6

Anne of Denmark (1574–1619), Queen of James I, 53, 55, 56, 60

Anson, George, 223

Arbuthnot, Charles (1767–1850), 151, 158–9, 178

Arbuthnot, Mrs, 154–5, 157, 159, 173, 174, 176

Armstrong, Archie, 55, 64

Arthur, King and the Round Table, 13–14

Ascham, Roger (1515–68), 45

Ascot, 93, 136, 180, 181, 190, 204, 265, 294

Ashley, Lord, 204

Ashmole, Elias (1617–92), 17, 18, 76

Asquith, Herbert Henry, Earl of Oxford and Asquith (1852–1928), 244

Asquith, Margot (wife of above) (1865–1945), 245, 249

Atlee, Clement (later Lord), 284, 285

Austin, William, 147

Bachelor, Thomas, 158, 175

Baillie, A. V., Dean of Windsor, 224n.

Baker, Sir George (1722–1809), and George III's insanity, 124–5, 126, 128, 130

Balmoral, 205n., 208

Baring, Hon. Susan, 224

Beatrice, Princess Henry of Battenberg (1857–1944), 211, 227

Beaufort, Joanna, 15n.

Bentinck, Lady Dorothy, Duchess of Portland, 104

Bentinck, Hans Willem, Earl of Portland (1649–1709), 88, 91

Birch, Henry, 233–4

Black, Sister Catherine, 264, 269

Black Book of the Household, 27–8

Black Death, 25, 32

Bloomfield, Benjamin, Baron (1768–1846), 159

Bolitho, Hector, 276, 277

Boswell, James (1740–95), 107–8, 119

Bradlaugh, Charles (1833–91), 216

Brett, Hon. Reginald (late Viscount Esher) (1852–1930), 222–3, 239, 240, 241, 246, 258, 260

Brighton Pavilion, 164

Brown, John (1826–83), and Victoria, 214–16, 220, 224

Brown, Margaretta, 176

Bruce, Lady Augusta, 213

Bruce, Lord, 73

Brummel, Beau (George Bryan) (1778–1840), 150, 151

Bryant, Sir Arthur, 255